Armed Humanitarians

Armed Humanitarians

The Rise of the Nation Builders

NATHAN HODGE

BLOOMSBURY

New York · Berlin · London · Sydney

Published by Bloomsbury USA, New York

All papers used by Bloomsbury USA are natural, recyclable products made from wood grown in well-managed forests. The manufacturing processes conform to the environmental regulations of the country of origin.

LIBRARY OF CONGRESS CATALOGING-IN-PUBLICATION DATA

Hodge, Nathan.
Armed humanitarians : the rise of the nation builders / Nathan Hodge. —1st u.s. ed.
p.   cm.
Includes bibliographical references.
ISBN: 978-1-60819-017-1 (hc)
1. Humanitarian intervention—Political aspects—United States.
2. Nation-building—United States. 3. United States—Military policy.
I. Title.
JZ6369.H63 2010
355.02'80973—dc22
2010025752

First U.S. edition 2011

1 3 5 7 9 10 8 6 4 2

Typeset by Westchester Book Group
Printed in the United States of America by Quad/Graphics, Fairfield, Pennsylvania

For Sharon

Contents

Port-au-Prince

February 2010

The Super Stallion shuddered to a halt, and the flight engineer signaled for me to follow. I stepped from the rear ramp, and hot exhaust from the giant CH-53 helicopter washed over me as I walked across the landing zone. I surrendered my helmet and float coat to the crewman, shouldered my rucksack, and followed my fellow passenger, a Marine Corps lieutenant colonel, to the rear gate of the U.S. embassy, Port-au-Prince.

We picked our way across the landing zone. A few paratroopers of the Eighty-second Airborne Division in soft patrol caps and wraparound shades were guarding the dusty, trash-strewn field. One of the soldiers, sucking impassively on his CamelBak canteen, waved us through to the embassy motor pool. The CH-53 then lifted off, the turbine engines briefly drowning out the jackhammer of the diesel generators inside the compound.

A Winnebago-sized truck with the logo of the Federal Emergency Management Agency was parked behind the high gates, its satellite antenna pointed skyward. Near another outbuilding, military cots were arranged in neat rows, complete with sleeping bags and mosquito netting. Crates of electronic equipment and medical gear were stacked on the gravel. On the inner lawn of the embassy, near a lap pool, was a small encampment where someone had pitched several pup tents, plus a few family-sized shelters. It looked as though someone had raided an out-doors store and dumped the contents on the embassy grounds.

The compound was swarming with uniforms. Some were familiar: Marines in dusty digital-pattern camouflage, Navy personnel in crisp blue utility suits, Army soldiers in combat fatigues. Some were a bit more exotic: Foreign Service officers in Patagonia hiking boots, contractors in 5.11 tactical gear, members of the National Disaster Management Agency in matching blue shirts, khaki cargo pants, and floppy-brimmed hats. Everyone seemed to be moving with brisk purpose.

Just a few weeks earlier, on January 12, 2010, a magnitude 7.0 earthquake had struck Haiti, the poorest country in the Western Hemisphere. The disaster killed over 200,000 Haitians and left the country without a functioning government. Official buildings were demolished, the local police force was paralyzed, and Haiti's splendid presidential palace, completed during the U.S. military occupation in the early twentieth century, was left in ruins. The quake also had decapitated MINUSTAH, the United Nations Stabilization Mission in Haiti. Hedi Annabi, the Tunisian diplomat who served as special representative of the Secretary-General and as head of the UN mission, was killed, along with his deputy, Luiz Carlos da Costa of Brazil. Dozens of international peacekeepers, police advisors, and civilian UN staffers died in the collapse of their headquarters.

The seismic shock had knocked out the control tower at Toussaint L'Ouverture International Airport and collapsed the north pier of the main port, cutting Port-au-Prince off from the outside world. Within hours of the disaster, however, the airport was up and running: A team from the U.S. Air Force's Twenty-third Special Tactics Squadron, 720th Special Tactics Group, had flown in to take over air traffic control so that search-and-rescue teams and medical aid could arrive. Within five days of the disaster, the Air Force had directed over six hundred takeoffs and landings on an airstrip that usually saw fewer than half a dozen flights a day.[1] The place was now crowded with canvas tents that served as an improvised headquarters for flight operations. Reinforcements arrived quickly. Days after the quake, soldiers of the Eighty-second Airborne Division's First Squadron, Seventy-third Cavalry Regiment began deploying to Haiti. They set up camp at an abandoned country club near the U.S. embassy.

In the weeks following the disaster, the U.S. force in Haiti and off the coast kept growing. Less than a week after the quake, fourteen hundred U.S. troops were on the ground, with another five thousand offshore. By the end of January, just over two weeks after the disaster, the Haiti earthquake relief mission involved twenty thousand U.S. military personnel, twenty-four ships, and more than 120 aircraft. It was an impressive military surge, but the U.S. mission involved an alphabet soup of civilian agencies as well. The U.S. Agency for International Development, or USAID, sent a Disaster Assistance Response Team for an initial assessment, mobilized search-and-rescue teams from around the country, and held emergency planning meetings with private relief groups and aid contractors. USAID, an autonomous federal agency indirectly overseen by the secretary of state, was designated as the lead agency for organizing the U.S. earthquake relief effort. A crisis-response team from the State Department's Office of the Coordinator for Reconstruction and Stabilization was on the scene as well.

The U.S. embassy had become the nerve center for a giant, quasi-military expedition, far removed from the world of traditional diplomacy. Everything here was "expeditionary," from the Meals-Ready-to-Eat rations and lukewarm bottled water to the bottled bug spray and droning generators. The embassy looked as though it was preparing for a siege: On the street outside, Marines in camouflage uniforms and boonie hats guarded the main entrance with M16 rifles, 12-gauge shotguns, and M249 light machine guns. A perimeter made of wooden traffic barriers and tape marked off an outer perimeter, while Haitians patiently queued up under the relentless midday sun for emergency visas. The scene represented a curious merger between military force and humanitarian aid, a blurring of the traditional lines of development work, diplomacy, and national defense. This was the new face of American foreign policy: armed humanitarianism.

The 2010 Haiti relief mission was a response to a natural disaster, but the massive military operation—and many of its distinct features—grew directly out of the experience gained in fighting wars in Iraq and Afghanistan. That spring, as the military began a phased withdrawal from Haiti, Army Major General Simeon Trombitas, the commander of Joint Task Force–Haiti, told me that the humanitarian operation, which placed unprecedented emphasis on openness and information sharing with nongovernmental organizations (NGOs) and civilian relief agencies, had been shaped by the lessons of combat. "Due to all of our services' experience in Afghanistan and Iraq, and working with the populations there, and with other agencies, we've developed great relationships working with our own other government agencies and NGOs," he said. "Here we've fine-tuned that, because they are the ones with the assets that deal directly with the people, and we can enhance what they do."

Still, it was striking to see how completely the military had embraced the humanitarian mission. Shortly after the quake, U.S. Southern Command, the military headquarters overseeing Haiti relief, had set up an online portal for sharing maps, satellite imagery, and other time-sensitive data with civilian aid groups. Within hours of the disaster, the Pentagon released footage of earthquake damage that had been collected by an RQ-4 Global Hawk, a pilotless spy plane. It was an unusual move. Ordinarily, access to images collected by the high-flying drone would be tightly restricted. But the Defense Department declassified the pictures as part of a larger push to share information with nongovernmental organizations and relief groups.

On the ground, the hierarchical, secrecy-bound military adopted a surprising mantra of trust and collaboration. En route to Haiti, I overnighted on the Navy amphibious ship USS *Bataan*, where I chatted briefly with a Navy Civil Affairs officer, who enthusiastically described how he was working with charities like Oxfam and Médecins sans Frontières. "We're trying to get to the NGOs and IOs [international organizations] and see how they operate," he told me. "We see what portals they use, how they operate. The attitude is, we know what we do, but we can learn from them."

The Haiti mission showed the extent to which the military had absorbed the principles of "soft power." In fact, that kind of collaboration with civilian agencies and nongovernmental organizations had become almost second nature. Although the Haiti mission was purely humanitarian, the U.S. military saw it as part of the same problem set they encountered in places such as Iraq and Afghanistan. "Foreign disaster relief is counterinsurgency, only no one is shooting at you (yet)," wrote Army Major Kelly Webster, chief of plans and regimental executive officer for the Second Brigade Combat Team, Eighty-second Airborne Division, shortly after the relief mission. "Making the mental switch from the former to the latter did not require a major paradigm shift."[2]

In other words, that paradigm shift had already occurred. A year and a half earlier, in late 2008, Linton Wells, a former Pentagon chief information officer, told me how he had pushed for military commanders to collaborate more freely with NGOs and aid groups, and not just for disaster response. Haiti, then, was more than an opportunity for the U.S. military to hone its humanitarian skills. It was a chance to prepare for a new kind of warfare, where the traditional lines between development, diplomacy, and military action were blurred. The challenge, Wells later told me in an e-mail, was to "figure out how to institutionalize the approach for the long haul in Haiti, ensure these capabilities (and other prototypes) get fielded rapidly in the next contingency, wherever it may be, and apply comparable approaches to support stabilization and reconstruction in Afghanistan, and to other theaters. Lessons learned from Haiti already are being developed."

I had first met Wells in early October 2008, when he was escorting reporters and officials around a technology demonstration in the Pentagon's central courtyard. The scene in many respects mirrored what I saw at the U.S. embassy in Port-au-Prince a year and a half later: A crew of fleece-clad twenty-somethings had erected a hexayurt, the cheap, eco-friendly shelter designed for refugee camps and rock festivals; two young tech-slackers dressed like roadies for a Seattle band circa 1991 were tethering an inflatable satellite dish to the lawn; a ponytailed man in a baseball cap plugged his MacBook into a nearby portable solar-power generator. It looked as though the hippies were invading the place, or so it might have seemed to the Pentagon bureaucrats who retreated to the courtyard to sip Diet Coke, smoke cigarettes, or hunt for cell phone reception.

This, however, was not a prank. It was officially sanctioned by the Defense Department. A colonel with a Special Forces tab inspected a rice cooker powered by a solar mirror; a two-star Army general appraised the hexayurt; Defense Department civilian employees wearing white Pentagon access badges peered at a portable water-purification unit. The demonstration, called STAR-TIDES (for Sustainable Technologies, Accelerated Research—Transportable Infrastructures for Development and Emergency Support), was organized to showcase new, low-cost tools for humanitarian aid, disaster relief, and postwar reconstruction. The Naval Postgraduate School had chipped in forty thousand dollars to fund the effort; the Joint Capability Technology Demonstrations Office, part of the Pentagon's Rapid Fielding Directorate, had provided another sixty thousand dollars.

The project was the brainchild of Wells. The former commander of a naval destroyer squadron, Wells looked every inch the retired Navy officer: He wore a regimental tie and round, steel-framed glasses; his gray hair was neatly cut and pomaded, with a side part. But Wells did not speak in the clipped tones of Pentagonese. Rather, he had a loose, professorial style, borrowing lots of buzzwords from the aid and development world. STAR-TIDES, Wells explained, was not some new agency of the Pentagon; their job was not to respond to the next Hurricane Katrina or deliver emergency rations to refugees in Darfur. Rather, the project would be more about "collaboration," "trust building," and "social networking" than leading the Army to build yurts during a humanitarian crisis. "We're not going to be planting a flag in the field and delivering MREs," he said, referring to Meals-Ready-to-Eat, the military's packaged rations. "Our job is to connect people who may have solutions."

At first glance, STAR-TIDES looked like little more than a public relations exercise—an interesting experiment in open-source technology, perhaps, or an advertisement for a kinder, gentler military. For manufacturers of solar power generators and water purification systems, it was a nice promotional boost, a way to reach potential government customers. But this was a radical departure from the standards of a decade earlier. Under the rubric of STAR-TIDES, Wells and his colleagues were trying to get the military to build new alliances and coalitions, not with other militaries, but with nongovernmental organizations, aid workers, diplomats, citizen activists, even the press. The idea was to overcome the uniformed military's traditional distrust of what they called the "unicorns-and-rainbows" crowd: aid workers, development experts, human-rights advocates. Wells gave a brief example to the reporters. One of his acolytes, Dave Warner, was able to persuade U.S. Central Command, the powerful military headquarters that oversees U.S. operations in the Middle East and Central Asia, to release a large amount of unclassified satellite imagery of Afghanistan, without restrictions, to nongovernmental organizations that were working on aid and reconstruction projects on the ground. In Wells's telling, this kind of data could be used for "nonkinetic" (i.e., nonviolent) ends: to win the support of the local population for road building projects.

"One of the roads went through a cemetery," Wells said. "And so the

[Afghan] government proposal was, 'Well, we'll just kick the people out and build the road anyway.' But Dr. Warner's point with the NGOs was, 'Let's not do that, let's work from the bottom up.' And so by working with the people in the village, showing them what the value of the road was, eventually the villagers moved their own graves to allow the road to be built. Rather than having the United States being blamed for some sort of sacrilege or violation of some ancient creed, it's turned out to have been an absolute win-win, because we've been willing to drink the three cups of tea, spend the time, and you had something worthwhile to offer."

This was a parable of sorts: Instead of using force—dropping a bomb, say, on a Taliban safe house or kicking down doors in the middle of the night—the military could collaborate with an NGO to win the support of the local population. It would, in development parlance, be a solution with local buy-in. And the happy villagers, presumably, would not be planting bombs on the new road or ambushing U.S. forces. Wells was also making a deliberate pop-culture reference: *Three Cups of Tea* is the title of a book by Greg Mortenson, a mountain climber who founded a charity to build children's schools in remote parts of Pakistan and Afghanistan. It turns out that the inspirational bestseller also had a cult following within the military: Mortenson had been invited that fall to the Pentagon for a private meeting with the chairman of the Joint Chiefs of Staff; later that year, he traveled to MacDill Air Force Base, Florida, to address senior officials from U.S. Special Operations Command.[3] *Three Cups of Tea* offered a tantalizing vision of the uses of soft power.

Wells's experiment was getting high-level attention. Among the visitors to the STAR-TIDES demonstration was General William "Kip" Ward, the head of AFRICOM, the U.S. military's newly created geographic command for Africa. AFRICOM itself was branded as an experiment in reorganizing the U.S. military for humanitarian emergencies and conflict prevention; it would be a "hybrid" organization with civilian and military experts on the payroll. A visit by the military's newest four-star combatant commander was a big deal for the STAR-TIDES organizers.[4] More important, the STAR-TIDES scenarios—disaster relief in Central America or the Western Pacific, stabilization and reconstruction in Afghanistan, refugee support in sub-Saharan Africa, disaster response in the United States (euphemistically referred to as "defense support to civil authorities")—were not plucked out of thin air. They were devised at the request of the combatant commands, the powerful regional headquarters the U.S. military uses to divide the globe into geographic "areas of responsibility."

STAR-TIDES, then, was not a mere curiosity. Wells and his fellow evangelizers may have been at the further edges of the movement, but they were part of a larger cultural shift within the defense and national security establishment: a consensus that the U.S. military needed to master the arts of diplomacy, learn the language of aid and development, and develop new cultural skills. It was an approach that would fundamentally alter the way that the U.S. government carried out diplomacy and delivered foreign aid. It would also transform the way the United States waged war.

After Wells delivered sound bites to a radio reporter and escorted some more VIPs around the courtyard displays, I asked him what motivated him to launch STAR-TIDES. "I spent sixteen years in the Office of the Secretary of Defense," he said. "And frankly, I saw too many young American men and women die, because our government doesn't do this 'Wrap up the conflict' very well, or in some cases avoid them."

What Wells was saying was the same thing I had been told dozens of times before, in some shape or form, by top officers, ordinary soldiers, and civilian officials: *We can get it right.* That phrase, variously put, distilled the bitter experiences of Iraq and Afghanistan: winning the war—and losing the peace.*

Just two weeks before the October 2008 STAR-TIDES demonstration, Secretary of Defense Robert Gates spoke at National Defense University in Washington. In his speech, he outlined his vision of the new American way of war. "What is dubbed the war on terror is, in grim reality, a prolonged, worldwide irregular campaign—a struggle between the forces of violent extremism and moderation," he said. "In the long-term effort against terrorist networks and other extremists, we know that direct military force will continue to have a role. But we also understand that over the long term, we cannot kill or capture our way to victory."[6]

---

* Shortly after taking office in January 2009, President Barack Obama employed that phrase himself when he addressed the U.S. military. In an interview with the Pentagon Channel, he said his biggest responsibility to the troops was to ensure he "gets it right," and that military power alone would not ensure victory in places like Afghanistan. "We are not going to win in Afghanistan or get an acceptable outcome in Afghanistan if we are only depending on our military," he said.[5]

Military operations, Gates continued, should be subordinate to programs to promote economic development and good governance in places at risk from extremism. And that strategy, he added, would require an effort to "tap the full strength of America and its people"—not just the uniformed military, but civilian agencies, volunteer organizations, and the private sector.

The United States fields the most well-trained, well-funded, and technologically sophisticated fighting force the world has ever seen. But that military was confounded by the complexity of fighting low-tech insurgents in places like Iraq and Afghanistan. For Gates and his allies within the Pentagon, victory over militant extremism depended on mastering the "three cups of tea" approach: digging wells, building schools, and repairing roads. What began in late 2001 as a global war on terror was quietly recast as a campaign of armed social work. And in the process, American foreign policy underwent a tectonic shift.

That shift had its modest beginnings in the post-9/11 U.S. intervention in Afghanistan. It accelerated in Iraq, as the United States became mired down in the vicious internal war that followed the decapitation of Saddam Hussein's regime in 2003. A series of dramatic, innovative nation-building experiments rescued the Iraq mission from complete failure, but in the process, the military overcompensated. The Pentagon became fixated on soft power as the answer for security problems such as terrorism and insurgency. Military commanders threw billions of dollars at quasi-development schemes in the hopes that a combination of aid money and armed social work would get at the root causes of violence in failing states. And top policymakers launched an initiative to refashion government around the tasks of state building. The short-term lessons drawn from Iraq took on a life of their own, as policymakers and practitioners looked to repeat the experiment on an equally grand scale in Afghanistan.

In a debate with Vice President Al Gore in 2000, the Republican presidential candidate, George W. Bush, outlined his vision of the U.S. military policy: "I don't think our troops ought to be used for what's called nation building," he said. "I think what we need to do is convince people who live in the lands they live in to build the nations. Maybe I'm missing something here. I mean, we're going to have a kind of nation-building corps from America? Absolutely not."

In the decade before Bush took office, the United States had been involved in armed humanitarianism, albeit in relatively modest contingencies. In Haiti, Somalia, Kosovo, and Bosnia, U.S. troops were committed to peacekeeping operations with limited goals and indeterminate ends, and military theorists and foreign policy thinkers worried that the United States was frittering away military power by playing global beat cop. The conservative argument against nation building was summed up in one neat phrase: Superpowers don't do windows.* By the time Bush left office, the United States had committed itself to nation building on an epic scale.

This shift toward nation building can be documented in many different ways. One of the starkest ways is cost. Since 2003, Congress has appropriated over $50 billion for Iraq relief and reconstruction, at one time considered the largest amount of U.S. taxpayer dollars ever committed to aid and reconstruction in a single country.[8] As of summer 2010 the war in Afghanistan has become a nation-building project as ambitious and costly as the reconstruction of Iraq. By mid-2010, the United States had spent approximately $51.5 billion on building the rudiments of a modern state in Afghanistan.[9] Those figures were only a fraction of the larger cost of staying on a wartime footing. In the decade that followed September 11, 2001, the Pentagon's base budget effectively doubled, not including additional funding to cover the cost of the ongoing wars in Afghanistan and Iraq.[10] For fiscal year 2011, President Barack Obama requested $733.3 billion in new budget authority for national defense: $548.9 billion for the regular operations of the Defense Department; $159.3 billion for ongoing military operations, primarily in Afghanistan and Iraq; and $25.1 billion for defense-related activities by other agencies, including money to support the nuclear weapons complex. The total national defense budget in fiscal year 2001, adjusted for 2010 dollars, was around $375 million. Foreign aid budgets grew dramatically as well. For instance, between 2002 and 2009 the U.S. Agency for International Development spent around $7 billion in Afghanistan.[11]

---

* That phrase, originally attributed to the former head of the CIA's Afghan Task Force, was the title of an influential article by John Hillen, a former Army officer who went on to serve as assistant secretary of state for political-military affairs under George W. Bush. The article was cited more often than read: Hillen was making a more nuanced argument about the management of alliances against the backdrop of the conflict in the Balkans. But because of its provocative title, it was often held up as an anti-nation-building screed.[7]

That amount roughly equaled USAID's global operating budget for fiscal year 2001.[12]

The manpower committed to this mission has also been extraordinary. By the end of his second term, Bush had embarked on a mission to reorganize government for this role, taking the first steps toward creating a standing nation-building corps. The State Department launched an effort to create a cadre of diplomatic first responders who would be on call to respond to humanitarian crises and take on nation-building assignments in war zones. And military planners began thinking in terms of the "long war," an era of persistent conflict that would require an unceasing cycle of deployments to places deemed vulnerable to violent extremism. In Iraq and Afghanistan, the practice of nation building was manpower-intensive, demanding a heavy U.S. troop presence to police some of the world's toughest neighborhoods. By mid-2010, troops in Afghanistan outnumbered those in Iraq, and casualties in Afghanistan reached record highs. Nation building is a hard, often risky business. As of this writing, forty-four hundred U.S. troops have died in Iraq. More than eleven hundred have died in Afghanistan. Those numbers do not include contractors and civilians, whose names rarely figure in official casualty tallies.

Weeks after the September 11 attacks in New York City and Washington, conservative writer Max Boot made a provocative argument in favor of a new kind of American imperialism. "Afghanistan and other troubled lands today cry out for the sort of enlightened foreign administration once provided by self-confident Englishmen in jodhpurs and pith helmets," he wrote.[13] Implicit in that clever shorthand was a critique: The United States lacked a talented class of colonial administrators capable of refashioning failed states and preparing the local inhabitants for eventual self-rule.

At first glance, it looks as if Boot's post-9/11 wish has been fulfilled—and that the United States is finally creating the twenty-first-century equivalent of the British Empire's Colonial Service. Over the 2000–2010 decade, a new class of nation builders has emerged: staffing Provincial Reconstruction Teams in cities in Iraq; constructing roads in rural Afghanistan; or training Kalashnikov-toting soldiers in Timbuktu. From West Africa to Central Asia, the old diplomatic cocktail-party circuit has given way to a new world of fortified outposts, where a new generation of diplomats, soldiers, and private contractors is working at the sharp end of U.S. foreign policy.

This is the world of muddy-boots diplomacy, practiced on a scale that would have been unthinkable a decade ago. Civil servants who once trained for peacetime development work now find themselves mediating tribal disputes in remote mountain provinces of Afghanistan. The State Department's Foreign Service officers find themselves evading roadside bombs—and sometimes returning fire in firefights. Army platoon leaders hand out microgrants to small-business owners in the restless Shia slums of Baghdad. And a new class of expatriate has taken up residence in an archipelago of miniature Green Zones. They live behind concrete blast walls and concertina wire, commute to work in armored trucks, and reside in the ultimate gated communities.

But the shift in many ways has been incomplete. As this book will show, there has been a horrific failure to equip ourselves for success in this mission. The military quickly learned that it was poorly equipped for nation building—lacking cultural knowledge, language skills, and local understanding to do the job right in places like Iraq. Civilian agencies of the U.S. government such as the U.S. State Department and USAID were poorly prepared for the mission as well. In military terms, they had no "expeditionary capability": They had no deployable reserve, no way to sustain people in the field, and few professional incentives for serving in combat zones. Their budgets were a fraction of the Defense Department's, and their personnel were stretched thin: The State Department has around sixty-five hundred Foreign Service officers and another five thousand Foreign Service specialists who work overseas; another fifteen hundred Foreign Service officers work for USAID, the Foreign Commercial Service, the Foreign Agricultural Service, and the International Broadcasting Bureau.[14] The U.S. Army, including active, reserve, and National Guard components, has an "end strength"—manpower authorized by Congress—of over one million.

The shortage of manpower was a chronic problem for this new enterprise. Sending thousands of civil servants to remote and often dangerous outposts had profound consequences. It was to create the world of the armed humanitarian: a landscape seen through bulletproof glass. An army of private security companies built a lucrative new business ferrying diplomats, civilian aid workers, and contractors around war zones. These hired guns provided bodyguard details, convoy escorts, and camp guards; they provided what the military calls "force protection"; they also created extraordinary distance between the representatives of the

U.S. government and the populations they were supposed to help. And the military's belated attempt to understand the "human terrain" it was operating in inadvertently sharpened the divide between the practitioners of this new foreign policy and the academic specialists whose expertise they sought to tap. This was one way the manpower gap was closed.

Equally problematic, this new mission blurred the lines between military force and humanitarian assistance. Over the course of the decade from 2000 to 2010, the Pentagon took on a greater share of overseas development assistance, work traditionally performed by civilians. In 2006, the Organisation for Economic Co-operation and Development, an international organization that tracks development trends, published a study of U.S. foreign aid. It found that over one fifth of official U.S. development assistance—22 percent, to be exact—flowed through the Defense Department. In 2002, that figure had been less than 6 percent.[15] And the 22 percent did not include the "security assistance" dollars the Pentagon committed annually to training and equipping foreign militaries and police forces.[16] The U.S. military had become a major player in the development world. And in many places, U.S. military money spent on development far outstripped the budget of traditional aid organizations. The aid workers there didn't wear Birkenstocks—they wore combat boots.

Despite working diligently to solve the bureaucratic problems of nation building, the new practitioners often came to a late realization: Building an effective state and a functioning civil society is a process that takes decades, often generations. Imposing it from the outside often feeds the perception that the intervening power is an occupier, not a nation builder. And they also faced an unhappy reality: Sometimes, the more you throw money, resources, and talent at a problem, the worse the problem becomes. The massive infusion of resources creates extraordinary opportunities for corruption in states that have weak rule of law and poor traditions of governance. Equally important, they had to confront the fact that the American public has little patience, particularly given the current economic state, for this kind of costly enterprise.

Many books have probed the military experience in Iraq and Afghanistan: memoirs of combat by platoon leaders, brigade commanders, and embedded reporters; searing critiques of military decisionmaking by investigative journalists; self-serving accounts by civilian decisionmakers.

But literature on the nation-building experience is almost nonexistent. Reporters who cover war often gravitate to the "bang-bang," but rarely hang around for the complex development work that follows military action. This book is about the rise of this new class of nation builder, and the experiences, frustrations, and lessons of nation building. It is a tale of courage, idealism, and commitment; it is also one of profligacy, waste, and disillusion. This is the defining experience for a generation of U.S. foreign policy practitioners.

Our decade-long affair with nation building was more than a break with the traditional world of diplomacy. For the military, it marked a shift away from fighting and winning conventional wars, as troops were reassigned to a constabulary mission. The military that had won a rapid victory over Saddam Hussein's army in 1991 and 2003 was now stretched too thin to handle major new emergencies. The military was grasping for a new way to describe this mission: It was something other than war— more a hybrid of police work and development. They settled on the term "stability operations" to describe this kind of approach.

The Pentagon's embrace of this new strategy can be charted out in a series of official documents. One week before the STAR-TIDES demonstration at the Pentagon, in October 2008, the U.S. Army released Field Manual 3-07, *Stability Operations*. The manual provided the military with a blueprint for rebuilding failed states. And it stated the obvious: Nation building requires a lot of "soft power" and the full participation of the civilian agencies of government if it is to succeed. According to the manual, the United States faced a new era in which "the greatest threats to national security will not come from emerging ambitious states, but from nations unable or unwilling to meet the basic needs and aspirations of their people."

The manual's foreword states:

> America's future abroad is unlikely to resemble Afghanistan or Iraq, where we grapple with the burden of nation-building under fire. Instead, we will work through and with the community of nations to defeat insurgency, assist fragile states, and provide vital humanitarian aid to the suffering. Achieving victory will assume new dimensions as we strengthen our ability to generate

"soft power" to promote participation in government, spur economic development, and address the root causes of conflict among the disenfranchised populations of the world.

The week the new Army manual was made public, I sat down with Clinton Ancker, the director of the Combined Arms Center Directorate at Fort Leavenworth, Kansas. During his Army career, Ancker had served with an armored cavalry unit in Vietnam and had spent nine years stationed on the border between East and West Germany in the late years of the Cold War. Ancker was also a historian, and he went on to be an intellectual mentor to many of the military officers who were leading battalions and brigades in Iraq and Afghanistan. He had helped lead the drafting of the manual, and he wanted to emphasize an important point. "There's a very clear message in the manual: that the Army should not be the lead on most of this, but a recognition that in many cases we will be when the operation kicks off," he told me.

Ancker, like many of his contemporaries, wanted a government that was better organized to carry out this mission, that would require a new kind of approach—neither purely civilian nor wholly military—to handle nation building. "In theory, in the best of all possible worlds, the military would never have to do stability operations because they are fundamentally functions of a government," he said. "If there is somebody else who is competent and capable of doing these things we would just as soon transition those tasks to them, because every soldier devoted to this is one who is not training for other missions or available for other missions. [But if] no one else can do it, we have to acknowledge that it's a task and we have to have thought about it ahead of time."

That manual was just one product of a period of introspection about the failure of the military efforts in Iraq and Afghanistan. The most famous document of this was Field Manual 3-24, the U.S. Army and U.S. Marine Corps's counterinsurgency manual, published in December 2006. That book became a surprise bestseller (and one of its authors, General David Petraeus, became a celebrity), but the manual represented only one aspect of the military's embrace of armed humanitarianism. In November 2005, the Defense Department issued Directive 3000.05, "Military Support for Stability, Security, Transition, and Reconstruction." It placed stability operations for the first time on a par with offensive or defensive combat. It stated: "Stability operations are a core U.S.

military mission that the Department of Defense shall be prepared to conduct and support. They shall be given priority comparable to combat operations and be explicitly addressed and integrated across all DoD activities including doctrine, organizations, training, education, exercises, materiel, leadership, personnel, facilities, and planning."[17]

This dull bureaucratic language obscured a stunning admission: The United States had failed to plan for the postwar occupation and reconstruction of Iraq. The counterinsurgency manual followed one year later, signaling a cultural shift within the land services, the Army and Marine Corps. In October 2007, the U.S. Navy released its "Cooperative Strategy for 21st Century Seapower," a document that, in essence, said that avoiding wars was as important as winning them. In June 2008, an entire section of the 2008 National Defense Strategy, a sort of "statement of purpose" for the Defense Department, was devoted to outlining the importance of working with civilian agencies. "Our forces have stepped up to the task of long-term reconstruction, development and governance," it read. "The U.S. Armed Forces will need to institutionalize and retain these capabilities, but this is no replacement for civilian involvement and expertise."

These documents, along with classified documents on development and deployment of forces, all provided guidance for a paradigm shift in U.S. foreign policy toward nation building. By October 2008, the same month of the STAR-TIDES demonstration, work was nearing completion on a "whole-of-government" counterinsurgency guide that would instruct policymakers on how to plan and respond to future interventions overseas. In parallel, the State Department was taking the first steps toward creating a new Civilian Response Corps, a sort of civilian equivalent to the military reserve that could be called up in an emergency for nation-building missions.

Nation building has also changed Washington. In parallel with the push to refashion government, a new class of theorists, consultants, and advisors set up shop among the think tanks and lobbying offices of downtown Washington and staked their reputations and careers on the nation-building enterprise. This paradigm shift has also created rich new opportunities for the government contracting firms, not only for traditional aid contractors but for defense firms looking to branch out into the stability operations business. Providing manpower, consulting services, and logistics for nation-building projects became a more promising growth business than building warships, helicopters, and tanks.[18] Aid contracting first became a big business with the Clinton administration's push to "reinvent government" in the 1990s. That same privatization dynamic was at work in the first decade of the twenty-first century, but on a much larger scale. The profit motive would often be at odds with the mission.

Wars of choice, such as the Iraq War, may prove the exception in American foreign policy, but the experience of administering Iraq, Afghanistan, and other frontier states will mold a new generation of soldiers, diplomats, and bureaucrats. This new doctrine—still a work in progress—will shape future interventions. Armed nation building fits neatly with new ideas taking hold in international relations. Concepts such as the "responsibility to protect" trump state sovereignty and can pave the way for humanitarian intervention in failing states, or states deemed to be failing. This is a new idea of a just war, a place where liberal interventionists and conservative hawks find common ground.

This embrace of nation building, however, carries serious risks. The more the military focuses on armed social work, the less it will focus on its main mission of fighting and winning wars. The United States may be less ready to respond to new crises because of the enormous drain on our resources posed by the nation-building mission. Sustaining these missions on borrowed money increases our national debt, diverts money from domestic priorities, and hands an enormous burden to the next generation of taxpayers. It threatens to diminish the standing of the United States, because the huge footprint that it requires feeds perceptions that we are an imperial power. It creates more, not less, temptation for the United States to intervene in putative failed states. It sends mixed messages about who we are as a nation, because we interact with the world through our most authoritarian institutions. More worryingly, armed nation building may begin to look like an attractive way to solve domestic problems. This is a noble but flawed undertaking. The tools are important to have, but they must be used judiciously.

This newest generation of nation builders had to learn the hard way, groping for solutions in often difficult circumstances. For guidance, the architects of this new approach looked to the lessons of the Vietnam War, and to the literature of nineteenth- and twentieth-century colonial administration. During Vietnam, the U.S. military and civilian agencies of government became heavily involved in what at the time was called the "other war": a massive civilian-led development campaign. Even though the Vietnam War ended in failure, some of the nation builders offered a new interpretation of the conflict: Many of the unique civil-military experiments in armed social work and reorganizing government had produced successes that, despite the fall of the Saigon government in 1975, could be repeated.

This book revisits some of that history, but it also describes what makes the experience of the past decade distinct from other foreign adventures. This new doctrine was an effort to get past the simplistic "shock and awe" view of American military might, and impose a more nuanced, and culturally sophisticated, way of doing business. Strenuously avoiding civilian casualties would become the prime directive for U.S. troops. And serious thinkers within government would look for ways to make U.S. intervention smarter, smaller, and less intrusive.

Despite this smarter approach, the outcome is not guaranteed. Iraq, as of this writing, is in the grip of a fresh wave of sectarian violence. Despite having stabilized to some extent, the country still could not manage to form a national government half a year after elections in March 2010. Overall violence is down, but the threat of renewed civil war is very real. In Afghanistan, the massive ramping up of U.S. military involvement and a parallel development effort had the perverse effect of enabling rampant corruption that undermined the trust of the Afghan people. U.S. troops, once greeted as liberators by Afghans weary of the Taliban's medieval rule and a quarter century of civil war, found that their welcome was wearing thin. Local resentment has grown over civilian casualties, and in many parts of the country the Taliban is managing to outgovern the coalition and the Afghan government. The practitioners of foreign policy were rediscovering the fundamental paradox of nation building: The more you help, the less you empower the host government.

This book, then, is an accounting. David Kilcullen, the Australian counterinsurgency guru, described this kind of mission as "armed social work." Poverty alleviation, job creation, and infrastructure development can be noble and altruistic enterprises; these projects are often taken on by self-sacrificing, service-minded people. But good intentions are not enough. As any student of aid and development should know, efforts to aid the developing world have often done more harm than good. To borrow a construct from the economist William Easterly, the U.S. government belongs to the world of the "planners," the topdown institutions that have consistently failed over five decades and trillions of dollars to find adequate remedies for poverty in the developing world. As they get further into the development business, the U.S. military faces the same dilemma. Underlying the whole enterprise is an assumption, questionable at best, that aid and development money can automatically bring down violence and promote stability in war-torn states.

Ultimately, there needs to be an acknowledgment of the limits to what we can accomplish. Without a reliable partner, the whole thing is doomed to fail. If the government we are helping is hopelessly corrupt, ineffective, and illegitimate, no amount of money or manpower will solve the problem. Building effective states can take decades, and requires a class of people who are committed to it. As experience in Iraq and Afghanistan showed, this is not a soldier's job, yet civilian agencies simply lack the personnel and the expeditionary capability to handle nation building in the world's most violent neighborhoods. We are still a long way from developing a real cadre of people who can handle this mission, and do it affordably. Furthermore, it's not primarily a task that can be accomplished by outsiders, be they in or out of uniform. Developing a functioning state and a thriving civil society is a process that has its own internal dynamic. We cannot remake entire societies no matter how much time we give ourselves. We cannot do it, and we can't afford it.

A few notes on terminology: This book traces the theory and practice of nation building, even in an era when official policy insisted that the term did not apply. The reluctant acceptance of the need to use that term—and the belated acknowledgment of its importance—is part of the story.

I have made a deliberate effort to avoid national-security jargon. In the U.S. military, the term "peacekeeping" has fallen out of fashion. "Stability operations," sometimes referred to as "Phase IV" or "post-conflict" operations, can apply to missions such as peacekeeping (the preferred phrase is now "peace operations"), disaster relief and humanitarian assistance, counterterrorism, counternarcotics, and counterinsurgency.[19] An argument persists about whether counterinsurgency falls under the rubric of stability operations or vice versa—the Army–Marine Corps manual describes counterinsurgency as a combination of offensive, defensive, and stability operations—but those definitions are of greatest concern to a professional military audience.[20] While it may offend the purists, I have chosen to use the terms "nation building" and "stability operations" interchangeably.

"Nation building" and "state building" are terms that have very specific meaning for academics and members of the development community. "Nation building" means building a collective political identity around the concept of a culturally unique "nation"; it is quite distinct from the task of designing and building institutions of state. The United States has been deeply involved in both: In Iraq, it tried to nurture and promote a sense of Iraqi national unity that superseded ethnic allegiance, even though certain state institutions were dominated by one group (the Interior Ministry was Shia-dominated, for instance) and parts of the country were pushing for the greatest possible degree of autonomy (Kurdistan wanted a regional government). In Afghanistan, the efforts to build a national army drawn from all of the country's ethnic groups was at its heart an attempt to promote national unity.

A note on sources: I have tried to depict as accurately as possible the world of the nation builder as I have encountered it. I have watched Army Human Terrain Teams negotiate with neighborhood leaders in Baghdad's Sadr City; accompanied military doctors to a rural clinic in Mali; observed Special Forces soldiers training the sneaker-clad troops of the Georgian army; and watched State Department diplomats negotiate with provincial leaders in Afghanistan. The ranks are those they held at the time they were interviewed. In addition to my firsthand reporting, I spoke to dozens of veterans of Provincial Reconstruction Teams, regional embassy offices, and Civil Affairs teams; tracked down retired Vietnam-era civilian and military advisors; and interviewed many generals and top civilian officials. Information not drawn from my own interviews, reporting, or observation is cited in the notes.

Many sources agreed to speak to me on the record; others, because of the nature of their work and their respective bureaucratic cultures, have asked to remain unnamed. The State Department, in particular, has a "don't-rock-the-boat" culture that discourages unscripted interaction with an independent writer and researcher. Nevertheless, many Foreign Service officers and many civil servants, contractors, USAID officers, and serving military personnel agreed to speak candidly to me. They felt the story was too important to remain untold.

PART I

Winning the War,
Losing the Peace

CHAPTER 1

Absolute Beginners

The rear ramp of the C-17 airlifter groaned open, bathing the cargo hold in a hot, stupefying glare. Two rows of Army infantrymen in coyote-brown camouflage filed out, dazed and blinking, into Afghanistan's noonday sun. A junior airman waved the soldiers away from the flight line, toward a row of sagging canvas field tents. The troops, soldiers of the Tenth Mountain Division, fresh from Fort Drum, New York, hauled their gear over to an assembly area. A few reporters who had hitched a ride on the same flight would hang back and wait for an escort. I dropped my bags in the dust and took in the scene. A pair of young airmen, a young man and a woman in T-shirts and fatigues, lounged on an empty pallet, swigging bottled water.

I had a panoramic view of Bagram Air Base, ringed on three sides by the jagged, white-capped walls of the Hindu Kush. Just a few months earlier, in the fall of 2001, this former Soviet base on the high desert plain of Parwan Province had been the frontline of battle between the Taliban and Northern Alliance fighters. And the scene here still looked like an outtake from *Apocalypse Now*, a wide-screen view of wartime devasta-tion. A pair of Chinooks—the hulking, tandem-rotor helicopters familiar from the old photos of the Vietnam War—lifted off from the airstrip, kick-ing up a ferocious swirl of dust. The carcasses of wrecked Soviet aircraft littered the revetments off the main taxiway. Out beyond the runway, ordnance disposal teams were combing the desert floor, probing for mines and unexploded shells.

In the prelude to the offensive that routed the Taliban in December of 2001, General Baba Jan, a swaggering Northern Alliance commander, had escorted reporters to the top floor of the Bagram control tower, a squat, three-story building with the windowpanes blown out, to point the way to Kabul, and to victory.[1] The tower had been a favorite target for Taliban mortar teams. The corroding skeleton of the main aircraft hangar was visible, improbably supporting the roof; an Army soldier, Specialist Jason Disney, had been crushed to death by a piece of falling scrap metal while clearing the building of debris the month before. The few buildings left standing were still perforated with bullet holes and shell fragments.

Before the Soviet-Afghan war, this had been the garden of central Afghanistan. Farmers tended orchards and vineyards on the lushly irrigated Shomali Plain, which doubled as a favorite picnic spot in the summer. In the winter, expatriates living in Kabul would drive the two-lane highway that skirted Bagram's western edge to go skiing near the Salang Pass. The slopes had no lift, and enterprising local truckers would drop skiers at the trailhead, drive the switchback road to the bottom, and then drive them back to the top of the mountain.[2] The idea of Ariana Afghan Airlines, the country's national carrier, offering package holidays to "Ski Afghanistan," did not seem too remote a prospect.[3]

A generation later, this bleak landscape was nearly uninhabitable. Bagram changed hands several times during fighting between the Taliban and the Northern Alliance. When the Taliban finally pushed their opponents from the Shomali Plain, their reprisals against the local villages for supporting the Northern Alliance were swift: demolition teams dynamited their mud-brick houses, burned the orchards, and destroyed the irrigation canals. By March of 2002 it was little more than a military staging area. In the Shah-e-Kot mountain range of eastern Afghanistan, Operation Anaconda was in full swing: Soldiers of the Army's Tenth Mountain Division, along with a contingent of Canadian soldiers, special operations teams, and Afghan irregulars, were engaged in a protracted fight against al-Qaeda footsoldiers entrenched in a series of bunkers and cave complexes in Paktia Province. Bagram was the logistics hub and headquarters for the battle; from the urgent pace with which the helicopters were shuttling off the airfield, it was clear that the fighting was still intense.

We had made a dramatic landing, with the C-17 hurtling down at a steep angle. A bulldozer and a dump truck were tethered to the floor of the aircraft. Buckled into my seat against the wall, I kept a nervous eye on the straps and chains that kept the bulldozer anchored to the deck of the cargo hold as the aircraft banked sharply. Before landing at Bagram, the C-17 had made a brief pit stop at Karshi Khanabad, a remote former Soviet air base in southern Uzbekistan. Several pallets of Pringles and Mountain Dew, destined for a makeshift commissary, had been bumped from the cargo hold to make way for the crucial heavy equipment. Karshi Khanabad was one of the staging areas of the new war; in the weeks after September 11, 2001, U.S. Defense Department officials and diplomats had negotiated overflight rights, access to airstrips, and refueling stops in remote locations along the southern rim of the former Soviet empire.

I had boarded the Afghanistan-bound C-17 at Incirlik Air Force Base, an American base in southeastern Turkey that was the home to aircraft enforcing Operation Northern Watch, the no-fly zone over northern Iraq. Incirlik was a well-established base. The Air Force had occupied the place since the Cold War, and the base was laid out in a neat suburban grid. It looked like Abilene, Texas. I arrived at Incirlik on a Civil Reserve flight, a commercial airliner chartered by the military. As the plane taxied in at Incirlik, the arriving U.S. troops puzzled over their travel orders, trying to get a fix on their final destination. A young woman in an Air Force uniform read her travel orders—her boarding pass listed her destination as Manas Air Base in Kyrgyzstan.

She wondered aloud: "Is that Kazakhstan or Kyrgyzstan?"

"Tajikistan," someone replied.

Once the plane departed Incirlik, however, we were entering a new geography: These new strategic outposts were in strange, unpronounceable places such as Uzbekistan, Tajikistan, and Kyrgyzstan. Even for a military used to cycling through deployments to Bosnia and Kuwait, the Pentagon's new map was still something of a mystery.

It was all supposed to be very, very temporary. That, at least, was the explanation Army Lieutenant Colonel Scott Donahue gave when he was asked why no American flag flew over the control tower at Bagram.

"You have to remember, if you study the history of this country, that's what caused the demise of some of these other nations that tried to come in here and help," he said matter-of-factly. "You come in here like a big brother to take over everything, there's a natural resentment."

It was a perceptive observation. During the 1960s and 1970s, politically non-aligned Afghanistan had been the scene of an international development contest between the United States and the Soviet Union. In the south, the United States Agency for International Development spent lavishly on infrastructure projects, building hydroelectric dams and irrigation canals in rural Helmand Province (Lashkar Gah, the provincial capital, was nicknamed "Little America") and building a sleek, modernist airport in Kandahar. In the north, the Soviets built a network of roads and the Salang Tunnel, which opened a year-round connection between the north of the country and Kabul. Despite these showpiece projects, the country remained at the bottom of the development scale. "Afghanistan's roads and highways, Russian-built in the north, American-made in the south, originally seemed like a decoration rather than a utility, neatly tied around the country like some superfluous and extravagant ribbon," an observer wrote in the early 1970s.

> Kandahar airport still remains only a splendid showpiece, an architectural masterpiece of concentric curves, a propagandist's pipedream costing 15 million American dollars. Equipped to welcome the biggest jets with runways designed as major staging arteries for flights to the East, the airport is a forlorn white elephant, virtually unused by the world's air routes.[4]

The disastrous Soviet intervention in the 1980s did little for the country. The Soviets tried a few hearts-and-minds projects, and built some grim socialist-style housing blocks in Kabul, but the indiscriminate use of force and the displacement of millions of Afghans left few positive memories of the Russians.

Donahue, a sunburned officer wearing square-framed engineer glasses, was in charge of Task Force Bagram, a team of Army engineers that had arrived the previous November to survey the place and see if it could be turned into a functioning base. In parallel, a team from the 744th Ordnance Company from Fort Meade, Maryland, set to work methodically clearing the place of mines and unexploded munitions. Their task was not to clear the surrounding Shomali Plain—that would take years—but to make it safe to work inside the base perimeter. Several times a day, the bomb squad held "controlled detonations" to destroy their deadly finds: artillery shells, mortar rounds, rocket engines, cans of machine-gun ammunition, even five-hundred-pound bombs. By that March, they had destroyed seventy-two hundred munitions at Bagram, the equivalent of thirty thousand pounds of high explosive.

More reinforcements were arriving from the United States, along with fresh contingents of NATO troops, including Polish sappers and British paratroopers. A squadron of tank-busting A-10 Thunderbolt II fighters from the Twenty-third Fighter Group was scheduled to arrive soon to provide air support for the ongoing campaign. But as the perimeter grew, Donahue said, the Army wanted to discourage the impression that it was here to stay. And one way to keep a small footprint was to enlist local help. Major Kevin Johnson, one of Donahue's subordinates, hired Afghan laborers to start clearing debris from the aircraft hangar. Local men got cash for hauling out trash and scrap metal. Unskilled laborers received 70 cents an hour; skilled workers got $1.70 an hour. The task force took the same labor-intensive approach to cleaning debris from the runway. The soldiers recruited two hundred day laborers, who lined up at one end of the runway, scouring the length of the fifty-six-hundred-foot airstrip, sweeping litter up with simple straw brooms. Donahue and Johnson struck a deal with local carpenters to start fixing up some of the battered buildings.

The whole point of the exercise was to give the local economy a lift. The Americans, after all, were the newcomers here, and paying for local labor and buying local tools was a quick and easy way to win hearts and minds. The Army was not here to do long-term development work; it needed to repair the buildings on base and make sure that the place was habitable during the winter. The repairs were part of a deal struck with Afghan commanders in return for the rights to use the base. "The agreement in theater is this: Every fixed building that we occupy, we will repair that building, and one more," said Donahue. "So it's a two-for-one."

The operation at Bagram was low-key and unobtrusive. Outside the razor-wire perimeter at the main gate, Afghan laborers in sandals and baggy *shalwar kameez* lined up patiently for a pat-down before being let on base; drivers in garishly decorated jingle trucks idled outside a sand-filled HESCO barricade; local entrepreneurs operated a small carpet shop and souvenir stands to cater to the new visitors. Commander Baba Jan's men wandered inside the perimeter, Kalashnikovs slung casually on their shoulders. One goal of these modest construction projects was what the military called "force protection." By spreading some dollars around the neighboring community and keeping local men employed, the military could build rapport with leaders. And befriending one's neighbors made it easier to collect intelligence and reduced the chances that the enemy would return to the area.

That equation, however, was about to change. A team of civilian contractors had recently arrived from the United States. They were here to scout the location for Brown & Root, then a subsidiary of the oil-services firm Halliburton. Brown & Root, renamed KBR later that year, was familiar to anyone who had visited the massive U.S. bases in the Balkans such as Camp Bondsteel, a sprawling camp in eastern Kosovo. The company had managed Camp Bondsteel as part of the Army's Logistics Civil Augmentation Program, or LOGCAP: it had a contract for the management of military installations overseas. Under LOGCAP, the Army could order individual "task orders" on an as-needed basis: The contractor built housing, provided clean water, and operated commissaries; it provided fuel and spare parts; and it maintained vehicles and equipment. In theory, outsourcing through LOGCAP freed up the downsized post–Cold War Army to do purely military tasks. The military could train and prepare for war, and leave the potato peeling and latrine cleaning to the contractors. And instead of training Army personnel, and paying for their training and long-term benefits, the Army could simply pay a one-time fee to a contractor.

Or so went the theory. In practice, it was expensive. LOGCAP was structured as a "cost-plus-award-fee" contract, meaning that the contractor would be reimbursed for the cost of work performed, plus a fixed percentage that would be considered profit. That meant there were few incentives to control costs. In a survey of outsourced work in the Balkans, government auditors found that Brown & Root charged the government for cleaning offices four times a day; servicing latrines three times a day; and conducting routine base maintenance around the clock. Commanders complained that the company padded payrolls by hiring oversized construction teams and cleaning crews that were often idle.[5]

Brown & Root won the original LOGCAP contract in 1992, for work in Somalia.[6] In 1997 and 2001, a rival company, DynCorp, outbid Brown

& Root for the second LOGCAP contract, but Brown & Root got a consolation prize: lucrative task orders in the Balkans. In December 2001, weeks after Bagram was captured by the Northern Alliance, the Army awarded a ten-year contract to Brown & Root for LOGCAP III. The contract had an initial ceiling of $300 million, an amount that would turn out to be a modest first installment. Brown & Root won the contract despite the fact that government auditors faulted the Army for failing to manage proper oversight of its work in the Balkans. Contracts to support the administration's war on terror followed in quick succession. In February 2002, the company won a sixteen-million-dollar award from the Navy for construction of an expanded detention camp at Guantánamo Bay, Cuba. By late April 2002, the Army's Operations Support Command in Rock Island, Illinois, which managed the LOGCAP program, had issued five task orders to the company and was preparing another; three of those jobs were in Central Asia. The U.S. military was preparing for a long stay in Afghanistan.

The military machine could not function without contractors, who maintained their equipment, provided translation services, and kept the camps running. Bringing in the big contractors, however, meant that fewer dollars would trickle down to the local economy. In the Balkans, Brown & Root hired an army of local people to do the cooking, cleaning, and construction, but in the new megabases such as Bagram, the company flew in third-country nationals—contract laborers from the Philippines, Sri Lanka, India, and Nepal—to dig ditches or ladle out food. By design or by accident, it mirrored the division of labor in the oil-rich Persian Gulf states, where imported workers did all the physical labor. Winning hearts and minds and boosting the local economy was not the point.

On the Shomali Plain, then, reconstruction got off to a modest start. During Afghanistan's civil war, villagers had fled the devastated agricultural region surrounding Bagram, and in the spring of 2002, the region was still in a shambles. The humble mud-brick compounds had been dynamited or destroyed; the fields were seeded with mines; and the main highway to Kabul was still pitted with the ugly, blossoming scars created by the impact of mortar rounds. The detritus of war still littered the road. On a drive outside the base, I spotted rusting hulks of armored personnel carriers, the occasional tank with its turret blown off, and a shipping container that had taken a direct hit, its shredded metal sides ballooned out. Green flags, symbolizing martyrdom, fluttered above roadside graves.

Around Bagram, the job of rebuilding fell to a relatively small contingent of Army Civil Affairs soldiers. When Dana Priest, a *Washington Post* military affairs reporter, visited the base that spring, she found a small group of reservists led by Major Bryan Cole, a Civil Affairs officer, leading a limited, ad hoc reconstruction effort. Cole's reservists were part of the 489th Civil Affairs Battalion, a unit based in Knoxville, Tennessee, that had around 120 soldiers in Afghanistan. They had two million dollars in seed money from the Army to jump-start the reconstruction process around Bagram.[7]

Priest, a perceptive reporter, had noticed an interesting shift in the 1990s, as U.S. policymakers turned increasingly to the military to solve political and economic problems. Priest had shadowed several of the "CINCs," the four-star commanders-in-chief of the military's geographic commands, and had seen how they had emerged as powerful regional proconsuls. General Wesley Clark, the head of U.S. European Command and Supreme Allied Commander Europe, and General Anthony Zinni, the chief of U.S. Central Command, held more power than any ambassador. They had aircraft and special operations teams at their disposal, they commanded the respect and attention of presidents and prime ministers, and they wielded more clout than the four-star service chiefs who were nominally their superiors. With little discussion or debate, America's military had been taking on a wider role in foreign policy. And nation building had by default been taken on by the combatant commands and the Civil Affairs and special operations units tasked to them.

That shift would begin to accelerate in Afghanistan, at first almost imperceptibly. In June 2002, a *New York Times* reporter visited a Civil Affairs team in Kunduz, a city that had been the final Taliban stronghold in northern Afghanistan. A small team there was working on a few small-scale projects, sprucing up a small schoolhouse with a fresh coat of paint and fixing windows. But the team had none of the resources to take on the more ambitious types of projects that Afghans were hoping for, like roadbuilding or bridge repair. In 2002, Civil Affairs teams in Afghanistan had an eight-million-dollar budget for the entire country, a relatively modest sum compared to the funds pledged at the December 2001 Afghanistan peace conference in Bonn. The soldiers avoided using the phrase "nation building" to describe their work.[8]

Civil Affairs troopers had one advantage over traditional aid workers, however: They were armed, and they could go to insecure areas that were off limits to many aid groups. That fact, combined with the military's "can-do" attitude and massive logistics capability, meant that the eight million dollars was just a start.

Civil Affairs is an unorthodox kind of soldiering. Unlike that of combat units—infantry, armor, artillery, and so on—the primary role of Civil Affairs is not "kinetic," because Civil Affairs troopers are not on the battlefield to seize territory and destroy things. Quite the opposite: Civil Affairs teams are supposed to step in after the fighting is over and restore essential services such as sewage, water, electricity, and roads. They dig wells, repair schools, and run small clinics. They forge relationships with local communities and nongovernmental organizations. Essentially, they are relief workers with guns.

The Civil Affairs community was unique in other ways. More than 90 percent of Civil Affairs troops are Army reservists, part-time soldiers with ordinary jobs in civilian life.[9] Civil Affairs shares a traditional affiliation with the Army Special Forces: Army Civil Affairs units were once subordinate to Army Special Operations Command, and for many years the Army had only one active-duty Civil Affairs unit, the Ninety-sixth Civil Affairs Battalion, stationed at Fort Bragg, North Carolina, the home of the Army's Special Warfare Center and School.[10] And like Special Forces, the Civil Affairs units were, at least in the pre–September 11 world, something of a stepchild. Civil Affairs was not considered a path to meteoric professional advancement; the Army classes Civil Affairs as a "functional area," essentially meaning that it is a secondary career for an officer.*

---

*In the weeks and months after the toppling of the Taliban regime, an operation in which Special Forces teams played an outsize role, it was easy to forget that for much of the 1990s, Special Operations had been something of a professional backwater. The world of Special Forces was also obscured by Hollywood mythmaking and its soldiers' depiction in the media as super-soldiers. One of the main missions, at least before Afghanistan, was the rather unglamorous work of "foreign internal defense": weeks and months spent patiently schooling ragtag third world armies in basic infantry tactics. As much as this task required good soldiering skills—and the Special Forces were very good at it—it also required some cultural sophistication and foreign-language skills. Along with the Civil Affairs teams and a small corps of Foreign Area Officers (military officers with advanced degrees in regional studies who worked as military attachés inside U.S. embassies) they were the Pentagon's informal diplomats, and its most experienced nation builders.

Civil Affairs had not, however, been conceived of as the primary development arm of the U.S. government. Its units were there to serve the immediate needs of the military commander on the scene; they were not equipped for any kind of long-term development effort. The idea was to step in, stabilize the situation, and get out. Patching up a road that was torn up by tank treads was one thing; helping create sustainable livelihoods in agricultural communities was quite another.

That was a job for another set of newcomers to the Shomali Plain: contractors from the U.S. Agency for International Development, or USAID. In July 2002, USAID awarded Chemonics International, a for-profit development firm, a $2.9 million contract for the Quick Impact Project, a short-term effort to repair the roads and the irrigation canals that once were the economic lifeline of the Shomali. The Quick Impact project was supposed to provide a quick infusion of jobs for returning families, and Chemonics hired three thousand local men to work as unskilled laborers rebuilding roads. The project would inject cash into the local economy, and help create the basic infrastructure that would connect communities to the capital.[11] The Quick Impact Project was also an important win for Chemonics: In 2000, its USAID contracts totaled $6.7 million.[12]

Development work and humanitarian aid may once have been the traditional domain of not-for-profit groups, charities, and international aid organizations such as CARE, Save the Children, and Médecins sans Frontières. Some nonprofits worked as "implementation partners" for government-funded aid schemes; others maintained their independence, refusing government funds. But foreign aid was also a tool of foreign policy. And it had increasingly become a for-profit business.

Chemonics was a good example. Founded in 1975 by Thurston Teele, a former Foreign Service officer, Chemonics was one of a number of private companies that had built a formidable business in the 1990s bidding for contracts from the U.S. government's aid agency. As part of an experiment in "reinventing government" led by the Clinton administration, USAID had become the government's primary laboratory for outsourcing.[13] USAID, which had deployed two thousand civilian development experts to South Vietnam at the height of the Vietnam War, had been gutted by a series of staff cutbacks; by 2002 it was basically a glorified contracting organization.[14] By the end of the 1990s, around half of USAID's funds for overseas development assistance were being channeled through private firms; the primary beneficiaries of U.S. development assistance were contractors. Ruben Berrios, a scholar who studied the emergence of for-profit companies in U.S. development assistance in the 1990s, reckoned that only a few cents of every foreign aid dollar actually ever reached the developing world. Hiring for-profit development companies often meant that much foreign aid was repatriated to the United States in the form of consultant salaries and other goods and services provided by contractors.[15]

This was the dirty little secret of U.S. foreign development assistance. While summoning visions of altruistic, self-sacrificing aid workers wearing sandals and digging wells, aid was really quite the racket. I had first encountered the world of the high-priced development consultant in the mid- to late 1990s, while living in Ukraine. To my eyes, at least, the life of a USAID contractor in Kyiv seemed to be one of enormous privilege, particularly in the down-at-heel world of post-Soviet Ukraine. Their employers paid astronomical sums to rent out smartly refurbished flats in the center of town; they were ferried around by drivers; they frequented a clutch of per diem–busting restaurants. This cosseted class also had its own unique vocabulary. Much discussion revolved around their "pay differential"— many of them, to my surprise, drew hardship pay—and they tended to ask other Americans how long they had been "in country," as if they were in the middle of a one-year combat tour. Ukrainians were referred to as "locals" (the word "native," evidently, had fallen out of fashion), and the USAID consultants had a uniformly low opinion of them. To my astonishment, few of the USAID contractors I met could speak passable Russian or Ukrainian. This, for them, was another stop on the USAID contracting circuit. Next year they would be in Bolivia, Bangladesh, or Albania.

Ukraine was a dysfunctional state run by retrograde former Communist officials. It had creaky infrastructure and poor rule of law; nevertheless, in most respects it belonged to the developed world. Still, like the rest of Eastern Europe and the former Soviet Union, Ukraine was a boom market for private-sector foreign aid contractors such as Chemonics and Booz Allen Hamilton as well as for large, not-for-profit entities like Counterpart International and International Relief and Development. They won USAID contracts to advise the Ukrainians on everything from agricultural-sector reform to media development.[16]

In the mid-1990s, Matt Bivens, a young freelance journalist, received a lucrative offer from Burson-Marsteller, a U.S. public relations firm, to work on a USAID contract promoting privatization in Kazakhstan. Burson-Marsteller, he later wrote, "made me an offer I couldn't refuse: $53,518 a year after taxes, insurance benefits, free housing, a driver, a maid, a $2,000 moving allowance, and an additional $25 per diem ($9,000 a year) in spending money. All told, a $70,000-a-year package; after only a few months, it would grow to $90,000."[17]

Bivens was twenty-six years old. In a scathing 1997 article in *Harper's*, he described the daily routine of a "cost-plus" USAID contractor in Kazakhstan. "The main event of every day was lunch," he wrote.

> Lunch was always at a fancy restaurant, with your driver waiting out front. More than thirty-five U.S. companies or organizations were on the AID payroll in Kazakhstan, offering advice on everything from drafting laws to wearing condoms, and every single one of them seemed to be as high on lunch as Burson-Marsteller was . . . Fridays I would retrieve a crumpled ball of business cards from my suit-coat pocket and incorporate them into a memo summarizing my work week: Monday met with so-and-so, discussed such-and-such. Tuesday met with such-and-such of the this-and-that group. Mostly I was describing lunch.[18]

Foreign aid budgets were often singled out by conservatives as a waste of taxpayer money—and aid programs to Eastern Europe and the former Soviet Union in the 1990s set new standards for corruption and mismanagement. In Russia, USAID hired the Harvard Institute for International Development to advise the government on privatization. The project was directed by Andrei Shleifer, a Russian-born émigré and tenured professor of economics at Harvard; another consultant to the project was Jonathan Hay, a Rhodes Scholar and former World Bank consultant. Both men, it turned out, had a massive conflict of interest: While helping the Russian government design the rules for a market economy, they were simultaneously making personal investments in Russia.[19] The U.S. government later implicated both men in a conspiracy to defraud the government, and Harvard University eventually paid $26.5 million to the U.S. government to settle a lawsuit after a U.S. District Court judge found Shleifer and Hay liable for breaching conflict-of-interest rules. Neither Shleifer nor Hay acknowledged any wrongdoing.[20]

Afghanistan would be the next big market for the USAID contractors. Much as KBR had arrived to scout Bagram Air Base for business opportunities with the Army, companies such as Chemonics, Bearing Point, and Louis Berger Group were positioning themselves to snag more contracts in Afghanistan. After all, USAID was as dependent upon companies like Chemonics to do its work as the Army was dependent on LOGCAP contracts to maintain its bases overseas. In government contracting parlance, Chemonics had a "track record"—it could be counted on to present a bid that would meet the Byzantine requirements of government contracting practice. As Joel Hafvenstein, a young Chemonics consultant, would note in his memoir of the aid business in Afghanistan, "Chemonics was nothing if not a proposal-writing machine. The company prided itself on being able to whip up a plan and a team to carry out pretty much anything USAID might want to do: clean up air pollution in Cairo, train Russian judges, help Ugandans export cut flowers."[21]

By the time Hafvenstein arrived to help close out the Chemonics Quick Impact Project on the Shomali Plain, a micro-economy had already sprung up in Kabul that served a small community of international relief workers and aid contractors, conspicuous in their white SUVs. Their drivers would park their vehicles outside the discreet restaurants that catered to Kabul's expatriate community, small oases behind compound walls where the development set could chill out, drink a few cans of imported Heineken, and live some facsimile of the high life.

At that point it was not clear what USAID's long-term plan for rebuilding Afghanistan was, or what the end-state was supposed to be. But the reconstruction of Afghanistan meant there would be a new destination for the lavishly paid class of aid consultants who would see Afghans through the windshields of their air-conditioned Land Cruisers. Watching the arrival of Development Inc. in Kabul, I wondered if this would be a new chance to get foreign aid right—or another opportunity for waste, fraud, and abuse.

For the time being, Afghanistan remained primarily a military mission. And Operation Enduring Freedom, the military's name for the post–September 11 campaign in Afghanistan, was first and foremost a punitive expedition. Major Bryan Hilferty, the spokesman for the Army's Tenth Mountain Division at Bagram, would conclude all of his press briefings with the same sound bite: "The hunt continues. The war against al-Qaeda in Afghanistan is not over."

After Operation Anaconda was wrapped up, in late March 2002, the press corps at Bagram rapidly dwindled: The dramatic battle in the mountains was over, and few reporters were attracted to the less alluring subject of rebuilding Afghanistan's shattered infrastructure. For the news media as much as the military, Afghanistan's long-term economic development was an afterthought.

Afghanistan had a transitional administration headed by Hamid Karzai, but little else that resembled a functioning national government or bureaucracy. The State Department needed the rudiments of a functioning embassy, both to conduct diplomatic business with the new government and to help get it on its feet. In March 2002, Ambassador Robert Finn, a career diplomat with some experience in the region, was dispatched to Kabul to set up an embassy. Finn had helped open the first U.S. diplomatic mission in the oil-rich former Soviet republic of Azerbaijan, and had previously served as ambassador to Tajikistan, the dysfunctional Central Asian state that bordered northern Afghanistan. At the time, the State Department had yet to begin normal rotational staffing for diplomats to Afghanistan. Kabul was considered a "hardship" rotation; most officers would stay for only weeks at a time. The high turnover meant there was constant waste and duplication of effort. There was no institutional memory to guide aid effectively.

Keith Mines was one of the Foreign Service officers who volunteered to "go TDY" (on temporary duty) to help get the embassy up and running. He arrived in Kabul in June 2002. The U.S. embassy in Kabul occupied a sandbagged compound near a traffic circle recently renamed for the martyred Northern Alliance commander, Ahmad Shah Massoud. After the city fell to the Northern Alliance in late 2001, a team of CIA and U.S. Special Operations commandos made their way through downtown Kabul to reclaim the embassy, which had been shuttered during Afghanistan's civil war and the years of Taliban rule. Gary Berntsen, a counterterrorism officer, was one of the first Americans to set foot in the embassy since 1989; he found rotary-dial telephones and official photographs of President Ronald Reagan and Vice President George H. W. Bush on the wall. On the floor of the ambassador's office Berntsen found a more somber memento: a photograph from the funeral of Adolph Dubs, the last U.S. ambassador to Afghanistan, who was killed in an exchange of fire during a botched hostage rescue attempt at a Kabul hotel in 1979.[22]

Among the many bureaucratic tribes in Washington, the Foreign Service had always conceived of itself as something of an elite. Foreign Service officers had to pass competitive entry exams, a written test and a more subjectively graded oral exam; obtain Top Secret security clearances; and pass a "suitability review." Foreign Service officers segregated themselves from the other civil servants within the State Department. FSOs, as they are called, are diplomats, not ordinary bureaucrats; everyone else is mere support staff, regardless of their pay grade or their expertise. Even the analysts at the Bureau of Intelligence and Research, the State Department's respected intelligence arm, were second-class citizens within the department. Until Colin Powell became secretary of state under George W. Bush, Foreign Service officers even had their own dedicated lounge inside "main State," the State Department's headquarters in Foggy Bottom.

Some Foreign Service officers were attracted to the job's prestige, and to the postings in European capitals. Mines was not one of them. He was the kind of Foreign Service officer instinctively drawn to what he called the "failed-state circuit." As a diplomat, he had served tours in Somalia and Haiti; he had made friends with Palestinians during a posting to Israel; and he had spent time overseas outside the protective embrace of the embassy. In the late 1970s, he had spent two years as a young Mormon missionary in Colombia, which was emerging from two decades of mayhem known as *la violencia*. His first experience was working in Barranquilla with a Colombian companion who spoke no English. He would go for weeks on end without any contact with other Americans.

Colombia taught him some valuable lessons. "That was the closest I have ever been to a foreign culture, living as we did directly among the people without any of the organizational protection from things foreign that is provided in military or Embassy service, business or even the Peace Corps," he later recalled.* That familiarity with life outside the embassy walls set Mines apart, as did his previous career: Before joining the Foreign Service, Mines was an Army infantry officer.

Mines, then, was unusually well prepared to work in the postconflict

---

* This section draws in part on *Wingtips on the Ground*, an unpublished memoir by Mines, who kindly gave permission to quote from his manuscript.

environment of Afghanistan. He was not drawn to the cocktail-party circuit, and he preferred hardship posts to plush assignments. Before he joined the mission in Kabul, Mines had been serving a relatively quiet posting in the political-military section at the U.S. embassy in Budapest. The evening of the 9/11 attacks, he collected all his old military gear and put it in a rucksack that he parked in the middle of the upstairs hall; the next day, he sent a letter to a reserve commander to offer his services. It was a symbolic gesture: The Army did not need an aging paratrooper. Mines eventually put his rucksack back in the closet, but he was on a war footing.

Like the other new arrivals at the U.S. embassy in Kabul, Mines was assigned space in cramped offices. But the job had an upside. Security in Kabul was reasonably good, and the capital was enjoying its first spring free of the Taliban. After a few days of orientation, embassy staffers were given a fair degree of freedom to move outside the fortified embassy perimeter. But there was no master plan for rebuilding Afghanistan; they would have to improvise.

In theory, the U.S. ambassador is the head of the "country team"; he or she is the top U.S. representative in a country, and all agencies of the U.S. government report to the ambassador. In practice, however, the military was running the show in Afghanistan. It owned a fleet of airlifters, fighter aircraft, and helicopters; it ran a massive logistics operation and a network of bases; and by late 2002, it had about seven thousand troops on the ground. It also had a clear mandate: Hunt for Osama bin Laden, destroy his network, and finish off the remnants of the Taliban. For the small embassy staff, the mission in Afghanistan was less than clear. Afghanistan barely had a functioning bureaucracy, and its economy seemed stuck in the Middle Ages. The traditional job of the diplomat, reporting on the political goings-on in a foreign capital, was hard to do when the institutions of government were still being rebuilt. For instance, Mines was instructed to prepare Afghanistan's new minister of commerce to brief some officials from Washington who would be paying a call on him. He walked through the minister's résumé with the minister's assistant. The biography went something like this: born, 1957; secondary schooling, Kabul Elementary and West Kabul High School, graduated 1975; graduate in engineering, University of Kabul, 1979; minister of commerce, 2001.

Mines inquired about the twenty-year gap in the minister's résumé.

"Oh, that," his assistant said. "Well, there was the *jihad* against the

Soviets; then there was the civil war; and then, of course, we had the war against the Taliban."

At that moment, Mines realized he was dealing with a lost generation; Afghanistan's governing institutions had missed the past twenty years of economic development and contact with the outside world.

Part of the diplomats' job was scouting local businesses to better understand the local economy, and figuring out how to get Afghanistan's economy back on its feet. Congress had inserted an extra $49.7 million in overseas humanitarian aid into a $20 billion emergency war spending bill in early 2002; $5 million was earmarked specifically for landmine victims. At an international conference in Bonn in December 2001, the international community pledged to back the creation of the International Security Assistance Force, or ISAF, a peacekeeping contingent that would initially provide security for Kabul. At a donors' conference in Tokyo the following month, donor countries promised $5 billion in reconstruction assistance to Afghanistan over a six-year period.

But the country could not move forward without some kind of collective political settlement, and that was where the diplomats could make a difference. The international community helped sponsor a *loya jirga*, a grand assembly, in June 2002. The *loya jirga* was the founding moment of the new Afghanistan, a council of national unity, attended by prominent community delegates and tribal leaders. In practice, it was Afghan tradition merged with twenty-first-century political theater: The event was broadcast on national television and radio, and the country watched the process of national reconciliation unfold. The United Nations had the lead for the event; Lakhdar Brahimi, a veteran UN peace negotiator, was the special representative overseeing the event. Behind the scenes, U.S. embassy staff helped stage-manage everything. The Germans brought in a huge Oktoberfest tent to house the delegates. Mines went around to NATO allies to beg donations of uniforms and equipment for the first *kandak* (battalion) of the Afghan National Army, which would provide security for the proceedings.

For Mines, watching the *loya jirga* was a heady experience. "It was national group therapy," he later recalled. "And it was precisely what the new nation needed. In the hall there was focus on each of the speakers, and throughout Kabul—in the cafes, homes, and parks—people were riveted. It was the cathartic experience that the Afghan nation had to have if it was to succeed in putting itself back together."

It was also a hopeful moment for the international community. ISAF, a small NATO force operating under a UN mandate, arrived to police the capital in late 2001. At the final session of the *loya jirga*, Mines noticed, the most enthusiastic applause was reserved for the commander of ISAF. After years of factional fighting and the near-destruction of Kabul, Afghans were grateful to see a force that was neutral and impartial. ISAF's mandate, however, extended only to the capital and its environs; outside Kabul, local warlords still held sway.

The triumph of the *loya jirga* was marred by a tragic event shortly afterward: the bombing of a wedding party at a village in Oruzgan by U.S. aircraft. The guests had been firing their Kalashnikovs into the air, a celebratory gesture the pilots mistook as an attack. Dozens of guests were killed.[23] It was not the first time civilians had been targeted by mistake: In December, U.S. forces acting on a tip from a local informant attacked a convoy in Paktia Province. But it was not a Taliban convoy; the trucks were actually ferrying a group of elders to Kabul to celebrate the inauguration of Karzai. It was a classic case of score settling: An informant had set U.S. troops up to kill off a rival.[24]

Not long after the *loya jirga*, the embassy hosted a visit from Paul Wolfowitz, the deputy secretary of defense. When an officer briefed the deputy secretary on the Oruzgan bombing, Wolfowitz quickly grew irritated. Why, he asked, had the briefers accepted the reports of civilian casualties at face value? Couldn't the Taliban have faked the incident? Perhaps it was staged to make the coalition look bad, he suggested. Did anyone actually *see* the bodies? Wolfowitz would hear none of it, and he chastised the group for falling for what, in his view, might easily have been Taliban propaganda. The people in the room were "stunned," Mines recalled.*

In public, at least, senior officials paid lip service to the importance of preventing civilian casualties. In a public town hall meeting during his visit to Afghanistan, Wolfowitz told a reporter, "We are always concerned when we believe that we may have killed innocent people. And we think that probably happened in that incident and we deeply regret that. But we have no regrets whatsoever about going after terrorists, or

---

* Asked about his recollection of the briefing, Wolfowitz told me through an intermediary that Mines's story "doesn't square with his recollection of this event from eight years ago," without offering any further account of what happened at the meeting.

people who harbor terrorists. And we have really very little doubt that there were such people in that area. It was a combat zone. Bad things happen in combat zones."[25]

Wolfowitz's attitude to Afghanistan's political end-state was even more revealing. The briefers cued up a slide for the high-level visitor that posed the crucial question: Would Afghanistan be a partner or a platform in the war on terror? Thus far, Afghanistan had been a launching pad, a base for a military campaign against al-Qaeda and their Taliban allies. Mines and his colleagues wanted to argue for a more robust state-building effort in Afghanistan: helping build state institutions and backing a capable national army under the control of the central government. At this point Karzai was the mayor of Kabul; most of Afghanistan was still ruled by strongmen who controlled private militias. And this task would require a commitment to extend the influence of the national government into the provinces, Special Forces soldiers to train and advise the new Afghan security forces, and civilian experts who could advise the new government on everything from education to agriculture.

But as the briefers quickly realized, the Pentagon leadership had already moved on from Afghanistan, and the focus had shifted to planning the campaign to unseat Saddam Hussein in Iraq. The Special Forces teams were needed elsewhere, and Afghanistan's military would have to do with secondhand equipment and an "economy of force" contingent. A vigorous state-building effort would have to wait. A question lingered for the next several years: What would have happened in Afghanistan if the United States had committed more resources early on, and not become distracted by Iraq? Would it have successfully kept the Taliban at bay—and kept Afghanistan from sliding back into war?

CHAPTER 2

The PowerPoint Warrior

The cavernous, air-conditioned auditorium of the Ronald Reagan Build-ing in downtown Washington was packed to capacity with Pentagon bu-reaucrats, defense contractors, and men and women in dress uniform. Covering a naval research and development conference was not the most exciting reporting assignment, but Admiral Vern Clark, the chief of naval operations, was scheduled to deliver the keynote address that day. After fortifying myself with cheap coffee and a stale bagel, I made my way into the hall and sank into a plush chair. I was prepared to doze quietly through another dull PowerPoint briefing.

Then the man in the mock turtleneck took the stage. Thomas Barnett, an obscure strategist with the Pentagon's Office of Force Transformation, strolled in front of the massive screen and cued up a slide. I was jolted in my seat by a jarring sound effect: *ching-ching!* the ominous prison-door clang from the crime procedural *Law & Order.*

For an audience used to monochromatic PowerPoint presentations from Pentagon officials, Barnett's approach was something completely dif-ferent: He prowled the stage restlessly with a wireless microphone, punching out his talking points with the patter of a Silicon Valley tech guru. He liked to use catchphrases ("disconnectedness defines danger") and Thomas Friedman-isms (Osama bin Laden and his ilk, he said, were "super-empowered individuals"). Key points were punctuated by an audio sample ("Yeah, baby!") from an Austin Powers movie. Barnett's style was over-the-top, but he was delivering an important message to the military and the defense industry: "We're a military that's built to fight other nation-states, other militaries," he said. "The security market has fractured dramatically over time."

It had already become a cliché to say that the world changed on September 11, 2001. But the Pentagon had not really changed as an institution. While U.S. troops were engaged in an unconventional war in Afghanistan, the Defense Department was still groping for an adversary worthy of an annual budget of roughly four hundred billion dollars. A decade after the collapse of the Soviet Union, the military was geared primarily toward conventional, state-on-state conflict. Air wings, Army divisions, and carrier battle groups were all trained and equipped for high-end warfare, and the Pentagon's guiding strategy document, the *2001 Quadrennial Defense Review*, still viewed China as a potential "peer competitor" that might someday challenge the United States.

Barnett had little patience with talk of a looming great-power struggle with China or a resurgent Russia that would provide an organizing principle for the Pentagon. "China and the United States going at it, out of the blue, is a load of crap in my mind," he said. The United States, he argued, was already deeply involved in a very new kind of war that would refashion the way the United States would be engaged in the world. And things would be that way for a long time.

Take, for instance, the new military outposts established on the periphery of the former Soviet Union to support Operation Enduring Freedom in Afghanistan. Although administration officials insisted they had no plans to maintain a permanent presence in Central Asia—in part out of deference to local political sensitivities—Barnett was blunt about the new U.S. military presence in Kyrgyzstan and Uzbekistan. He predicted that the United States would be in these new outposts for decades to come. "I believe fifty years from now, [those bases] will be as familiar to us as Ramstein Air Force Base," he said, referring to one of the giant U.S. installations in Germany. It was an arresting prediction, particularly considering the Bush administration's efforts to portray those bases as a temporary expediency for the war on terror. And it was particularly startling to hear it from a Pentagon strategist.

In August 2002, Barnett was employed by the Office of Force Transformation, a new office within the Pentagon devoted to big-picture thinking about how the U.S. military should respond to future strategic threats. The head of the Office of Force Transformation was a retired Navy vice admiral, Arthur Cebrowski, who had been tapped by Secretary of Defense Donald Rumsfeld to be the Pentagon's in-house intellectual. From the beginning of his tenure, Rumsfeld had made it clear, in his typically brusque way, that he saw the military services, particularly the Army, as hidebound, Cold War–era bureaucracies that were wedded to parochial interests, especially when it came to procuring new equipment. The defense secretary had a point. While the military had made great technological strides in developing precision weaponry and designing elaborate command-and-control networks, the Defense Department had remained mired in mid-twentieth-century business practices and organizational behavior. And although the services paid a lot of lip service to "jointness"—under the sweeping changes enacted under the Goldwater-Nichols Act of 1986, they were required to coordinate their efforts and their procurement—they zealously fought to preserve their individual budgets. The Pentagon bureaucracy, Rumsfeld famously complained, was "one of the world's last bastions of central planning."[1] The Office of Force Transformation was supposed to help drag the military and the defense bureaucracy into the Information Age.

Cebrowski, who had been a fighter pilot in Vietnam and a Navy aircraft carrier commander, was Rumsfeld's chief evangelist for this new way of doing business. He had helped popularize a concept called "network-centric warfare," a vision of harnessing the power of information technology to dominate future battlefields. Network-centric warfare borrowed its trendy lexicon from Silicon Valley, but stripped to its essence, it was a vision of rapid, decentralized decisionmaking.[2] Much as dominant private-sector firms such as FedEx, Walmart, and Amazon .com could leverage information technology to move inventory rapidly and stay ruthlessly lean and efficient, the U.S. military wanted to use information to create a permanent advantage against all adversaries. By knitting together sensor information—drawn from cameras perched on satellites, surveillance planes loitering overhead, shipboard radars, even precision weapons themselves—and disseminating it across a network, the U.S. military would have total information superiority, empowering it to move at lightning speed. "Peer-to-peer" communication would trump traditional top-down military hierarchies.

It was an intoxicating vision. The first laser-guided "smart bombs" were used in the Vietnam War, but the U.S. military's stunning victory in Operation Desert Storm in 1991 had given the world the first real glimpse of this kind of overwhelming technological and informational advantage. The recent campaign in Afghanistan affirmed this vision: A handful of Special Operations troops with satellite communications, access to overhead surveillance, and the ability to call in smart weapons had been able to dispatch Taliban fighters with lethal precision and unprecedented speed. That vision of a technologically superior, network-enabled military appealed not only to the military but also to defense contractors and their supporters in Congress. In fact, large defense firms were particularly enamored of the concept. "Network-centric" became a convenient marketing term for any costly, high-tech piece of military gadgetry, and industry executives liked to tout the "net-centricity" of whatever piece of hardware they were selling.

In the summer of 2002, network-centric warfare was still all the rage inside the Pentagon. Yet Barnett's briefing was not a sales pitch for network-centric warfare. He was there to tell the military and the defense industry something they did not want to hear. Before joining the Office of Force Transformation, Barnett had been a strategic researcher and professor at the Naval War College in Newport, Rhode Island, where Cebrowski had served as president. In 1999, the young scholar had written an article for *Proceedings*, the professional journal of the U.S. Naval Institute. "The Seven Deadly Sins of Network-Centric Warfare" was a pointed critique of Cebrowski's vision. "If absence makes the heart grow fonder, network-centric warfare is in for a lot of heartbreak, because I doubt we will ever encounter an enemy to match its grand assumptions regarding a revolution in military affairs," he wrote. "The United States currently spends more on its information technology than all but a couple of great powers spend on their entire militaries. In a world where rogue nations typically spend around $5 billion a year on defense, NCW [network-centric warfare] is a path down which only the U.S. military can tread."[3]

The article caught Cebrowski's attention, and he encouraged Barnett's inquiry. With some nudging from the admiral, Barnett began studying problems of globalization and how they might shape future conflict. In 1999, Cebrowski and Barnett teamed up with top executives at the Wall Street firm Cantor Fitzgerald to present a workshop on how information technology and the rise of the global economy were changing national security. It was an eye-opening experience for both men. Encouraged by Cebrowski, Barnett began to devise a grand strategic briefing that depicted a new map of the world. Instead of the old Cold War map in which the world was divided between East and West, Barnett's map showed a bifurcated world with a "functioning core" of states integrated into the global economy, and a "non-integrating gap" that covered Central Asia, the Middle East, most of Africa, and a fair chunk of Latin America. These "gap" states were the parts of the world that were poorly integrated into the global economy; they were prone to wars, insurgencies, and humanitarian crises. And they were the parts of the world, Barnett theorized, where the United States would find itself rebuilding failed states, policing conflicts, or fighting preemptive wars against terrorists.*

As an adjunct to this theory, Barnett forwarded a second, equally important, idea. The U.S. military, he argued, was well equipped for the "regime change" mission. It could take on any conventional military force in the world, and its air wings, armored divisions, and carrier battle groups were primed for violent, short-duration conflicts. But the military was ill equipped for the civilizing mission required in the "gap." In Barnett's view, the U.S. military needed to be divided into two forces: a conventional military force—borrowing from Thomas Hobbes, Barnett dubbed this "Leviathan"—that could demolish any opposing country's forces; and another, hybrid, force, called "SysAdmin," that would be equipped for nation-building missions. It would have experts in governance, infrastructure, and humanitarian aid; it would be flexible enough to work with civilian agencies, aid workers, private voluntary organizations, and contractors; and when not cleaning up after Leviathan, the system administrators would be involved in cooperative training exercises and other quasi-diplomatic missions around the globe. They would include a sort of constabulary force of lightly armored soldiers and Marines, aid workers, diplomats, and legal specialists. Its workforce would be older and more experienced.

What Barnett was articulating was not a particularly original idea. In

---

*Barnett also seemed to draw inspiration from the pop-globalization writings of Thomas Friedman, who once postulated the "Golden Arches Theory of Conflict Prevention," according to which no two nations with McDonald's franchises—nations that are part of the global economy—had ever gone to war. Friedman's observation would be undermined by the 1999 NATO bombing campaign against Serbia.

the late 1990s, Marine Corps General Charles Krulak wrote an article outlining a "three block war" scenario in a hypothetical African country in which Marines would have to conduct a peacekeeping mission, conduct raids, and hand out humanitarian aid, all in a day's work.[4] Nor was it that new: The Romans, for instance, had two distinct words for war: *bellum*, which applied to military campaigns against the armies of other empires or city-states; and *guerra*, which described combat against tribes on the periphery of the empire.* The U.S. military, Barnett was basically saying, wanted *bellum*: a straightforward fight against an enemy whose soldiers wore uniforms and had regular military formations. What it was engaged in, however, was *guerra*, the thankless, ambivalent task of playing globo-cop. And it was not equipped to handle the latter.

Had the Berlin Wall never come down, Barnett probably would probably have made a career as a Kremlinologist, counting ICBM payloads in advance of arms control talks with the Soviets. But his timing was off: He graduated from Harvard University's Soviet area studies program in 1986, just as Mikhail Gorbachev began accidentally dismantling the Soviet system through *perestroika* and *glasnost*. He completed his Ph.D. in 1990—his dissertation compared Romanian and East German policies in the Third World—just a year before the final collapse of the Soviet Union.

Before joining the faculty at the Naval War College, Barnett worked at the Center for Naval Analyses and the Institute for Public Research, federally funded nonprofit research organizations. It was not the fast track to a traditional academic job in a political science department, but it gave Barnett extensive contacts with the post–Cold War military as well as with the U.S. Agency for International Development, where he worked

---

* The defense analyst D. Robert Worley outlined precisely this point in a publication funded by the U.S. Army War College, "Waging Ancient War: Limits on Preemptive Force" (Carlisle, Pa., 2003). He called for developing a "*guerra* strategy" that he argued would be more appropriate for dealing with terrorists and other nonstate actors in poorly governed regions of the world. *Guerra* would be a nation-building campaign that demanded minimal, not overwhelming, use of force. And more important, *guerra* would require a new kind of hybrid force. "Humanitarian interventions in failed and failing states require expeditionary forces designed for peace operations that may evolve into nation-building," he wrote (p. xi).

on the "reinventing government" push that gutted the agency in the 1990s. When the U.S. military became involved in a number of nation-building exercises in Haiti, Bosnia, Kosovo, and Somalia, the military establishment seemed to view these involvements as exceptions.

Despite the military's attitude toward nation building, military personnel who had direct experience in those operations seemed to be developing an alternative view. Barnett encountered a number of individuals whose careers had become defined by what he would later describe as the hybrid nation-building "SysAdmin mode." There was retired Army Lieutenant General Jay Garner, who led a humanitarian rescue mission in northern Iraq in 1991 in the aftermath of Operation Desert Storm. There was General Eric Shinseki, who led the NATO Stabilization Force in Bosnia. In other words, despite the fact that nation building was not in fashion in the military in the first decade after the end of the Cold War, the U.S. military was gaining a fair amount of practical experience in nation building, whether it wanted to or not. After September 11, 2001, Cebrowski tasked Barnett with refining a global strategy briefing.

"Art," Barnett later recalled, "You're asking me to come up with the grand strategy for the United States after 9/11."

"Yes," Cebrowski said.

"Well, can't I just go ask those who know what it is?" Barnett responded.

"They don't know," Cebrowski replied. "If they do, they can't articulate it. Or they're too busy to articulate it, and they wouldn't articulate it to you anyway."

Barnett drew up the slides and began working on the presentation that would later be called "the Pentagon's new map." The ideas drew heavily on the globalization theory, and his storytelling style seemed inspired by pop-sociology books such as Malcolm Gladwell's *The Tipping Point*. Military officers were not initially receptive to the ideas outlined in the briefing. Barnett's motivational-speaker style could be glib and off-putting, and his early briefings were often met with scorn. And as critics of the Office of Force Transformation liked to point out, aside from a few pet projects, Cebrowski and his crew of strategy geeks controlled few budget lines, which were the real measure of power in the Pentagon. (As Barnett recalled later, "You're just a crank then. You're naïve. You're immature. And they demean your message by demeaning you.")

But it was Barnett's predictions of a long-term presence in the "gap" that proved most controversial—and, briefly, landed him in hot water. I wrote a short article on Barnett's August 2002 presentation for *Defense Week*, the trade paper I worked for in Washington. The piece juxtaposed Barnett's predictions of long-term bases in Central Asia with a policy statement from Rumsfeld ("We don't have any particular plans for permanent bases"). Although *Defense Week* had a tiny circulation, its articles were often picked up in the *Early Bird*, the Pentagon's daily clipping service; those stories circulated among hundreds of thousands of Defense Department personnel. Barnett recounted what happened next in his 2004 book, *The Pentagon's New Map: War and Peace in the Twenty-first Century*. "Well, the day the article appeared in the Pentagon's Early Bird news service, I got a phone call from OSD's [Office of the Secretary of Defense] policy shop, asking, in effect, who I was and why I was saying these things," he wrote.[5]

A few weeks later, Barnett was summoned to give his briefings to a collection of DASDs ("daz-dees," deputy assistant secretaries of defense, political appointees who supervised offices within the Pentagon). A representative from the Office of the Under Secretary of Defense for Policy Doug Feith was also in attendance. When the "core-gap" briefing was over, everyone in the room turned to the representative from Feith's office. "Nothing I see here goes against the stuff we're trying to do in our shop," the representative said with a shrug.[6] Barnett was off the hook. His brief wasn't at odds with the long-term planning in the Pentagon; he had in fact distilled it quite nicely. The U.S. military was planning to ramp up its involvement in those regions of the globe deemed most vulnerable to violence and political instability. Barnett's vision of the world would take on an unexpected clarity, and his briefing would soon become quite famous within defense circles.

The former Soviet Republic of Georgia is blessed with a Mediterranean climate, mountain landscapes, and a rich tradition of wine and hospitality. But its history since independence in 1991 had been an unhappy one. It was poorly integrated into the global economy, it had suffered from years of civil war, and it was near the top of the scale on any corruption index. In short, it looked like the ideal place to experiment with molding a new state.

Georgia's first postindependence president was Zviad Gamsakhurdia, a onetime Soviet political prisoner and literature professor. Gamsakhurdia was no dissident in the Vaclav Havel mold; he was erratic and dictatorial, and he shut down opposition newspapers and jailed political opponents. Ethnic minorities in the provinces of South Ossetia and Abkhazia particularly loathed Gamsakhurdia, who attracted some especially nationalistic followers. Georgia was soon faced with separatist movements on several fronts, including the resort region of Abkhazia on the Black Sea coast and the mountainous enclave of South Ossetia, just an hour's drive north of the capital, Tbilisi. The country was divided into armed camps.

Ousted after a round of street-fighting in 1992, Gamsakhurdia sought refuge across the border, in Russia's Chechen Republic, where a mercurial former Soviet Air Force general named Dzhokhar Dudayev was leading a campaign for independence from Moscow. Gamsakhurdia died under mysterious circumstances in 1993—perhaps a suicide, perhaps killed by his own supporters—as Georgia became engulfed in a ruinous civil war. By the early 1990s, the Mkhedrioni, a militia run by a posturing thug named Jaba Ioseliani, had emerged as Georgia's most powerful military force. Ioseliani, who had been convicted of bank robbery in Leningrad, styled himself as a playwright and an intellectual. His fighters, accessorized with Armani knockoffs and heavy weaponry, had a preference for running extortion and protection rackets. They were very good at intimidating ordinary Georgians, but were an absolute failure as a military force. Ragtag separatist armies in Abkhazia and South Ossetia, sometimes with assistance from Russia, succeeded in beating back the Georgian military and driving ethnic Georgians from their homes.

By the late 1990s, those ethnic conflicts had cooled down—or at least, the separatist boundaries were frozen in place, leaving hundreds of thousands of Georgians displaced from their homes. Georgia had stabilized somewhat under the rule of President Eduard Shevardnadze, a former secretary general of the Georgian Communist Party and onetime member of the Soviet Politburo. Shevardnadze, known as the "Silver Fox" for his political longevity, was well known in Western capitals: He served as Mikhail Gorbachev's foreign minister, and played a key role in allowing the Warsaw Pact states to go their own way during the wave of democratic transformations that swept Eastern Europe in the late 1980s.

Shevardnadze was a canny political operator, and he had cultivated closer ties with the United States. Under his leadership, Georgia joined the Partnership for Peace, a club for NATO aspirants, and he signed off on the Baku-Tbilisi-Ceyhan pipeline, a new route for transporting Caspian oil from Azerbaijan that was favored by the United States. Still, despite paying lip service to democracy, Georgia under Shevardnadze was something of a gangster's paradise. The old nomenklatura was still a presence, and corruption and cronyism were a fact of life. Seen from afar, Georgia sometimes looked like Havana under Fulgencio Batista: exotic yet familiar, freewheeling and corrupt, a place to celebrate life or go on vacation, but certainly not a smart place to invest your money.*

In 1998, AES, a U.S.-based global power company founded by two veterans of the U.S. Department of Energy, won a tender to oversee the privatization of Telasi, the electricity distribution company in Georgia's capital city, Tbilisi. The whole AES Telasi exercise was a fiasco: Georgian customers, pensioners and large state enterprises alike, were used to receiving power for free; Georgia relied heavily on power imported from Russia, and its energy distribution infrastructure was a shambles. A metering scheme introduced by AES was a flop, especially when official monthly salaries were often less than a monthly electricity bill. Power outages were a routine part of life, and candlelight ceased to be romantic for the beleaguered Georgians. It was an unhappy first encounter with globalization and American know-how.†

In Barnett's terms, Georgia was a classic "gap" state: It was poorly integrated in the global economy, and its main trading partner was Russia, which hardly made it a promising model for greater global connectivity. In mid-2002, it was to become a laboratory for the U.S. government to remake this impoverished republic in its own image.

In late April of 2002, the U.S. Defense Department announced a major new initiative: the Georgia Train and Equip Program, an effort to build a new Georgian military from scratch. The program would begin

---

* Hugh Rodham, the brother of First Lady Hillary Clinton, dabbled in a deal to grow and export hazelnuts from Georgia. The arrangement fell through when it came to light that Rodham's local partner was Aslan Abashidze, a rival of Shevardnadze.
† Paul Devlin, an independent filmmaker, shot a brilliant documentary about AES Telasi, entitled *Power Trip*. As he concluded work on the film, AES was forced to put the money-losing company up for sale. The enterprise was acquired by Russia's United Energy Systems.

in the classroom: U.S. advisors would lead a course for the Georgian military staff to ensure that Georgia's Land Forces Command, Border Guards, and other security agencies had professional staff organizations capable of communicating with NATO militaries and with each other. The advisors would then start building individual Georgian army units, one battalion at a time. Army Special Forces soldiers would do most of the hands-on training, teaching Georgian recruits battlefield first aid, radio procedures, land navigation, and marksmanship. By graduation, Georgians would be able to master small-unit infantry tactics, and a smaller, more capable group would be trained as commandos.

For a country of Georgia's size, the scope of the program was ambitious: The first phase of the program was valued at $64 million, a relative pittance by Pentagon standards, but a substantial amount of money for Georgia—several times greater than the country's regular annual defense budget. And in addition to training, the United States would provide weapons and ammunition to the Georgians, as well as around a dozen Vietnam-vintage UH-1 Huey helicopters. That fall, as the training program got under way, I traveled to Georgia to see firsthand what this experiment looked like.

Out at the Krtsanisi training range, a former Soviet tank-driving range on the southern outskirts of Tbilisi, the U.S. military trainers wore holstered sidearms. The pistols, I was told, were for self-protection against stray dogs that tended to wander around the dilapidated compound. Krtsanisi was the main venue for Georgia Train and Equip Program, a state-building exercise that was being overseen by soldiers from the Tenth Special Forces Group. When I arrived in October 2002, the trainers had been here for only a few months; the Georgia Train and Equip Program was still in its infancy, as was the new Georgian military.

Out on the firing range, the Georgian recruits were lined up in their mix-and-match uniforms. Some had old Soviet desert fatigues that looked like hand-me-downs from the 1980s war in Afghanistan; a few had U.S. Army surplus uniforms. On the range, Sergeant First Class Keith Peterson patiently helped one of the Georgians zero his rifle, a basic exercise in rifle marksmanship. Peering into his spotting scope at a paper target 100 meters downrange, Peterson ordered the trainee to squeeze off another round; a Georgian translator relayed the order to the trainee, whose scruffy Puma sneakers showed beneath his camouflage uniform. *Crack!* The trainee flinched from the recoil. "Is he jerking?" asked Peterson. The translator relayed some more instructions; Peterson then ordered another shot. After another shot downrange, Peterson looked satisfied that his student's rifle sights were correctly aligned: "That weapon is zeroed."

The exercise at the firing range required an extra bit of patience: Special Forces soldiers had to work through a team of around two dozen Georgian interpreters who translated their instructions into the exotic Caucasus language. While working in Georgian was something new, training foreign militaries was nothing particularly novel for the Special Forces, who in peacetime had become the Pentagon's dedicated cadre of soldier-diplomats. Special Forces troops were all required to acquire at least one foreign language: Training third world militaries, a mission called "foreign internal defense," was one of their primary jobs. It was a valuable and relatively low-cost sort of military exchange program. U.S. Special Operations Command would routinely send small teams on Joint Combined Exchange Training exercises, or JCETs ("jay-sets") to dozens of countries around the world, usually for a few weeks at a time. Local militaries would receive invaluable training from some of the best tacticians in the business. As a quid pro quo the Special Forces would build contacts with local officers and NCOs, and familiarize themselves with a terrain they might someday find themselves operating in.

The Georgia Train and Equip Program was a JCET on steroids. Most JCETs involved small teams of around a dozen or so Special Forces troops, although some larger exercises might involve a few more soldiers. The Georgia program soon involved a total of around 150 trainers. (In terms of the number of uniformed personnel, it was closer in size to the U.S. involvement in Colombia, which had been a major recipient of U.S. military aid as part of a massive counternarcotics program, Plan Colombia. In early 2002, the Defense Department had around 250 uniformed personnel stationed in Colombia, a country with nearly ten times the population of Georgia.[7])

The Georgia Train and Equip Program was also a major opportunity for the Pentagon's logistics support contractors. U.S. trainers enjoyed hot meals in a shiny new mess hall built by KBR, the subsidiary of the Houston-based oil services company Halliburton that had been scouting Bagram Air Base in Afghanistan earlier that spring. Prefabricated buildings were parked around the camp, which was a hub of construction activity. A contingent of KBR contractors lived on the base, and they could also be spotted cruising around downtown Tbilisi in their SUVs. At Betsy's, a boutique hotel overlooking Tbilisi's main boulevard, the influx of Defense Department money was the talk of American expatriates who gathered to trade gossip over Saperavi wine. Well-paid jobs out at Krtsanisi were there for the asking, especially for anyone with any Georgian language skills and familiarity with Tbilisi. AES Telasi may have been a failed venture, but U.S. military involvement meant that there would be no shortage of lucrative expat jobs in Tbilisi.

Georgian troops were not the only recipients of American largesse. At the Tbilisi Marriott, a smartly refurbished hotel on Tbilisi's Rustaveli Boulevard, I met a U.S. government consultant who was working with Georgian government officials to help create the Georgian equivalent of a U.S. National Security Council. The program, he told me, had the backing of U.S. National Security Advisor Condoleezza Rice. The idea was to create U.S.-style institutions in the post-Soviet state and to ensure a smooth succession of power when Shevardnadze left office in 2005. The United States had an eye on this region, and wanted to be sure it knew the key players in the next administration.

What, exactly, was the reason for lavishing strategic attention on this tiny country of around four and a half million people on the southern edge of the former Soviet Union? The ostensible reason was the Pankisi Gorge. This mountainous corner of northeastern Georgia was the traditional home of the Kists, ethnic cousins of the Chechens. When Russia launched a second campaign to reclaim the breakaway Chechen Republic in 1999, the Pankisi Gorge became a safe haven for Chechen refugees and a staging area for some Chechen rebels. After September 11, reports surfaced of Arab jihadis who had filtered into the region to turn it into a regional base. Whether al-Qaeda ever had a serious foothold in the Pankisi is now in doubt, but a somewhat lurid account in *Time* magazine described an al-Qaeda operation in Pankisi Gorge as belonging to

> a multi-layered, interlocking, region-wide organizational struc-
> ture, with decentralized planning and procurement systems.
> The Pankisi groups, using sophisticated satellite-based and en-
> crypted communications, sometimes concentrated on their own
> operations—including refugee work and recruiting for Khattab,
> the Saudi-born guerrilla commander in Chechnya believed to

have been close to Osama bin Laden. At other times they lent a hand to the broader "jihad" against the U.S. and its allies. For the Pankisi operatives, this meant trying to target U.S. and western interests in Russia and Central Asia using poison and bombs.[8]

The idea, then, was to get the Georgians to do their bit for the Bush administration's Global War on Terror. That, at least was the official line: Georgia was not supposed to use U.S. military assistance to attempt to regain control of secessionist territories like Abkhazia or South Ossetia. That kind of move might spark a full-scale war with Russia, which overtly backed the secessionists in the guise of "peacekeeping" forces stationed in the breakaway republics. U.S. trainers were adamant that they were there for training purposes, not to help the Georgians build proficiency and weapons stockpiles to retake the rebel territories by force. In an interview from Tbilisi, Lieutenant Colonel Robert Walte-meyer, the commander of the first U.S. training group, said his men would account for "every bullet" in the program. "We're not leaving war stocks here," he promised.

The Georgia Train and Equip Mission, then, was a form of preventive state building: The United States would help Georgia better police its borders, making it a less attractive place for extremists to do business. This was exactly what Barnett's vision of the "SysAdmin" hybrid looked like: Americans quietly helping a poorly developed (or, in his parlance, a "disconnected") country better control its territory, ensuring that it did not become a haven for transnational terrorists. During an appearance at the Pentagon with Secretary of Defense Donald Rumsfeld, however, the Georgian minister of defense, David Tevzadze, strayed a bit from the script. Asked about al-Qaeda's phantom presence in the country, the minister said, "You know, actually, for me personally, it is very difficult to believe in that, because to come from Afghanistan to that part of Georgia, they need to [cross] at least six or seven countries, including [the] Caspian Sea. No, al-Qaeda influence can't be in the country."

So some wishful thinking was at work here: The Georgians were eager recipients of money, training, and expertise, and they were willing to play along with the convenient fiction that the Pankisi Gorge was a hotbed of international terrorism, al-Qaeda's strategic outpost between the Black Sea and the Caspian Sea. And U.S. policymakers seemed to overlook the fact that the program would be training and equipping a country with an unresolved civil war on its hands. Tevzadze denied that training by U.S. forces might be used in any effort to reclaim separatist regions such as the self-proclaimed Republic of Abkhazia on the Black Sea coast. The Georgian military didn't intend to deploy U.S.-trained troops there because, Tevzadze said, "at least in the nearest future, we will not . . . try to come to a military resolution of the problem."

That description would prove entirely accurate. Georgia would not use U.S. military aid to reconquer lost territory—in the nearest future.

The Georgia Train and Equip program was ambitious, but it was a sideshow compared with the regime-change mission the Bush administration was preparing to launch in Iraq. Within months, Waltemeyer and his Special Forces soldiers would be in northern Iraq, helping organize Kurdish and Arab militias to topple Saddam Hussein. The Georgia Train and Equip Program continued for the next several years, with little public interest or scrutiny in the United States. Within a few short months, events in Georgia were overshadowed completely by events in the Middle East.

On the eve of the invasion of Iraq in March 2003, Barnett, who had become a star on the military speaking circuit, wrote an essay in *Esquire* magazine outlining his support for the invasion of Iraq. He did not justify his support in terms of unearthing Iraq's weapons of mass destruction, which at that point was providing the main justification for going to war. This new campaign, he suggested, would not end with the overthrow of Saddam Hussein's regime. The true rationale was provided by his now-famous briefing, dubbed "the Pentagon's new map."

Overthrowing Saddam Hussein was "not only necessary and inevitable, but good," Barnett argued. "When the United States finally goes to war again in the Persian Gulf, it will not constitute a settling of old scores, or just an enforced disarmament of illegal weapons, or a distraction in the war on terror. Our next war in the Gulf will mark a historical tipping point— the moment when Washington takes real ownership of strategic security in the age of globalization."

The real reason the United States was going to war, he argued, was a long-term civilizing mission—in contemporary terms, integrating a "gap" state into the global economy. It was a nation-building argument, not a regime-change one. "The reason I support going to war in Iraq is not simply that Saddam is a cutthroat Stalinist willing to kill anyone to stay in power, nor because that regime has clearly supported terrorist networks over the years," he wrote. "The real reason I support a war like this is that the resulting long-term military commitment will finally force America to deal with the entire Gap as a strategic threat environment."[9]

Accomplishing that mission, however, would not prove as easy as overthrowing Saddam Hussein.

CHAPTER 3

"Beat 'em Up and Go Home"

As the UH-60 Black Hawk skimmed low over the desert of southern Iraq, I noticed the "fun-o-meter" patch the pilot, Chief Warrant Officer Ryan Newman, had fixed to back of his flight helmet: ARE WE HAVING FUN YET OR WHAT?

It was late March 2003 when I flew into Iraq in the passenger compartment of Newman's helicopter, perched on a carton of field rations. I was one of several hundred journalists the U.S. Defense Department had invited to cover Operation Iraqi Freedom, the military campaign to oust Saddam Hussein and hunt for weapons of mass destruction. It was a master stroke of public relations. My embed assignment was with the Sixth Battalion, 101st Aviation, part of the 101st Airborne Division. Six Bat was a "general support" aviation unit: basically, a battlefield taxi service. This aircraft was delivering Meals-Ready-to-Eat and water destined for a Pathfinder infantry unit. I was a piece of spare cargo, and things were off to a rough start. The night before the battalion crossed north into Iraq, its staging base in Camp Udairi, Kuwait, saw a real missile attack. Startled from their cots by a deafening crack, soldiers donned gas masks and climbed back in their sleeping bags. The all-clear sounded soon after over the camp loudspeakers.

It was friendly fire. As it turned out, we had heard the impact of a U.S. Patriot missile smacking into a Royal Air Force GR4A Tornado fighter.

The missile battery failed to pick up the aircraft's IFF (identification friend or foe) beacon, an electronic signal that is supposed to prevent fratricide.[1] Both crew members were killed. Word of the incident spread quickly, but although it occurred within earshot, I did not learn the full details until I heard about it from the BBC (a young company commander, better prepared than I, had remembered to pack a shortwave radio). My pessimism deepened when I learned of a grenade attack the previous night in neighboring Camp Pennsylvania. A U.S. soldier, Sergeant Hasan Akbar, had lobbed some grenades in a 101st Airborne command tent. The attack claimed the lives of two officers, and several others were injured.* To me, at least, it didn't seem an auspicious day to be going into a combat zone.

Captain Dana Bult, a signals officer, was designated as my escort. I had been bounced from several helicopter flight manifests like a piece of excess baggage; the night before we were to leave, Bult informed me that she had a spot for me on board her aircraft. I reported to her tent about an hour before the next wave of helicopters was scheduled to take off. She was talking distractedly on a field telephone; I waited outside. As it happened, her husband had been staying in the tent where the grenade attack took place. By sheer luck, he had been in the shower at the time of the attack. A military operator had connected her with her in-laws so she could tell them he was all right. After hanging up the handset, she grabbed her rucksack and hauled it to a waiting Humvee. She was perfectly collected. We headed to the flight line.

Bult's attitude—businesslike, intent, focused on the task at hand—was reassuring. In the weeks I had spent in Kuwait, waiting for the war to begin, most of the soldiers in the battalion had been preoccupied with military chores: assembling their equipment, spray-painting helicopter blades to protect them from erosion, practicing "dust landings" in the desert sands of the Udairi range. There was little time for introspection. To unwind at night, soldiers passed around DVDs to watch on portable video players. *Black Hawk Down* was a particular favorite.

---

* Akbar would later be convicted of murder and sentenced to death by a court-martial. Incidents of fragging, murder of fellow soldiers or superior officers, were extremely rare in the Iraq War. A 2009 shooting spree by a soldier at a stress treatment clinic at Camp Victory, Baghdad, however, put the spotlight on the psychological toll of combat.

Shortly after Six Bat's arrival in Kuwait, the battalion commander, Lieutenant Colonel Chuck Fields, had given the soldiers a short pep talk. Fields had fought in the first Gulf War; he was with the "ready brigade" that airlifted helicopters to Saudi Arabia in August 1990, after Iraq's invasion of Kuwait, as part of a quick-reaction force assembled to defend the kingdom's oilfields from Saddam Hussein. "We're ten times more prepared than we were last time," he said.

The buildup in Kuwait had been under way for months, and Fields was confident of a successful reprise of Desert Storm. Chief Warrant Officer Shawn Mertens, another Black Hawk pilot, summarized the confidence in what was supposed to be a conventional military mission to defeat the Iraqi army and unseat Saddam Hussein. "We're supposed to beat 'em up and go home," he told me.

Mertens neatly described the operating assumption at the time. The United States was going to war in Iraq for a host of reasons: intelligence speculation about the regime's ties to terrorists, a desire to upend the regional political order, unfinished business from the 1990–91 Gulf War. The campaign was largely billed as a hunt for weapons of mass destruction, although Deputy Secretary of Defense Paul Wolfowitz, perhaps inadvertently, let slip in a May 2003 magazine interview that the case for war was built around that selling point "for reasons that have a lot to do with the U.S. government bureaucracy."[2]

But as much as Saddam was an odious tyrant, he presided over a functioning state. The ruling Ba'athist Party—a thugocracy, really—held power through an ugly combination of patronage, repression, and political murder. Saddam's malignant cult of personality was the state's official ideology. The economy was a wreck: The state was the largest employer, and the country's infrastructure had suffered through years of neglect, underinvestment, and sanctions. The disastrous UN-backed Oil-for-Food program had only created more opportunities for those with ties to the corrupt regime to enrich themselves. The U.S. invasion would destroy the regime, but a new system would have to be rebuilt from scratch.

The 101st Airborne Division had detailed terrain maps, access to up-to-the minute satellite pictures, and signal intercepts from the Iraqi military's communications systems. But its familiarity with the cultural terrain it was about to occupy was marginal. Back at Fort Campbell, the public affairs office, the division's media-relations shop, had printed up a short handbook called *A Soldier's Guide to Iraq*. It was rudimentary at best, and a section on cultural considerations was particularly comical. It depicted "the Arab" as a sort of B-movie villain: Arabs are crafty, feckless, preoccupied with honor and shame. A few excerpts:

> To show politeness when asked a yes or no question, the Arab will always answer yes, whether true or not. A flat "no" is a signal that you want to end the relationship. The polite way for an Arab to say "no" is to say, "I'll see what I can do."

> Arabs, by American standards, are reluctant to accept responsibility. They will accept shared responsibility, but if responsibility is accepted and something goes wrong, the Arab is dishonored.

> The Arab approach to time is much slower and relaxed. If God wills things to happen, they will, so why rush. Relationships are more important than accomplishing an act.

> An Arab sees friendships with anyone outside the family as meaning, "You scratch my back and I'll scratch yours."

The handbook also offered a few pointers for dealing with the press. Some tips were practical ("Don't lie"); others encouraged spin ("Do not provide the enemy with propaganda material by complaining about things"). It had few specifics on Iraqi, as distinct from Arab, culture, although page 8 also featured a small map that crudely outlined "dissident areas" (predominately Shia and Kurdish). It gave no hint of the ethnic and sectarian conflict the invasion would inadvertently ignite.

Prior to the division's departure to Kuwait from Fort Campbell, I watched a briefing by a young Civil Affairs major on Iraq. It was embarrassingly brief. The takeaway: Iraq had three major groups, Shia and Sunni Arabs, and the Kurds up north. They didn't always get along. The Shia and the Kurds will probably be friendly, because they were oppressed by Saddam. And don't eat with your left hand; Arabs consider that unclean. He glossed over a slide on arts, monuments, and national archives ("There's a lot of stuff here," he said), and he was stumped by a basic question on the distances between Baghdad and the borders of Syria and Turkey.

An Army lawyer also gave an overview of "ROE," the rules of engagement on the battlefield. Soldiers received two "ROE cards": a green one for "pre- and post-hostilities" (in preparation for the invasion and after victory, respectively) and an orange one titled "ROE during hostilities." The orange ROE cards outlined the basic rules for engaging enemy forces and also gave instructions for dealing with civilians. Rule 1: "You may stop civilians and check their identities, search for weapons and seize any found. Detain civilians when necessary to accomplish your mission or for your own safety. Use the Four S's when dealing with civilians demonstrating some form of hostile intent."

The Four S's were a simple formula for using "graduated force" against civilians: "1. SHOUT verbal warning to halt; 2. SHOW weapon and intent to use it; 3. SHOVE use non-lethal physical force; 4. SHOOT to eliminate the threat. Fire only aimed shots. Stop firing when the threat is neutralized." These guidelines were to be followed whenever troops set up a roadblock or a security perimeter in Iraqi towns and cities. A series of bullet points on the back of the card outlined a few possible scenarios, like a civilian deliberately driving a vehicle at friendly forces (response: shoot to eliminate the threat) or a young civilian woman pointing out to the enemy the location where friendly troops were concealed (response: shoot to eliminate the threat).

The rules seemed to encourage the assumption that civilians were potentially hostile, not potentially friendly. At the top of both cards, in boldface type, was the prime directive: NOTHING IN THESE RULES PROHIBITS YOU FROM EXERCISING YOUR INHERENT RIGHT TO DEFEND YOURSELF AND OTHER ALLIED FORCES. The U.S. military's preoccupation with what it called "force protection" would have serious consequences. And the forces the invasion would unleash—sectarian conflict from within, a new front for international *jihad*—would create the conditions for a deadly internal war.

The 101st Airborne reached the outskirts of Najaf in early April 2003. It was the division's first real encounter with the Iraqi population; it also served as a test of how Iraq's Shia community would receive the Army—as liberators or as occupiers. For Shia believers, Najaf was a holy place. It housed the shrine of Imam Ali, considered by Shia to be the rightful successor of the Prophet Muhammad; after Mecca and Medina, it was the third most important site for Shia pilgrims. Standing atop a Humvee outside the gates of the city, Army Major General David

Petraeus turned to his boss, the commander of V Corps, Lieutenant General William Wallace. "There sure are a lot more civilians on the battlefield in this particular scenario than there were at the NTC or at JRTC," he said.

Petraeus was referring to the Army National Training Center at Fort Irwin, California, and the Joint Readiness Training Center at Fort Polk, Louisiana. Those two "dirt" training facilities were where the Army conducted its full-dress rehearsals for war. A month-long stay "in the box" at NTC or JRTC was the closest you could get to combat without real shooting. At Fort Irwin, Army units would play a sophisticated version of laser tag against an OPFOR ("opposing force") that was usually configured like a Soviet armored formation. For maximum realism, the OPFOR even had a fleet of Warsaw Pact equipment—tanks, helicopters, armored personnel carriers.* It was practice for the type of conventional, tank-on-tank engagement the Cold War military had always prepared to fight: the Soviets crashing through the Fulda Gap in West Germany. What the Army called "COBs"—civilians on the battlefield—were notably absent from the NTC war games. Now, Army commanders were very rapidly learning that civilians were not just an unexpected obstacle that could be easily circumvented.

On April 3, a delegation of soldiers of the First Brigade of the 101st Airborne entered the city to pay a visit to Grand Ayatollah Ali al-Sistani, the leading Shia imam. As the soldiers approached the Shrine of Ali, a large crowd of Shia men began to assemble; they quickly blocked the streets near the shrine. Rumors swirled that the foreign soldiers would try to enter the Shrine of Ali, or that they would detain Sistani. As the crowd grew, someone began to pitch stones at the American soldiers. Lieutenant Colonel Chris Hughes, commander of the Second Battalion, 327th Infantry Regiment, decided on a show of restraint. He ordered his soldiers to drop to one knee and point their weapons to the ground. "We're going to withdraw out of this situation and let them defuse it themselves," he said through a bullhorn. "All vehicles turn around."[3]

A CNN reporter on the scene said Hughes's decision to call off the visit and avoid a confrontation prevented U.S. troops from making enemies of

---

*The Army also had a similar facility in Germany, the Joint Multinational Readiness Center in Hohenfels. The Marine Corps did similar training at Twenty-nine Palms in the Mojave Desert.

the civilians in Najaf. But the gesture actually had been proposed by Kadhim Al-Waeli, an Iraqi exile employed as a cultural scout and advisor to the First Brigade of the 101st Airborne. He was the one who suggested that U.S. soldiers drop to one knee to show respect as they approached the Shrine of Ali. A violent confrontation was averted by a suggestion from a native-born Iraqi; this was broadcast on CNN and Al-Jazeera.[4]

"I'm your Google. You don't have to go to Google, just ask me," Al-Waeli had told Hughes. "I'm not a genius, but I was born in Iraq. I know that culture, I know the people." That sort of advice was indispensable—and it was in extremely short supply. The Army had envisioned the creation of a three-thousand-strong force that would be charged with interpreting for coalition forces, acting as cultural guides, and helping handle refugees. The Iraqi volunteers, dubbed the Free Iraqi Forces, were supposed to act as senior cultural advisors, giving commanders insights into Iraqi attitudes and customs and helping smooth interactions with ordinary Iraqis.[5]

It was a good idea in theory. But in practice, the creation of the Free Iraqi Forces was a fiasco: Only a very small number of Iraqi exiles actually stepped forward to volunteer, and even fewer were prepared to deploy in time for the fighting. Many of those who did show up for training were not in particularly good shape.[6] Few had combat experience. The Army quickly had to lower its expectations. Even an otherwise glowing Pentagon news story about Task Force Warrior, the Army's program for training the exiles at Taszar Air Base, Hungary, acknowledged that trainers had to dumb down the curriculum. A caustic e-mail by a major assigned to Task Force Warrior was passed around within the military community: "Never in the history of the U.S. Armed Forces have so many done so much for so few," he observed.[7] The program in Hungary produced only a few dozen graduates in time to join the war.

Chris Straub, a retired Army officer and former member of the Senate Intelligence Committee staff with extensive experience working with Iraqi exile groups, blamed the relatively low pay—Free Iraqi Forces were paid one thousand dollars a month—for the poor turnout. The U.S. government did not want it to look as if it was raising a force of mercenaries, but Iraqi exiles could make much more money working as interpreters for Titan, the firm that held the main linguistics contract for the Army. "We [the U.S. government] were competing against ourselves," Straub later observed. Straub had been hired as a Pentagon contractor to recruit

Iraqis for the Free Iraqi Forces from half a dozen exile groups that qualified for U.S. assistance under the Iraq Liberation Act, signed into law in
1999 by President Bill Clinton. Free Iraqi Forces were supposed to provide an Iraqi face for the U.S.-led invasion, but Straub said the names of
most volunteers were provided by the Iraqi National Congress, an Iraqi
opposition group led by the exile politician and neoconservative favorite
Ahmad Chalabi. "A lot of them didn't show up," Straub said. "Lots of
them were old." But Straub believed that the program, despite its faults,
paid dividends. He later told me, "In my mind [the Najaf incident] paid
for the program."

In Najaf, the 101st Airborne Division also discovered that it would
have to take on some distinctly nonmilitary missions: restoring essential
services for the besieged city. Temperatures in early April were already
rising into the nineties, and the city was running short of potable water.
The unit shipped in a thousand gallons of water for local residents in
neighborhoods occupied by the First Brigade, and made plans to deliver
diesel fuel to restart a pumping station that had been out of service for
several days.[8] Even as the U.S. military delivered a swift, overwhelming
defeat, another kind of war was taking shape. And those small hearts-
and-minds victories could not alter perceptions in the Arab world that
the United States was an occupier.

The march to Baghdad continued at whiplash pace. Soldiers and Marines on the ground would quickly learn that civilians were the defining
feature on this new terrain. Days after the 101st Airborne Division's uneasy first encounter with the residents of Najaf, Lieutenant Nathaniel
Fick, a platoon leader with the Marine Corps's First Reconnaissance Battalion, was ordered to scout the Iraqi military airfield at Qalat Sukkar, an
air base that would be used as a staging point for the final assault on
Baghdad. As they approached the chain-link fence surrounding the airfield, a message came over the radio network from company headquarters. "All personnel on the airfield are declared hostile."[9]

Fick paused, and prepared to override the order. He wanted his unit to
stick to the established rules of engagement. He then changed his mind,
trusting that the order might save Marines' lives by giving them crucial
seconds to respond to an ambush or attack. As the Marines moved forward, Fick heard a short burst of gunfire, and a snatch of radio traffic:

Something about men with weapons, and possible muzzle flashes. Not long after, Fick's Marines were approached by a small group of villagers pulling two bundles. The Marines unwrapped the blankets: The villagers were carrying two young boys hit by the Marine gunfire. One boy had a bullet wound in the leg; the other was punched through by four bullets. "In horror, I thought back to our assault on the airfield a few hours before," Fick later wrote. "The pieces fell into place. Those weren't rifles we had seen but shepherds' canes, not muzzle flashes but the sun reflecting on a windshield. The running camels belonged to those boys. We'd shot two children."[10]

As the platoon pushed farther through Muwaffiqiya, the Marines shot a civilian who had failed to stop at a traffic checkpoint. It was a classic "escalation of force" scenario. As they pushed farther north, Fick ordered one of his Marines to commit a small act of vandalism. They cut down an octagonal traffic sign with the word STOP written in Arabic. It would be perfect, he thought, for their traffic checkpoints. It might even save a life.[11]

Fick finally drew a line. His platoon was ordered to search an abandoned amusement park on the Tigris River for pro-Saddam *fedayeen*—the word "insurgent" had not yet come into vogue—when a battered old sedan rolled up to their position. Inside the car they found a badly injured teenage girl, quite possibly wounded by U.S. fire, and her frantic parents. Fick had to decide between staying with the original military mission of searching the park to find a possible cache of surface-to-air missiles or helping the girl. The Marines chose to help the girl. After cleaning and dressing the girl's suppurating wound, they sent her family to an aid station at a higher headquarters, with a handwritten note from Fick instructing U.S. forces further down the line to provide medical aid.

For Fick that encounter marked a sort of break with his conventional military training. But the decision did not rest easy with him. "I kind of berated myself for a few years, thinking I had made the wrong choice . . . We didn't find the surface-to-air missiles and some helicopters then get shot down, and did our decision to help end up costing the lives of many?" he later told me in an interview. "And only recently have I sort of found peace with this decision."

The point was, Fick continued, "that most of us—most of us in the NCO corps and the junior officer corps—wanted to default to doing the right thing." In that case, doing the right thing meant setting aside a purely military mission—hunting for a weapons cache—in order to aid innocent civilians who had been caught in the crossfire.

But the biggest disappointment, Fick told me, was that no civilian reconstruction effort seemed to materialize in the wake of the destructive military campaign. The U.S. military's success in Iraq had been catastrophic: the regime had been shattered, but Iraq's creaky national grid was failing and its economy was in ruins. No one had stepped in to fill the void. Where was USAID? Where were the civilian relief agencies? The realization was dawning that the United States needed to fix things, and fast.

"It's really startling," Fick said. "We expected there to be this army of reconstruction people descending on the city. And once the supply lines from Kuwait were open, once we had fought our way to Baghdad, there were going to be trucks, you know, convoys of trucks full of equipment and people coming in behind us. And they didn't come. And the disillusionment set in pretty quickly."

Fick and his Marines were perhaps only dimly aware of a Pentagon-led effort to launch reconstruction projects and take the lead on administering Iraq. In January 2003, the Defense Department created the Office of Reconstruction and Humanitarian Assistance (ORHA), an "interagency" office that brought in officials and experts in postwar planning and reconstruction from the State Department, USAID, and other government agencies.[12] On March 1, 2003, just a few weeks before the invasion, U.S. Central Command prepared CONPLAN (Concept Plan) AURORA, a planning document that outlined the "Phase IV" plan for rebuilding Iraq.* Secretary of Defense Donald Rumsfeld tapped retired Army Lieutenant General Jay Garner to run what was supposed to be Iraq's caretaker government.

Garner had won acclaim in 1991 for overseeing Operation Provide Comfort, a relief effort to save thousands of Kurdish refugees who had fled to the mountains of northern Iraq after a failed uprising in the wake of Saddam Hussein's defeat in Operation Desert Storm. When allied forces and relief workers scouted the region in early April 1991, they estimated

---

* Details of that plan are still not public. On April 1, 2010, U.S. Central Command released a redacted version of the document in response to a Freedom of Information Act request. Nearly all of its twenty-seven pages were blacked out.[13]

that as many as a thousand people a day were dying of disease and expo-
sure in the mountains along the Turkish border. Garner led an improvised task force of NATO troops to help protect the civilians, deliver
food aid, and set up refugee camps.

It was a muscular model of postwar disaster relief. U.S. military aircraft enforced a no-fly zone overhead, keeping Iraqi government forces in
check and delivering relief supplies by air. Garner, then a major general,
led Joint Task Force–Bravo, a multinational contingent built around the
Twenty-fourth Marine Expeditionary Unit, to the town of Zakho.* His
task was to prepare the town for an influx of Kurdish refugees coming
down from the mountains. The entire operation lasted just three months:
Garner crossed back into Turkey on July 15, and the camps were handed
to United Nations control. Operation Provide Comfort was a success: The
Kurds came down from the mountains but did not remain stranded in
refugee camps, dependent on international aid. Most Kurds returned
home, many of them after passing through a tent city in Zakho designed
by Fred Cuny, a Texan who ran Intertect Relief and Reconstruction, a
small private company based in Dallas that specialized in disaster relief.[14]

The key to Operation Provide Comfort was its flexible, improvised
design: Garner pulled together a loose coalition from different nations
operating under varying rules of engagement. Everything was "done with
a handshake," as he explained later. Flying into northern Iraq on a helicopter with Lieutenant General John Shalikashvili, his boss, and with General Colin Powell, chairman of the Joint Chiefs of Staff, Garner explained
how the arrangement with other allied nations would work.

Garner recalled that Powell asked to see his MOU, a formal memorandum of understanding between the different component commanders
from different nations contributing to the force. "General Powell, there
isn't one," Garner responded. "We didn't sign an MOU."

Powell flushed for a minute. "If I'd known that, I'd never have let you
start this operation," he said. Pausing for a moment, Powell added, "If I'd
done that, you'd still be back in Turkey trying to get an MOU signed, so
you did the right thing."

---

* The Twenty-fourth Marine Expeditionary Unit was commanded by Colonel James
Jones, who would later go on to be NATO's supreme allied commander–Europe and the
head of U.S. European Command. In 2009 he was named National Security Advisor to
President Barack Obama.

Equally important, Garner also collaborated with civilian relief workers and nongovernmental organizations, a major departure from standard military practice. Military commanders were trained to guard access to information, and the idea of civilian relief agencies being allowed to participate in planning meetings or set foot inside an operations center was anathema. Likewise, relief groups had also been quite wary of cooperating with the uniformed military, but Garner held a "town hall" meeting to build rapport. "We have to demonstrate you can trust us," he told them. "We're going to go full open kimono." Garner gave NGOs and aid workers the opportunity to hitch rides on his helicopters and vehicles and granted access to the task force's civil-military operations center so they could coordinate relief efforts.

Initially the relief workers may not have been comfortable around the military, but they quickly discovered the phenomenal logistics capability the armed forces had. Security and mine clearance also helped lay the foundation for effective relief. What started as a military operation became a unique hybrid experiment in collaboration among the military, international organizations, civilian aid workers, and private relief groups.

But the lessons of Operation Provide Comfort were largely forgotten within the institutional military, in part because of the spectacular success of Operation Desert Storm, the conventional fight between U.S. and Iraqi forces. As Garner later told me, "It was kind of lost in the shuffle." His operation was viewed as a minor epilogue to victory, and little effort was made to study it. And Garner would never have a real chance to apply his experience. ORHA's lines of authority in Iraq were less than clear, its staff was spread thin, and its planning guidance was almost nonexistent. Colonel Mike Fitzgerald, a deputy planner at U.S. Central Command, later recalled that the only ORHA-related planning document he ever saw was a "one to two page document that said these are your essential tasks. It didn't tell him [Garner] where he was lined up in the chain of command and who he responded to."[15]

Less than a month after his arrival in Iraq in April 2003, Garner was replaced by Ambassador L. Paul Bremer, a career diplomat who became the head of the Coalition Provisional Authority, a revamped occupational government that was funded through the Pentagon. As U.S. proconsul, Bremer reported directly to the president through the Defense

Department. The military, through its new proconsul, retained the lead in rebuilding Iraq.

In civilian life, Lance Corporal John Guardiano was an editor; in Iraq, he would become entangled in municipal affairs. Guardiano had enlisted in the Marine Corps at the late age of thirty-four, in a put-up-or-shut-up fit of post-9/11 patriotism. After boot camp at Parris Island and training as a field radio operator, he joined a reserve Civil Affairs unit based in Washington, D.C. His actual Civil Affairs qualifications were minimal: The unit was supposed to provide him with training in the basic tasks during his weekend reserve duty, but he was called up for active duty before he ever got around to the training. Anyway, Marines were expected to be riflemen first.

Guardiano was activated in February 2003 in preparation for the invasion of Iraq. His unit, the Fourth Civil Affairs Group, was broken up into four- and five-man teams and parceled out to frontline Marine units preparing to cross the berm into Iraq.* Guardiano was assigned to the First Battalion, Fourth Marines. They crossed into Iraq in late March. After a short mission to Nasiriyah, Guardiano's Civil Affairs team set up shop in Hillah, a mostly Shia town about sixty miles south of Baghdad. The Marines had been told to expect surrender en masse by Iraqi military units after the invasion. That never happened. The enemy dispersed, and Marines shifted into an uneasy constabulary role. Guardiano went out on routine patrols with the infantry, anxious to find the "bad guys." They rarely found them: the *fedayeen*, former Ba'athist paramilitaries, had gone to ground. The unit's mission shifted—subtly, almost imperceptibly at first—to rebuilding.

The Marines Civil Affairs team began arranging meetings with sheikhs and tribal leaders. The First Battalion, Fourth Marines set up an office at the municipal hall, where a Marine commander played the role of local grandee: meeting petitioners, hearing complaints, weighing requests for assistance. The occupying Marines also created a city council to create some semblance of a local government. Many Ba'athists had fled or gone underground, and the unit's encounters with most Iraqis

---

* At the Iraq-Kuwait border was a ten-kilometer-deep linear obstacle complex comprising massive tank ditches, concertina wire, electrified fencing, and of course berms of dirt.

were positive. Guardiano felt that by and large, the residents of Hillah were genuinely grateful to the U.S. military for ousting Saddam.

Not everything was rosy. Hillah and the surrounding province was now home to fifteen thousand disgruntled ex-soldiers. On May 23, 2003, in the second decree he issued as head of the Coalition Provisional Authority, Bremer disbanded the Iraqi army. This act had far-reaching implications: It made it difficult to reconstitute the Iraqi military and security forces to assist in restoring law and order, and it created a pool of angry, unemployed men with military training who became willing recruits for the insurgency. When unemployed soldiers found out that the American military was providing stopgap salary payments to some local municipal employees, their discontent grew. One group of ex-soldiers even organized a small rally in protest outside the municipal hall. Guardiano wrote an opinion piece that touched on the protest in the *Wall Street Journal*. "The soldiers' complaint was not that the United States is too heavily involved in Iraqi affairs," he wrote. "They were instead complaining that we are doing too little to help them. They want more help, not less; they seek greater engagement, not a withdrawal of American military forces. The difficulties here aren't the result of the U.S. being heavy-handed. Rather, they result from our inability to bring greater resources to bear."[16]

The biggest frustration for the Marines, then, was the absence of outside help from the rest of the U.S. government. Political advisors from the State Department, it seemed to many in the military, were a no-show. Guardiano saw no nongovernmental organizations on the ground in Hillah, either. The only civilian representative of the U.S. reconstruction effort in the area was an elderly man working as a USAID contractor who had showed up to help advise the new city council. Recalling it later, Guardiano said, "We wanted the State Department. We wanted the UN to help. I mean, very badly."

Guardiano and the Marines were puzzled. Although Hillah was seeing sporadic violence, it seemed secure enough to begin work on "Phase IV," the military's shorthand for postconflict operations. "Honestly, that caused us to scratch our heads somewhat," he said. "By our standards . . . well, you have to understand, it's a little unfair—because we were walking around with guns. You're there with a Marine infantry regiment . . . But the point is, we would have escorted the UN, we would have escorted the NGOs. We would have been their security guards, happily."

In fact, the United Nations had established a mission in Iraq after the fall of Baghdad. UN Secretary General Kofi Annan had sent one of his most capable diplomats, Sergio Vieira de Mello, as his special envoy. But on August 19, 2003, a truck bomb laden with explosives detonated outside Baghdad's Canal Hotel, headquarters of the UN mission. Vieira de Mello and twenty-one others were killed; after the bombing the United Nations pulled out nearly all its staff. Nevertheless, Guardiano and the Marines began reaching their own conclusion: They had been left holding the bag. "I think part of it, candidly, was an antimilitary bias," Guardiano said. "And I think a lot of us felt that way: They don't want to be seen with the Marines, they don't want to be seen with the military."

For Guardiano, as for other troops on the ground, a shared perception was beginning to take shape: Although Marines and soldiers were at war, the rest of the government was not. They would have to go it alone. And to make matters worse, they would have to tackle postwar reconstruction missions while being shot at. The collapse of Saddam Hussein's regime created a power vacuum within Iraq, and U.S. troops would quickly find themselves in the middle of a vicious internal war.

A civilian reconstruction effort was taking shape, however slowly. By late March, as U.S. troops reached the outskirts of Baghdad, humanitarian assessment teams from USAID had progressed no farther than Umm Qasr, the Iraqi port just over the border from Kuwait. "We don't operate in a combat environment," Donald Tighe, a spokesman for USAID's Disaster Assistance Response Team (DART) in Kuwait, explained to the *Christian Science Monitor*. "We have begun the assessment process in areas declared secure by the military."[17]

The reality was a bit more complex. As a USAID official who was on the ground in Kuwait at the time later explained to me, the DART teams were in a bind, because they had no security of their own, and traveling with the military was initially not considered an option, because nongovernmental organizations that worked with USAID to implement their programs insisted on strict separation from the military mission. No one had planned to deliver aid in an active combat zone. The official said, "The USAID DART was refusing to leave Kuwait, because they were told the only way they were going to have security inside was with the military. And they were like, 'Nope! None of our NGO [non-governmental organization] partners will have anything to do with us, oh no, no, no!'"

In essence, the war in Iraq was widening the military-civilian rift that had been exposed in Afghanistan. Part of the problem was political. Some charities, such as the U.K.-based Oxfam, refused government funds to finance operations in Iraq, partly because of their objections to the war.[18] Many aid groups opposed efforts to place humanitarian projects under military supervision on principle: The International Rescue Committee, CARE, and WorldVision all refused to take part in a thirty-five-million-dollar USAID program to rebuild Iraqi schools and health clinics because, they argued, it undercut their independence and neutrality.[19] But the problem was also bureaucratic. The organizational culture of USAID was not geared toward working in a combat zone, and despite the small experiment in armed social work that had begun in Afghanistan, the agency was waiting for a formal end to hostilities—a sort of punctuation mark—to begin their work.

USAID's work began to pick up momentum in April 2003. On April 2, the agency announced $200 million in food aid for Iraq, a contribution that would be funneled through the World Food Program, and also began parceling out the first major aid contracts. On April 11, the agency announced an initial $7.9 million award to the North Carolina–based Research Triangle Institute, or RTI, to promote Iraqi participation in local government. It also gave a twelve-month contract to Creative Associates International Inc., an international consulting firm, to revitalize Iraqi schools. Finally, it announced a major overhaul of Iraqi infrastructure projects, awarding an emergency infrastructure repair contract to Bechtel, a construction firm based in San Francisco. The contracts would go toward repairing airports, dredging and upgrading the port of Umm Qasr, and repairing and rebuilding hospitals, schools, irrigation systems, and some ministry buildings. That contract had an initial ceiling of up to $680 million payable over eighteen months.[20]

But it was clear that USAID was farming out work to the usual suspects: established, well-connected firms such as Creative Associates International, RTI, and Bechtel. Much like Afghanistan, Iraq was shaping up as a bonanza for Beltway bandits. In an opinion piece in USA Today, Andrew Natsios, the head of USAID, defended the contract awards as a wartime necessity:

> Instead of the usual procurement process allowing all firms to
> compete for contracts—a process that takes six months—the
> U.S. Agency for International Development used expedited pro-
> cedures under federal law, allowing it to limit the number of
> competing firms to shorten the decision time. Naturally, the
> USAID issued invitations for bids (known as Requests for Pro-
> posals or RFPs) to multinational firms with a proven track re-
> cord of tackling major reconstruction projects in post-conflict
> countries such as Bosnia and Haiti. And since the war in Iraq
> had not yet begun or is still underway, RFPs went to firms with
> security clearances.[21]

As in Afghanistan, preference would go to large international firms
and established consultancies. It was a continuation of business as
usual for USAID: outsourcing their work to the development-industrial
complex.

In parallel, the State Department was scurrying to find volunteers to fill
the ranks of the newly created Coalition Provisional Authority. One internal notice in July 2003 sought volunteers for "TDY POLADS" (temporary
duty political advisors) in Iraq. Volunteers would serve three-month rotations. Arabic language skills were preferred, but not required. The notice
also outlined the incentives: Volunteers would receive 25 percent danger
pay, plus a 25 percent differential (an extra salary allowance). In essence,
volunteers would receive a 50 percent pay boost for service in Iraq. They
would also be able to bank their pay, since housing, meals, travel, and
laundry would all be provided in lieu of a per diem. Equally important, the
State Department was not planning to break or curtail regular diplomatic
assignments for temporary duty in Iraq. The bureaucratic routine of bidding for embassy assignments or jobs within the Washington bureaucracy
would not be interrupted.

These temporary assignments meant, in essence, that service with the
Coalition Provisional Authority would be a "ticket-punching" exercise:
Volunteers would go on a brief assignment to a war zone, add another
line to their résumés, but not hang around long enough to accomplish
anything. In short, the diplomatic corps was not on a war footing.

The high turnover rate among civilians assigned to the CPA made a
poor impression on the military, particularly those working staff positions
in Baghdad. Most Army units were expected to serve one-year rotations in

Iraq, at a minimum; as the situation worsened, units often found their tours were extended by several months.

Colonel Peter Mansoor, commander of the "Ready First" First Brigade, First Armored Division, arrived in Iraq in late May 2003; his unit effectively administered several districts in central and northeast Baghdad, an area of seventy-five square miles that was home to 2.1 million Iraqis. By late 2003, Mansoor's brigade was already deeply involved in the stability operations across the Tigris River from the CPA headquarters in the Green Zone. They had helped to form neighborhood and district advisory councils to create some facsimile of local government, had begun training Iraqi security forces, and had undertaken Civil Affairs projects. But their encounters with the civilian-led occupation authorities were rare—and immensely frustrating. In his memoir of his tour in Iraq, *Baghdad at Sunrise: A Brigade Commander's War in Iraq* (2008) Mansoor recalled a dispiriting trip into the Green Zone, Saddam Hussein's former palace complex on the west bank of the Tigris river, where the CPA had set up shop. Insulated behind the blast walls, HESCO barriers, and razor wire, CPA staff rarely seemed to venture outside the fortified perimeter.

"What we really needed was an embedded team of interagency advisors configured to help the brigade combat team deal with issues of governance, economics, and rule of law," he wrote. "But the Ready First Combat Team was based on the east side of the Tigris River and rarely saw CPA personnel in our area. Furthermore, Ambassador Bremer had centralized decisionmaking in his palace headquarters in the Green Zone, which made support for brigade combat teams difficult if not impossible."[22]

Not only did the CPA's Humanitarian Action Coordination Center and representatives of the U.S. Agency for International Development ensconced in the Green Zone seem detached from what was happening on the ground, but the staff at CPA seemed young and underqualified. Mansoor recalled meeting a twenty-something employee of the State Department, who, despite her youth and inexperience, had been assigned as the coordinator for local governments throughout central and northeastern Baghdad. "I took her to a meeting of the Adhamiya District Advisory Council a few days later, gave her a personal briefing on our operations at my brigade headquarters, and invited her to return to coordinate complementary efforts," he wrote. "I never saw her again."[23]

Within the Green Zone, the CPA had its own internal conflicts. Faced with unfilled billets in the CPA, the Defense Department made the decision to hire "3161 appointees" to supplement members of the military and the diplomatic corps staffing the CPA. These were direct hires who would typically serve in Iraq on one-year contracts (3161 refers to the section of the U.S. Code that regulates the hiring of civilian experts). Many 3161 appointees were drawn from the private sector. They were experts in the oil sector, municipal services, and transportation; in order to recruit them temporarily from the private sector, 3161s were paid at the top of the government pay scale. At one memorable DoD-to-State transition meeting for 3161s in Baghdad, a visiting State Department personnel specialist announced, with some bewilderment, "Some people here make more money than the ambassador." The 3161s also clashed with the Foreign Service culture: Many of them had never worked in an embassy or learned how to clear a diplomatic cable, but they also felt that diplomats had few real-world skills to offer when it came to repairing Iraq's creaking infrastructure, and spent little time meeting their Iraqi counterparts.

An advisor to the Transportation Ministry recalled that a Foreign Service officer visited the ministry he was supposed to be advising only once. "It was a forty-five-minute, senior-level event and everyone came away talking about 'the relationship,'" the advisor said. "Unfortunately, the minister never gave it another thought." The 3161 advisor, on the other hand, visited the ministry several times a week. "We spoke to our Iraqi counterparts every day," the advisor told me. "I sometimes went to the ministry (escorted by ten heavily armed friends) with no fixed agenda, but invariably something arose once I started talking to my Iraqi counterparts. And besides, the Iraqis made it to work. Why should we cower in the Green Zone?"

The greatest media scorn, however, was reserved for the political hacks who seemed to dominate the CPA. Although the CPA staff had been drawn from various government agencies, and included a smattering of officials from other coalition states, it also had a fair share of ideologically motivated operatives who seemed to view their jobs primarily in terms of securing President Bush's reelection in 2004. The CPA press office was a particularly egregious case: It was led by Dan Senor, a former press secretary for Spencer Abraham, the Michigan Republican who was then secretary of energy. Senor headed an office that included a healthy number of former Bush campaign workers, political appointees, and former Capitol Hill staffers. The Associated Press found that more than one third of the CPA's press office staff had Republican ties.[24]

And then there was the "brat pack," a group of politically connected youngsters inside the CPA. Ariana Eunjung Cha, a *Washington Post* reporter, profiled one group of twenty-something volunteers who served short tours with the CPA in Iraq. They included a twenty-eight-year-old legislative aide to Republican Senator Rick Santorum, a twenty-four-year-old Web site editor, and the twenty-eight-year-old daughter of the neoconservative pundit Michael Ledeen. They were all in their twenties or early thirties; few had any overseas experience; and they had been hired for low-level jobs. But because of high staff turnover and a lack of volunteers, they very quickly found themselves occupying positions of serious responsibility and drawing six-figure salaries. How did they manage to land these important jobs? "For months they wondered what they had in common, how their names had come to the attention of the Pentagon, until one day they figured it out: They had all posted their resumes at the Heritage Foundation, a conservative-leaning think tank," Cha wrote.[25]

Less well connected but equally inexperienced were Ray LeMoine and Jeff Neumann, a pair of enterprising misfits on a Valium- and liquor-fueled buddy trip to Iraq who also managed to land jobs in the CPA. LeMoine and Neumann, who previously had run a business selling YAN-KEES SUCK T-shirts at Boston's Fenway Park, ended up running the CPA's NGO Assistance Office after taking a bus trip to Baghdad on a lark in January 2004. As outsiders to government, they were perceptive observers. And they quickly found the CPA's appearance of purposeful administration was little more than illusion. Their description of the "Bremer Look" (the CPA chief favored a navy-blue blazer, khaki trousers, and regimental tie, plus a pair of desert tan combat boots) was particularly withering. "By the time we arrived in Iraq, the Bremer Look had fully penetrated the CPA," they noted. "Like a news anchor wearing a suit jacket and tie but naked below the desk, the Bremer Look suggested both serious work and slightly reckless adventure. Considering that most Iraqis wore plastic sandals, and didn't live in palaces or travel by helicopter, they associated the Bremer Look with American arrogance . . . Fact is, most CPA combat boots never left the Green Zone. The Look, like the CPA itself, was all image."[26]

Bremer would later write a self-serving memoir, *My Year in Iraq: The Struggle to Build a Future of Hope*. LeMoine and Neumann provided more insights about their own failures. In a heartbreaking summary of their time in Iraq, *Babylon by Bus*, they wrote: "In the end, it was our work that would come to define our time in Iraq. There is no point in romanticizing what we did. We thought we were helping Iraqis. We were wrong. Because of our failure, we'd leave the Middle East in a state of regret."[27]

The biggest U.S. experiment in foreign assistance since the Marshall Plan was being run by amateurs. In an October 2004 U.S. Institute of Peace interview, Colonel Lloyd Sammons, a reserve Special Forces officer and a lawyer who served as a military assistant in the governance section of the CPA, described the atmosphere of deep disillusion that set in within the CPA under Bremer. The political appointees seemed more preoccupied with making the administration look good than actually improving the lot of ordinary Iraqis. Frustrated by the remoteness of the CPA and his isolation in the Green Zone, Sammons staged a minor act of rebellion. In the small shared office space, he started posting the names of soldiers whose deaths had been announced in Defense Department news releases and put up a sign on his desk that said, "Why I am here?" in bold-face type.

Sammons departed Iraq in frustration. "I'm a big boy and I recognize things aren't perfect in this world, but to me it was sad," he later said. "Frankly, I left early. Nobody threw me out, but I knew that I was probably reaching an untenable level of anger and sadness. I would rant and rave right outside of Ambassador [Richard Henry] Jones's office while visiting his MA [military assistant]. Jones had to hear me. When Bremer would walk in every once in a while (he had to pass my desk on the way to the john) I'd just look at him like he was a piece of shit, and that's how I felt about him . . . I don't know every inside deal and everything, but I'm not an idiot. You can sort of smell when you're losing."[28]

CHAPTER 4

The Other War

The string of grenades went off in quick succession: *pop-pop-pop.* I was down the block at the Mustafa Hotel, a four-story hotel on a traffic circle in Kabul's Shahr-e-Naw district. The Mustafa was a sketchy place—it had been the favorite haunt of an American bounty hunter who was later arrested for running a private jail in Kabul—and I was convinced that someone, someday, would try to blow the place up. But it served decent kebabs and kept beer in stock, and I liked the manager, Wais Faizi, a fast-talking guy with a New Jersey accent and a vintage Camaro. I excused myself from my lunch on the terrace and went out onto the street to see what the matter was.

At the intersection of Chicken Street and Interior Ministry Road, an agitated Afghan National Police officer was waving his Kalashnikov rifle to keep curious onlookers away from the scene of the attack. A few photographers were hanging out around the traffic barrier. They wanted to get closer to the scene, so I followed them as they ducked down a side alley and wound their way down to the middle of Chicken Street, a dusty lane filled with carpet shops and souvenir stores selling antique daggers, Martini-Henry rifles, and pirated DVDs. The body of a man in a scorched *shalwar kameez* was lying on the pavement, his arms blown off and his torso squeezed like a tube of toothpaste.

This was the body of the bomber, who had detonated a series of hand grenades concealed beneath his shirt. Dressed like a beggar, the man had approached a group of soldiers from the International Security Assistance Force, the NATO-led peacekeeping mission in Afghanistan. The bomber had been trying to follow them into a carpet shop when he detonated his improvised suicide vest. The soldiers escaped, but others were not so lucky. The blast killed Jamie Michalsky, a young American woman who had recently served with the Army in Afghanistan and was on a visit from Uzbekistan, where she worked as a contract linguist.[1] It also killed Feriba, a third-grader who attended a nearby school, and who hawked English-language papers on the street to foreigners. She was the main breadwinner for her family.[2]

It was a relatively primitive attack. Afghan reporters from a local news agency later discovered the identity of the suicide bomber, a mentally ill man named Matiullah who had been recruited at a refugee camp near Peshawar, Pakistan, by a splinter faction of the militant group Hezb-e-Islami.[3] But the attack had a strategic effect: It deliberately targeted a place frequented by foreigners, and it sent a message that the people who were in Afghanistan to help rebuild the country were also targets of the insurgency.

In a modest way I was one of the people aiding the reconstruction of Afghanistan. I had returned to the country in September 2004 to cover the upcoming presidential elections and had stayed on to take a job with the Institute for War and Peace Reporting, a U.K.-based charity that was teaching basic journalism skills to a new generation of Afghan reporters. Accepting the post was in part a move dictated by necessity: Very few U.S. news organizations were willing to keep a full-time correspondent in Kabul, and living and working in Afghanistan on $150 or $200 per article, the going rate paid by many newspapers, was a losing proposition. So this job allowed me to remain in Afghanistan.

I may have been a reluctant member of Development Inc., but autumn 2004 was a unique time to be in Afghanistan. Unlike Baghdad, which was in the grip of a violent insurgency, Kabul was a relatively peaceful place. I could live in a residential neighborhood without having to retreat inside a guarded compound. It was easy to move around the countryside. To report a story outside the capital, I could simply hire a truck and go. That freedom had its limits: Parts of the south and the east were still home to the remnants of the Taliban, but violent crime actually seemed as big a worry as political unrest. The U.S. military maintained an almost invisible presence in much of the country. Part of the reason for this invisibility was the size of the contingent, which hovered at around fifteen thousand troops. It was also a "force protection" mind-set that kept U.S. forces sequestered behind blast walls. On a reporting visit to Bagram Air Base, the public affairs major who arranged my interview asked me how I'd gotten to the base. When I told him that I'd taken a taxi, he looked at me as though I was deranged.

It was generally an optimistic time. On October 9, 2004, Afghanistan held its first direct presidential elections. Millions of Afghans went to the polls, and U.S. and NATO troops stepped up security around the country to make sure the elections took place. Out on the Shomali Plain, which was still devastated after the war two and a half years earlier, I saw the first signs of economic optimism: brick factories, which were providing the materials to help rebuild the capital.

But the Taliban and its allies, who had been driven from power in 2001 by the United States and the Northern Alliance, were readying a comeback. In villages on the Shomali Plain, agitators from Pakistan were rumored to be meeting with village elders to encourage them to fight the Americans. At the time, the U.S. military was focused on rescuing Iraq from its downward spiral, not on the possibility of a resurgent Taliban. And the attack on Chicken Street was a sign that the mayhem on the distant Afghanistan-Pakistan frontier could also reach the capital. After taking in the scene of the bombing, I hurried back to my guest house to type an e-mail to an editor in the United States: "Any interest in a story on the bombing?" "Thanks," he wrote, "but we'll pass." He was expecting a heavy run of domestic news. The 2004 U.S. election campaign was in full swing; another big story of the day was that Delta Airlines was experiencing financial turbulence. In other words, Afghanistan was a forgotten war. And that was a shame, because Afghanistan was the scene of an important new experiment in the way that aid was being delivered.

A few months before the invasion of Iraq, a Pentagon official, Joseph Collins, traveled to Afghanistan on a fact-finding trip. Collins, a retired Army colonel, was known as something of an Afghanistan watcher: He had begun studying the country in the late 1970s, and his Ph.D. dissertation at Columbia focused on Soviet policy in Afghanistan. After a career in the Army, he worked as a public policy researcher in Washington. But his research career was put on hold in 2001, when he was asked to join the incoming administration of George W. Bush. Collins first served as special assistant to Deputy Secretary of Defense Paul Wolfowitz, and was promoted shortly thereafter to a new job within the Office of the Secretary of Defense.

Collins was deputy assistant secretary of defense for stability operations, an obscure directorate inside "OSD Policy," the policymaking shop in the Office of the Secretary of Defense. Stability operations was something of an orphan inside the DoD bureaucracy. Collins described his office as the "junk drawer of OSD policy" because of the mixed bag of missions under his purview: evacuating U.S. citizens from combat zones, humanitarian mine clearance, civil-military operations, peacekeeping, and humanitarian aid.[4]

In theory, the Pentagon was not supposed to be the lead U.S. agency for aid to Afghanistan: That was supposed to be the job of the U.S. Agency for International Development. In the year following the defeat of the Taliban, USAID had initiated its first quick impact projects: rebuilding schools, delivering new textbooks, and providing food to returning Afghan refugees. And Afghans were voting with their feet: By official estimates, around two million Afghans had returned from the refugee camps of Pakistan and the cities of Iran. At the same time, the military was getting more deeply involved in the business of humanitarian aid. By late 2002, around two hundred Army Civil Affairs specialists were on the ground in Afghanistan, repairing schools, boring wells, and opening medical clinics. They had refurbished the National Veterinary Center and the National Teachers' College in Kabul.[5] Collins's office oversaw that portfolio of humanitarian projects.

During his fact-finding trip to Afghanistan, Collins received a briefing from a British army officer, Colonel Nick Carter. Carter showed Collins a PowerPoint slide that sketched out a novel military organization that would be tailored to Afghanistan, something called Joint Regional Teams. The idea was to jump-start development projects in rural Afghanistan by organizing eight or ten of these units—essentially, supersized Civil Affairs teams—and stationing them out in the provinces. Each JRT would field a force of fifty to one hundred uniformed personnel. A larger "force protection" component of the team would guard the small outpost, run patrols, and provide overwatch (where one small unit supports or covers the activities of another). They would expand the presence of the military in Afghanistan, and by extension, serve as a counterweight to the militia commanders who still held sway in the countryside. Afghanistan at that point still had an extremely fragile central government, and the *jang salaran* (warlords) who had been put on the U.S. payroll during the campaign to oust the Taliban now stood in the way of creating a functioning Afghan state.

Carter, a former battalion commander with the British army's Royal Green Jackets regiment, would later be credited with the idea of the JRTs, but the plan was also being presented by other British officers assigned to Coalition Joint Task Force-180, the military headquarters that ran the war from Bagram.[6] The approach drew inspiration in part from the British army's experience in policing low-intensity conflicts in Northern Ireland and Cyprus. Carter was a recent veteran of Kosovo, where he had been charged with policing Kosovo's divided city of Mitrovica as part of KFOR, NATO's Kosovo force. Patrolling Mitrovica was equal parts police work and military operation: keeping the ethnic Serb and Albanian communities at bay, preventing ethnic reprisals, and searching for illegal weapons.[7]

Military planners believed the Joint Regional Teams would create a more visible coalition presence in Afghanistan outside the capital. By the summer of 2002, Kabul and its environs were reasonably secure, a development that was credited to the presence of the International Security Assistance Force, a small UN-mandated peacekeeping contingent that had arrived in December 2001. But ISAF did not patrol outside the capital, and policymakers in Kabul and Washington wanted to find a way to spread the "ISAF effect" into the regions.

Collins brought up the topic of Joint Regional Teams in a meeting with President Hamid Karzai. The Afghan president liked the idea, but he didn't like the name. "It doesn't work," Karzai said. "The word 'joint' doesn't exist in Dari or Pashto."

Officials in Kabul would have to come up with a new name. They settled on Provincial Reconstruction Teams, or PRTs. It was in part a political calculation: Warlords had their regions, the reasoning went, but the new Afghan state had provinces.

The PRTs were a more muscular version of the Civil Affairs teams already on the ground. With a security contingent to both guard their base and provide transport, they could go into harm's way to do development work. Collins, who came from the world of special operations and low-intensity conflict, liked the idea. On his return to Washington, he presented the idea to Doug Feith, the head of the Pentagon's policy office.

Collins would not take credit for inventing the PRTs, but he was key to propagating the concept within the Pentagon. The experiment had previously been tried on a small scale by the Coalition Joint Civil-Military Operations Task Force (CJCMOTF, pronounced "chick motif"), an ad hoc organization that originally oversaw the U.S. military's humanitarian operations in Afghanistan. CJCMOTF formed something called Coalition Humanitarian Liaison Cells ("chick licks" or "Chiclets"), six-man Civil Affairs teams augmented by a few civilian experts who accompanied Special Forces troops working out in the field.[8]

But for the concept to work on a larger scale, it would need funding, and some more personnel. Traditional Civil Affairs teams did not have the right skills for long-term development projects. They could drill a well here or repair a school there but could not necessarily do anything about the underlying problems of poverty and development that afflicted Afghanistan. In the new PRT model, the civilian experts—diplomats, agricultural experts, and development specialists—could focus on the tasks of long-term economic development. It was agreed that the PRTs would include civilian members drawn from development organizations such as USAID or the U.K.'s Department for International Development, the U.S. Department of Agriculture, and the U.S. State Department. The diplomats were supposed to act as local political advisors and report back to their embassies on the situation in the provinces. Real development experts could help plan more ambitious development projects such as building highways or repairing hydroelectric dams.

That fall, work got under way on planning, and military officials laid out a timeline for staffing the new Provincial Reconstruction Teams. The first was a U.S.-led team in eastern Afghanistan that opened in January 2003 at Gardez. Shortly thereafter, teams were established at Bamyan, home of the giant Buddha statues dynamited by the Taliban in 2001, and in Kunduz, the last city in northern Afghanistan held by the Taliban. The British opened the first non-U.S. team in Mazar-e-Sharif, a city in northern Balkh province that was the scene of an ongoing feud between two warlords, the Tajik leader Ustad Atta Mohammad Noor and his rival, an Uzbek general named Abdul Rashid Dostum. Plans were in the works for additional teams to be deployed around the country by the late summer of 2003.[9]

Collins presented the idea to the press in a December 2002 briefing and relayed an important message to the public as well: Major combat in Afghanistan was essentially over, and the emphasis would now shift. Beginning on January 1, 2003, the military would "be transitioning to focus on stability operations."[10]

In theory, the creation of these new teams—they had yet to be officially renamed PRTs—would bring the military and the civilian agencies closer together. The military headquarters at Bagram and the embassy in Kabul were physically and psychologically separated. Up until that point, each had basically done its own thing, meaning there was little "unity of effort" by the various U.S. agencies tasked with rebuilding Afghanistan. It was a bureaucratic problem with real implications. Without some elementary coordination, aid would be wasted: the same school might be repaired twice, unnecessary wells would be drilled. Savvier local leaders could persuade multiple donors to fund the same project, essentially double- or triple-dipping in reconstruction funds while depriving needier and less well connected communities of essential funds.

But the creation of the PRTs inadvertently expanded the military's remit. Collins noted that Lieutenant General Dan McNeill, commander of Combined Joint Task Force 180, and General Tommy Franks, the head of U.S. Central Command, "will be the people who are running these operations out in the field."[11]

The creation of the PRTs was, in effect, the first step toward what the Pentagon strategist Thomas Barnett had called the "SysAdmin" force: a new kind of organization, part military, part civilian, that was uniquely suited for the task of nation building. Afghanistan would serve as the first laboratory for this experiment. But it was easier said than done. When I met with Collins shortly before my departure for Afghanistan in September 2004, he made a blunt appraisal of NATO's efforts to contribute to this new mission. "The performance of our European brethren is pretty pathetic," he said. "Pretty pathetic." The problem was that "everybody wants to help, but nobody wants to put out. NATO is incredibly badly organized, the NATO nations are incredibly badly organized. The Germans complain all the time about their overstretch, and they've got less than three percent of their force abroad."

By early 2003, although the headlines about Iraq were eclipsing all news from Afghanistan, U.S.-funded reconstruction work in Afghanistan had slowly begun to pick up its pace. The first wave of quick-impact projects had been wrapped up, and work was beginning in earnest on more ambitious projects such as repairing Afghanistan's "ring road," the highway network that would connect the country's major cities. Plans were also in the works to repair the country's hydroelectric dams, which could generate inexpensive power and speed rural electrification. In its fiscal year 2003 budget request, the State Department also recognized a new development priority: weaning Afghan farmers from their dependence on growing opium poppy. Opium had emerged as Afghanistan's main cash crop: It was easy to grow, transport, and store, making it the perfect hedge for a lawless and uncertain time. A portion of the department's International Narcotics Control and Law Enforcement budget would go toward poppy eradication, police training, and employment schemes in opium-growing areas.

Simultaneously, the Bush administration's philosophical opposition to this mission was quietly set aside. George W. Bush had declared his aversion to nation building during the 2000 presidential campaign. A few months after he declared "Mission accomplished" on the deck of the carrier USS *Abraham Lincoln*, however, he recast the occupation of Iraq in clear nation-building terms. In a speech before the United Nations on September 23, 2003, half a year after the Iraq invasion, Bush used the success of the Marshall Plan, Europe's postwar recovery, as a selling point for a massive assistance package for Iraq. The reconstruction of Iraq, he said, would be "the greatest financial commitment of its kind since the Marshall Plan." Bush glossed over a key distinction: The United States did not rebuild postwar Europe in the midst of a shooting war. More important, the Marshall Plan hinged on facilitating trade, not handing out aid, and a great deal of American money went directly into backing the European Payments Union, which served as a clearinghouse for transactions between European nations.[12] It was, according to the historian Nicolaus Mills, a "blood transfusion" that encouraged the European states to make their own investments in infrastructure and social welfare programs to improve the lives of their citizens.[13]

While less ambitious in scale than Iraq's reconstruction, efforts to rebuild Afghanistan were also ramping up. "That opposition to nation-building is a fig leaf that dropped a while ago," a spokesman of the U.S. embassy in Kabul, Alberto Fernandez, told the *Washington Post*. "We're up to our ears in nation-building."[14] Between 2002 and 2003, the United States poured around $900 million into humanitarian aid and assistance to Afghanistan, eclipsing the $296 million the United States initially pledged at the first donor conference in Tokyo.[15]

Not everyone was pleased with the U.S. government's new enthusiasm for this approach, however. Traditional nonprofit aid groups such as CARE and Save the Children greeted the creation of the Provincial Reconstruction Teams with skepticism. In the 1990s, armed intervention in Kosovo and East Timor had troubled many traditional aid and relief groups, who felt they were being crowded out of the traditional "humanitarian space" by the military. The PRTs, they argued, "blurred the line" between humanitarian workers and the military, making it difficult for locals to distinguish between the coalition forces and the "true" humanitarians.

Militaries, they argued, served the interests of policymakers in their respective capitals; they were not guided by principles of neutrality and impartiality that humanitarian agencies traditionally aspired to. And they tended to deliver aid in a way that was likely to suit the short-term aims of military commanders on the ground, rather than considering broader development imperatives or the needs of the local community. Most important, associating with the military violated a deep taboo among traditional humanitarians at a fundamental level: In their view, it created a perception that humanitarian actors are not neutral players in a conflict, and this makes it harder for them to act impartially and effectively. Two researchers for Save the Children U.K. outlined their worries in a paper published in late 2002:

> If humanitarian actors are not perceived as neutral by the parties to the conflict, their impartiality and trustworthiness will be in doubt, and their access to all people in need, as well as their own security, will be in jeopardy ... Any integration of humanitarian aid into wider political and military strategy compromises humanitarian principles, making it harder for humanitarian actors on the ground to assert their independence and impartiality, and to negotiate access to people in need. Associating with a military force in a conflict zone implies that the agency in question is in some way identifying with that group, against others.[16]

In fact, the traditional humanitarians felt that the PRTs and the military's embrace of the humanitarian mission put them directly in harm's way. In the past, humanitarian aid groups had relied on their neutrality for protection. Even in strife-torn regions such as Afghanistan, they would avoid hiring armed guards for fear that it would compromise their impartiality. If members of the uniformed military dug wells or rebuilt schools, they feared, it would become impossible for the local population to distinguish between combatants and humanitarians.

In Afghanistan, however, arguments about preserving the traditional humanitarian space seemed increasingly quaint. In late March 2003, a Red Cross water engineer from El Salvador named Ricardo Munguia was driving along a road in southern Uruzgan province when he was pulled over by gunmen at a roadblock. He was pulled from his car and shot dead, in plain sight of other Afghan aid workers. Munguia's killers apparently knew he was an aid worker: One of the gunmen reportedly pulled his trouser leg up to show Munguia an artificial limb he had received from the Red Cross in Pakistan.[17]

The death of Munguia sent a tremor through Afghanistan's small community of expatriate aid workers.[18] The insurgents were beginning to deliberately target humanitarian aid workers and their local employees, who presented a much easier target than foreign military forces. Killing aid workers served a dual purpose. It telegraphed a message of intimidation to Afghans: collaboration with foreigners might cost you your life. And it was what the military called an "information operation," a dramatic attack that would guarantee headlines, magnifying insurgents' power and omnipresence.

Sarah Chayes, a former radio correspondent who had settled in Kandahar to work for an Afghan charity, saw how the death of Munguia further soured relations between the U.S. military and the nongovernmental organizations. "For international aid workers in Afghanistan, the only available target upon which to vent their frustration was the U.S. presence there," she later wrote. "And so humanitarian workers, Europeans as well as many Americans, opposed the presence far more vocally than Afghans did. They said it was the U.S. troops who endangered their lives, since the U.S. troops were doing reconstruction, and 'insurgents' could not distinguish between soldiers and aid workers."[19]

Chayes worked on development projects in Kandahar as a field director for Afghans for Civil Society, an independent charity founded by

Qayum Karzai, President Hamid Karzai's older brother. In *The Punishment of Virtue*, an account of her first few years in Afghanistan, she described how poorly the international aid system had delivered on promises to rebuild Afghanistan. But she disagreed with the humanitarian aid purists. She felt that the presence of U.S. troops had in fact brought security to Afghanistan. In fact, the military's deepening involvement in the humanitarian enterprise seemed to threaten the image of lofty neutrality that was carefully cultivated by the international aid community. "Aid workers have trouble accepting that they are now in the crosshairs themselves," she wrote. "When one of them is killed deliberately, the loss sparks shocked hurt feelings as well as grief. For the unconscious belief persists: If humanitarian workers are being targeted, there must be some mistake."[20]

Michelle Parker tightened the straps in the passenger seat of the old Huey helicopter as it prepared to lift off from Kabul Airport. It was a painfully early hour, and Parker had never flown on a helicopter before. As she anxiously waited for liftoff, she noticed a slight Afghan man tethered to a harness in the front of the passenger hold. He was carrying a Kalashnikov rifle. *Can he stop an RPG with that thing?* she wondered. *Really, what is he going to do—annoy some farmer?*

Just a few weeks earlier, a helicopter carrying workers for the Louis Berger Group, a U.S. construction firm that had a major contract from USAID to rebuild Afghanistan's main highways, had crashed after coming under fire in southern Afghanistan. The pilot was killed, and a civilian worker was injured.[21] The diminutive Afghan was supposed to provide some modicum of security for the flight down to Jalalabad, where Parker, a young USAID employee, would be taking up her new assignment with the Jalalabad PRT.

It was July 2004. Parker had been in the country for about two weeks, and she was being accompanied down to Jalalabad by her predecessor, a former Marine who had been promoted to USAID regional development advisor at Camp Salerno, a large U.S. firebase in southeastern Afghanistan (a firebase is a base supplying fire support to coalition forces). At the time, USAID still faced a logistical nightmare getting its employees and contractors out to the field: The agency had no aircraft of its own, Afghanistan had only a couple of unreliable commercial carriers, and the military owned most of the helicopters. On military flights, civilians were the lowest priority for seats: They flew "space available," meaning they could be bumped from their seat on the aircraft by the lowest-ranking private or a pallet of bottled water. And to further complicate matters, USAID usually had to rely on "implementing partners," its contractors and their subcontractors, for transportation. They had few options.

Parker's predecessor, however, had figured out how to work the system. He had been scouting an electrification project at Torkham, the border town that is the crossing point from Pakistan's Khyber Agency to Afghanistan's Nangarhar Province. He convinced some of the USAID senior engineers to make a fact-finding trip to Torkham, the main customs station on the highway between Peshawar and Jalalabad. Having senior officials on board helped him line up the helicopter flight, and they could drop Parker off in Jalalabad. After rising at the crack of dawn, going down to the airport, and waiting for liftoff, Parker weighed the situation: It was her first job after graduate school; it was her first trip on a helicopter. As the helicopter lifted off, Parker breathed in: *Okay, welcome to your new job.*

The flight was stunning. The chopper wound through the jutting canyons of the Kabul Gorge, passed over the sparkling reservoir behind the Surobi Dam, and then dropped low, hugging the plains of Nangarhar Province, until it arrived at the Jalalabad PRT's camp. The USAID team touched down at a primitive landing zone, by a swampy area behind the PRT site.

At the landing zone, Parker and the USAID team were met by an Army Civil Affairs major. *Here's a strapping young lad*, she thought to herself with a laugh. And then it started to sink in: She would be living alone on a military base with all of these young men, many of whom were barely old enough to buy beer. The soldiers unloaded Parker's gear, and then, after grabbing a quick breakfast, the entire team walked over to a convoy of pickup trucks and SUVs for the two-hour ride to the border.

Another major was standing by the trucks with an enormous plug of chew in his mouth. He sized up Parker, a Georgia native with the looks of a hometown sweetheart, strapped into body armor and ready for the journey.

"So," he drawled with an exaggerated southern accent, "You a Republican or Democrat?"

"How about undecided?" Parker shot back.

"I'll take it, you're hired!" the officer said approvingly. "I think we just got an upgrade in AID people."

When Parker arrived in Nangarhar Province, the Provincial Reconstruction Teams were still a novelty. Parker had first heard of them just a few months before, when she was finishing a graduate degree at the Institute for Conflict Analysis and Resolution at George Mason University. An instructor had suggested that she research a paper on this new experiment; aside from a critique written by Barbara Stapleton, then of the Agency Coordinating Body for Afghan Relief, an alliance of charity organizations, there almost was no literature on the subject. So Parker went straight to the source: She began lining up interviews with people in the Pentagon who were involved with setting up the PRTs. She couldn't get an appointment with Joseph Collins, so she arranged an interview with Dave des Roches, a gregarious West Point graduate who worked on Collins's staff and had worked behind the scenes to set up the first PRTs. Parker interviewed des Roches at a bar.

She also paid a call on the Afghanistan desk at USAID. After she concluded her interview, the official she was interviewing made her a recruitment pitch. Parker had already worked on a USAID project in Nepal; she was finishing graduate school; and she probably knew more about PRTs than anyone else right now. Did she want to apply for a job?

At the time, tenured USAID officers had few incentives to work and live on a military outpost on the Afghanistan-Pakistan frontier. Culturally speaking, the USAID bureaucracy primarily viewed itself as an altruistic organization, not an arm of the U.S. national security establishment. Volunteering for this quasi-military duty was not a career-enhancing move. What's more, USAID tenure and promotion boards weren't quite sure how to review or evaluate someone who had served on a PRT: It didn't fit the traditional job description for a USAID worker, and very few volunteers came forward within the bureaucracy in the early days of the PRTs.*

---

* In fact, it would take another two years before USAID's human resources department would add Afghanistan PRT jobs to the "bid list," so it was next-to-impossible for a tenured USAID Foreign Service officer to get an assignment to a team. Complicating matters, career USAID Foreign Service officers couldn't legally report to a personal services contractor, and until 2006, the head of the USAID PRT office in Kabul was a personal services contractor.

Consequently the agency had to turn to contractors such as Parker. USAID had a mechanism, called a personal services contract, which basically allowed USAID to beef up its foreign service by hiring individual contractors. The PSCs, as they were called, worked directly for USAID. They held temporary positions within the civil service, but they had none of the long-term benefits that USAID personnel enjoyed. Within the caste system of USAID, they were temporary hires, bureaucratic second-class citizens.

These shake-and-bake USAID officers were not an easy fit with the military culture, either. Parker's predecessor had clashed with the military members of the Jalalabad team. As a former Marine officer, he was unimpressed by what he saw as sloppy soldiering by the Army reservists and National Guard soldiers on the outpost. He reprimanded them for discipline infractions such as failing to arm their weapons when they went "outside the wire." For their part the troops resented being dressed down by an aid worker. When Parker arrived at the Jalalabad base, she was unsure how she would fit in, both as a civilian and as a woman.

Parker's first day on the job was not easy. Before the drive to Torkham, the security team held a predeparture briefing, which was routine before a military convoy. The PRT had never had a civilian female team member, and they were unsure how the conservative, male-dominated Pashtun community of Torkham would respond to her presence. "Michelle, if you feel at all uncomfortable, let us know and we'll sweep you into the car," said one of the members of the security team.

And Parker had to adjust to military culture as well. As she climbed inside the truck, she found her boots on the top of some odd black box in the passenger compartment. "What's that?" she asked. One of her colleagues silenced her: their interpreter was in the car. He was a local hire and had no security clearance. You had to be careful not to talk about the equipment in front of them. It was her first encounter with what the military calls OPSEC (operational security): keeping a lid on classified information, keeping operational plans closely held, not revealing sensitive information about equipment or intelligence collection capabilities. OPSEC was not a phrase that was usually employed in aid and development circles.

They arrived at Torkham. Sure enough, Parker found herself the lone woman at the meeting with local leaders on the electrification project. Everyone seemed to be staring. She was uncomfortable, and her headscarf kept slipping off, but she didn't want to show any fear. She kept her composure, and the meetings, about an electrification project and a government proposal to move the border post, went without a hitch. On the ride back to Jalalabad, she reviewed her first day on the job: the insane helicopter ride from Kabul, the gorgeous ride down to the Khyber Pass. Not a bad first day of work. She was hooked.

Parker was a natural for the role: As a woman she felt no peer pressure, no need to fit in with the "band of brothers" culture of the military. She would never be part of the boys' club. For her, as a strong, independent woman, living alone on a military base, it was liberating to be outside the group. There was no need to pander. She could do her job without feeling as though she had to toe the military's line.

More important, she could be a player. For a relatively junior civil servant, she wielded a significant amount of power. In addition to the "quick impact" funds at her disposal, she ended up working behind the scenes to start a road project that would link the homelands of the remote Shinwari tribe, in the Shinwar District of Nangarhar Province, with Highway 1, the main road that linked the region with the capital. Constructing the road was an important political move that helped placate the tribal leadership and improved the aid workers' relations with the provincial government. Parker had a fair degree of autonomy, serious resources, and a heavily armed contingent of soldiers to help her get the job done. In many respects it was a powerful, almost intoxicating, experience. She ended up staying in Afghanistan for the next twenty-nine months and eventually was promoted to the civilian equivalent of a brigadier general before she was thirty-two.

Launching the PRTs in Afghanistan also hinged on recruiting diplomats to fill State Department positions on the teams. But within the Foreign Service, details were still scant about what, exactly, the job entailed. All they knew was that it meant an assignment to a combat zone, far outside the confines of the capital and the embassy. It was a potentially dangerous job, one for which few Foreign Service officers were trained.

John Mongan, a junior diplomat, first heard about the PRTs during the 2003 "bid cycle," the time of the year when Foreign Service officers apply for their next rotational assignment. Mongan was intrigued by the idea of joining a PRT: As a student he had considered joining the military and

was enrolled in the Reserve Officers Training Corps. And he was fasci-
nated by America's experiments in counterinsurgency during the Vietnam War. "Everybody else in my ROTC and poli-sci classes were studying
wars we had won," he later recalled. "And it made sense to study a war you
had lost, because we pretty much know how to fight a major tank battle in
Europe."

Mongan also had some experience in conflict zones; he had joined the
Foreign Service after a stint in Kosovo with the international charity
Mercy Corps, where he had worked setting up food distribution networks. The idea of being a diplomat had initially sounded very stuffy and
boring to someone like him, but full-time jobs with nongovernmental
organizations were hard to come by, and his parents wanted him to get a
job and get on with his professional life. He took the Foreign Service exam
and passed. While waiting for his security clearance to come through, a
time-consuming process of background checks that usually took several
months, he took the job in Kosovo.

NATO's bombing campaign over Kosovo began three weeks after he
joined the Foreign Service. Since he spent some time there, he was eager
to continue with his Foreign Service career and put his Kosovo experience to work. First, however, he had to complete his A-100 class, the orientation and training course for new Foreign Service officers. After he
completed the course, in 1999, the State Department informed him it
was sending him to Angola.

Mongan was unhappy with the Angola assignment. Eventually he
heard through the bureaucratic grapevine ("I met a guy, who knew a guy,
who knew a guy") that James Dobbins, a veteran diplomat who had been
President Clinton's special envoy to Somalia, Haiti, Bosnia, and Kosovo,
was looking for a staff assistant. Mongan was able to get an introduction,
and was offered a one-year assignment as Dobbin's aide.

It was an educational year. Dobbins had one of the longest diplomatic
résumés in Washington; he had also served as the Bush administration's
special envoy on Afghanistan. But after his assignment with Dobbins,
Mongan found that there were few really hands-on nation-building
jobs in the Foreign Service. Then, in mid-2003, he read an internal cable
saying the State Department was looking for volunteers for something
called a PRT in Afghanistan. He was intrigued. He contacted the officers
running the program to volunteer for it. Initially he was told that he was
"under grade"—too junior—and that he was ineligible because he had

never held a job providing relevant experience in political affairs. But few Foreign Service officers were clamoring for the chance to live on a remote Army outpost in the middle of a combat zone, and Mongan eventually got the call to work at a PRT in Ghazni, southwest of Kabul.

He arrived later that summer in Kabul on an Air Azerbaijan flight— Afghanistan's national carrier, Ariana, was considered too risky for U.S. government personnel—after about two weeks of rudimentary training in Pashto, one of the languages of Afghanistan.

He had a week of orientation at the embassy, and then they tried to figure out how to get him down to Ghazni. Much like USAID, the embassy had not completely figured out how to support its personnel in isolated parts of Afghanistan. Meanwhile, Mongan went to the embassy's political section to try to get information on Ghazni. The people there could not really help him, saying, "None of us have been down there in a while." The deputy chief of mission's sole advice to Mongan was, "Don't try to be a player out there."

Like their USAID counterparts, State Department PRT team members were orphans within the bureaucracy. James Hunter, another Foreign Service officer who served on the Asadabad PRT at roughly the same time as Mongan, described the experience thus: "When you walked out of the Kabul embassy, you dropped off the face of the earth." At the time, the embassy's PRT section had only two officers who supported the field staff, and both had to juggle that responsibility with other embassy jobs.

Eventually, Mongan managed to get a lift to Ghazni, a two-hour drive from Kabul, with the deputy chief of mission. The DCM was new to Afghanistan; he had never traveled outside the capital, and wanted to see a PRT. By hitching a ride with the senior diplomat, Mongan felt a little bit like a kid being dropped off at college. But it had its advantages. "It probably gave the PRT and the battalion head a completely mistaken sense of the influence and heft I happened to have back in Kabul," he later recalled. "I guess in the first few weeks that helped."

Over the next few weeks, Mongan settled into his new situation. The base at PRT Ghazni was manned by soldiers of the Virginia National Guard. The Provincial Reconstruction Team had only a small civilian contingent: a USAID representative who had been there since earlier in the spring and a U.S. Department of Agriculture officer. The State Department had sent a retired Foreign Service officer to Ghazni, but he had lasted only two months.

The DCM's advice to Mongan was repeated by others who worked on the PRTs. In essence, it meant "Keep your head down." The primary function of the diplomats on the PRT was to observe and report back to the embassy, nothing more. They would keep an eye on the local situation, as well as on what the other U.S. agencies were up to. They were not there to influence local decisionmaking or contribute to the larger effort being led by the military.

Diplomats did not fit neatly into the military organization. They were not on the same rotational schedule, and they reported through a different chain of command. And there was a serious communications problem. The military maintains its own classified networks, but the State Department had not provided for secure communications outside the embassy. The entire time Mongan was posted to Ghazni, he had to use a Hotmail account to communicate with his superiors in Kabul. That meant he had to send an unclassified version of his reports, with sensitive information stripped out. If he needed to relay something classified, he would add it to a summary report that the Provincial Reconstruction Team's military staff typed up and sent nightly to their brigade headquarters. A State Department officer assigned to the brigade was supposed to pass on any relevant information on the situation in Ghazni to the embassy in Kabul.

Or so went the theory. Mongan assumed that his State Department counterpart would pass the reports on to the embassy in Kabul and that someone in the embassy would bother to read them. Neither, it turned out, actually happened, even though one of Mongan's main responsibilities was keeping tabs on the political situation in Ghazni. Eventually, Mongan had to send e-mail from the PRT commander's account and call his superiors in Kabul to make sure some of his reports got through to the embassy. Other Foreign Service officers serving on PRTs encountered the same problem.

And then there was the issue of whether the civilians should be armed. Both the military and the State Department were ambivalent. This was, after all, a relatively small and isolated military outpost, and everyone needed to pitch in to provide security. But no one was clear on whether the civilians on the PRT should also carry weapons. Mongan and the other civilian members of the PRT traveled with the military on patrols, sometimes going into the city of Ghazni to meet up with some of the local government officials, sometimes driving out to rural districts. About once a month the PRT members would load up their vehicles and form a convoy for a five-day patrol to some of the more remote areas of the province. Most of the districts were pretty secure, but about four districts were marked red on the map. The PRT commander wanted everyone carrying a weapon whenever they went there.

The embassy did not want Foreign Service officers openly carrying weapons, but maintained something of a "Don't ask, don't tell" policy. And if having Foreign Service personnel carrying pistols and carbines made State Department officials uneasy, it didn't please some military commanders either. Mongan once attended a brigade commanders' conference where a State Department employee arrived with a pistol strapped to his hip, raising a few eyebrows among the military men in the room. Another Foreign Service officer on a PRT showed a bit more chutzpah. Whenever he showed up at the embassy he would leave his pistol in his truck, but he would come walking into the embassy with the empty holster still strapped to his thigh.

Despite the bureaucratic ambiguities, Mongan loved working on the PRT. It was "the best job of my life," he later told me. He was living at a combat outpost, free of the dull certainties of embassy life; he enjoyed a good working relationship with the other civilians on the team; and his commander had a clear grasp of the mission. He discarded the DCM's cautious advice, and became closely involved in overseeing local projects. Like Michelle Parker, he discovered that a relatively junior officer had real power on a PRT. As he later recalled, "The embassy tends to have a very conventional outlook. And when they said 'Don't try to be a player,' what they meant is 'Keep us informed on what's going on, and don't try to get involved in it.' The problem is, of course, most diplomats being diplomats, and not physicists, don't know what Heisenberg's uncertainty principle is. You can't passively report on something—if you're in the room, you're influencing it! And you may as well influence the shit out if it instead of influencing it passively. And there were a couple of times . . . where I probably got in front of myself. But at a certain point the embassy was willing to trust me to go ahead with what I thought was a good idea."

Like Parker, he was hooked. But at that point the PRTs were still an obscure experiment in militarizing aid and development.

Despite those first hesitant steps toward creating a cadre of muddy-boots diplomats, there was a sense within the Bush administration that the

State Department was still not pulling its weight in nation building. In early 2004, Michael Coulter, a Republican political appointee within the State Department's Bureau of Political-Military Affairs, had a conversation with Deputy Secretary of State Richard Armitage about the apparent lack of State Department commitment to the civilian reconstruction mission. The PRTs seemed like a worthwhile experiment, but there were no standard guidelines for how, exactly, they were supposed to do their job, whom they were supposed to report to, and how they fit in with the overall mission.

Coulter later recalled that the discussion got Armitage fired up. He had served three combat tours in Vietnam as a patrol boat officer and advisor to the South Vietnamese navy. Within a week, he instructed Coulter to pack his bags for Afghanistan, where he would be the eyes and ears for Armitage. Armitage's advice: "Don't spend a single night in Kabul; hitchhike around the country with our staff." Coulter's initial title was "roving PRT person."

The problem was, getting around Afghanistan was not easy. At that point the State Department still had few people stationed outside Kabul, and the embassy usually depended on the military to ferry its personnel to remote outposts. Even though Coulter was relatively senior, he had a difficult time following Armitage's directive. Eventually he found a solution. In spring 2004, the Twenty-fifth Infantry Division's commander, Major General Eric Olson, took over as the head of Combined Joint Task Force-76. Coulter was essentially seconded to Olson as a political advisor, and in return, he had authority to hop around the country on military aircraft. It was, to use State Department slang, a classic bureaucratic "drug deal."

By autumn 2004 the U.S. military wanted to expand the number of PRTs around the country. The plan was to gradually hand over control of PRTs to NATO, starting with the teams in the relatively stable and secure northeastern portions of Afghanistan and then moving around the map counterclockwise. It was part of the exit strategy: As NATO took control, this would presumably free up more U.S. forces that were desperately needed in Iraq. But Coulter discovered that the NATO allies were not always enthusiastic about the PRT mission. In northern Kunduz Province, he found, the Germans were extremely risk-averse. They allowed the Provincial Reconstruction team members to leave the camp only if they could be accompanied by armored ambulances; night patrols were rare; and the Germans were bound by restrictive rules (called "caveats") that prevented them from taking part in combat unless they were under direct attack. That approach created a security void that insurgents would soon fill.

In early October 2004, I paid a visit to Kunduz, where about 280 German soldiers were stationed along with a handful of U.S. government civilians and about a dozen U.S. soldiers. Lieutenant Colonel Thomas Scheibe, spokesman for PRT Kunduz, made it eminently clear to me that the Germans were not eager to work outside the wire, emphasizing that basic security was the job of local police. "We are part of ISAF," Scheibe told me. "Security *assistance* force."

But that attitude was problematic. A month earlier, in September 2004, the city of Faizabad, in the remote northeastern province of Badakhshan, had been the scene of a riot. Fired by rumors that local women had been sexually assaulted by foreigners, local men had burned down the offices of two foreign aid agencies in the town, where fifty-five members of the PRT Kunduz had recently established a security contingent. Around a dozen German soldiers were working at the airport when the riots began. Hoping to consolidate his forces, the German commander ordered the team members back to base but they couldn't get away. When the German troops reached the town, they ran straight into the rioters. "They stopped immediately and saw about a thousand people. The street was full," Scheibe told me. "And they were not friendly-looking . . . so [the German soldiers] decided to go back another way."

After beating an initial retreat, the German commander led a team out to do some reconnoitering. By then the riot was over; it all ended when a local Afghan commander threatened to shoot rioters. Several aid workers were beaten, and they had to be spirited away by UN workers and Global Risk, a private security firm. The Germans were supposed to be responsible for the four northeastern provinces of Afghanistan, generally considered the most secure part of the country. Although they took their own protection very seriously, caveats meant that security in the north would start to unravel. In June 2004, eleven Chinese laborers who were working on a road construction project south of Kunduz were gunned down in their tents. Not long after that, the convoy of Afghanistan's vice president, Nematullah Shahrani, was hit by a roadside bomb. The night after I left Kunduz, two rockets hit the Kunduz PRT; four soldiers were injured, one seriously.

This new model of militarized aid to Afghanistan, then, was a completely hit-or-miss affair. In early 2003 and 2004, the PRTs were still very much a work in progress, and policymakers were still wrestling with basic questions of how to support this experiment. State Department personnel still had few career incentives for working in isolated military outposts; they were not trained to work in an active combat zone; and once in the field, they were all but forgotten by their parent organizations.

And there was another reason why the reconstruction of Afghanistan would have to wait: The machinery of government was still focused on the war in Iraq. As employees of the U.S. diplomatic mission in Kabul had realized in their 2002 briefing with Deputy Secretary of Defense Paul Wolfowitz, senior leaders in Washington had shifted resources and bureaucratic attention to the Iraq campaign, which was starting to unravel in the face of an accelerating civil war.

The military's focus in Afghanistan, then, moved away from stability operations. Emphasis shifted to "Find, fix, and finish": killing the remnants of the Taliban instead of focusing on securing the needs of the population. Troops and resources would be needed for Iraq, and rebuilding Afghanistan was a manpower-intensive business. A civilian official recalled realizing how far the pendulum had swung away from development work during a briefing with Major General Jason Kamiya, who was the chief operational commander in Afghanistan as of March 2005. Kamiya and his staff had paid a visit to central Afghanistan after a severe spring flood, and PRT members had prepared a briefing on relief distribution. Kamiya told the team leader: "I don't give a fuck about this flood! What are you doing to kill the enemy?"

Kamiya remembered it differently. That remark, he said, was "one hundred eighty degrees from my philosophy." But he acknowledged that there was sometimes friction among the military command, the PRTs, and the development agencies that led to constant misunderstandings. In PRT briefings, people sometimes misinterpreted his questions about how development projects fit into the larger security picture. "This is Ph.D.-level work," he said. "You're just trying to mentor both the military side as well as showing your development partner, who is looking skeptically at someone in uniform, it's not 'my way or the highway.'"

Afghanistan had started to slip away. Even though the reconstruction effort there was relatively modest in scale, many of the tensions between military and humanitarian missions were already apparent. The entire enterprise seemed chronically short of money, manpower, and time. Equally important, the traditional humanitarian aid community was alarmed by what it saw as a dangerous blurring of the lines, with uniformed soldiers taking on a greater share of development work. Soon, those tensions would become even more pronounced in Iraq, where the U.S. military was beginning to spend much more heavily on infrastructure and governance projects than ever before. In a bid to stop Iraq's deadly spiral, a key new instrument—cash—would become as important as any weapon system in the arsenal.

CHAPTER 5

Cash as a Weapon

In October 2003, I attended the annual conference of the Association of the United States Army, the service's professional association, in Washington. Amid the displays of high-tech weaponry mounted by military contractors such as Raytheon, Boeing, Lockheed Martin, and BAE Systems was the charred hulk of a High Mobility Multipurpose Wheeled Vehicle, a truck better known as a Humvee, that had struck a command-detonated mine in Afghanistan. The engine block was destroyed, leaving tendrils of blackened steel where the front axle had once been, but the passenger compartment was intact—the windshield wasn't even cracked.*

This was an M1114, an armored version of the truck. The detonation of a roadside bomb—say, an artillery shell detonated by remote control—would throw out a lethal blast wave and a shower of hot, sharp fragments. An "up-armored" Humvee had a hardened passenger compartment that cocooned its occupants behind ballistic glass and heavy steel doors, diminishing the risk of injury from an explosion.

---

* The Humvee was never designed to be an armored vehicle. While the ballistic windshield of an "up-armored" Humvee could stop armor-piercing 7.62mm rounds from a Kalashnikov rifle, and its front axle could withstand a 12-pound contact-mine detonation, its drive train and suspension were not originally built to handle the extra weight of heavy steel armor. More important, the vehicle's flat-bottomed design would not dissipate the energy of a blast when the vehicle was hit from below.

Many military units had arrived in Iraq in "soft-skin" Humvees, four-wheel-drive utility trucks with flimsy canvas doors, or no doors at all. The vehicles were not designed for combat: They were supposed to be an all-purpose pickup for troops operating safely in the rear. It reflected the U.S. military's conventional view of war. Either the environment was considered "permissive," and troops could drive around in Humvees, or it was frontline combat, and they would be in tanks. For this new type of combat arena the military needed a different mode of transport: one that was light enough for ferrying soldiers around narrow urban streets but robust enough to withstand gunfire or a mine detonation. The U.S. military had a few vehicles that fit the bill, but only in very limited numbers.

In October 2003 Congress was weighing the Bush administration's $87 billion emergency spending request for fiscal year 2004 to pay for the ongoing wars in Afghanistan and Iraq, and Armor Holdings, a company that made Humvee armor, expected that the bill would pay for more of the vehicles. Anticipating rapid demand for vehicle protection, the company had also developed something called the HArD-Kit (HMMWV Armored Demountable Kit), a bolt-on armor system that could be installed on Humvees in the field. Bob Mecredy, president of Armor Holdings' aerospace and defense group, told me that the damaged chassis on display at the conference "couldn't be a better advertisement" for the effectiveness of the M1114.

Congress passed the bill, and tacked on extra funds for up-armored Humvees. When the Bush administration submitted its supplemental-funding request to Congress, it asked for $177.2 million to buy approximately 747 up-armored Humvees. House and Senate conferees, however, recommended a total of $239 million, enough to buy 1,065 of the vehicles. Congress also inserted funds to pay for radio frequency jammers capable of blocking the signal from cell phones or pagers, which were often used to set off roadside bombs remotely. Still, the new armored vehicles could not get to Iraq quickly enough. In a town hall meeting with Iraq-bound troops at Camp Buehring, Kuwait, in December 2004, a Tennessee National Guardsman, with some prompting from a reporter, asked Secretary of Defense Donald Rumsfeld: "We've had troops in Iraq for coming up on three years and we've always staged here out of Kuwait. Now why do we soldiers have to dig through local landfills for pieces of scrap metal and compromised ballistic glass to up-armor our vehicles and why don't we have those resources readily available to us?" Rumsfeld's answer: "You go to war with the Army you have, not the Army you might want or wish to have at a later time."[1]

The statement spoke volumes about the military's preparedness for this new mission. In the months after the invasion, the military ramped up delivery of up-armored Humvees to Iraq, and they did save lives. But they would also create the phenomenon of the "urban submarine": U.S. troops and reconstruction specialists driving around in these boxy, bullet-resistant vehicles seemed all the more remote from the population they were supposed to be aiding. The business of nation building in Iraq was extremely dangerous and deadly, but the military needed more than lethal weaponry to get the job done.

On May 7, 2003, the U.S. military command in Iraq issued a fragmentary order (in military parlance, a "FRAGO," used to inform units of a refinement to the operations plans) titled the "Brigade Commander's Discretionary Recovery Program to Directly Benefit the Iraqi People." The FRAGO gave unit commanders the authority to spend cash that had been confiscated from the Ba'athist regime and direct the money toward humanitarian assistance and development.[2] The money included around $900 million that had been seized by U.S. forces during the invasion, much of it discovered in Saddam Hussein's palaces. The following month, the Coalition Provisional Authority formalized the program, authorizing commanders "to take all actions necessary to operate a Commander's Emergency Response Program."[3]

This Robin Hood scheme would quickly evolve into something more ambitious. Left essentially to their own devices, military units on the ground in Iraq would devise their own approach to repairing and stabilizing Iraq. Unlike the civilian-led administration, which had relatively little manpower at its disposal, the military had 150,000 pairs of boots on the ground. And it had a new tool for promoting Iraq's self-government, security, and reconstruction: cash, and lots of it.

The Commander's Emergency Response Program (CERP, pronounced "surp") quickly became a preferred tool for U.S. military commanders trying to solve problems on the ground. The program allowed military purchasing officers to authorize large cash expenditures using standardized forms, so it was a quick way to spread cash around in the communities where they operated. Used to pay for local development projects, CERP became the most important nonlethal instrument in the U.S. military's tool kit. Within the first six months in Iraq, commanders burned through around $78.6 million, buying neighborhood generators, paying Iraqis to pick up trash, repairing schools, and procuring computers or air-conditioning units for municipal and provincial offices.[4]

It seemed to be an easy way to buy goodwill. Soon, however, the military spent down the cash confiscated from Saddam Hussein's regime. In the fall of 2003, the administration of President George W. Bush included a request for more CERP funds as part of the $87 billion emergency spending package to pay for the ongoing costs of the wars in Iraq and Afghanistan. Around $18.7 billion in supplemental money was earmarked for the Iraq Relief and Reconstruction Fund. The bill passed by Congress included $180 million for CERP funds. Oversight of reconstruction funds, however, was extremely haphazard. Coalition officials were given "footballs," bricks of $20 bills delivered by the Federal Reserve Bank of New York, and loaded them into trucks and Chevrolet Suburbans to deliver them around the country.[5] Stuart Bowen, appointed as special inspector general for Iraq reconstruction in early 2004, recalled seeing bags of dollar bills being literally hauled out of the Republican Palace, the headquarters of the Coalition Provisional Authority. "What I saw was troubling: large amounts of cash moving quickly out the door," he later wrote.[6]

In the northern Iraqi city of Mosul, spreading around CERP funds quickly became a major priority. The 101st Airborne Division under Major General David Petraeus arrived there in late spring of 2003. Mosul was an ethnically mixed city, with a Sunni Arab majority in some areas, as well as a sizable population of Kurds, Assyrians, and Turkmen. Mosul was a potential tinderbox, and with the strongman gone, dormant ethnic rivalries threatened to reignite. The city was also a key trade center, and the division began spending money across the board to keep Mosul stable. In a press briefing shortly after the division's arrival in Mosul, Petraeus ticked off a laundry list of projects his troops had undertaken:

> Our soldiers have deployed throughout our area of operation, securing cities and key infrastructure facilities; helping the new interim city and province government get established; conducting joint patrols with Iraqi policemen and manning police stations in the city; helping organize and secure the delivery of fuel

and propane; assisting with the organization of the recently be-gun grain harvest, a huge endeavor in this part of Iraq; building bridges and clearing streets; helping reopen schools and Mosul University; assisting with the reestablishment of the justice sys-tem in the area; distributing medical supplies; helping with the distribution of food; guarding archaeological sites; working to restore public utilities, and ninety percent of Mosul now has power and water.[7]

Petraeus also began paying salaries to government workers. The divi-sion used national bank funds that had been safeguarded during the looting, paying the salary arrears of government workers who had not received paychecks since the collapse of the regime in April. It was an important move: The public sector employed a large segment of the Iraqi population, and keeping civil servants on the payroll was one way to keep a lid on discontent.

Essentially, Petraeus was trying to prime the pump, both politically and economically. The lightning advance on Baghdad in 2003 had decapitated the old regime, but the dearth of postwar planning meant that military commanders on the ground would have to improvise. Faced with a popu-lation that had no recent experience of representative government, and an almost crippling dependence on the state for everything from bread ra-tions to fuel vouchers, smart leaders like Petraeus realized that they would have to step in and perform many of the functions of the Iraqi state. But they needed more than just military manpower for the job: American sol-diers could never be a substitute for local Iraqi administrators from the communities they were supposed to serve.

That approach, however, would require some finesse. Bremer's first move as the head of the CPA was to issue a sweeping de-Ba'athification order, which in effect barred thousands of low-level civil servants from work. Under Saddam, Ba'ath Party membership had been obligatory for many professionals, including doctors, professors, and schoolteachers. Petraeus would seek, and receive, an exemption from Bremer in order to keep some of those institutions functioning.

Petraeus was careful not to clash openly with Bremer, but Colonel Lloyd Sammons, who worked in the CPA's governance office, noted that Petraeus was conspicuously absent from the regular meetings in Bagh-dad on provincial affairs. "The military commanders were also supposed to come in for these meetings," Sammons later noted. "Every commander came in except one, and that was Petraeus. General Petraeus never showed up at the time I was there. He blew them off."[8]

In Mosul, as in other cities throughout Iraq, soldiers who were trained as aviators, infantrymen, or artillery gunners were having to adapt to a new job description: aid worker. Lieutenant Katrina Lewison, a young West Point graduate from western Kansas and now a Black Hawk pilot, was one of the soldiers who unexpectedly found herself on a quasi-humanitarian mission. On paper, she was a platoon leader with the Sixth Battalion of the 101st Aviation; in practice, she was a construction boss, supervising a team of sixty Iraqi day laborers.

Lewison's career in the construction business began on Mosul's unemployment line. Each day, hundreds of jobless men from Mosul would line up outside the front gate of the airfield where the helicopter unit was based. A minor local sheikh named Doctor Mohammed had presented himself to the division on the day it arrived in Mosul, sending out a handwritten note, in stilted English, that was hand-carried to the airfield by an elderly man. Major Fred Wellman, the battalion executive officer, went to meet Doctor Mohammed. Over a gelatinous plate of lamb meat, Wellman agreed to help start building clinics and schools in the local villages.

The sheikh emerged as a trusted labor broker, and helped Lewison to hire carpenters to do some construction jobs. "After I hired one family, they had other family members and friends, and with the sense of family honor, I could hold one man responsible for all the family members, and they knew that if one person did something wrong that I would fire all the rest of them," she said. To Lewison, the employment scheme seemed to be working. Iraqi men were getting cash, and they were staying off the streets.

The division's approach to governing Mosul—in essence, spreading cash around and trying to restore essential services—had its hazards, however. The Civil Affairs approach meant getting outside the wire and working among the population in Mosul. But that hearts-and-minds work was often hard to square with the imperatives of what the military called "force protection." On August 2, 2003, Lewison received permission to accompany her husband, Lieutenant Tyler Lewison, on a local reconstruction project. Tyler Lewison's unit was assigned to a Civil Affairs project at the University of Mosul, and reopening classes was a point of pride for Petraeus. For Katrina Lewison, the mission was supposed to be a break from the routine. August 2 was Tyler's birthday, and Katrina, who did not get to see much of her husband while on deployment, had received permission to accompany Tyler's unit for the day.

As the soldiers left one of the university buildings and climbed into their Humvee, someone tossed a hand grenade at their truck. Amid the noise and confusion, the soldiers sped away; a warrant officer was bleeding from a shrapnel injury in the neck, and Katrina Lewison had been nicked by a grenade splinter.

Iraq had no clear frontline, and the troops there faced a war in which the adversary's primary weapon was the roadside bomb, termed by the military parlance an improvised explosive device, or IED. At the beginning of the war, the IED was not expected to be the main threat. But as the U.S. military settled into an uneasy routine of occupation in the summer of 2003, insurgents began seeding the roads with improvised bombs. They observed the patterns of the U.S. patrols, counted how many vehicles were in each different convoy, and noted what kinds of vehicles they used and how vulnerable they were.

During its stay in northern Iraq, the 101st Airborne Division became the region's largest single employer. The division had around twenty thousand troops at its disposal, and it could saturate Mosul and Nineveh Province with patrols and Civil Affairs projects.[9] Under Petraeus's leadership, things were starting to get up and running, but the question remained: What would happen after the division went home? In late January 2004, the 101st Airborne Division began rotating home to Fort Campbell, Kentucky, and it handed over responsibility for the area to Task Force Olympia, an eight-thousand-strong force built around the Third Stryker Brigade Combat Team, Second Infantry Division, commanded by Brigadier General Carter Ham.[10] (A Stryker is a type of eight-wheeled, armored combat vehicle.)

The Third Stryker brigade was designated as a reserve force for Multi-National Corps-Iraq, meaning that it was on call to support other units outside of northern Iraq, so it was stretched a bit thin. It also had far fewer CERP funds at its disposal than the 101st. A RAND research report noted that the 101st Airborne Division spent around thirty-one million dollars in reconstruction funds during its stay in northern Iraq; the arriving Stryker brigade had less than half that amount, around fifteen million. The 101st Airborne Division also had an engineering unit that was able to take on ambitious projects to rebuild roads and irrigation systems, repair a major bridge between Irbil and Mosul, and reopen Mosul University.[11]

Using cash as a temporary fix had its risks: Although it kept some of the holdover institutions running, new, fully functioning Iraqi civil and political institutions had yet to emerge. So when the money ran out, it could all fall apart. Watching the Mosul handover from his office in CPA-Baghdad, Lieutenant Colonel Lloyd Sammons warned in October 2004 that things would not turn out well. Before leaving Iraq, he took a trip to visit an Army Reserve Civil Affairs group in Mosul, and he relayed his concerns to an interviewer from the U.S. Institute of Peace. "They were very worried, and they had a good reason to be worried," Sammons said. "General Ham had replaced General Petraeus in charge of the Stryker force in the north. Ham was a nice guy, but he was no Petraeus. Petraeus walked around with two stars on his shoulders and two stars in his pocket. You could tell. You could feel it. I hear now they call him King David over there."[12] More important, Petraeus could commandeer more cash and other resources than Ham.

Petraeus was on an upward career trajectory. Less than half a year after the 101st Airborne Division returned from Iraq, he was rewarded with a third star and command of Multi-National Security Transition Command Iraq, which was responsible for training and equipping the Iraqi military and police forces. Ham, meanwhile, presided over a dwindling supply of emergency funds, and his troops could not always follow through on humanitarian aid and reconstruction projects begun by the 101st Airborne Division.

"The Iraqis were furious because Ham couldn't fund a lot of the projects that had been promised by Petraeus," Sammons complained. "Do you think that maybe the Civil Affairs people are going to have a hard time working and living in that situation? We're talking mainly about reservists who, for the most part, were not equipped to handle a lot of violence. A lot of them are very smart. You have Ph.D.s and you have people with real world experience who know how to do things and are no idiots. I don't know how they managed in the long term, but I can't imagine that they've had an easy time of it."

Sammons's worries prove to be well founded. Mosul may have been judged a success during the 101st Airborne Division's stay, but things rapidly went south after the handover to the Stryker brigade. Major Tim Vidra, an Army reservist, was one of the soldiers who found themselves in the difficult position of trying to rebuild Mosul as a violent insurgency gained momentum. For Vidra and soldiers like him, figuring out who, exactly, was in charge—whom to work with—became one of the primary challenges in the frontier chaos of post-Saddam Iraq.

In July 2004, Vidra was on reserve duty at U.S. Northern Command in Colorado Springs. It was a convenient part-time assignment; Vidra was attending graduate school, and Colorado Springs was a good place to hang out, take courses, and do reserve work at the same time. As the Iraq War entered its second year, however, Civil Affairs specialists were in especially high demand. Vidra was involuntarily transferred to a Civil Affairs unit that was preparing to deploy to Iraq. The Army gave him six days' notice. After reporting to Fort McCoy, Wisconsin, he received an assignment to Bravo Company, 448th Civil Affairs Battalion, which would be supporting the Stryker brigade that replaced the 101st Airborne Division in Mosul.

Bravo Company's first assignment was to support Fifth Battalion, Twentieth Infantry Regiment, a unit of the Stryker brigade that had been sent out to patrol the area surrounding Tal Afar, a rough border town in Nineveh Province not far from the Syrian border. Tal Afar was a magnet for insurgent groups, but the battalion, which was sent to pacify the town and the surrounding area, had only 650 soldiers to patrol an area about twice the size of Connecticut. There was no local police force, and only a few Iraqi National Guard troops supplemented the U.S. soldiers. A particularly heavy battle erupted on September 4, 2004, after insurgents shot down an OH-58 Kiowa reconnaissance helicopter. When a scout platoon moved in to secure the crash site and evacuate the pilots, dozens of insurgents converged on their position, and Bravo Company had to fight through an ambush to rescue the embattled platoon. The incident could have turned into another Mogadishu-style debacle, but digital networking tools—which gave the commander on the scene a precise, up-to-the-minute picture of the location of friendly forces—helped identify the crash site and escape routes. More than a hundred insurgents were killed in the firefight; only one Iraqi National Guard trooper was killed.[13]

Despite the Stryker brigade's digital equipment, the Civil Affairs soldiers went blind into Tal Afar. The day before he was sent from Mosul to Tal Afar, Vidra had sat in on a half-hour briefing on current operations in the area in which the briefers made scant mention of Civil Affairs. As it turned out, the Civil Affairs unit that Vidra's team was replacing was somewhat dysfunctional. They hadn't gone "outside the wire" (off their base) in two months because of the heavy fighting. The team that preceded his had been pretty intent on finding chores they could do within the confines of the base, and there were no ongoing reconstruction projects in the city. Vidra's team would have to start from scratch.

Much as Civil Affairs means working outside the wire, it also requires finding key local leaders who can help identify the needs of the local community. And with Iraq's administrative and governance institutions still in tatters, that was a challenge. U.S. forces had detained the mayor and the police chief, who were allegedly colluding with the insurgents. With little formal civilian leadership in the city, it would be hard to begin any meaningful reconstruction work. The U.S. military handpicked a new mayor for Tal Afar (a former Ba'athist general) and a new police chief (the leader of a local Shiite militia, as it later emerged).

The biggest chore for Vidra's Civil Affairs team members, however, was dealing with a huge population of displaced people outside the city. Before insurgents moved in, Tal Afar had been a city of around 200,000 people, but around 190,000 people had fled into the neighboring desert because of the heavy fighting. The Civil Affairs team had to help the Iraqi Red Crescent Society deal with 190,000 internally displaced people in the deserts outside Tal Afar. Actually, Vidra said, the insurgents had made a tactical error. "They really paid a price by allowing civilians to flee, because it let us use our weapons systems more effectively against them. They didn't make that mistake again. In later fights, the insurgents would threaten the population and tell them they had to stay in the city to give them more cover."

For a spell the fighting died down in Tal Afar. U.S. security forces tried to screen the civilians flooding back into the city, but their efforts were only marginally effective in culling out insurgents. The soldiers set up checkpoints on the main roads into the city, but insurgents would just take the small back roads. Vidra's Civil Affairs team had to help get some very basic services back online. U.S. forces had turned off electricity to the city during the fighting to try and disrupt the insurgents. After the major fighting was over, the Civil Affairs team had to figure out how to turn it back on.

After that first attempt to pacify Tal Afar, top generals and experts from the U.S. Army Corps of Engineers flew in to assess the situation and find out what was going on. The planners in Baghdad had ambitious designs to rebuild the town, but they had some unrealistic expectations. For instance, they devised U.S.-style contracting schemes, and one of the selection criteria was that the winning bidder had to have a bank account so the Corps of Engineers could wire money to them. Iraq's banking system was in shambles at that point, and Vidra had to explain to the planners that the only place Iraqis could open an account was in Baghdad. "They [were] trying to use a selection criteria for Tal Afar that was meaningless, they couldn't do it," Vidra later recalled. "Tal Afar had a total cash economy."

By the end of September 2004, Tal Afar saw a brief period of calm, and Vidra had begun to initiate a series of small-scale construction projects. But the Fifth Battalion 20th Infantry Regiment was redeploying, and their leadership didn't seem particularly interested in supporting the hearts-and-minds mission. The only way the battalion's commander would allow Vidra to go into town was if he was accompanied by a full infantry company, and that meant he couldn't do his job. The 5-20 was a very good infantry unit, but they really hadn't caught on to what Civil Affairs teams could do.

About six weeks after its arrival in Tal Afar, Vidra's Civil Affairs team was transferred out of Tal Afar, and he was sent back to Mosul, where his team was attached to First Battalion, Fifth Infantry Regiment. This unit's operational area had recently shifted to cover the southern portions of Mosul, including a particularly rough neighborhood known locally as Palestine, which had historically been a center of insurgent activity. Few local leaders were willing to step forward to assist the Americans in reconstruction projects. Collaborating with coalition forces could be a death sentence for Iraqis. The Palestine neighborhood had a bad reputation: A number of former generals in Saddam's army lived there, and they may have been helping organize attacks on coalition forces.

Vidra learned firsthand how dangerous it could be. On a trip to the neighborhood on February 22, 2005, Vidra went out to take a look at neighborhood generators used to supplement power when the electrical grid was down, which was fairly often. He was interviewing the generator operator through an interpreter when a sniper opened fire. When the men sought cover on the other side of the building, they were caught in a burst of machine-gun fire. Vidra was hit in the abdomen with a tracer round—probably one that ricocheted, for the injury was considered relatively light—a "return to duty" injury. His wound was cleaned up and he was back at work the next day. The soldier standing next to him was shot in the neck, but miraculously the bullet missed any major veins or arteries. They were both very lucky.

The security situation in the Mosul area had been deteriorating since late 2004. In November the local police force walked off the job en masse, and the chief of police fled the city. The U.S. Marines had begun an assault on Fallujah, in Iraq's western Anbar Province, and a number of insurgent fighters fled north into Mosul. Insurgents had used Nineveh Province as a staging area in the past, but as more fighters came north, the entire region erupted. For several days, the U.S. military nearly lost control of Mosul. U.S. combat engineers were deployed to secure the bridges that went through central Mosul. The U.S. troops were reinforced by a contingent of Kurdish *peshmerga*, and another Stryker battalion that had been preparing to go into Fallujah was pulled back and sent to reinforce Mosul.

One particular town, Hammam al-Alil, the largest town outside Mosul in the battalion's operating area, was spiraling dangerously out of control. A substantial portion of the Iraqi National Guard walked away from the brand-new training center the U.S. military had just built for them, and the place was ransacked. The situation was touch-and-go, and as the battalion moved into the area, Vidra persuaded the commander to focus his CERP money on the town of Hammam al-Alil. It was the only U.S. development work going on there at the time. During the spike in violence, USAID forbade its representatives to go to Mosul.

Attacks on U.S. forces in the town had crested in the last week of 2004, when there were thirteen incidents. As Vidra started spending money in the town, he charted the dollars invested and the projects started against the number of incidents. He saw an interesting correlation. The more money he spent, the fewer attacks there seemed to be. The Civil Affairs team collected intelligence from the local population as they spent money, and it seemed to promote a virtuous cycle: The more information the military units had, the more effective they were in their targeted raids on insurgent safehouses. The more insurgents killed or captured, the fewer the number of attacks. Information also made it a lot easier to run development projects. Vidra spent $1.6 million in Hammam

Al-Alil over the course of about six months—roughly the cost of a new Stryker vehicle.[14] By the time Vidra handed over the mission to his successor, attacks in the town were down to zero.

This approach was not about sustainable development or meeting the long-term needs of the population; it was about using money as a weapon. The projects that Vidra focused on—keeping fighting-age Iraqis off the streets; discouraging the population from supporting insurgents; and repairing infrastructure—were all of direct benefit to U.S. forces. A good example was a roadbuilding project funded by Vidra. The Stryker unit had to traverse a twelve-mile dirt road that connected the town of Hammam Al-Alil to a major north–south highway, and U.S. troops had lost two Strykers to improvised explosive devices on the road. Vidra was able to go out and find a Kurdish contractor to come in and pave the highway with asphalt, making it much harder for insurgents to bury roadside bombs.

Vidra's team also funded short-term employment in a manner that supported U.S. troops. Roadside debris was often used to conceal IEDs. The Civil Affairs team hired Iraqis to collect trash in their neighborhoods. If teams paid residents of a neighborhood to pick up litter, and U.S. troops were attacked there, the residents did not get paid. It was a simple, almost coercive relationship, but it reduced attacks on the troops. Some Civil Affairs units focused on giving away school supplies to children or handing out soccer balls and stuffed animals. It made for nice press back at home, but to Vidra, it seemed like a waste of time. The whole point of Civil Affairs operations, he thought, was to try to dissuade an unemployed young Iraqi man from pulling a trigger or laying a land mine. He explained his philosophy this way: "The project I worked on was not necessarily, 'Hey, let's go drill a well for people, it's the right thing to do.' Because the need was overwhelming—every town needed help, because there was no government to help support them. Every town needed roads paved, every town needed schools done, every town needed medical clinics, supplies. And so the question came down to, 'Well, where can I be the most effective?' And so you ask your commander, 'Where do you need results?' You need results in town A, B, and C, and then you tailor your program to achieve those results."

It was one of the things they didn't teach in Civil Affairs school. Some in uniform were attracted to Civil Affairs because it seemed like a humanitarian mission. "A lot of Civil Affairs people came in and said,

'That's great, I'm so happy I'm in the Civil Affairs, we're not in the part of the military that kicks down doors and conducts ambushes and things like that—we're here because we're great humanitarians and we want to hand out food biscuits to starving babies,'" Vidra reflected. "No. The role of Civil Affairs is to support the infantry commander. And if he wants to lessen attacks on his troops, you need to go out and develop Civil Affairs strategies to support that goal. So you develop relationships with people in the community by using money and you can influence people's behavior by doing that. By starting those jobs programs, by pumping money through the mayor or other means."

Those humanitarian projects may have had a beneficial effect, but that was not the main reason the military was doing them. In his handover memorandum to his successor in May 2005, Vidra emphasized that point:

> Our ultimate goal here is to get out of the country all together. In order to do this, civil institutions need to be robust enough to serve the needs of the people. The more projects that the military does, the more the local populace will turn to the coalition to fix their problems and not the local government. Right now, one of the biggest things holding back the local governments is the lack of money. With no budget, it is hard for the local governments to do anything.
>
> CA [Civil Affairs] projects are at best a short-term band aid-like fix to a much larger problem. The fact of the matter is that most CA projects are not sustainable in the long term (in terms of being able to totally replace the functions of a local government). Good luck.

As the military was taking on a growing share of humanitarian aid and development work in Iraq, it was becoming increasingly difficult for traditional aid and relief groups to operate. One obstacle was security. After the August 2003 bombing of the UN headquarters in Baghdad, it was clear that international organizations and humanitarian workers were considered legitimate targets by insurgents.

Another obstacle had been the Coalition Provisional Authority itself. On October 25, 2003, the CPA issued Order 45, which compelled all non-governmental organizations to register with the occupation authorities or be barred from operating inside Iraq. Among other things, the CPA demanded that international and local NGOs provide detailed information on their activities, including full addresses, lists of employees, sources of funding, proof of nonprofit status, and lists of ongoing projects inside Iraq.[15] To the CPA, it may have seemed like a reasonable measure to ensure that insurgents did not use obscure civil society groups as front organizations for fundraising or money laundering. It also was aimed at ensuring that NGOs did not abuse their exemption from paying import duties. But to traditional aid groups such as Oxfam or Médecins Sans Frontières, it looked like a brazen effort by the U.S. occupational authorities to exercise unprecedented control over Iraqi civil society and neutral international groups. It looked like the kind of authoritarian move the rulers of Russia, Uzbekistan, or Zimbabwe might try. The NGO Coordination Committee in Iraq, an umbrella organization that represented dozens of established international organizations, protested that the rules were intrusive and potentially dangerous, especially for groups that wanted to keep a low profile in Iraq.[16]

Ray LeMoine and Jeff Neumann, the authors of *Babylon by Bus*, who had lucked into jobs in the CPA's NGO Assistance Office, watched communications break down between the international aid establishment and the CPA. The humanitarians insisted on maintaining their neutrality, while CPA officials seemed unperturbed that they were relying increasingly on the military to achieve humanitarian goals. "By early February [2004], Jeff and I could already see the seeds of Iraqi dissatisfaction germinating," LeMoine and Neumann wrote. "The U.S. government and its CPA in Iraq didn't seem to care that using an army to achieve humanitarian aims sends the wrong message to the local population. Tanks and machine guns are never associated with hospitals and schools. If the Pentagon-powered CPA insisted on using Army Civil Affairs units instead of NGOs to lead Iraq's rebuilding effort, confusion was going to be the result. Bremer's Order 45 became our introduction to the wholesale misdirection of power that was the CPA."[17]

But the point was academic because the military was the only organization that could operate with relative freedom inside an increasingly violent country. What's more, the U.S. military had the cash. By the end of his tour, Major Tim Vidra, the Civil Affairs officer in Mosul, was contracting about a million dollars' worth of projects per month—a staggering amount of money for a junior officer to be overseeing, and an enormous "burn rate" (spending rate) for development work.

Back in Tal Afar, after Vidra's short-term job in the town ended, Major Brian Grady stayed on as a Civil Affairs team leader. He inherited some of the same local relationships for a new battalion that was stationed there. About half of Grady's time was spent on project development and project management, parceling out the unit's CERP funds on a wide range of projects. One of his major efforts was a clean-up campaign for Tal Afar streets that was supposed to deter insurgents from laying IEDs. Like Vidra, he tried to use cash as an incentive to discourage insurgents from laying ambushes or roadside bombs. Grady did it through the mayor of Tal Afar at the time and paid biweekly. "I wrote into the contract or the proposal that if we got an IED . . . on a portion of that route during that two weeks, they didn't get paid. It didn't work so well, but we tried." So spending money was not a panacea. Grady reckoned his Civil Affairs team distributed about fourteen or fifteen million dollars throughout Nineveh Province during its ten-month rotation there.

The other half of Grady's time he spent as a sort of political advisor to the battalion commander when he went on missions to meet with either tribal leaders or local government representatives. The violence in Nineveh continued, and much of the military's work concentrated on feel-good projects. A *Stars & Stripes* reporter described Grady's delivering school supplies and toothbrushes to children at a remote school near the Syrian border. "The visit was a spur-of-the-moment stop for the Stryker Brigade Combat Team," the reporter wrote. "Soldiers piled up backpacks filled with school supplies and warnings about unexploded ordnance on the ramps of two Strykers while soldiers and translators asked the school principal to let the children out of class to have at them."[18] The positive atmospherics were of little consequence. In retrospect one can see that CERP projects and Civil Affairs work were well intentioned but misguided, and officers were spreading around funds without much thought to the longer-term implications.

More important, there was no systematic way of tracking the funds, how effectively they were spent, and whether or not the cash got into the wrong hands. The aims, Grady concluded, were good, but projects were implemented with little oversight: "It was mostly a waste of money that [would have] needed a robust support structure to see it spent at all responsibly." It was a quick fix, not a strategic development effort, and it could fuel corruption. But strict oversight and fiscal responsibility were not the primary criteria: Officers were under pressure to spend CERP money, and quickly. It was considered an important item on the commander's "to do" list.

Iraq continued its downward spiral into violence, and U.S. military commanders groped for a new approach that required more than just military manpower and know-how. Money may have been an important new tool in the military's arsenal, but it needed more serious planning and oversight if it was to bring political results. All the good intentions in the world plus a heap of cash could not fundamentally change the problem: The United States was trying to stabilize a country that did not have stable civil and political institutions. The invasion had demolished the old order, and its military architects had neglected to plan for a new one. And American solutions were never going to be as effective as Iraqi ones.

PART II

History Lessons

CHAPTER 6

The Phoenix Rises

In early February 2005, a group of government and defense industry officials crowded the exhibit hall of the Marriott Wardman Hotel in Washington, D.C., for a symposium on the newly fashionable subject of special operations and low-intensity conflict. The war in Iraq was less than two years old, and many members of the audience were fresh from their first tours there. The defense industry–sponsored forum was an opportunity to reflect on the frustrating first year and a half in Iraq, which had seen lackluster performance by the Coalition Provisional Authority and rising casualty count. At that point, the war had claimed the lives of over fourteen hundred U.S. troops, but the complex and deadly insurgency showed no sign of abating. A panel on "capabilities and gaps" featured a briefing by Brigadier General Joseph Votel, who was then head of a new Army task force for battling roadside bombs. What had begun as a ten-man cell at the military headquarters in Baghdad by July 2004 had morphed into a full-fledged task force for fighting roadside bombs, which were growing in their sophistication and lethality. The Pentagon eventually poured billions into fielding radio-frequency jammers to counter these devices, but insurgent technology—often shared through the Internet—was often one step ahead of the defense countermeasures.

While defense contractors and government officials swigged coffee and picked at cheap pastries, Lieutenant General Jerry Boykin, the deputy undersecretary of defense for intelligence and warfighting support, took the podium. He opened his remarks with a disclaimer. "Let me say that I did clear this speech with public affairs," he said. "Nothing that I will say today represents the official position of the Department of Defense. Let's get that out of the way in case the inspector general happens to be in the audience."

The mostly male, middle-aged audience erupted in hearty laughs. It was a defense insider's joke: Boykin had become the focus of a media firestorm in late 2003, when a defense writer, William Arkin, broke the story in the *Los Angeles Times* of how Boykin, a born-again Christian, had been delivering speeches to evangelical groups that cast the Bush administration's war on terror in terms of a Christian crusade. One Boykin gem: He told an Oregon congregation that George W. Bush "was appointed by God." And in a speech at a church in Daytona, Florida, Boykin described his encounter with a Somali warlord. "I knew that my God was bigger than his," he said. "I knew that my God was a real God and his was an idol." Boykin typically appeared in uniform at these events.[1]

Arkin's report had put an uncomfortable spotlight on Boykin, who had spent most of his career in the secretive world of Special Operations. Boykin was a public relations liability for the Bush administration, which was trying to persuade the world it was not at war with Islam. An investigation by the Pentagon inspector general concluded that Boykin failed to properly vet his speeches and make clear that his religious pronouncements were not official policy.[2] It was, in essence, a slap on the wrist. Boykin stayed on in the job.

Despite the disclaimer, Boykin's remarks that morning were provocative. In Iraq and Afghanistan, he told the audience, the military was undergoing a fundamental shift in the way that it fought. The military would no longer be preoccupied with traditional military tasks. It was no longer focused on enemy formations—tracking Saddam Hussein's armor brigades or looking for Soviet strategic nuclear forces. It was about identifying and targeting specific individuals. Information collected by a soldier on patrol or captured by a surveillance aircraft loitering overhead could be used to capture or kill members of the insurgent underground in Iraq and Afghanistan. In Boykin's jargon, "operationalizing intelligence," once the domain of the elite and secretive counterterrorism world, was now a task for the conventional military.

"What we're trying to do is get the rest of the military to recognize today that our real battle in Iraq and Afghanistan is a battle for knowledge, it's a battle for information, it's an intel battle," he said.

Waging the offensive in Iraq and Afghanistan was about mapping out and recognizing networks: identifying insurgent cells, mapping out how they were organized, and connecting the dots. It was closer to detective work than fighting a conventional enemy. For this new mission, it was important to reorganize, at some fundamental level, the way the national security bureaucracy was structured, and how military and civilian organizations shared information, Boykin said: "Intelligence today that never would have been of importance to the soldier on the street, collected from the national foreign intelligence program, is now important to the ordinary soldier out on the street. And the intelligence that guy is collecting—that guy running around in a Humvee—he's getting information that is now important all the way to the top, all the way to the national foreign intelligence program."

Now, intelligence was driving military operations. "Every high-value target that we capture today has intelligence value in the interrogation and debriefing of those targets," Boykin said. "We need to recognize that now."

It was an approach that would have sounded familiar to a British officer in Northern Ireland, or an Israeli officer policing the Palestinian territories. But Boykin reached for a different analogy. Pressed to provide further clarification on the issue by a member of an audience, Boykin made a direct comparison to the 1980s campaign against Communist guerrillas in El Salvador and to the Phoenix program, a CIA-orchestrated program put in place during the Vietnam War. "I think the basic principle [of Phoenix and El Salvador] was to kill or capture," he said.

> I will tell you, I wouldn't call it the Phoenix program, but I think we're doing a pretty good job of it right now. It's not just SOF [special operations forces], it's conventional forces that are out there capturing. I think we're running that kind of program right now. I think this secretary and this administration understand this is a war, we're going after these people, killing or capturing these people is a legitimate mission for the department and for the interagency. I think we're doing a pretty good job . . .

> We're doing what the Phoenix program was designed to do,
> without all of the secrecy.

Boykin was reaching back to one of the more controversial lessons of the Vietnam War. During the Vietnam War the U.S. government—after initial frustration and setbacks—embarked on a sweeping reorganization of its mission in Southeast Asia. Phoenix was just one piece of this, although it was perhaps one of the more infamous. At its core, Phoenix was an intelligence program: an attempt to map out and identify what was called "Viet Cong infrastructure," the underground political organization of the Viet Cong. That meant collecting human intelligence at the local level: maintaining dossiers on individual members of the Viet Cong infrastructure who had infiltrated villages in Vietnam, and targeting them. "Targeting" could mean capture or arrest, or persuading Viet Cong cadres to defect through an offer of amnesty. Yet critics of the Phoenix program maintained that in practice, it led to a program of targeted killing: Thousands who were identified as Viet Cong sympathizers were also killed.

Apologists for Phoenix maintained it was not a deliberate assassination program. In 1971 testimony on U.S. assistance to Vietnam, William Colby of the CIA offered some interesting statistics: Since the program began in 1968, Phoenix had accounted for the capture of 28,978 members of the Viet Cong infrastructure, 17,717 members of the Viet Cong had defected, and 20,587 had been killed. Colby claimed that most of those deaths were incidental—most of those killed had been involved in firefights with the regular military or South Vietnamese paramilitaries and identified after the fact. He insisted that Phoenix was not designed primarily as an assassination campaign, while not ruling out that Viet Cong sympathizers or innocent civilians had been the victims of premeditated killings.[3]

Colby may have missed a larger point. But Colby, who was CIA director from 1973 to 1976, and others saw Phoenix as a success, part of a larger set of bureaucratic tools that had proved themselves in Vietnam. In his introduction to *Lost Victory*, his intimate but rather self-justifying postmortem on the Vietnam War, Colby alluded to "right" lessons that could be drawn from Vietnam:

> We must distinguish the strategy, or lack thereof, from the tactics
> and judge them separately to find which are worthy of adding to

our national arsenal and which clearly were mistaken and should be rejected. We must sort out the optional from the inevitable aspects of our effort there, the choice of strategy and arms from the certain side effects of the presence of a large military force in an ethnically and culturally foreign community.[4]

With the military groping for the "right" approach to Iraq, that reading of the Vietnam War was deeply appealing. In 2005, General Peter Schoomaker, the Army chief of staff, wrote a foreword to the paperback edition of *Learning to Eat Soup with a Knife: Counterinsurgency Lessons from Malaya and Vietnam*, a book first published in 2002 by Lieutenant Colonel John Nagl, an Army officer who had recently served in Iraq as the operations officer of the First Battalion of the Thirty-fourth Armor Regiment. Coming from the highest-ranking general in the Army, the foreword was a top-level endorsement. "The organizational culture of the U.S. Army, predisposed to fight a conventional enemy that fought using conventional tactics, overpowered innovative ideas from within the Army and from outside it," Schoomaker wrote of the experience in Vietnam. "As a result, the U.S. Army was not as effective at learning as it should have been, and its failures in Vietnam had grave implications for both the Army and the nation."[5]

Schoomaker could as easily have been talking about Iraq in 2005. In a new preface to the 2005 edition of his book, Nagl wrote about the "searing" experience of fighting insurgents in Iraq's Anbar Province. "The task force was built around a tank battalion that had been designed, organized, trained and equipped for conventional combat operations. The enemy we confronted was implacable, ruthless, and all too often invisible."[6]

As Nagl learned, Phoenix-like human intelligence collection was essential to success. "Understanding tribal loyalties, political motivations, and family relationships was essential to defeating the enemy we faced, a task more akin to breaking up a Mafia crime ring than dismantling a conventional enemy battalion or brigade," he wrote. "'Link diagrams' depicting who talked with whom became a daily chore for a small intelligence staff more used to analyzing the ranges of enemy artillery systems."[7]

Equally important, Nagl argued that the chores of stability operations were a central part of the mission, not just a helpful adjunct to the overall mission. Commander's Emergency Response Program (CERP) money was crucial for building the trust of the Iraqi people. Nagl's reading of the Vietnam War was shared by others. Lieutenant General David Petraeus, in Iraq as the head of Multi-National Security Transition Command Iraq, had written his Ph.D. dissertation on the military's failure to absorb the lessons of Vietnam.[8] Andrew Krepinevich, the author of another influential book, *The Army in Vietnam*, had argued that the Army had failed to learn the "right" lessons, stubbornly clinging to large-unit operations and heavy firepower instead of adopting the practices of counterinsurgency.

The rediscovery of the lessons of Vietnam was spreading to Afghanistan as well. A few months earlier, when I had visited a German-run Provincial Reconstruction Team in Kunduz, northeastern Afghanistan, I met a young U.S. Foreign Service officer who was detailed to the team. He told me that the military was considering whether the PRT experiment might work in Iraq. "This is a test case—we'll have to see if the PRT concept brought any added value to reconstruction," he told me. "There's no reason not to try. This is the first time this has been done since the CORDS program in Vietnam."

He was referring to Civil Operations and Revolutionary Development Support, a Vietnam-era pacification program whose principles were now being revived for the twenty-first century. The main lesson being drawn from Vietnam had more to do with what was referred to during the Vietnam as "the other war." In Iraq, the U.S. military and the rest of the national security establishment were painfully relearning lessons about armed nation building that had been discarded after Vietnam, even though they were reluctant to use the term "nation building."

In the late summer of 1972, Army Captain John Morris received a call from his boss: A very important man would be paying him a visit, and he expected Morris to prepare a briefing. Morris was an Army senior district advisor in Binh Son, the northernmost district in South Vietnam's Quang Ngai province; his small advisory team was responsible for an area that ran from the coast to the southern border of the Chu Lai combat base. About twenty kilometers southeast of the district center where Morris lived was My Lai hamlet, the site of the 1968 massacre of Vietnamese civilians by soldiers of the Army's Americal Division.

His advisory team had seen its fair share of visitors from Saigon, and Morris prepared his usual briefing. The colonel mentioned a name, Sir Robert something, but it didn't ring a bell for Morris. "What should I tell him?" Morris asked the colonel. "He works for the president, tell him everything!" the colonel barked.

The visitor arrived in a helicopter escorted by four heavily armed Cobra helicopter gunships. *That's unusual*, Morris thought. *I've never seen that. This must be an important guy!*

Morris's guest was Sir Robert Thompson, a renowned British counter-insurgency guru and an expert in guerrilla warfare and colonial policing. At the time, Thompson was known as one of the architects of the successful campaign by the British colonial government against Communist guerrillas during the Malayan Emergency of the late forties and fifties. It was considered a textbook example of how to fight insurgents. Even though thousands of British and Commonwealth troops were deployed, the strategy was not primarily military. The British retrained the corrupt and unprofessional Malayan security forces, reached out to disaffected ethnic Chinese to reconcile them with the government, and undertook a vigorous program of "civic action"—essentially, rural development projects—in parallel with hunting guerrillas in the jungle. The British also imposed emergency regulations (a form of martial law) and in some cases resettled parts of the rural population in fortified "new villages." They drew heavily on criminal investigative techniques, using informants and link analysis to map out the guerrilla "infrastructure"—its leadership network—and empowered police with special counterterrorism authority. It was the remedy to counter Mao Zedong's prescription for revolutionary war, in which the guerrilla is described as a fish swimming in the sea of the peasantry.[9]

Thompson was also something of a Vietnam hand. In 1961, he had gone to Saigon as the head of the British Advisory Mission to South Vietnam, a small team of Malayan Civil Service veterans who provided counterinsurgency advice and guidance to the Saigon government.[10] In the mid-sixties, as the U.S. military involvement deepened, he published trenchant critiques of U.S. policy, arguing that the both the U.S. government and its critics had failed to understand the nature of the war as a political, not a military, struggle.[11] In October 1969 Thompson was named a special consultant to President Richard Nixon and sent to South Vietnam to give a candid, firsthand appraisal of the situation; he traveled extensively through South Vietnam on a series of fact-finding visits.[12]

Thompson's visit to Quang Ngai in 1972 was part of an assessment of the progress of "Vietnamization": the Nixon administration's plan for a gradual exit from Vietnam. The plan hinged on continued pacification of the South Vietnamese countryside, containment of the invasion threat by North Vietnam, and the withdrawal of U.S. ground combat troops. Small advisory teams stayed on to provide a crucial on-the-ground link between the U.S. military and the government of South Vietnam. They supervised training of regular South Vietnamese units and local and regional militias, coordinated air strikes and artillery fire, and collected intelligence. Combat advisors had preceded the entry of U.S. conventional forces in 1965, and they would be a key part of the exit strategy.

Morris had arrived in South Vietnam in November 1971. First assigned to the 101st Airborne Division at Da Nang Air Base, he had the unglamorous job of running a wash rack: preparing vehicles to be shipped back to the United States or to be scrapped. It was a dismal chore. Most of the other officers were "short-timers" preparing to rotate home, and the enlisted men, who would be going back to the field after they were done washing trucks, weren't particularly motivated. At that point, for infantry officers there were few open assignments with regular units, as U.S. ground forces were starting to withdraw. Morris, a West Point graduate, was able to pull some strings. With some persistence, he landed an assignment with Military Assistance Command Vietnam (MACV), which ran the advisory mission to South Vietnam.

The nine-man team he joined lived in a small compound inside a larger compound manned by South Vietnamese Regional Forces troops—sort of a rural Vietnamese version of the National Guard. Serving as an Army advisor was an unconventional job for a regular infantry officer. Leading indigenous forces traditionally was a more of a job for Special Forces. It was closer to colonial policing than serving in a Cold War army that had been designed primarily to fight the Soviets in Europe. Even for someone from the "can-do" culture of the Army and West Point, the advisory job required something of a cultural adjustment. Over the bar in the team house, someone had posted a quote from T. E. Lawrence's "Twenty-seven Articles," wisdom Lawrence imparted to British liaison officers leading Arab irregulars battling against the Ottoman Empire during World War I. The quote read: "Do not try to do too much with your own hands. Better the Arabs do it tolerably than that you do it perfectly. It is their war, and you are to help them, not to win it for them."

One of Morris's main jobs was flying over the area to do surveillance and observation; he usually could find an available helicopter about twice a week. Another task for the advisors was filling out the Hamlet Evaluation System (HES) reports, detailed monthly surveys whose purpose was to measure both the level of security in the countryside and the progress of development. Security was graded on an A to E scale: A, B, and C represented varying degrees of government control; D and E representing "contested." Another grade, V, meant full Viet Cong control.[13] Morris thought the HES reports were a pain. It was a time-consuming process, and required answering what seemed to be inane questions such as "How many people in your village have a TV set?" In Morris's rural district, the nearest television station was well out of broadcasting range.

Morris rolled back the yellow covers on the classified maps and launched into a discussion of security in his district. He pointed to the map to show Thompson the progress of the South Vietnamese government's accelerated pacification campaign, how much territory the government controlled, and how much was in the hands of the Communists. The government controlled pretty much everything between the north–south highway and the South China Sea; to the west of the highway, things were also reasonably secure; a bit further inland, security was a bit more tenuous. Out toward the mountains was pretty much Indian country. Thompson stopped Morris for a moment. "What time of day are you talking about?" he asked.

"During the day," Morris replied.

"Well," said Thompson, "What if I asked you, how much of that map you control after two A.M.?"

Morris pointed to the thin line of the north–south highway, bounded on one side by rice paddies and by the old French railroad on the other. "See that line there—Highway 1?" Morris said. "That's questionable—how much we control and how well we control it."

By that point in his tour, Morris thought he was pretty familiar with the local picture. He recounted a favorite anecdote for Thompson. One night, Morris's Vietnamese interpreter had roused him from his bunk: A remote observation post near a bridge was under attack. Morris, still groggy, bumped his head as he walked inside the South Vietnamese tactical operations center, which was built by the much shorter Vietnamese. His counterpart wanted to request U.S. naval gunfire, and Morris got on the radio to a destroyer off the coast. After being obliged to listen to a short lecture on naval gunfire—the shipboard Navy officers, Morris noticed, tended to treat Army officers with condescension—he got the target cleared. The naval gun hit the target; a couple of guerrillas were killed, and a few friendlies were wounded. During the attack, Viet Cong sappers had destroyed one of the supports to the bridge.

Morris went out to survey the scene the following morning. He found the destroyed bridge, but interestingly enough, he also discovered that local commerce had not been interrupted. The truck drivers who were hauling the rice harvest were driving over a culvert that was a well-established bypass. The Viet Cong had surely seen the culvert when they got there, but, strangely, they hadn't destroyed it. The bridge was rebuilt shortly thereafter, and the outpost came under attack. The next time, Morris found, the guerrillas knocked out the culvert and not the bridge. It was an illuminating moment for Morris. The insurgents they were fighting were locals who needed the bridge as much as the Government of South Vietnam and its allies did. And they didn't want to destroy the route for that rice crop.

Thompson's visit underscored how U.S. military advisors like Morris had learned by experience. By November 1972, when Morris's one-year Vietnam tour ended, the United States seemed to have turned a corner in Vietnam. Cease-fire talks with Hanoi were under way, the South Vietnamese army had repelled a major conventional offensive by the North Vietnamese Army earlier in the spring, and security throughout the country had significantly improved. By that time, however, the war had cost $150 billion (over three quarters of a trillion dollars in today's dollars), and the American public was weary of a costly and frustrating intervention on behalf of the corrupt and ill-formed regime in Saigon.[14] This was the fundamental flaw of the nation-building approach: Creating stable, accountable, and effective local institutions took years. That kind of involvement required an extraordinary commitment in money, manpower, and resources, and the outcome was not guaranteed. Still, counterinsurgency experts like Thompson were optimistic. They felt that the war was winnable and that the United States and South Vietnam had essentially come to grips with South Vietnam's domestic insurgency. In 1974, a year before the final humiliating collapse of the Saigon government,

Thompson wrote: "The greatest myth, widely accepted in the United States and elsewhere, was that the war was unwinnable. Certainly it was unwinnable in the conventional sense but then this was not a conventional war. It was also unwinnable by the United States. It was winnable only by South Vietnam with American assistance."[15]

In Malaya, preventing a revolutionary takeover had hinged to some extent on addressing some of the basic grievances of the local population: allowing some degree of political participation and paving the way to eventual independence. After years of failure and setbacks in South Vietnam, U.S. policymakers and their counterparts in Saigon had settled on a new approach. Success would not depend on overwhelming U.S. military force, but on a hybrid of development work, military action, intelligence gathering, and political reform. Armed social work would save South Vietnam, not firepower.

The turning point, at least for the U.S. military, was the appointment of General Creighton Abrams, who succeeded General William Westmoreland as MACV commander in June 1968. Distilled to its essence, Westmoreland's approach had been "enemy-centric." He directed his subordinates to undertake large-unit "search and destroy" missions to find enemy forces and kill them. Abrams's approach was the opposite of attrition. His mantra was "Clear, hold, and build." The focus was on providing security to the population in safer areas, winning the population over with development work, and then gradually spreading security outward to less secure areas, like ink on a blotter.

This experiment was not new. In addition to borrowing from the British experience in Malaya, the Americans were consciously reaching back to an idea attributed to Marshal Hubert Lyautey, a French general who managed the colonial administration of Morocco earlier in the century. Some *tache d'huile* ("oil spot") concepts had been tested early by the Americans in South Vietnam. The Marine Corps Combined Action Program sent squads of Marines to rural hamlets to live and patrol alongside local militia. Serving in a Combined Action Platoon was a dangerous job: the Marines lived in small, isolated villages, essentially cut off from the umbilical cord of larger units. But Thompson praised them as a model for the "successful 'strategic hamlet' defended by its own people."[16] But the Combined Action Program was a piecemeal experiment in counterinsurgency that the Americans essentially shunted aside in favor of firepower-intensive, large-unit action.[17]

The most sweeping reorganization of the U.S. mission in Vietnam began in 1967, during Westmoreland's command, with the creation of CORDS, a hybrid civil-military organization that was created to back the government of Vietnam's "new model" pacification program. CORDS merged the U.S. Embassy Saigon's Office of Civilian Operations with the military's Revolutionary Development Support staff, bringing together for the first time the military and civilian nation-building effort under a single umbrella.* As early as 1966, the U.S. government recognized that the "other war," the nation-building effort, was being given short shrift.[18] But before CORDS, there was little unity of effort given to the problem, and the military paid little attention to it. The State Department was largely focused on traditional diplomacy and intrigue in the capital, USAID was off pursuing its development projects and paid little attention to the larger issues of counterinsurgency strategy, and the military was focused primarily on finding and killing the enemy. The agencies had different bureaucratic agendas and cultures. To lash together the various agencies of government more effectively, President Lyndon Johnson tasked Robert Komer, a career intelligence official and talented national security bureaucrat, with the job of running CORDS. Colby was Komer's deputy.

Komer, known as "Blowtorch Bob" for his abrasive, hard-driving style, was given ambassadorial rank, unprecedented power for a civilian, and, crucially, was made part of the military chain of command: Komer reported directly to Westmoreland and later to Abrams, the commanders of MACV. He was no mere civilian figurehead: Komer led a mixed civilian-military staff drawn from the military, the State Department, the U.S. Information Agency (the external propaganda arm of the U.S. government), USAID, the CIA, and the White House. Four regional deputies were assigned to each of the four corps-level commanders, and hybrid civilian-military teams were assigned to 250 districts and forty-four provinces of South Vietnam. Soldiers reported to civilians, and vice versa.[19]

Komer recognized that the conventional military tended to focus on finding and killing the enemy. Even though the U.S. agencies and the

---

* William Colby would later quietly change the R in CORDS to stand for "rural" to soften the implication that development would be imposed on the population in a draconian, top-down way.

South Vietnamese governments had forwarded a few piecemeal programs to promote rural security and development before then, Komer
later noted that "pacification remained a small tail to the very large conventional military dog."[20] Placing the military's pacification programs
under civilian leadership, he found, gave the civilian experts greater influence over the project. The main problem, in his view, was a lack of
managerial focus, not of armed might. In essence, the U.S. government
was putting into practice strategies that had been advocated by veterans
of colonial administration like Thompson, who believed the problems of
guerrilla war could basically be solved by intelligent civilian administration, better policing, and political reconciliation.

Land reform was an example of how this could work. The Communists had made a promise of land redistribution to win support.[21] With
U.S. government encouragement, the government of President Nguyen
Van Thieu forwarded a program called "land to the tiller," whereby the
government of South Vietnam gave deeds to tenant farmers who actually
worked the land. By early 1973, the government distributed over 2.5 million acres, helping undercut the Communists' promise. In his conversation with Thompson, Morris discussed the land program; as Thompson
noted, Thieu's government was consciously borrowing from a lot of the
same programs that Ho Chi Minh had originally used to gain his political capital with people in that region there.

Nonetheless, the military was resistant to taking on what were essentially nonmilitary jobs, even after Abrams took command of MACV. In
a 1970 commanders' meeting, Abrams complained that the 173rd Airborne Brigade had brought all of its parachutes and rigging equipment
to Vietnam, perhaps in the hope that they could get in some D-Day-style
combat parachute jumps. "They've *got* all that stuff," he said. "What are
they doing? It's *never* going to be used here—*none* of it! And the reason
is that that's not what you need. Really, in order to help this thing along,
you've got to do something *else*. That's no good, parachuting around the
country. It isn't going to advance the cause by a nickel."[22]

Even in 1970, three years after the creation of CORDS, the military officers had failed to see the nature of their work. Abrams complained point-
edly, "And I think everyone, especially the military officers, has got to
realize—. I mean, you can say, 'Jeez, it's nonmilitary, I mean that's not what
the military is supposed to be doing.' No shit! *Too bad!* That's not what
we've got. We've got something *else*! And we've got to do what this thing

needs, and the problem is to understand what is best and what it does most need, and then go ahead and do it!"[23]

In 1969, David Passage, a junior Foreign Service officer, was assigned to CORDS. It was his second overseas posting. His first State Department assignment was to the U.S. embassy in London—a plum job, but at the height of the war, he knew sooner or later his number would come up for Vietnam. Like most of the other junior Foreign Service officers in his CORDS training class, he was young and single—somewhat expendable, in the view of the bureaucracy.

Prior to arriving in Saigon he attended a six-week course at the Foreign Service Institute's Vietnam training center. Each class received lectures on the history and economy of Vietnam, and the culture of the region. They learned some rudimentary Vietnamese, and talented linguists were singled out for further language instruction. Instructors also led classes on insurgency and guerrilla warfare that drew on the experience in Vietnam and other counterinsurgency campaigns, including the Hukbalahap Rebellion, a Communist guerrilla movement in the Philippines that was put down in the early 1950s with U.S. assistance. Finally, Passage and his fellow Foreign Service officers received a week's training at Fort Gordon, Georgia.

Most of the CORDS team members would be assigned to small advisory teams in the provinces, but Passage was assigned to work directly for William Colby, the career CIA officer who had been seconded to USAID to work as Komer's deputy. He lived in a USAID compound halfway between downtown Saigon and Tan Son Nhut airport. The USAID presence in South Vietnam at the time was enormous. Between 1962 and 1975, South Vietnam was the largest single recipient of USAID funds; at the height of the war, the agency spent over a quarter of its total annual budget there.[24] The agency's commitment to South Vietnam also carried another price: The memorial wall at USAID headquarters in Washington lists fifty-three agency employees who were killed in Vietnam and Laos.

Passage was assigned to MACV headquarters. His office ran the Hamlet Evaluation System, the complicated and time-consuming security and development reports that were so widely disliked by advisors like John Morris. The reports required answering lengthy multichoice questionnaires on questions of nation building (or "economic development" in the parlance of the time) and security. The HES reports were highly politicized, and could have serious implications for advisors' careers: If a report was too negative—showed too many enemy-held villages—the advisors weren't doing their jobs. But if the advisers were too positive—didn't report any contested hamlets—they couldn't show progress. Passage's job was to "adjudicate" the report to provide a reality check against the self-reporting bias of the advisors. The whole point of the exercise was to create accurate metrics, a practice that appealed to the technocratic sensibilities of the time but was also a way of countering the phenomenon of "ticket-punching." Most civilian and military personnel served one-year tours, which meant that little if any collective wisdom about the place was accumulated. As one CORDS official put it: "We don't have twelve years' experience in Vietnam. We have one year's experience twelve times over."[25]

CORDS staff in Saigon would review the monthly tactical operations center reports, or TOC summaries, for each province and compare them with the HES reports. The TOC summary was basically a digest of radio traffic and incident reports: the Viet Cong overrunning a hamlet; the assassination of a village official; the request for an air strike or artillery fire. Passage would then go out to the field to compare notes with the advisors on the ground. He had blanket travel orders with the military, which meant he could fly within the country on military aircraft on a "space available" basis. He could hop military flights on Air America, a CIA front company that operated an airline within South Vietnam. He would make the arrangements with the province senior advisor and visit district-level teams. Armed with the HES reports and the radio summaries, he would sit down with the advisor and ask, "Are we talking about the same place?" He found that some advisors were honest and can-do, but others were so cynical by that point that they saw no reason to justify staying in Vietnam.

Passage spent about fifteen days per month traveling around one of South Vietnam's four corps (Vietnam was divided into four tactical zones by the military). He was issued a weapon to carry when he was out in the field. He was also given an International Harvester Scout, a small four-wheel-drive truck, a sort of civilian equivalent to a Jeep. After a field trip he wrote a short summary on how pacification programs were doing and where CORDS needed to focus more effort. That short memorandum was included in a larger report that was summarized and sent to Ellsworth Bunker, the U.S. ambassador in Saigon, to Abrams, to Komer, and to the president.

The other part of Passage's job was the "dog and pony show." A regular series of congressional delegations visited Saigon on brief fact-finding junkets, and Passage was Abrams's command briefer on pacification. His briefing usually followed briefings by bright, squared-away military officers; Abrams sandwiched him in between J-2 (intelligence) and J-3 (current operations). Passage also briefed Thompson.

Despite the massive U.S. involvement in the hearts-and-minds effort, however, Passage was pessimistic about the government of South Vietnam, upon which the responsibility for winning ultimately would rest. Despite reforms by the government of Nguyen Van Thieu, and the appointment of more competent Vietnamese generals, the simple fact, he felt, was that the government of South Vietnam was hopelessly corrupt and inept. He was learning the hardest lesson of U.S. intervention: Pouring millions of dollars of aid into building military, political, and civil institutions sometimes had the paradoxical effect of weakening the host government. U.S. assistance to a kleptocratic government only created more opportunities for corruption. And time was not on the side of the intervening Americans. Passage's final briefing for a congressional delegation was for Senator Margaret Chase Smith, Republican of Maine. As he went through the pacification brief, he ended by concluding: "I have spent fifteen of the last thirty days in the field, and I can detect no improvement in the loyalty of the rice farmer whose father grew rice and whose children and grandchildren will grow rice. They think the GVN [government of Vietnam] is beastly and corrupt."

In Passage's view, the operation, CORDS and the U.S. government pacification effort, was a success, but the patient was irretrievably ill. The population was still sitting on the fence, and massive U.S. aid only made things worse. The U.S. government, Passage felt, never tried to root out the corruption in the government of South Vietnam, but unless the government was able to win the loyalty of its own people—to get them off the fence, and volunteer information about where the enemy was—they would be at a hopeless disadvantage. The main lesson, at least in Passage's view, was that sometimes less is more. The larger the involvement, the more likely it was to fail.

In Vietnam, Passage was a mid-rank Foreign Service officer, an FSO 5 going on FSO 4, so he had little power.* He resolved that one day, if he had the chance, he would do things differently, and get it right. He continued to work with the military during his diplomatic career and had a chance to put the principles he had learned in Vietnam into practice—in El Salvador. Between 1984 and 1986, he was deputy chief of mission and chargé d'affaires at the American Embassy in San Salvador, at the height of that country's civil war. Every key member of the military and diplomatic team in El Salvador had served in Vietnam, and they were determined to avoid the massive involvement that had undermined Vietnamese self-reliance. "We were convinced that we could do it right and it worked," Passage told me. "We . . . turned it around. It was El Salvador's fight, not ours, and they were going to win it."

There would be no massive U.S. military presence in El Salvador: Less was more. The Reagan administration, its hands tied by a Democratic Congress, avoided the temptation of committing massive amounts of men and matériel that would undermine the will of the host country to fight for its own survival. "We would train the Salvadorans to fight . . . but we would not advise them," Passage told me.

The United States compelled the government of El Salvador to make significant internal reforms; retrained the Salvadoran military, which had been guilty of grotesque human rights abuses, and, most important, kept the U.S. military footprint small—no more than fifty-five trainers were in the country at a time. In Passage's view, El Salvador was a model of successful counterinsurgency.

As a retired diplomat, Passage was often invited to lecture senior military officers on counterinsurgency. But he found that the Vietnam conflict remained a taboo subject: "The military as a whole did a reasonably complete job of putting Vietnam aside. We were simply not allowed to use Vietnam as a case study. We used Angola and Mozambique. Anytime anybody suggested Vietnam, a sort of advanced palsy or Saint Vitus' dance would take hold."

This changed after the Iraq invasion. In early 2006, Passage, then a retired ambassador, received a letter from the U.S. Army's Command and General Staff College at Fort Leavenworth, Kansas. The Center for Army Lessons Learned was convening study groups under the direction

---

* Foreign Service ranks go in reverse numerical order: The lower the number, the higher the rank.

of Lieutenant General David Petraeus, who was leading an effort to write a new counterinsurgency doctrine. The team drafting the manual wanted input from civilians who had experience in the mission of armed nation building in Vietnam, and Passage was uniquely qualified.

The U.S. military, chastened by the horrific failures in Iraq, was about to undergo a serious culture shift. Confronted by failure, commanders would reach out to diplomats, development experts, even human rights advocates for fresh insight into what was now acknowledged as a nation-building mission. In part, commanders were searching for a bureaucratic fix. "Getting it right" meant that the rest of government would sign on for the mission, and the military would not have to go it alone. That was supposed to be the template for success in Iraq, as well as in Afghanistan.

Getting nation building right, however, ignored some larger historical lessons. When U.S. intervention was massive, and intrusive, it threatened to wreck local self-reliance. Building a functioning state and a robust civil society was a difficult, drawn-out process that took decades, even lifetimes. But like the generation that preceded them in Vietnam, the military planners and policy practitioners dealing with Iraq's implosion were can-do types who thought that "we" could somehow save the situation if enough energy, ingenuity, and resources were brought to the mission.

CHAPTER 7

The Accidental Counterinsurgents

In late 2005, the journalist Thomas Ricks paid a visit to Fort Leavenworth, Kansas. Leavenworth was home to the Army's Command and
General Staff College, the midcareer school for Army officers, and Ricks
had been invited to give a talk to a lecture hall packed with majors, many
of whom had seen recent action in Iraq. At that point, he was in the
midst of writing a new book on the war in Iraq, then entering its third
deadly year. For Ricks, a longtime military correspondent for the *Wall
Street Journal* and the *Washington Post*, the decision to invade Iraq had
been a devastating strategic blunder, followed by a series of frustrating
missteps by U.S. military commanders. The title of his book was *Fiasco*.

Ricks had been working on his manuscript around the clock, seven
days a week. When he finished the first draft of a section, he would
e-mail it to every soldier mentioned in the passage. When he finished a
second draft he would repeat the process. One soldier wrote back, "I am
in Iraq, just got back from a firefight, but give me a couple of weeks and I
will tell you more." He was writing history as it unfolded, in near-real
time.

Ricks also immersed himself in French counterinsurgency theory,
scouring old volumes and memoirs in a search for answers to the questions he had brought home from his reporting trips to Iraq in 2003 and
2004. "I would read it and again and again find the key to the problems

that had bothered me," he told me. "How should troops deal with prisoners? How should commanders think about the enemy? What is the proper command structure in an operation like this? It was all there."

Those same questions were on his mind when he drove out to Fort Leavenworth. *I need to leave them with something concrete.* The room had a green chalkboard. He began his talk by writing one word, in block letters: GALULA.

Then he turned and looked up at the thousand or so majors in the auditorium, and asked, "Who knows what this word is, or means?"

Two or three hands went up.

Oh no, Ricks thought. "If there was anything you take away from this lecture," he continued, "you need to go and find out who David Galula was, and what he wrote, and how it might help you in Iraq."

Galula, a French theoretician of irregular warfare, fought in North Africa, Italy, and France during the Second World War, and later observed revolutionary wars in Indochina, Greece, Algeria, and China. In 1964, Galula published an influential volume, *Counterinsurgency Warfare: Theory and Practice*. The book elaborated a simple, compelling idea: Insurgency is at heart a struggle for the support of the population. Eighty percent of the counterinsurgent's task was civilian in nature: administering aid, building roads, policing villages. It is a manpower-intensive task, and Galula stated that the armed forces are usually the only organization equipped to handle the mission. But soldiers are no substitute for civilians. "To confine soldiers to purely military functions while urgent and vital tasks have to be done, and nobody else is available to undertake them, would be senseless," Galula wrote. "The soldier must then be prepared to become a propagandist, a social worker, a civil engineer, a schoolteacher, a nurse, a boy scout. But only for long as he cannot be replaced, for it is better to entrust civilian tasks to civilians."[1]

Galula was writing primarily about twentieth-century insurgencies, anticolonial liberation movements or Communist insurrections, but his description seemed to neatly describe how so many nation-building tasks had fallen to the military in places like Afghanistan and Iraq. The Army had published an interim counterinsurgency manual in October 2004, but the literature on the subject was still scarce. Many of the classic counterinsurgency texts were out of print. In the Pentagon library there had been a waiting list to check out the lone copy of Galula's book.

Fortunately, a boutique publisher in St. Petersburg, Florida, had stepped in to provide reprints of many of the classics. Hailer Publishing was founded by Jamie Hailer, a thirty-something devotee of military history and strategy who had a day job in the business planning department of General Dynamics Ordnance and Tactical Systems, an ammunition manufacturer. Hailer had done graduate work at Missouri State University, where he first read Galula, and he had first toyed with the idea of starting a publishing company when he tried to find a copy of *From Dreadnought to Scapa Flow*, a five-volume series on the history of the Royal Navy. When Hailer looked for a used set on the Internet, it priced out at $1,200.

But Hailer's decision to launch a publishing venture was sealed in late 2004, when he read an article in *Inside the Pentagon*, a defense trade paper published in Washington. The reporter, Elaine Grossman, described the reading list that Colonel H. R. McMaster had prepared in advance of the Third Armored Cavalry Regiment's deployment to Iraq. On the top of that list was Alistair Horne's *A Savage War of Peace: Algeria 1954–1962*, but it was out of print.

Grossman had surveyed top officers, retired intelligence officials, and strategists about what was on their essential reading list, and found that some of the most enthusiastic suggestions were for hard-to-find books like Galula's. "May I suggest that you run—not walk—to the Pentagon library and get in line" for Galula's book, a retired CIA officer with Vietnam experience told Grossman. The book should be read as "a primer for how to win in Iraq."[2]

Hailer decided to reprint the Galula book, as it seemed to fill the most urgent need. "Guys came back [from Iraq] and said, 'What are we doing?'" Hailer later told me. "That's what frustrated me: We are fighting a unconventional war, and all these books are out of print. It's like taking an economics course and Adam Smith's *The Wealth of Nations* is out of print."

He found a copy in the University of South Florida library and tracked down the company that had acquired the book's original publisher, and offered to pay royalties for reprint rights. The publisher agreed. Hailer then found a Florida firm that could make a high-quality scan of the original book and located a printer in Minnesota that could handle the job. By October 2005, the book had sold around twenty-four hundred copies. The Army's Command and General Staff College had ordered fifteen hundred of them.[3] The books were a key addition to the Fort Leavenworth bookstore.

Ricks later got a note from a friend at the Command and General Staff College who had asked a young officer he knew about Ricks's talk. "Oh, that reporter?" the friend said. "He got up and mentioned some French guy and said we were stupid if we didn't know who he was."

In early 2006, a quiet revolt was gathering momentum at Fort Leavenworth, home to the Army's Command and General Staff College, the midcareer school for Army officers. Located on the west bank of the Missouri River, this historic Army outpost was once the jumping-off point for the settlers headed west on the Santa Fe and Oregon trails; the wide trail ruts left by the thousands of wagons are still visible from the commanding bluffs above the river. The sturdy, nineteenth-century brick houses and manicured lawns give the place the feel of a Midwestern college, although the uniformed student body, Civil War cannons, and equestrian statues were a reminder of the place's martial purpose. A stint running Fort Leavenworth was seen as something of a career killer—or at least not the place to be if you wanted to go on to become a four-star combatant commander or Army chief of staff. In October 2005, Lieutenant General David Petraeus began a new assignment commanding the Combined Arms Center at Fort Leavenworth. Petraeus had returned to the United States after two and a half years in Iraq, first as commanding general of the 101st Airborne Division, then as the head of the Multi-National Security Transition Command Iraq, which was charged with training Iraqi security forces. His predecessor at Fort Leavenworth, General William Wallace, had been promoted to the unglamorous job of running U.S. Army Training and Doctrine Command at Fort Monroe, Virginia, which oversaw the service's schools and training facilities.

Just a few months after Petraeus arrived at Fort Leavenworth, things took a dramatic turn for the worse in Iraq. On February 22, 2006, bombers struck the al-Askari mosque in Samarra. The mosque was a major Shia shrine, where the earthly remains of the tenth and eleventh imams were buried, and the attack, orchestrated by al-Qaeda in Iraq, had a very deliberate aim of starting a full-blown civil war in Iraq. In the weeks following the Samarra mosque bombing, a wave of sectarian reprisals swept Iraq. During one thirty-hour period alone, eighty-six bodies were found dumped on the street in Baghdad, with the bodies of many victims bearing signs of

gruesome torture. Neighborhoods of the capital were being systematically ethnically cleansed.[4]

News of the Samarra mosque bombing reached Fort Leavenworth in
late February of 2006, while Petraeus was hosting a conference to review
the first draft of FM 3-24, the Army's new counterinsurgency field manual. The document was supposed to be much more than a professional
handbook: It was supposed to serve as a template for reforming the Army,
and fixing Iraq in the process. It was also intended to launch a broader
conversation about reinventing government. The meeting, convened by
Petraeus and Sarah Sewall of the Carr Center for Human Rights Policy at
Harvard's Kennedy School of Government, was a chance to test-market
the new counterinsurgency document to the broader foreign policy community. Representatives of other government agencies, the human rights
community, think tanks, and even a few journalists were invited to offer
critiques.

Work had begun in earnest on the new counterinsurgency manual in
late 2005, when Conrad Crane, a retired Army lieutenant colonel who
had graduated in the same West Point class as Petraeus (1974), brought
together a small writing team to produce an early first draft. Lieutenant
Colonel John Nagl, the armor officer who wrote the influential *Learning
to Eat Soup with a Knife: Counterinsurgency Lessons from Malaya and
Vietnam*, was a member of the team. Colonel Peter Mansoor, the armored brigade commander who had administered parts of Baghdad in
2003 and 2004, would later help revise the final version of the document.
But the most remarkable thing about the writing process was the amount
of input that came from nonmilitary people. Harvard's Sewall played a
unique role.

Sewall is not just a tenured academic but also a Pentagon and Washington policy insider. During the Clinton administration she served as
the first deputy assistant secretary of defense for peacekeeping and humanitarian assistance. Before that she served as senior foreign policy advisor to Senate Majority Leader George Mitchell on the Democratic
Policy Committee and the Senate Arms Control Observer Group. Under
Sewall's leadership, the Carr Center for Human Rights Policy had quietly
emerged as an influential player in military and national security circles.
In November 2005, working with the Strategic Studies Institute at the
Army War College at Carlisle Barracks, Pennsylvania, the Carr Center
had cosponsored a colloquium on irregular warfare in Washington.

Sewall invited Lieutenant Colonel Erik Kurilla, the commander of the First Battalion, Twenty-fourth Infantry Regiment, part of the Stryker Brigade that had recently policed Mosul, and other officers, but the panelists were not all military. To place emphasis on the issues of minimizing the use of force and reducing civilian harm, Sewall invited representatives of NGOs such as Human Rights Watch, Refugees International, and the International Rescue Committee, all organizations that normally were reluctant to be associated with the military.

These groups often had an adversarial relationship with the military, but Sewall managed to persuade senior officers to sit at the same table with human rights advocates. Getting academics and representatives of nongovernmental organizations to show up was also a struggle. Tyler Moselle, a research associate at the Carr Center, helped Sewall work the phones to persuade nonmilitary participants to attend the conference. "We open up the window and try to rush as many people in the room and then close the window," he said.

The role of the Kennedy School of Government was particularly important because the military and the scholarly worlds had been at odds since the Vietnam War, and the estrangement and mistrust had continued for decades. Introduction of an all-volunteer military widened the rift, as did policies like the military's ban on gays and lesbians serving openly in uniform. The Bush administration's disastrous preemptive war against Iraq was not particularly popular with academics nor with human rights advocates, either. But Sewall and Moselle believed they were on a mission; they justified the Carr Center's close collaboration with the military as working within the system to minimize the use of force and reduce civilian harm. When people asked Moselle to describe his job, he liked to say, "We try to humanize the military."

But it was a two-way street. Petraeus and the counterinsurgents also needed the imprimatur of the Kennedy School. They wanted to reach policy wonks, think-tankers, and academics who would help shape the debate about armed nation building. Equally important, they wanted to cultivate prominent journalists. Peter Maass, the journalist who had written a thoughtful profile of Lieutenant Colonel John Nagl for the *New York Times Magazine* in 2004, shared a panel with Kurilla at the Carr Center's 2005 conference on irregular warfare.

It was easy to understand why journalists gravitated to articulate officers with Ph.D.s such as Petraeus and Nagl. Counterinsurgency was an irresistible story of military reform. Smart counterinsurgents such as Colonel H. R. McMaster and Nagl favored a subtle, culturally nuanced approach that emphasized development work over violent action, and they found common cause with journalists who had witnessed firsthand U.S. troops' uncomprehending first encounters with Iraqis. A subtle cultural prejudice may also have been at work. Sophisticated officers with Ph.D.s made for better protagonists than old-school knuckle draggers who preferred to kick down doors in a fruitless hunt for insurgents.

For Greg Jaffe, then a reporter for the *Wall Street Journal*, media-savvy officers such as Nagl—sometimes nicknamed "COINdinistas" because of the military's inevitable reduction of the word "counterinsurgency" to an acronym, COIN—were an irresistible story. "The counterinsugency narrative became an interesting one to me when I was trying to figure out how the hell we were losing this war," he told me. "And the COIN folks were offering compelling alternatives that you could write about."

Jaffe was one of the reporters invited to the February 2006 drafting session for the counterinsurgency manual. "To be honest, I think a big part of that was not that they were desperate for our opinions, but they wanted to socialize the document to a certain extent," he said. "And reporters are going to write about it if they have access to it and access to the people who are writing it."

The military's embrace of counterinsurgency was not, however, a strictly top-down affair. In many respects, it was a grassroots movement. As many career soldiers returned from frustrating first tours in Iraq and Afghanistan, they began searching for new intellectual guidance that would explain how to set things right.

In generations past, the military's middle management—the noncommissioned officers, platoon leaders and company commanders—had limited say about how the military organized, trained, and equipped. They had few forums for a free and open discussion of the problems they faced in the field. Of course, they might consider submitting articles to military journals such as the Naval Institute's *Proceedings* or the Army's *Parameters* quarterly, but these publications have a fairly long lead time, limited space, and strict editorial guidelines. Professional conferences like the Association of the United States Army symposia offered some outlet for professional discussion, but little opportunity for dissident opinions.

In the post-9/11 era, however, a new generation of professional soldier was able tap the power of the Internet. In 2005 and 2006, as the official counterinsurgency doctrine took shape, the middle ranks of the military, the men and women who were most heavily engaged in nation building, began using Web 2.0 tools—digital communication, e-mail, and social networking—to share their experiences. And the shift to nation building took on a whole new momentum. In 2000, Army Majors Nate Allen and Tony Burgess created a Web site, Companycommand .com, that was modeled on a hunting-and-fishing discussion forum and was meant to serve as a professional forum for young officers. On Compa nycommand.com, officers could trade tips on everything from navigating Army bureaucracy to negotiating with village elders. The Web site, which allowed open discussion threads, quickly caught on; a year later, Allen and Burgess founded a site for lieutenants, Platoonleader.org.[5]

The sites were an extraordinary networking tool for junior officers and a medium for immediate and open exchange. The Army establishment, however, was terrified about these discussions taking place on the civilian Internet, potentially in full view of the enemy, although officers were supposed to be self-policing in virtual chat rooms. Eventually both sites were firewalled and brought onto Army servers. To log on, a person needed an Army Knowledge Online account, an official Army e-mail address. The forums continued to be useful for sharing practical advice, but they were not always the best venue for debate. Everything posted would be potentially visible to the person's chain of command.

What the counterinsurgency movement needed was a more freewheeling and unmoderated forum. On official Defense Department sites, users were logged in under their full names and ranks, and people who held unpopular opinions or questioned established policies couldn't do so without fear of retribution. Perhaps more important, the counterinsurgency proponents wanted a forum where they could engage communities *outside* the military: from academia, from nongovernmental organizations, even from the media. After all, nation building demanded civilian expertise as much as it required technical military proficiency.

At the senior level, there was Warlord Loop, an invitation-only e-mail list founded by a retired Army colonel, John Collins. The discussion group included senior military officers, some experienced NCOs, plus a smattering of civilian experts and even a few select reporters. But Warlord Loop was exclusive, limited to a few hundred members.

A new outlet appeared in 2005, with the publication of Small Wars Journal, an online magazine devoted to the study of counterinsurgency and internal war. Small Wars Journal originally looked more like a traditional outlet for scholarly writing and magazine-length articles, but the Small Wars Journal Web site also featured a resource page with reading lists, links to other agency Web sites and archival materials on everything from histories of British involvement in peacekeeping to small wars in the twentieth century. Very quickly, Small Wars Journal attracted an online audience, and it became home to a lively discussion forum and a blog.

The founders of Small Wars Journal, Dave Dilegge and Bill Nagle, had worked together at the Marine Corps Warfighting Laboratory at Quantico, Virginia. The site indirectly evolved from the MOUT Homepage, a site originally developed by Dilegge when he was working as an analyst on urban warfare (the acronym MOUT stands for "military operations in urban terrain"). MOUT Homepage was a useful resource for a small community of military experts and scholars who studied urban warfare, and it gradually evolved into an online publication called the Urban Operations Journal. The publication was funded through the Defense Technical Information Center and was on an official site of the Defense Department.

Having an official site had its advantages. Dilegge and Nagle could post items stamped "For Official Use Only" (a designation often used to restrict the circulation of sensitive but unclassified government documents); they also posted after-action reports and other unclassified information that the military wanted to confine to the small community of urban operations specialists. But the official approval process on a government Web site made posting slow and was cumbersome. Dilegge found that it took only a few minutes to draft a post, but it took two to three days for it to go live. The site was not kept up-to-date, and with time, Urban Operations Journal became a dormant page.

After Iraq and Afghanistan, however, Dilegge and Nagle noticed a surge in interest in some of the topics once covered by Urban Operations Journal. In Iraq especially, bypassing the urban areas was no longer an option. It was central to the fight. They took the old template of the Urban Operations Journal and repurposed it. Small Wars Journal would be broader and more inclusive, and would cover the full range of issues: cultural awareness, civilian-led reconstruction and development, counterinsurgency theory and practice. The two men were skilled networkers, and were able to solicit contributions from rising stars within the community—Nagl and Bing West, a former Reagan defense official who wrote the cult Vietnam book *The Village*. Small Wars Journal became a must-read for people in uniform who were looking for answers to the problems they faced in Iraq and Afghanistan.

Small Wars Journal later had a rogue twin in Abu Muqawama, a blog founded in early 2007 by Andrew Exum, a former Army Ranger who had served in Afghanistan and Iraq. If Small Wars Journal became an established forum for serious-minded discussion, Abu Muqawama was its hip, snarky counterpart. Exum, a native of east Tennessee and a graduate of the University of Pennsylvania, founded Abu Muqawama almost on a dare while on a year-long fellowship in Washington. The name was an inside joke: Exum, who had received a master's degree at the American University of Beirut, was a student of Lebanese politics. Exum and his office-mate, Seth Wikas, kept a Hezbollah flag in their office, which features the phrase *al-muqawamah al-islamiyah fi lubnan*: "The Islamic resistance in Lebanon." The nickname Abu Muqawama means "father of the resistance" in Arabic. The name was suggested by Wikas.

The first post described Abu Muqawama as "a resource and clearinghouse for information relating to contemporary insurgencies." At first Exum used the pseudonymous blog to highlight links to articles on events in the Middle East and Iraq. Exum had written a serious memoir of combat, *This Man's Army: A Soldier's Story from the Front Lines of the War on Terrorism*. Now he quickly found his voice as a blogger; he had a talent for writing sharp, witty posts laced with pop culture references and subversive humor. The readership of the blog grew exponentially: When he began posting in the spring of 2007, he had around a hundred visitors a day; a year later, his readership had spiked to about three thousand a day. It was a wide and influential audience. Exum had a stable of serious contributors, and his site became both a serious discussion forum as well as a sort of gossip site—a Gawker for the counterinsurgency set.

When Exum founded the blog in early 2007, the counterinsurgents—as the name implied—still viewed themselves as outsiders, a group of insurrectionists bent on challenging conventional thinking within the military. But they were already on the way to becoming the new establishment.

By midsummer 2006, the Army was in the throes of a full-blown intellectual revolt. A few months earlier, *Military Review*, the journal published by the Combined Arms Center at Fort Leavenworth, published an article by Brigadier Nigel Aylwin-Foster, a British Army officer who had served in Iraq with the U.S.-dominated command from December 2003 to November 2004. Aylwin-Foster's piece captured many of the U.S. Army's failures. He wrote:

> My overriding impression was of an Army imbued with an unparalleled sense of patriotism, duty, passion, commitment, and determination, with plenty of talent, and in no way lacking in humanity or compassion. Yet it seemed weighed down by bureaucracy, a stiflingly hierarchical outlook, a pre-disposition to offensive operations, and a sense that duty required all issues to be confronted head-on. Many personnel seemed to struggle to understand the nuances of the OIF [Operation Iraqi Freedom] Phase 4 environment. Moreover, whilst they were almost unfailingly courteous and considerate, at times their cultural insensitivity, almost certainly inadvertent, arguably amounted to institutional racism.[6]

It was a devastating critique of the U.S. Army's performance in Mesopotamia, published in one of the Army's leading professional journals. Although many disagreed with points in Aylwin-Foster's critique, the failures in Iraq had indeed spurred profound self-criticism within the Army. Also widely circulated at the time was "Twenty-Eight Articles: Fundamentals of Company-Level Counterinsurgency," an article by David Kilcullen, a reserve lieutenant colonel in the Australian Army who was seconded to the U.S. State Department as chief strategist in the Office of the Coordinator for Counterterrorism. Kilcullen had completed a doctoral dissertation on Indonesian insurgent and terrorist groups and counterinsurgency methods, and a version of his article was circulated widely by e-mail. It contained a striking injunction: "Practice armed Civil Affairs. Counterinsurgency is armed social work; an attempt to redress basic social and political problems while being shot at."[7] That article was also published in *Military Review*, giving it an official imprimatur.

Fort Leavenworth, the intellectual home of the Army, was caught up in the service's mood of profound professional introspection. Invited there for a series of briefings on the new manual, I was told that two thirds of the students at the School of Advanced Military Studies were now writing theses on the trendy new topic of counterinsurgency. A visit to the campus bookstore would also demonstrate this hunger for new ideas and receptiveness to criticism. One of the top-selling books at the store was *Fiasco: The American Military Adventure in Iraq*, a new hardcover by Tom Ricks, the renowned *Washington Post* military-affairs reporter who had visited Fort Leavenworth in 2005 and recommended that officers start boning up on their French counterinsurgency theory. Ricks was particularly scathing in his treatment of Major General Ray Odierno, the commander of the Fourth Infantry Division, whose division was known in 2003 and 2004 for an aggressive, "guns-up" posture that alienated Iraqis and set back efforts to win over the population.

Another item stacked up on the display table: *In the Belly of the Green Bird: The Triumph of the Martyrs in Iraq*, an insider's account of Iraq's burgeoning civil war by Nir Rosen, a young American journalist and fluent speaker of Arabic who had managed to report from inside Iraqi cities that had come under the control of the insurgency. In some military circles Rosen was regarded with suspicion for his willingness to report from the other side, but the popularity of the book suggested that there was an intellectual curiosity about the internal dynamics of Iraq's sectarian conflict.

Through the late summer and early fall of 2006, Fort Leavenworth hosted a procession of journalists to introduce both U.S. and overseas audiences to the main tenets of the counterinsurgency manual. Visiting media could meet the rising stars of the counterinsurgency community, including Colonel Peter Mansoor, who had grasped the basics of armed nation building during a tour as brigade commander in Baghdad. They could visit the Center for Army Lessons Learned, where the service engaged in institutional self-scrutiny. As icing on the cake, they could sit down with the general for the "Engine of Change" briefing, a PowerPoint presentation delivered personally by Petraeus. It was a conscious effort to sell the new doctrine, but also an opportunity to explain to a military audience what kinds of skills the Army wanted to master. I was reporting for *Jane's Defence Weekly*, the U.K.-based military magazine; *Jane's* reached a key audience for the U.S. military, professional military readers in both the United States and other NATO countries.

Petraeus met me in his office, which had dark wood paneling and leather chairs and was festooned with martial awards and memorabilia. Like the general's uniform, replete with a serious array of badges, patches, and tabs, it bespoke an impressive military career. During our hour-long conversation, the soft-spoken general favored the politically correct language of nation building and diplomacy, emphasizing the military's need to master a new set of "soft" skills: language and culture. Within the Army, Petraeus said, there was "a pretty big realization that if you want to be good at this kind of stuff . . . if you want to operate effectively in a different culture, then you've got to understand the nuances of that culture, you've got to be sensitive to the various aspects of that culture, that specific culture. Not the Arabic culture writ large, but the Iraqi Arabic culture."

It was a realization of a hard lesson. The mission in Iraq would require a nuanced understanding of politics, ethnicity, and religion at the local level. U.S. troops would have to overcome their ignorance of local language. Producing a large cadre of fluent Arabic speakers seemed a tall order for the military, but, Petraeus said,

> You certainly ought to have a survival level of that language. It's something like you recall in the NATO days, it was *Gateway to German*, or *Gateway to Italian*. Every American soldier had to go through this in the first two or three weeks that he or she was in theater. And that turned out to be useful, in fact all of us can still parrot our phrases, you know, "*Wo ist der Bahnhof?*" and all that other stuff. But you took stuff away from that that was really important. We sought to do that.

The new battlefield, Petraeus said, was no longer the blue team (the good guys) squaring off against the red team (the bad guys). He recalled the moment when he stood atop a Humvee outside Najaf in 2003 and realized that there were a lot more civilians on the battlefield than there ever were at the National Training Center. The business of nation building required patience, and the counterinsurgent needed to serve as a public ambassador for the mission. That meant explaining the mission to, and engaging with, the press. "It's not optional to deal with the [press], just like it's not optional to deal with the civilian population," he said. "It's not optional to work with local leaders. It's not optional to do nation building. You've got to do all of those, or you will not succeed at the National Training Center, and you will certainly not succeed in Iraq or Afghanistan."

It was more than just an overhaul of training that Petraeus and the counterinsurgents wanted to impose on the Army. They wanted to develop a new generation of officers and soldiers who were comfortable with the chores of nation building, men and women who were willing to immerse themselves in foreign cultures, and who were as skilled at managing reconstruction funds as they were in sending tank rounds downrange. That would require a shift in the way that the military selected people for promotion. In colonial militaries such as the British Army, serving with "indigenous" or "native" forces was traditionally a prestigious assignment. In the U.S. Army, volunteering to serve on a Military Transition Team— the thankless, often dangerous job of mentoring Iraqi military units or training Afghan police forces—was still largely viewed as a professional dead end. It was in many respects a repeat of the Vietnam War, when the path to rapid advancement was having an assignment to a line unit, not a job as a district or a province advisor. And after Vietnam, those kinds of advisory jobs were largely relegated to Special Forces. Petraeus wanted to make sure that an advisory tour was no longer a bar to professional advancement.

Advisors, he said, needed to be given priority for "branch-qualifying" jobs. They needed to be given preference for promotion to important leadership jobs: a battalion command or an operations officer or executive officer in a brigade.

> We want to make sure that if someone volunteers to be a MiTT or a SPTT—a Military Transition Team member or a Special Police Training Team member or leader—that they are then rewarded for that. And in all the traditional ways that we reward people: They get their share of decorations and promotions and selection for command and everything else. So we have to insure that our personnel system, the Human Resources Command,

rewards them by then giving them follow-on assignments that insure their upward trajectory.

But, Petraeus added, a successful counterinsurgency campaign in Iraq would require a serious nonmilitary component. "Some of these are national issues. And I think the State Department is starting to look at the overall national government response to conduct of counterinsurgency."

Later that month the State Department would be holding a conference on the subject, and he would be making a presentation. What Petraeus seemed to be driving at—although he was careful not to step "outside of his lane" as a general officer—was that the United States might need an increase in the size of the diplomatic corps. "It'd be interesting to ask what the size is of the Foreign Service officer community in the State Department," he said. "Far be it from me [to say]. I think people should ask: What is the capacity?"

And, Petraeus added: "I think you might want to go see the assistant secretary for pol-mil"—John Hillen, who was preparing the ground for the counterinsurgents in Washington.

John Hillen, the head of the State Department's Bureau of Political-Military Affairs, got the phone call from Petraeus in early 2006. The general was just back from Iraq, and he needed a favor. Hillen knew Petraeus from Army circles—not especially well, but they had a mutual friend in Lieutenant Colonel John Nagl, the influential armor officer who had made waves with *Learning to Eat Soup with a Knife: Counterinsurgency Lessons from Malaya and Vietnam*, the newly popular book on counterinsurgency. Hillen and Nagl had been friends for two decades: They shared the same supervisor at Oxford University, where Nagl was a Rhodes Scholar and where both men earned doctorates. They had known each other as young lieutenants in the Army and had both served in the first Gulf War.

During Operation Desert Storm, Hillen was the senior scout platoon leader for then Captain H. R. McMaster, who commanded Eagle Troop of the Second Armored Cavalry Regiment in the Battle of 73 Easting, a tank duel with the Iraqi Republican Guard in late February 1991.[8] McMaster's Abrams tank and Hillen's Bradley fighting vehicle were within fifty meters of each other during the fight, which led to the destruction of over one hundred Iraqi armored vehicles and the decimation of a Republican Guard brigade. As their careers advanced, Hillen and Mc-Master stayed in touch: They were all part of a relatively small circle of Army officers with Ph.D.s who all knew one another, at least by reputation, and who tracked one another's professional rise.

Petraeus was part of that circle as well: He had completed a Ph.D. at the Woodrow Wilson School of Public and International Affairs at Princeton University. "I'm sitting here writing this field manual, and it's great, I got Nagl, I got all the right people," Petraeus said. "And we have reaffirmed the age-old counterinsurgency tenet: Eighty percent is political, twenty percent is military."

"Great," Hillen laughed. "You reinvented the wheel."

The two men were sharing an insider's joke: That 80 percent political, 20 percent military formula was, at least within progressive military circles, a piece of accepted wisdom, a formula borrowed from David Galula. The irony was not lost on Petraeus.

"I'm sitting around here, Ranger Hillen, and I'm looking at all uniforms," he said. "And I'm writing a book that says eighty percent is a nonuniformed task. What's wrong with this picture? Where's the rest of the government?"

Petraeus was slowly coming around to a larger point. The new counterinsurgency manual was intended for the Army and the Marine Corps; the general wanted someone to evangelize the concept throughout the rest of the government. The military desperately needed civilian support, and Petraeus needed a point person in Washington to help organize a governmentwide conference that would introduce the gospel of counterinsurgency to a wider government audience.

"That's a good point," Hillen said. The reason for Petraeus's phone call was starting to dawn on him. "Do you have anybody in mind?"

"You're the point person for the rest of the government," Petraeus said. Petraeus and his team were planning to roll out the new counterinsurgency manual early in the fall, and they wanted to capture the maximum attention of the Beltway policymaking elite. The governmentwide counterinsurgency conference—advertised as "jointly sponsored" by the State Department and the Pentagon, although the Defense Department would provide most of the funds for the event—would be their coming-out party.

Hillen's first thought was, *Shit, well that's not what my bureau does.* (The National Security Council, part of the Executive Office of the President, is supposed to be the main forum for coordinating national security issues at the senior level.) And Hillen's second thought as the phone conversation unfolded was that everything that he had accomplished thus far during his tenure had been done outside the traditional budget authority of the State Department. For instance, Hillen had helped push through the Section 1206 program, also known as "Global Train and Equip." Foreign military assistance—providing equipment and technical support to foreign militaries—was traditionally overseen by the State Department, but Section 1206 of the Fiscal Year 2006 defense budget gave the Defense Department authority to do the job (referred to as "building the military capacity of partner nations"). For instance, Section 1206 funds helped Pakistan acquire helicopters, spare parts, and night-vision equipment so it could combat Islamic militants in its tribal areas and do it quickly. To critics it represented the steady erosion of the State Department's traditional diplomatic activities and the accumulation of even more power by the Defense Department. But the military liked Section 1206 funding. It was faster and easier than the traditional security assistance programs that required a lot of cumbersome oversight and took years to execute. Section 1207 authority, another new mechanism, allowed the secretary of defense to transfer funds to the State Department so they could provide civilian stabilization and reconstruction assistance. Those funds were used to train local police capacity in Haiti's Cité Soleil and clear unexploded ordnance in Lebanon. In Colombia, the State Department and the Pentagon used Section 1207 to fund health and education programs in areas recently won back from guerrillas.[9]

In essence, Sections 1206 and 1207 quietly expanded the foreign policy powers of the Pentagon under the banner of "interagency cooperation." But Hillen had pushed for it, along with his boss, Secretary of State Condoleezza Rice. As a former soldier, he was the ideal advocate for pushing what was essentially a military agenda, raising consciousness within the larger civilian bureaucracy about "their" role in counterinsurgency. It would require a plan of action, training, and—most important—money. Petraeus promised to help come up with the funds for the conference, and he brought in Jeb Nadaner, deputy assistant secretary of defense for stability operations, as cosponsor. Hillen was energized, and he started work on organizing the conference.

The conference, Hillen told me, was "the first step" toward creating a new consensus in Washington, a push to reorganize the foreign policy apparatus around the tasks of nation building. It succeeded in recasting the conversation about national security, and the mission of the twenty-first-century diplomatic service. "That's the basic genesis: a phone call from Petraeus to me at my desk, and a willingness to just jump out there and try this," Hillen said.

Within Washington, however, Hillen ran into bureaucratic resistance in his attempt to build a "whole-of-government" counterinsurgency approach. For one, he faced questions from the National Security Council, which in theory was supposed to coordinate the "interagency" issues that cut across government departments. Not long after he started organizing, Hillen received a call from the NSC; his efforts had prompted "a lot of concern" about a potential bureaucratic land grab by the military. Part of the problem was conceptual: Since September 11, 2001, U.S. foreign policy had been reorganized around the response to terrorism, not insurgency. The State Department had a counterterrorism office that was focused on a much narrower set of problems: tracking, finding, and combatting transnational Islamic terror groups. The counterinsurgents were talking about something bigger. They were framing the problem in terms of nation building. And the set of tools they wanted to develop could apply as easily to Haiti as they could to Iraq.

Part of the problem was cultural. In January of 2006, Hillen flew out to Iraq for a short fact-finding trip. The brief stay of about five days was frustrating. To get around the country, Hillen had to draw on the old-boy network from his days in the military, hitching rides on helicopters and a C-12 transport plane. He spent one night out in the field with the Third Armored Cavalry Regiment, commanded by his old friend, Colonel H. R. McMaster. The visit to Iraq cemented Hillen's views: The 80 percent political side of counterinsurgency was missing from the equation. A traditional mind-set still prevailed: Diplomats should stay inside the Green Zone, while the military conducted its business out in the Red Zone—all of the rest of Iraq. Something had to change. "I only spent two hours in the Green Zone," he told me. "And it drove the State Department nuts. They were like, 'What's the assistant secretary doing out of the Green Zone?'"

Not long after his trip to Iraq, Hillen began planning a fact-finding visit to Afghanistan. He wanted to examine the civilian-military experiment under way in Afghanistan's provinces, and outlined his plans in an e-mail to the U.S. Embassy in Kabul. The embassy staff, however, initially opposed Hillen's plans to travel outside of Kabul, and a chain of e-mail correspondence followed. The argument from Kabul was that Hillen, as the assistant secretary of state, should be spending his time in Kabul with the Afghan ministers of defense or interior, not mucking around in the countryside visiting military units or Provincial Reconstruction Teams. What was there for him to do in Khowst, or in Ghazni, or some other combat outpost in the provinces? Shouldn't he be spending time meeting his counterparts in the capital?

As Hillen's correspondence with the embassy made it clear, a Red Zone–Green Zone mentality still prevailed in the diplomatic corps. When Hillen scrolled down to the bottom of the e-mail chain, he noticed a note appended from Ambassador Ronald Neumann, a tough, salty-tongued Vietnam veteran who had succeeded Zalmay Khalilzad in the ambassador's post. He had written a note to one of his officers, perhaps not thinking it would find its way back to Hillen. As Hillen recalled, it said: "Tell Assistant Secretary Hillen we're not his fucking travel agency."*

Still, after a few months of persuading, Hillen received the National Security Council's blessing to begin working on whole-of-government counterinsurgency guidelines. "Which is probably why Dave [Petraeus] cannily pushed it off on me," Hillen told me. "I mean, why should he get the crap beat out of him in Washington for three months, when I was willing to do it?"

The governmentwide counterinsurgency conference was held at the Ronald Reagan Building in downtown Washington that September. The agenda read like a roster of luminaries from the counterinsurgency world: An opening panel on counterinsurgency best practices featured David Kilcullen, the Australian military officer who had won a cult following with his "Twenty-Eight Articles," and Colonel H. R. McMaster, the former commander of the Third Armored Cavalry Regiment in Tal Afar. Day 2 featured a keynote address by Petraeus, who was introduced by Sarah Sewall of the Carr Center for Human Rights Policy.

---

*Neumann said he didn't recall that remark, or any such exchange with Hillen. "He may have clashed with someone in Kabul and it may not have come up to me," he said. But ferrying officials from Washington around the hinterlands, Neumann added, was definitely a problem. "We didn't control much aviation, so when people wanted to get around it wasn't so easily done," he told me.

If the concept of armed nation building was already taking hold within the military, the conference brought the concept to a wider audience: the civilian agencies of the federal government. A briefing paper distributed to participants made the aim of the conference clear: The U.S. government should "reframe the GWOT [global war on terror] as global COIN [counterinsurgency]." That new acronym marked a clear break with the concept that had provided the intellectual framework and justification for five years of war under President George W. Bush. And it heralded a more sweeping, long-term campaign that would see the United States intervening to support governments that were combatting locally organized, globally networked extremists, not just in Iraq and Afghanistan but around the globe. At the heart of counterinsurgency was political, social, and developmental work, meaning that civilian agencies needed to work more closely with the military and absorb counterinsurgency principles in their planning. The conference packet featured a logo that presented the idea visually: a circle in which the blue silhouette of a soldier is flanked by two bureaucrats, a man in a suit and tie and a woman in a pant suit; they face off against a cartoon insurgent, a shadowy figure holding a Kalashnikov rifle. The circle was bounded by the phrase "United States Interagency Counterinsurgency Initiative"; a crest, top and bottom, read "whole of government" and "whole of society."

This was more than the usual series of lectures and workshops. It was designed to set the agenda for something quite radical: refashioning the U.S. government around stability operations and nation building. This would be a generation-long effort, something that would require reorganizing the agencies of government around the mission of advising, rebuilding, and sometimes directly administering vulnerable states. Hillen's co-host, Jeb Nadaner, the deputy secretary of defense for stability operations, ticked off a list of new "capabilities" the U.S. government would require. At the top of the list was a deployable "civilian reserve," analogous to the military's reserve system, that could send civilian experts to crisis regions on short notice.

It was, in short, a call to reform the U.S. diplomatic and foreign aid establishment and place it on a war footing. Nadaner said that this new force, like soldiers, would need to take part in military exercises, and they would need protection in the field. This dedicated cadre of nation builders might even extend outside the federal government: It might include members of state and local government, private-sector experts, even representatives of nongovernmental organizations. "We're going to need a national movement, if we want to see the civilian reserve develop into the institution it needs to become," Nadaner said.

In essence, the counterinsurgents were mobilizing around a vision of a reinvented federal government, a sort of Colonial Office for the twenty-first century. It would have a cadre of skilled development experts and administrators who could work in collapsed states and war zones; a corps of social scientists who could help the military navigate this complex ethnic terrain; a military advisory force that would help build the key security institutions of developing countries. In theory, it would unite the practice of development, defense, and diplomacy. The foundation was now being laid for all three. The next several years would be a test: of whether the United States was equipped for nation building, and if nation building could succeed.

At that stage, Iraq was still in the throes of a civil war. U.S. assistance had yielded some tenuous successes, including a series of national elections in 2005. Afghanistan had receded from the headlines, but it, too, was beginning to face growing instability as the Taliban regrouped and as guerrillas built a recruiting and organizational base across the border in Pakistan. Even as the United States looked for a smarter approach, the internal dynamics in both countries meant that the nation-building mission would still have to be done under fire.

PART III

Theory into Practice

CHAPTER 8

Wingtips on the Ground

Sending diplomats and aid experts to Provincial Reconstruction Teams and other war-zone assignments was a good idea, in theory. Civilians had the kind of expertise in governance, state building, and development that few soldiers had. But the State Department and other civilian agencies were even less prepared than the U.S. military for the violent, chaotic situation they faced in Iraq and Afghanistan. Nation building required more manpower than those organizations had on hand, and the larger the mission grew, the more it exposed the shortcomings of the civilian bureaucracy.

It was tough, unglamorous work, and diplomats were being asked to tackle a completely unfamiliar set of problems. Instead of their traditional responsibilities of reporting back to Washington on the high-level goings-on in foreign capitals, they were becoming involved in the complexities of local and provincial administration. They were overseeing water and sewage repair, trash collection, and rural electrification, all while occasionally being shot at.

Diplomatic and government agencies had been involved in administering and rebuilding Iraq since the invasion in 2003, but there was still no comprehensive way to organize and mobilize them. Unlike the military, which had realistic predeployment training and predictable rotation cycles, the civilian bureaucracy had a more haphazard approach to

sending employees "downrange." Military units typically trained together before deploying to Iraq or Afghanistan; by contrast, civilians
usually arrived as individual replacements on Provincial Reconstruction Teams or in regional embassy offices. This lack of esprit de corps
often created unnecessary friction. It was also a question of training.
The State Department offered a rigorous area-studies and language
training to diplomats going to traditional embassy assignments, but
that kind of specialized preparation was nonexistent for nation-building
assignments.

In the summer of 2005, the State Department began planning Provincial Reconstruction Teams for Iraq. The idea was to deploy a Provincial
Reconstruction Team in each of Iraq's eighteen governorates (provinces)
as part of a push to extend the central government's control to Iraq's regions, something the military desperately wanted. Greg Bates, a retired
Marine Corps officer who had worked in Iraq since the days of the Coalition Provisional Authority, was part of the team recruited by the State
Department to help jump-start the effort. Bates had wide civilian and
military experience in the Middle East. He had worked in naval intelligence, had served a tour with the CPA as a Foreign Service officer, and
had worked as a USAID contractor for a local governance program in
Iraq. By his third tour in Iraq, as director of operations for the State Department's Iraq Reconstruction Management Office, a shortfall in civilian
personnel had become glaringly obvious. Multi-National Force Iraq, the
U.S.-dominated military command, was "screaming to get civilians back
in the provinces," Bates said.

The aim in Iraq was not to reproduce the Afghanistan experiment.
Iraq was much more developed: It had infrastructure, a centralized administration, and a literate population. What it needed most was effective provincial- and national-level government institutions. Planners
started work on a new template for civil-military teams in Iraq. Whereas
PRT commanders in Afghanistan were almost exclusively military, the
Iraq teams would be civilian-led, and they would focus more on governance than on rural development projects. Mentoring Iraqi officials, not
building infrastructure, would be the main focus. The catchwords for
the program, "capacity building" and "sustainability," were borrowed
from the world of development. The planning team presented their proposal to Ambassador Zalmay Khalilzad, who had moved on from Afghanistan to become the U.S. ambassador to Iraq, and General George

Casey, the top U.S. commander in Iraq, in September. The team feared that "reconstruction" in the name might suggest to Iraqis that they would have a giant pot of construction funds at their disposal, but they stuck with PRT, which was by that time familiar to the members of Congress who controlled the purse strings.

Training would be a problem for diplomats and other civilians assigned to this new mission. At that point, diplomats headed to Iraq could expect to go on a three- or five-day security course where they would learn the fundamentals of working in a hostile environment—basic first aid, evasive driving, and weapons handling—but there was no PRT-specific training. No system was in place to ensure proper coordination with the military or to pass on lessons that had been learned in the field. (There would be no formal predeployment training program for PRTs until February 2007, when the Iraq "surge" began.)

Then there was the question of who would provide security. Foreign Service officers, USAID employees, and other civilians assigned to PRTs would require protection while out in the field. The first three teams would be working out of regional embassy offices, so they could rely on private security details provided by Triple Canopy, DynCorp, or Blackwater, the three U.S. security firms that had security contracts with the State Department. But in other provinces, the PRTs would have to be located on forward operating bases, where security and transportation would have to be provided by the military. That would require intricate negotiations between the different bureaucratic tribes in Iraq: the State Department, the Defense Department, and the Multi-National Force Iraq headquarters.

The national coordination center for Iraq PRTs was established at the beginning of October 2005. Around the same time, the U.S. Embassy Baghdad released Baghdad Cable 4045, a coordinated memorandum between the embassy and Multi-National Force Iraq to the State Department headquarters that outlined the PRT program, what it was supposed to accomplish, and how diplomats and the military were directed to do it. By late November, two teams were up and running. The first was in Mosul, the city where Petraeus had made his mark as a military administrator, and the second in Hillah, where Marine Lance Corporal John Guardiano had learned hard lessons about municipal politics in Iraq. A third team was established in Kirkuk by mid-December. But the PRTs were slow to build momentum. Under the original timetable, around fifteen PRTs were supposed to be established by mid-2006. By June 2006 there were only five. Secretary of Defense Donald Rumsfeld—not a huge fan of the concept, according to those involved in the project—demanded a sixty-day "proof of concept" before allowing the program to move forward.

Rumsfeld's skepticism came in part from the apparent lack of commitment from civilian agencies to the Iraq mission. Keith Urbahn, a Rumsfeld associate, told me that Rumsfeld's objections to the PRTs "were not with the concept itself," but with the lack of nonmilitary personnel committed to the task:

> The goal of the PRTs was exactly what senior military commanders had been asking, even pleading for, since 2003: more interagency support and competence in reconstruction activities in Iraq and Afghanistan which were nonsecurity and non-DoD related. The problem with the PRT concept was the commitment (or lack thereof) to staff them with non DoD personnel—State, Agriculture, etc. . . . Rumsfeld and other senior DoD officials recognized that absent commitments beyond comforting words of assurance, DoD would be carrying the burden for PRTs. And sure enough, that's what happened, especially in Iraq, when many PRTs had dozens of uniformed personnel and no more than a few civilians.

By February 2006, plans were finally in the works to roll out the rest of the teams, including an Italian-led team and a British-led team. But many issues were still unresolved. In June of 2006, James Jeffrey, a senior advisor to Secretary of State Condoleezza Rice, conceded that there was friction between the military and the diplomatic corps over coordinating aid and reconstruction efforts at the regional level. Each PRT had up to one hundred personnel, so establishing more contingents would involve major security demands and put additional strain on military resources.

"The military would like to see thousands of civilians throughout the country and that would require tens of thousands of folks securing them," Jeffrey told reporters at a breakfast in Washington. "That's a very big issue. It would be either billions of dollars and huge numbers of PSDs [personal security details] running around the country, and that's already a political and security problem, or it would require a lot of troops."

Planners faced another problem: Civilian agencies had a hard time finding people willing to serve in Iraq. Once again, the military would plug the gap, providing much of the manpower.

Iraq's deadly downward spiral continued through 2006. That spring, Congress appointed the Iraq Study Group, a bipartisan panel of ten Beltway worthies charged with assessing the situation in Iraq. The panel, chaired by former Secretary of State James Baker and former Representative Lee Hamilton of Indiana, reached a depressingly obvious conclusion: U.S. troops were overstretched and Iraq was engulfed in civil war. With one hundred Americans dying every month and the war reaching a "burn rate" of $2 billion a week, there seemed to be no clear exit. That November, the American public, wearying of violent headlines from Iraq, handed a defeat to the Republican Party in the midterm elections, and the Democratic Party gained control of both the House and Senate. After the crushing electoral loss, President George W. Bush fired Defense Secretary Donald Rumsfeld. Robert Gates, a national security veteran who had served as director of Central Intelligence under Bush's father, was announced as Rumsfeld's replacement.

Rumsfeld's dismissal was the first real acknowledgment by the administration of the severity of the Iraq situation. Early in the war, officials had been relentlessly upbeat, even as postinvasion casualties climbed. Even the word "insurgent" was verboten. In Rumsfeld's lexicon, the insurgents were "dead-enders," isolated Ba'athist regime holdouts, and assorted criminals. "The reason I don't use the phrase 'guerrilla war' is because there isn't one, and it would be a misunderstanding and a miscommunication to you and to the people of the country and the world," he had said in late June 2003. Iraq had "looters, criminals, remnants of the Ba'athist regime, foreign terrorists who came in to assist and try to harm the coalition forces, and those influenced by Iran," but "that ... doesn't make it anything like a guerrilla war or an organized resistance."[1] He was still saying this two and a half years later.

Even after General John Abizaid, the top U.S. commander in the Middle East, broke with the party line the following month to describe the situation in Iraq as a "classical guerrilla-type campaign," the secretary of defense clung to his "freedom is untidy" interpretation of events in Iraq. Both Rumsfeld and National Security Advisor Condoleezza Rice even floated an absurd comparison between postwar Germany and present-day Iraq, suggesting early on that the attacks in Iraq were reminiscent of the few isolated cases of postwar violence by Nazi saboteurs. That mendacious retelling of history was quietly dropped as casualties mounted.

The United States needed a radically different approach. The Iraq Study Group recommended a traditional "diplomatic offensive" that would force Iraq's neighbors to broker reconciliation within Iraq. U.S. forces should scale back to a supporting role; combat forces should begin a withdrawal from Iraq. The report concluded that it was time for a "responsible transition," but President Bush opted for a different course. On January 10, 2007, he announced a "new way forward" for Iraq, a "surge" of five additional brigade combat teams to Iraq—a total of more than twenty thousand additional troops, with the main effort focused on securing the Iraqi capital. It was a break with a strategy of gradual disengagement. General George Casey, who had assumed the top command in Iraq in June 2004, had concentrated his efforts on handing off provinces to Iraqi control and confining U.S. troops to megabases away from population centers. That would all change. As part of the surge, U.S. forces would move to small combat outposts in residential neighborhoods, where they would work to expand security, block by block. To seal the deal, Bush selected a new top commander, General David Petraeus, the godfather of the counterinsurgency movement. Ryan Crocker, a career Foreign Service officer and fluent Arabic speaker, was named as Petraeus's civilian counterpart; he replaced Zalmay Khalilzad as U.S. ambassador to Iraq.

The surge plan was influenced in part by "Choosing Victory: A Plan for Success in Iraq," a paper authored by Frederick Kagan, a scholar at the neoconservative American Enterprise Institute, and retired General Jack Keane, a former Army vice chief of staff. The paper had been put forward by AEI in part as a response to the Iraq Study Group's report. It was rolled out at a December 2006 event at AEI's headquarters and then at a January event attended by Senators John McCain and Joseph Lieberman. The AEI report foreshadowed some aspects of the plan that Bush adopted, and the new Iraq strategy was also shaped by the newly adopted counterinsurgency manual. The new doctrine was not presented as Iraq-specific—it was supposed to be a generic guide for U.S. forces supporting a "host nation" government involved in battling an insurgency—but it was very much written with Iraq in mind. David Kilcullen, the Australian counterinsurgency guru who was heavily involved in crafting the document, called it "a manual on how to win in Iraq."

The counterinsurgency manual was meant in part to force a rethink of the military's fixation on "force protection," the fortress mentality that kept U.S. troops hunkered behind the walls of large, fortified bases. It featured a series of thought-provoking "paradoxes" that would encourage commanders to think more carefully about the application of lethal force and about preventing civilian harm:

Sometimes, the more you protect your force, the less secure you
    may be
Sometimes, the more force is used, the less effective it is
Sometimes, doing nothing is the best reaction
Some of the best weapons for counterinsurgents do not shoot

These sounded like politically correct talking points, or a clever way of selling counterinsurgency to the public, but they had a very real aim: collecting intelligence. If U.S. forces relied on blunt tools such as airstrikes or artillery, killed civilians at checkpoints, and generally kept everyone back one hundred meters from their convoys, as signs on their vehicles warned, they would never collect any meaningful information about the insurgency. A key appendix on using social network analysis and other intelligence tools drove the point home: In many respects the campaign would resemble policing a beat, as the military patrolled an area and mapped out and identified the insurgent networks and how they operated.

The field manual devoted an entire chapter to "unity of effort," the bureaucratic term for tightly integrating development work, diplomacy, and military operations. The Departments of State, Justice, and Treasury would all have to send representatives to work and live with the military and provide advice on governance, law enforcement, and finance. USAID would also have to subordinate its development programs to counterinsurgency strategy. The focal point of the development agency's efforts in Iraq was the Community Stabilization Program, a massive jobs and public-works program for Iraq. The program was supposed to keep young (fighting-age) Iraqi men away from the insurgency by putting them to work or enrolling them in vocational programs. The

tab for the Community Stabilization Program was a whopping $644 mil-
lion, more than the agency allocated to the Child Survival and Health
Programs Fund and the Development Assistance account for all of Asia
and the Near East in fiscal year 2005. The contract was controversial.
Many established nongovernmental organizations were skeptical that
such an ambitious program could be managed effectively (Mercy Corps, a
major U.S. nonprofit, declined to bid on the project for that reason). There
was also concern that the program was too overtly tied to counterinsurgency aims, rather than development goals, and was a textbook example
of how military operations and development work had become inter-
mingled. International Relief and Development, a large, well-established
USAID implementing partner, won the contract.

The surge also required a parallel diplomatic effort, a doubling of
the number of Provincial Reconstruction Teams and civilians serving
outside the Green Zone. Those new teams, called "embedded" or e-PRTs
because they would be attached directly to brigade combat teams or
regimental combat teams, were to be a key piece of the new Iraq strategy.
They were supposed to streamline military operations and civilian reconstruction efforts, which in the past had often been badly coordinated.
They were civilian-led by design (in Afghanistan, PRTs were led by military officers).

Unfortunately this civilian surge got off to a rough start, and the State
Department was slow to fill billets on the new Provincial Reconstruction
Teams. Further complicating matters, the Pentagon and the State Department could not agree on lines of responsibility, staffing plans, and
objectives for PRTs. According to a House Armed Services Committee
report, the State Department did not plan on "backfilling" these positions
until the end of September 2008, when the military surge would already
be winding down.[2]

On October 25, 2007, Harry Thomas, director-general of the Foreign
Service, sent out an announcement to staffers informing them that the
State Department had decided to begin "directed assignments" to fill an
anticipated shortfall of 48 diplomats in Iraq. Around 250 Foreign Service
officers received an e-mail informing them that they had been selected
as qualified for the posts. If enough of them did not step forward, some
of them would be ordered to Iraq. In theory, Foreign Service officers
were supposed to be available for worldwide deployment. Refuse an assignment, and you had to resign your commission. But this was the first

time since the Vietnam War that the State Department had contemplated ordering diplomats to serve in war zones.[3]

The following week, State Department management held a "town hall" forum at its Foggy Bottom headquarters whose purpose was to explain the decision to order Foreign Service officers to Iraq to make up for the lack of volunteers. The meeting turned into a bitter confrontation between diplomats and their senior management. One diplomat, Jack Croddy, seemed barely able to contain his rage as he took his turn at the microphone. Standing before the hundreds of diplomats assembled in the State Department's main auditorium, the gray-haired senior Foreign Service officer's face flushed and his voice quavered: "Incoming is coming in every day, rockets are hitting the Green Zone. So if you forced-assign people, that is really shifting the terms of what we are all about. It's one thing if someone believes in what's going on over there and volunteers, but it's another thing to send someone over there on a forced assignment. I'm sorry, but basically that's a potential death sentence and you know it."[4]

A wave of sustained applause swept through the auditorium. News accounts of the acrimonious town hall forum further bolstered a perception within the military that Foreign Service officers were elitists who refused to perform their duty while those in uniform made all the sacrifices. Many diplomats had served in harm's way since September 11, 2001, and the State Department did eventually find volunteers to fill the positions. Still, the damage to the reputation of the Foreign Service was lasting. In an open letter to colleagues posted on the State Department's Web site, John Matel, a career Foreign Service officer serving as the head of a Provincial Reconstruction Team in Iraq's Anbar Province, fretted that the Marines he served alongside would think of the government civilians as "wimps and weenies" because of the furor. "I personally dislike the whole idea of forced assignments, but we do have to do our jobs," he wrote.

> We signed up to be worldwide available. All of us volunteered
> for this kind of work and we have enjoyed a pretty sweet lifestyle
> most of our careers. I will not repeat what the Marines say when
> I bring up this subject. I tell them that most FSOs are not wimps
> and weenies. I will not share this article [about the town hall
> meeting] with them and I hope they do not see it. How could I

explain this wailing and gnashing of teeth? I just tried to explain it to one of my PRT members, a reserve [lieutenant colonel] called up to serve in Iraq. She asked me if all FSOs would get the R&R, extra pay etc. and if it was our job to do things like this. When I answered in the affirmative, she just rolled her eyes.[5]

Ted Andrews, a veteran Foreign Service officer, was on vacation in Florence with his wife in October 2007 when he picked up a copy of the *International Herald-Tribune* and spotted an article about the contentious town hall meeting at the State Department. He turned to his wife and drily remarked, "I wonder where I'm going."

Andrews didn't consider himself much of an adrenaline junkie. He was enjoying a peaceful diplomatic assignment in Brussels with his family, and he had no plans to volunteer to go into a war zone. Reading about the town hall tirade by Foreign Service officers, however, helped change his mind. A few weeks later, he signed up for a State Department billet on an embedded PRT in Iraq. "I don't want to sound like a great patriot," he told me the following December, as he neared the end of his tour in Baghdad, "but I didn't like the press. It made the State Department look pretty ridiculous—the people who were so vocally and openly complaining. And also the head of our personnel department is someone I really admire, and he was going out there and beating the drum for this. He's not a fool, so I said, 'All right, we'll go, because we've got one boy next year going to college.'" Pausing briefly, Andrews added, "I don't want to sound flippant. I thought it would be—it wouldn't be appropriate to say fun—I thought it would be really interesting sort of work." (Andrews's understatement was deliberate. Several of his colleagues, including a member of the PRT, were killed in the bombing of the Sadr City District Advisory Council in June of that year.)

Andrews was not a stranger to conflict; he had previously worked in Somalia, and he was posted to Kenya at the time of the 1998 embassy bombing in Nairobi. But until the "town hall" fiasco, he hadn't been particularly eager to volunteer to go to Iraq. The Foreign Service did offer sweeteners for serving on a PRT: They allowed families to stay at whatever post the diplomat was already assigned to, sparing them a disruptive move back to the United States. That meant children could stay in school, and they wouldn't have to move for just one year or thirteen months. The State Department also offered generous leave packages.

During their year-long deployment, diplomats serving on PRTs could take three long R&R breaks or two long R&Rs and three shorter breaks. It added up to a total of about two months of leave. By contrast, a typical Army tour in Iraq during the surge was fifteen months.

But Andrews's training for Iraq was abbreviated at best. The position he put in for was scheduled to begin in April; then the start date was moved up to March. Prior to deployment, he went through a five-day security course refresher, a version of the "crash and bang" course taught in West Virginia to teach basic survival skills for assignments to dangerous places. The first three days included intensive first aid; the training also featured a familiarization course on improvised explosive devices, the main threat in Iraq. The trainers showed gruesome videos of roadside bombs going off to remind trainees of how serious the dangers were. It was like a wartime version of the classroom scare movies they show in driver's education: If diplomats were riding along in a military vehicle, it was as much their job as it was a soldier's to stay alert and look out for a possible attack.

The diplomats also received a brief overview of weapons handling. It wasn't particularly intensive training. They took turns firing pistols, and learned the difference between the 9mm weapons carried by diplomatic security and the ones used by the military. Trainers also familiarized them with the ubiquitous AK-47, so they could recognize its distinctive sound, and the M4 carbine, the Army's standard carbine. Then they drove through a course where they saw simulated ambushes and roadside bomb attacks. The whole thing was sobering, but brief. Many people finished the course at noon on a Friday and flew out of Dulles International Airport to the Middle East at nine that night.

Diplomats assigned to PRTs were also supposed to get specific training in the United States on how the teams operated. Andrews never got around to that, because of the rush to get diplomats to the field during the surge. Likewise, he never had the chance to attend a mandatory orientation for e-PRT team members that was supposed to be held in one of Saddam Hussein's former palaces inside Baghdad's International Zone (also called the Green Zone). Andrews was originally scheduled to arrive on Easter Sunday, 2008, the day that insurgents unleashed a barrage of rocket and mortar fire on the IZ. The indirect-fire attacks continued for several more weeks. Andrews was sent instead to Camp Taji, a large base north of Baghdad, where he began his assignment with the Third Brigade

Combat Team, Fourth Infantry Division, which was responsible for the volatile Baghdad neighborhoods of Sadr City and Adhamiya.

"I've never taken the orientation class," Andrews said with a laugh. "They have an orientation for us, three days in the IZ at the palace, at the head office for the PRTs. I never took it, because there were all the rockets, and they said, don't come here." He continued with a chuckle. "I came straight to . . . Taji, and started working around. I learned everything on the job!"

Part of the job was to provide a civilian face for the brigade's "engagements" with local politicians and local business leaders in discussions about Civil Affairs projects. They were also there to provide some guidance and advice to local district councils. Living on a base, wearing body armor, and riding in military convoys was physically taxing: The middle-aged diplomat shed around twenty pounds during his deployment. And he had learned that progress in Iraq would be slow. "They're not going to have a 'victory-over-terrorism day,'" he said. "Just one day you're going to realize, we've gone six months without a big incident. And that's what normalcy will be."

The military took the lead in almost everything related to reconstruction. The e-PRT didn't have transport of its own, so Andrews and his colleagues had to hitch rides around the brigade's area of operations on military convoys. In briefings for the press or meetings with local dignitaries, the brigade commander was clearly in charge, although Andrews or another civilian was often at his elbow to provide some quiet advice. Andrews's case was somewhat extreme, but it reflected the general lack of training and preparation the State Department gave to diplomats, more than five years into the Iraq War. A picture Andrews kept on the wall of his office slyly underscored the absurdity of the situation. It showed a wrecked vehicle in the tank graveyard at Taji. On the rusting hulk someone had spray-painted DAD— STUCK IN IRAQ—SEND MONEY.

When Petraeus took command in Iraq, he selected a team of experts, called the Joint Strategic Assessment Team, that was tasked with creating a unified civil-military plan for the country. It was to combine all the elements of nation building: economic development, intelligence gathering, and security measures. Petraeus also invited David Kilcullen, an Australian counterinsurgency expert, to serve as his personal counterinsurgency advisor in Iraq. Kilcullen arrived in early 2007, and over the next year he traveled throughout the theater, serving as a sort of roving emissary for Petraeus. His role was to be an evangelizer for counterinsurgency "best practices," hammering home the basic principles of protecting the population, promoting development, and breaking the cycle of violence. It was an unusual choice to bring in a foreigner to tell the U.S. military how to do its job. In some respects, Kilcullen was reprising the role of Sir Robert Thompson, the Malaya counterinsurgency expert who had provided expert advice (and prescient warnings) to the U.S. military during the Vietnam war: a smart, articulate outsider who could tell the military what they did not want to hear.

In the small clique of counterinsurgency theorists, Kilcullen was a star. A reserve lieutenant colonel in the Australian Army, he had been seconded to State Department's Office of the Coordinator for Counterterrorism as an expert on guerrilla warfare.[6] His exotic résumé read like a document from another era. He had made use of the Australian Army's generous leave to conduct field work in West Java for a doctoral dissertation on Indonesian insurgent groups. As a soldier he had taught tactics at the British School of Infantry; served on peacekeeping operations in Cyprus and Bougainville; and worked as a military advisor to the Indonesian Special Forces.[7] He had also worked in several countries of the Middle East. Perhaps most famously, he negotiated a ceasefire after a border clash between Australian troops and the Indonesian army, police, and militia in October 1999, during the UN-mandated intervention in East Timor.[8] The incident occurred in the town of Motaain, close to the border with Indonesian West Timor. The Indonesian army was using an old Dutch map that showed Motaain west of the border; the UN's map, printed in Indonesia, showed Motaain in the east.[9] Television footage shot at the time showed Kilcullen crossing Motaain Bridge in the open, with his hands up, to meet with his Indonesian counterparts, compare maps, and broker a ceasefire.[10]

Kilcullen had also participated in the drafting of the Army–Marine Corps counterinsurgency manual. But his participation at the Fort Leavenworth counterinsurgency seminar in February 2006 was interrupted by an urgent phone call. There had been a bombing at the al-Askari mosque in Samarra. Kilcullen needed to get to Iraq as quickly as possible. What Kilcullen found on this trip to Iraq was dispiriting: The U.S. military had been slow to respond to the accelerating internal war. On a visit to the deputy of Muwaffak al Rubai'e, Iraq's national security advisor, Kilcullen noted the disconnect as U.S. military briefers delivered an eye-glazing, acronym-laden PowerPoint presentation filled with "metrics" detailing the latest trends in Iraq. The American briefers were focusing mostly on their recent raids against insurgent groups and ignoring the impact that the burgeoning civil war was having on the population. "[I]t took approximately four and a half months, from the Samarra bombing until mid-July 2006, for these slides to begin reflecting what the Iraqi political staff (who worked less than 50 yards from the briefing room but were not allowed into it) had told me the very week of the bombing: that Samarra was a disaster that fundamentally and irrevocably altered the nature of the war," Kilcullen wrote.[11]

Iraq's violent civil war continued for the rest of the year. In parallel, Kilcullen and his allies within the national security bureaucracy started working on a way to salvage the situation and get the rest of the government more fully involved in the mission. By late 2006, counterinsurgency was all the rage within military circles, even as commanders on the ground were still trying to get a grip on its practice. The same could not be said for the civilian side of government—even if, as theory held, civilian-led nation building was the most important part of a counterinsurgency campaign.

Shortly after the September 2006 U.S. government counterinsurgency conference in Washington, Kilcullen and a few others within the State Department started working on a new interagency counterinsurgency guide, a handbook for civilian policymakers that was supposed to drive home the importance of nation building. A less-than-subtle agenda was at work: If the Army–Marine Corps counterinsurgency manual was supposed to push the uniformed military to embrace "soft power," the new guide was supposed to get diplomats, aid officials, and other civilians to get in touch with their hard-power military side.

But the new document needed to be more than just a Cliff's Notes version of the Army–Marine Corps counterinsurgency doctrine. The new guide was a manual on how to win Iraq, but it wasn't necessarily going to help in Afghanistan or in any other future contingency. It focused heavily on twentieth-century Maoist-style insurgencies, rather than on the sophisticated, globally connected insurgencies the U.S. government was expected to face in the future. Kilcullen wanted a document that took a more contemporary view of the problem. More important, he wanted to force policymakers to think about a larger issue: when—and when not—to intervene. Kilcullen made little effort to conceal the fact that he viewed the decision to invade Iraq as a grave strategic mistake, and he wanted to make clear that aiding a government involved in counterinsurgency did not have to require deploying a large, conventional U.S. military force. The counterinsurgents once again reached for historical precedent. Air Force Lieutenant Colonel Edward Lansdale, one of the models for the eponymous character in Graham Greene's *The Quiet American*, was sent as an expert advisor to the Philippine leader Ramon Magsaysay during the Communist-dominated Hukbalahap rebellion. The United States supported El Salvador's counterinsurgency with a limited number of military advisors in the 1980s. This new document studied the problems of intervention, and showed when and how to intervene.

The first draft of the document ran to around two hundred pages. That was too long for the kinds of busy senior policymakers—cabinet members, National Security Council staffers, presidential envoys—that Kilcullen and the counterinsurgents wanted to reach. It needed to be fifty pages, tops, with a crisp executive summary. Kilcullen decided to refocus the document. Just two weeks after the near revolt at the State Department over news of the directed assignments, Kilcullen hosted a workshop in a rented conference room at a hotel in Arlington, Virginia. Representatives of over half a dozen government agencies and from think tanks, academia, the media, and several foreign embassies participated. Kilcullen, who only recently had returned from Iraq, tried to relay the gravity of the situation to the attendees. "This doctrine that we're looking at here actually saves lives," he said.

During his recent tour in Iraq, Kilcullen had traversed the violent landscape, visiting e-PRTs, brigade commanders, and Iraqi officials in a frenetic effort to reinforce the basic principles of counterinsurgency: unity of effort, civilian and military cooperation. "To fix that, we had to sit out in the field with these e-PRTs, work out their problems, and identify what's going on," he said.

> And it's easy to say that, but doing that involves transiting areas. We lost aircraft trying to get out to e-PRTs . . . We had a Humvee crew drown in their vehicle when they were hit by an IED getting out to the e-PRT to talk about their command and control structure. Moving through ambush after ambush to deal with

little problems that could have been solved in a handbook written
a thousand miles away that just didn't come in time. So we had to
be out there doing it—and eventually losing people to snipers and
to IEDs and so on to make this thing work.

The effort carried a price, he grimly concluded. "I reckon conserva-
tively we lost about a dozen people because we didn't have a doctrine," he
said.

As Kilcullen concluded, the manual was supposed to spell out the
roles of civilian and military agencies that would be involved in these
sorts of interventions for the foreseeable future: "It's so that you don't
hunker down in some building with people shooting at you and some
full colonel saying, 'What are you supposed to be doing here?' and we
certainly don't need to lose people trying to get out and explain stuff that
people should already know."

This new document was just one part of the solution. The civilian
agencies of government needed to be more "expeditionary"—more military, better able to deploy on short notice, practiced in cooperating with
the military, ready to work in war zones. The U.S. military has a deep
bench: In addition to an active-duty force, it has an extensive reserve
system that it can call on in a crisis. During the Cold War, the National
Guard and the reserves were standing by for "the big one" if war broke
out with the Soviet Union. In the post-9/11 era, the military drew heavily
on reserves, especially Army National Guard units, to support rotations
in Iraq and Afghanistan. The system worked, despite the strain of repeated deployments. But the diplomatic corps and the civilian agencies of
government had no civilian equivalent. Absent a large reserve, nation-
building missions would continue to depend heavily on civilian contractors who could deploy to a crisis zone on short notice.

With the creation of the Office of the Coordinator for Reconstruction
and Stabilization in August 2004 the State Department took the first ten-
tative steps toward building a more "expeditionary" diplomatic corps.
The new office, known as S/CRS (S stands for State Department's Office of
the Secretary), was supposed to be the home for a new kind of diplomat,
"muddy-boots" Foreign Service officers and civil servants who would
work outside the walls of the traditional embassy and focus on working
in conflict and postconflict environments. It was a direct response to the
failures in Iraq, where the diplomatic corps had been slow to mobilize for

the reconstruction. In theory, members of the new office would be the diplomatic equivalent of Special Forces teams, ready to parachute into remote, often hostile, places with minimal support to prevent a localized conflict from becoming a regional crisis.

The creation of the new office was exciting news for adventurous young diplomats like John Mongan; Mongan learned about S/CRS as he was preparing to deploy to a Provincial Reconstruction Team in Afghanistan. Mongan needed a new assignment after his one-year tour, so he approached the new office, submitted a résumé, and made a point of keeping in touch with them while he was in the field. It sounded like a perfect fit. Mongan wanted a job that would allow him to keep working in trouble spots, instead of rotating back to a routine management job in Foggy Bottom. He turned down other State Department jobs, having gotten a promise from the new head of S/CRS that he would have a place within the new organization. But when Mongan began his job, at S/CRS in August 2005, he learned that he would not be returning to the field anytime soon. His first task at S/CRS was to write up a recruiting paper so they could begin filling the first fifteen one-year positions for something called the Active Response Corps, or ARC, which would form the core of the new civilian reserve. In other words, S/CRS had not even begun staffing its first diplomatic crisis-response team.

In its first year of existence, S/CRS invested in building a Washington office but put little money into training, which was essential if the State Department wanted to have bureaucrats standing by for deployment. To work in these war zones, they would need hostile environment training and language skills; they would have to be adept at negotiating with local warlords, nongovernmental organizations, and military officers; and they would need to take part in training exercises. Part of the problem was managerial. Secretary of State Colin Powell founded S/CRS shortly before he left the administration, so the initiative foundered without high-level backing. And in January 2006, his successor, Secretary of State Condoleezza Rice, launched "transformational diplomacy," a broader effort to put the State Department on a war footing by shifting more assignments within the Foreign Service from coveted embassy slots in Europe to posts in the developing world. In parallel, Rice restructured USAID, folding its planning staff into the State Department and elevating the USAID administrator to a rank equivalent to that of deputy secretary of state. Although the move stopped short of merging USAID completely with State, it further marginalized an organization that should have played a key role in fixing failed states.

The first test of the Active Response Corps was in Sudan's Darfur region. In May 2006, the Darfur Peace Agreement, signed in Abuja, Nigeria, brought a fragile accord between the Khartoum government and one of Darfur's rebel factions. S/CRS sent Eythan Sontag, one of the eleven officers of the Active Response Corps, and Keith Mines to help implement the peace agreement by persuading other rebel groups to join the peace process. Mines was now stationed in Ottawa as a political officer and had volunteered for duty as a standby officer. The ARC team had to scout a location for a modest, fortified headquarters on the outskirts of El Fasher; hire a small local staff of drivers, custodians, and interpreters; and set up a remote office using a Very Small Aperture Terminal, a satellite Internet connection.[12] Both Sontag and Mines were former Army officers, and they gravitated to work in crisis zones. The government needed more than just a self-selected group of civil servants and diplomats standing by to be international first responders, but at that point the Active Response Corps had a full-time staff of only a dozen people.

ARC's deployment to Darfur, then, was a trial run of something much more ambitious. Just a few weeks after announcing the Iraq surge, in his 2007 State of the Union address, President Bush proposed a dramatic initiative, the creation of a volunteer Civilian Reserve Corps: "Such a corps would function much like our military reserve. It would ease the burden on the Armed Forces by allowing us to hire civilians with critical skills to serve on missions abroad when America needs them. And it would give people across America who do not wear the uniform a chance to serve in the defining struggle of our time."

In theory, the CRC would be a sort of supersized Peace Corps, stacked with experts in nation building. It would be a complex, three-tiered organization, built in stages. The first stage would comprise active and standby components drawn from government ranks. The active component, around 250 strong, would be trained to deploy within forty-eight hours. The standby corps, about 2,000 individuals drawn from around eight federal agencies, would be available to respond within thirty days of a crisis. The second stage, creating the reserve component, would be a much more ambitious, long-term project. It would be drawn from a roster of citizens in all walks of life who were willing to serve as temporary

U.S. government employees in support of overseas reconstruction and stabilization operations: civil engineers, agricultural experts, city managers, public health officials, police officers, corrections officials. They would provide the boots on the ground and the expertise that the government simply did not have.

Officials within S/CRS acknowledged that this stage would be easier said than done. How would reservists be paid? What would happen if they were injured or killed on the job? Would they be considered full government employees, or would they be glorified temps? None of the details were clear, and there were thorny legal issues that would have to be resolved. When military reservists are called up, their employers are required by law to release them and rehire them when their service is complete. If a volunteer for the Civilian Response Corps were not offered similar legal protection, they would have little incentive to leave their jobs and deploy to a war zone or a postconflict environment.

The biggest problem, however, was the budget. If the goal was to have a real "whole of government" nation-building team—a true twenty-first-century Colonial Office—it would need full funding from Congress. Without money to cover the cost of salaries, buy war-zone survival equipment, and develop a training program, the whole thing would be an exercise in paper shuffling.

In its brief existence S/CRS managed to lure some motivated and talented people. Beverli DeWalt, a member of the Civilian Response Corps, Active component, joined the Foreign Service in November 2003 and served her first tour in Islamabad as a consular officer. She spoke Urdu, a key language, and had served at the U.S. mission to NATO in Brussels as a political officer specializing in Iraq and civil-military issues. In 2008, she worked at the U.S. embassy in Pristina to help pave the way for Kosovo's declaration of independence. That same year, she served for about six months as a political, governance, and women's issues advisor at the Kapisa and Parwan Provincial Reconstruction Team in Afghanistan. In short, she was the kind of person who was a natural fit with the new kind of diplomacy.

But this new breed of diplomatic first responder was not a natural fit with the culture of the State Department, in which everything revolved around the embassy hierarchy. They were still bureaucratic orphans. And the deployment cycle for active-duty members of the Civilian Response Corps was a strain; they often spent six months in the field, then six months back at home. Back-to-back rotations were difficult for the military, but at least the troops could rely on an extensive support network for their families back at home. It was an imperfect system, but the expectation of spending time in the field was built into the system, part of the normal cycle of deployment. The Civilian Response Corps did not have that infrastructure. Unlike regular diplomatic assignments, their postings to the field were "unaccompanied," meaning that their spouses, if they had them, could not go with them. It made for a less than ideal social life, and was a major disincentive for joining the State Department's nation-building force.

I asked DeWalt if she had a family. "Mom and Dad," she said quietly. "A sister." Was anyone else in the small group at S/CRS married? Did they have children?

"Let me go through this," she said. "The director does, but he doesn't really deploy much." Ticking off the rest of the group on her fingers, she continued, "Single, single, single—sensing a theme here?—married with one kid. The majority are single."

S/CRS's corps of diplomatic first responders was the exception: Most diplomats were still being posted to dangerous places without much thought or preparation. James Hunter was the first Foreign Service officer stationed to the Asadabad PRT, a remote firebase in a high-walled mountain valley in Afghanistan's Kunar Province, not far from the Pakistan border. Hunter was the lone PRT civilian at the outpost, where a contingent of sixty-seven American troops, a mix of regular Army and Special Forces, and later Marines, defended the base. Fortunately, the military scrapped plans to withdraw some of the soldiers guarding the base. Otherwise, maintaining Americans in each guard position—a necessity, since the base was ten miles from the border with Pakistan— would have taken up all the time of everyone on the base, Hunter included. The small fort was under attack on average at least once a week. One night they could even observe the Taliban fighters coming down on the opposite side of the valley, setting up mortars to fire at the base. Hunter grew accustomed to the distinctive sound of incoming 107mm rockets whistling across the valley. A few even flew right over his position. It sounded just like in the movies.

Out in Asadabad, Hunter felt as if he was at the very end of the line. As far as the embassy in Kabul was concerned, "We fell off the face of the earth." He had to send in reporting cables, minus the sensitive information, by Hotmail account: The embassy had not yet arranged for secure communication with Kabul. Still, Hunter threw himself into his work, compiling detailed biographical files on the major tribal players and local officials in Kunar and Nuristan provinces. By the time he left his "bio files" extended to about 350 pages; the document provided the U.S. mission with key insights into the "human terrain" of this part of Afghanistan.

Still, it was a job that required skills that were not remotely part of Foreign Service training. The PRT worked with people from the Korengal Valley, a densely forested river valley in Kunar Province that was home to a proud, insular tribal community that offered a haven for insurgents. A convoy traveling through the valley in the spring of 2005 hit an ambush. The column of vehicles was stuck on the road while gunfire cracked overhead. At one point, Hunter borrowed an M4 carbine from the driver, climbed out of the truck, and began returning fire—firing aimed shots, just as he had been trained to do in the military. "I didn't spray and pray," he recalled.

During the hour-long fight, Hunter also helped hand up ammo to the turret gunner in the Humvee who was sweeping insurgent positions with his machine gun. His actions sent a message to the soldiers that the lone civilian could also handle himself in a firefight, although he knew that many of his colleagues back at the embassy in Kabul would prefer that he never pick up a weapon. Hunter was not one to overdramatize: Later he self-deprecatingly said, "It sounds a lot more dramatic than it felt like at the time. And my role was a minor one."

The incident drove home how the diplomatic service was quietly becoming more militarized. It also underscored a lingering gap. The State Department and other civilian agencies were struggling to find enough personnel to support the nation-building effort, and the military was stretched thin. That gap would be filled by another force: an army of contract hires.

CHAPTER 9

Kalashnikovs for Hire

The conflicts in Iraq and Afghanistan transformed the American way of war. Many of the changes were technological: The proliferation of robotic systems, digital communications, and high-end surveillance equipment gave military commanders an extremely fine-grained picture of the battlefield. Advances in battlefield medicine and protective gear made the individual soldier much more likely to survive contact with the enemy. The pairing of new precision weapons with twenty-first-century command and control gave the U.S. military unprecedented reach, lethality, and accuracy. But another, equally potent transformation was also under way: the privatization of armed force. The conflicts in Iraq and Afghanistan were accompanied by a phenomenal expansion of government outsourcing.

By the summer of 2008, the number of civilian contractors supporting U.S. military operations in Iraq, Afghanistan, and the Balkans matched the number of deployed troops one to one. In Iraq, the contracted workforce at its peak was 190,000, roughly equal to the total number of uniformed personnel.[1] In Afghanistan, contractors also outnumbered troops: By December 2009, the number of Defense Department contractors in the country had reached 104,100, greater than the total number of U.S. troops (98,000) that were expected to be in the country after new reinforcements arrived.[2]

The phenomenal rise of battlefield contracting completely changed the incentives for serving the government overseas. It created a perception that money came first and service second. But without the contracted workforce, the U.S. military could not stay on an expeditionary footing. Contractors serviced and maintained sophisticated military equipment; ran city-sized forward operating bases and airstrips; supervised an army of imported laborers who worked in dining facilities, cleaned latrines, and delivered fuel; and provided intelligence support, translation services, and myriad other services. Manpower was needed for nation building, too, but when a U.S. citizen could earn a six-figure salary working as a contractor, why would she take a pay cut to serve as a temporary government bureaucrat seconded to the State Department or USAID? If the government needed a civilian nation-building corps, it was competing with private companies for talent.

The business of diplomatic protection was the starkest example of this manpower crisis. The State Department did have a small cadre of diplomatic security officers who provided protective services to ambassadors and other VIPs. They specialized in what was called "close protection," or personal security details—PSDs, to use the inevitable acronym. Personal security work was essentially VIP protection, guarding a "principal," and it implied that some lives were worth more than others. It required a different mind-set than soldiering. When an infantry team hits an ambush, soldiers are taught to respond, return fire, and then counterattack. But in close protection, the idea is to get the principal "off the X"—away from the point of contact. If a PSD doesn't provide the principal with a cover and evacuation force, they are potentially leaving the principal in the open to get shot.

With more diplomats and Foreign Service types working in harm's way on nation-building missions, however, there were simply not enough PSDs to keep up with the new demand. The government turned to the private sector, creating a new boom market for bodyguards. This army of private soldiers became one of the most problematic aspects of the American experiment in nation building.

"What's your blood type?"

It was an unusual question for a driver to ask when picking up a passenger at the airport. But this was not your ordinary car service: We were about to make the drive between Baghdad International Airport and downtown Baghdad, a dozen kilometers away. "Route Irish," as the military designated the Baghdad airport road, was a magnet for suicide car bombers and rocket-propelled grenade teams. By December 2005, when I touched down at Baghdad airport, stories about the world's most dangerous road were already journalistic cliché. U.S. and Iraqi troops had in fact stepped up patrols along Route Irish, but the journey to the center of Baghdad was still a white-knuckle ride.

I was in Iraq as a guest of Erinys, a British security firm. *Expert*, a Russian newsmagazine, had sent me on assignment to tag along with Erinys's "Russians," a group of professional soldiers from the former Soviet Union. Though most of the company's expatriate management was British, North American, or South African, they also employed a handful of Slavs: The team meeting me at the airport was composed of Russians and Ukrainians, and their team leader was a former French soldier. It was a reminder of how much the United States relied on a multinational army of hired help to keep the occupation functioning. I had flown into Iraq on a Royal Jordanian flight crewed by South Africans, disembarked under the gaze of an armed Fijian employed by a company called Global Strategies Group, and queued for a visa with guest workers from South Asia.

We entered the underground parking garage at the airport, where the gun trucks of different security firms were idling before making the next dash down Route Irish. The place fairly reeked of testosterone. As we suited up in body armor and helmets for the ride into town, the competing teams sized each other up. It was easy to spot the road warriors with the U.S. firm Blackwater, who were mounting up in their South Africa–built Mamba mine-proof vehicles. They cultivated a look of deliberate menace, favoring Terminator-style wraparound shades, goatees, and lots of tattoos. Another protective team in the garage sported Mohawks. Erinys had a spiffier, more corporate image. Its contractors wore blue polo shirts and khaki trousers, though they were unmistakably well armed. It was easy to detect a sort of hierarchy here. At the top, U.S. Special Operations veterans could command salaries of up to a thousand dollars a day to guard diplomats and VIPs. Further down the chain, veterans of cash-strapped former Soviet armies earned two hundred dollars a day or less to ferry around civilian engineers and guard supply convoys. At the bottom of the pay scale, Ugandan soldiers earned a thousand dollars a month to guard dining halls. (Security was particularly tight at military dining facilities after a suicide bomber struck one at Forward Operating Base Marez near Mosul in late 2004.)

Today's mission was fairly straightforward: to deliver the new arrivals from the airport to the company's headquarters just outside the International Zone. As the convoy of armored trucks rumbled past the outer perimeter of the airport, the contractors racked back the slides on their Kalashnikov rifles: We were entering the Red Zone (in military protocol, a "red" weapon has a round in the chamber and is ready to fire). Out on the Baghdad airport road they would have to be on maximum alert, watching in all directions for any potential attacker. As they hurtled along at high speed, the lead driver called out possible threats on the radio: a car rolling up on an access road, a taxicab that was slow to pull over to the right, an oncoming highway overpass (bridges and overpasses were a favorite ambush spot). As the three-vehicle convoy blew through traffic, I could see the turret gunner in the lead truck scanning the traffic with his rifle. The contractors stopped only for coalition checkpoints, which they flashed through after showing a vehicle pass.

Night was falling, and a fine cloud of dust further obscured visibility on the highway. Did that scrap of trash on the side of the road conceal a roadside bomb? Was that taxicab tilting on its suspension because of a heavy suitcase, or a bomb in the trunk? Was that man watching the traffic from a plastic chair acting as a spotter for insurgents, or was he just bored and unemployed?

The convoy finally exited the highway and entered a traffic roundabout that led to a residential neighborhood. This was Mansour, an upscale residential neighborhood of Baghdad not far from the International Zone. Baghdad in late 2005 was the scene of a brewing sectarian war, and the entrances to streets were barricaded by concrete barriers. High blast walls pasted with posters from the recent general election shielded many of the houses. Our convoy pulled into a side street barricaded with more concrete and razor wire. Iraqi guards with Kalashnikovs pulled aside a traffic barrier, and we rolled into Erinys headquarters, a couple of villas fortified by blast walls plus an assortment of trailers.

After I stowed my gear in a trailer, the tattooed former British soldier who was a manager for the firm gave me a short tour of the compound.

Erinys contractors' stay in Baghdad was an all-inclusive deal: The company provided all the necessities—weapons, body armor, tactical gear, polo shirts. A small canteen provided three meals a day, usually sandwiches or burgers for lunch, and rice and kebabs for dinner. Accommodations were basic. Some staff lived in the trailers parked outside, and the Russian team bunked in a couple of small rooms inside the main house, where they shared a single desktop computer for e-mailing friends and family, and had a satellite television with a subscription to Russian channels. The atmosphere was sober. After a mission, they could lift weights outside, chat online, or clean their weapons. On Thursday nights there was a barbecue. In Iraq, the mission roster was usually pretty light on Fridays. Alcohol was available: Unlike U.S. troops, who were under General Order No. 1, which prohibits alcohol consumption, contractors could unwind over beers. But the Slavs, playing against type, did not indulge. They told me they needed to stay sharp on the road.

The manager then escorted me to the roof of the villa. From the top floor we had a spectacular panorama of Baghdad by night, and a commanding view of the surrounding streets. Aside from the unsettling sight of some tracers arcing in the distance, it was almost pleasant in the cool evening breeze. But my companion had not brought me up here to appreciate the view. "If we get attacked, we need you to get up here as fast as you can," he told me.

The roof of the villa was sandbagged, an Alamo in the event of an attack. My companion then pointed out the main approaches to the neighborhood, with a traffic roundabout here, a checkpoint there, and then another fortified compound that belonged to an Iraqi politician. "The good news is," he said, "they'll have to get through two firefights to get here."

But he was getting around to another point. "I want you to carry a weapon." I hesitated, but only for a second: I was here as an observer, not as a participant, and the only thing I was planning on shooting were pictures. In the Red Zone, the contractors were on their own. In theory, if they came under attack they could call for backup from the military. In practice, they weren't counting on a quick reaction force to save them. The company armorer issued me a 9mm pistol, two magazines of ammo, and a holster. For good measure, he put a Kalashnikov rifle in my trailer. If the place did come under attack, I was expected to pitch in.

If you needed a journalist to help out in a firefight, then you were probably already done for. But the contractors were mindful of incidents like the ambush of a KBR supply convoy in April 2004, in which half a dozen unarmed civilian truckers were killed, along with two Army soldiers who were escorting their convoy. It later emerged that the convoy drove down a road that was supposed to be off limits, but an officer who was supposed to send an e-mail about the no-go route inadvertently sent the memo to himself.[3] Also in April 2004, four Blackwater guards blundered into an ambush in Fallujah. The mutilated and burned bodies of two of them were strung up from a bridge, an image that blanketed international news channels.

The situation also underscored the lawlessness of Iraq. Erinys contractors were contractually limited to defensive work. Under guidelines issued by the coalition, they were not allowed to participate in offensive combat operations. They could use force to protect their clients, defend installations and equipment, and protect themselves.* Multi-National Force Iraq was supposed to issue weapons cards authorizing contractors to carry certain light weapons, but the guidelines also made it clear that they were not combatants. It was an important legal distinction for the military, which wanted to ensure that civilian contractors didn't cross the line into being active combatants. In mid-2005, the Defense Department had quietly revised the Defense Federal Acquisition Regulation Supplement, or DFARS, to underscore the rules governing contractors who deployed with or supported the U.S. military overseas. According to a notice issued by the Defense Department, DFARS "has been amended to caution that contractor personnel are not combatants and shall not undertake any role that would jeopardize that status."

The careful bureaucratic language could not change a simple fact: Contractors in Iraq fell into a legal gray area. They carried weapons and worked on behalf of the U.S. government (in the case of Erinys, their main client was the U.S. Army Corps of Engineers Gulf Region District),

---

* The contractors received laminated "rules for the use of force," or RUF cards, similar to the "rules of engagement" cards issued to soldiers. A RUF card issued in May 2005 said private security contractor personnel were authorized to use deadly force only when necessary in "self-defense, defense of facilities / persons as specified in their contract; prevention of life-threatening acts directed against civilians; or defense of Coalition-approved property specified within their contract."

although they wore no uniforms and did not report to the military chain of command.

Sending diplomats and aid experts to rebuild Iraq sounded like a good idea: Civilians had the kind of expertise in governance, state building, and development that few soldiers had. But the State Department and other civilian agencies were even less prepared than the conventionally trained U.S. military for the kind of hit-and-run warfare they faced in Iraq and Afghanistan. Nor had the State Department originally planned that its embassies would become fortresses.

At the height of the Cold War, U.S. diplomatic missions were designed around a single architectural principle: openness. The United States was locked in an ideological struggle with the Soviet Union, and its embassies were supposed to convey a message of progress, innovation, and accessibility. After the Second World War, the State Department was able to tap foreign credits from Lend-Lease settlements and postwar reconstruction funds to pay for new embassies, consular offices, and cultural centers. According to Jane Loeffler, a historian of U.S. diplomatic architecture, this novel financing arrangement allowed the State Department to fund new embassies with minimal congressional interference and to commission designs that celebrated transparency and modernity.[4]

These new embassy buildings, Loeffler writes,

> became symbols of the United States and its desire to be perceived as an energetic and future-oriented nation. Thus the buildings themselves served as cultural advertisements, propaganda perhaps, but nothing less than reflection of architectural theory married to political necessity. Not surprisingly, the symbols themselves were ambiguous—at once elegant and refined, decorative and flamboyant. Though often concealed behind wood, metal, or masonry screens, the buildings called attention to themselves with the openness of their glass walls, their overall accessibility, and their conspicuous newness.[5]

The violent, tumultuous 1960s and 1970s forced something of a rethink in U.S. embassy design. The Viet Cong assault on the fortresslike U.S. embassy compound in Saigon during the 1968 Tet Offensive was a

tactical failure, but it had a profound symbolic effect. Images of the evacuation of the U.S. embassy in Saigon in 1975 and the storming of the U.S.
embassy in Tehran in 1979 further underscored the vulnerability of U.S.
diplomatic missions overseas. The decisive shift away from open embassy
design occurred in the aftermath of the suicide bomb attack on the U.S.
embassy in Beirut in 1983, an incident that claimed the lives of seventeen
Americans and thirty-four Lebanese employees and decimated the CIA's
Middle East operation, which was based out of the compound.

In the wake of the bombing, Secretary of State George Shultz appointed a retired admiral, Bobby Inman, to head an advisory panel on
diplomatic security. His report, which came out in 1985, identified vulnerable facilities overseas, and it recommended stringent new building
standards for U.S. embassies.* No more sleek, smoked-glass facades:
Buildings would have blast-proof walls and windows and would be surrounded by high walls, security cameras, and monitors. The panel recommended that the State Department embark on a long-term plan to
renovate or replace office buildings at 126 overseas posts in order to reduce their vulnerability to attack. Instead of the open plan, embassies
would have to be designed around a new principle: "setback." New embassy compounds would have layered defenses. They would be built at
least one hundred feet from the street, have a more forbidding outer perimeter, and be far less accessible.[6] And they would no longer be situated
in busy downtown areas and open to visitors, which would make the job
of public diplomacy much harder. The embassy and its inhabitants would
become more isolated from the world outside.

Equally important, the Inman report called for creation of a Bureau of
Diplomatic Security. The bureau was given a wide remit: issue security
clearances for diplomatic personnel; conduct background checks; investigate passport and visa fraud; and supervise the security of diplomatic and
consular offices. It was also to provide bodyguard details for the secretary
of state, the U.S. ambassador to the United Nations, and foreign VIPs visiting the United States. Diplomatic Security special agents are federal law
enforcement officers. In the United States, they help guard foreign embassies and consulates. Overseas, they serve as regional security officers responsible for embassy security and the safety of diplomatic personnel.

---

* The Inman report's formal title is "Report of the Secretary of State's Advisory Panel on
Overseas Security."

The bureau, however, was not equipped to handle a massive nation-building enterprise. The Inman panel originally recommended a force of 1,156 special agents, hardly enough to take on the full range of missions at the time. (Two decades later, the bureau had grown to about 1,450 special agents.) In the mid-1990s, the bureau began quietly augmenting its force with contracted personal security specialists, first hiring contractors to provide security in Haiti, then deploying them to the Balkans, Gaza, and the West Bank. The State Department also contracted Dyn-Corp to provide personal security details to President Hamid Karzai of Afghanistan in 2002.[7]

The invasion of Iraq and the deployment of diplomats and civilians to work in reconstruction projects created an explosion in demand for contracted security. The Coalition Provisional Authority was a major customer for private guards. It hired a previously obscure company called Blackwater to provide a high-end protective detail for Ambassador Paul Bremer, the head of the CPA. The U.S. Army Corps of Engineers Gulf Region District, which oversaw massive infrastructure projects in Iraq, also hired its own army of private security operators to ferry its engineers and specialists around the country. Through the Corps, the military even hired a contractor to oversee the other contractors. With so many private security convoys operating on the roads, competing firms needed to find a way to share intelligence about threat conditions: routes that were safest to travel, places where roadside bomb attacks and ambushes were taking place, no-go areas where coalition forces were conducting combat operations. They also needed to reduce the risk of shooting at each other or being shot at by coalition forces. Well-armed private security details often traveled in unmarked vehicles. They were easy to mistake for insurgents, and on more than a few occasions, private security details and military forces mistakenly shot at each other (something euphemistically referred to as "blue-on-white" incidents, a reference to friendly, or "blue" forces, and contractors, referred to in military shorthand as "white" forces).[8]

In May 2004, the British security firm Aegis Defence Services Ltd. won the first Reconstruction Security Support Services contract to build the Reconstruction Operations Center as a hub to oversee a network of reconstruction projects. The ROC was supposed to serve as an interface between uniformed troops and private security. It tracked contractor vehicles with transponders and distributed sanitized military intelligence such as the grid coordinates of recent roadside bomb attacks and information on threat levels. It was also supposed to introduce some kind of accountability and oversight. Security operators were supposed to file route plans and report weapons discharges. The system evolved into a network of six regional ROCs as well as a national intelligence center in Baghdad. The company subsequently won two extensions to a contract initially worth $293 million, and the ROC contract effectively put Aegis on the map.

Iraq in 2003 and 2004 was a Klondike for security firms. Previously unknown firms such as Custer Battles, a start-up founded by two former Army Rangers, scored multi-million-dollar awards to provide security in the chaotic postwar environment. As the *Wall Street Journal* reported, no banks would lend new firms money, so the Coalition Provisional Authority had to lend Custer Battles $2 million. It arrived in the form of $100 bills that one of the company founders had to stow in a duffel bag and deposit in a Lebanese bank.[9] What private security providers called the "Baghdad bubble" created enormous new opportunities in a relative niche market for high-end security services. In early 2003, before the ouster of Saddam Hussein's regime, ArmorGroup had conducted a survey of the total global market for "high-end" protective security (bodyguard services for government clients in war zones and other high-threat areas). They estimated a total global market of $900 million per year. In 2007 the company repeated the survey. The estimated value of the security market had risen to $2.5 billion.*

Before Iraq, low-key British firms such as Control Risks and Global, companies often staffed by former commandos from British and Commonwealth armies, dominated the private security field, providing bodyguard services, security consulting for high-risk regions, and occasionally kidnap-and-ransom negotiation services. But with the American government now the biggest customer in Iraq, there were glowing prospects for U.S. firms—especially when they could recruit U.S. citizens with security clearances.

The biggest players in this new market were three U.S. firms: Blackwater,

---

* Peter Singer, the author of the authoritative study *Corporate Warriors: The Rise of the Privatized Military Industry*, reckoned in 2004 that the size of the global market for private military companies was around $100 billion. But that figure included logistics and construction firms like KBR, consulting and training companies like MPRI, and major defense contractors like General Dynamics and Lockheed Martin, which maintained complex military equipment. ArmorGroup's survey was limited to companies that provided armed protective services in high-threat areas.

Triple Canopy, and DynCorp. In early 2004, as the Coalition Provisional Authority prepared to hand over power to a provisional Iraqi government, the State Department issued additional task orders to its Worldwide Personal Protective Services contract to hire additional contracted security for the planned opening of the U.S. embassy in Baghdad on July 1, 2004. DynCorp was unable to meet the rush requirements for additional guards and personnel, so the State Department signed a second contract, with Blackwater.[10] Meanwhile, Triple Canopy won a key contract to provide protective services for the Regional Embassy Office in Basra.[11] In July 2005, the State Department formalized the arrangement, selecting the three U.S. security firms to compete for task orders under the new Worldwide Personal Protective Services (WPPS) II contract, a program worth a potential $1.2 billion to each contractor over five years to provide protective services to U.S. diplomatic personnel in war zones. WPPS II task orders included missions in Afghanistan, Bosnia, Iraq, and Israel. The private guard force would help protect a gargantuan new embassy rising on the Tigris River, a billion-dollar complex the size of Vatican City that would house a thousand diplomats.[12]

The new U.S. Embassy Baghdad was the logical culmination of the Inman standards. Many details of the design remained classified, but a Senate Foreign Relations Committee report in 2006 offered some hints of the scale of the project, and the degree to which this giant fortress would isolate U.S. diplomats from the Red Zone of Baghdad. The building would be "hardened" (reinforced to withstand rocket and mortar attacks); self-sufficient (it would have its own generating station, wells, and wastewater treatment facilities); and it would have extraordinary "setback" (the walled perimeter would be ringed with multiple layers of defense, plus an emergency entrance-exit). Loeffler, the historian of U.S. diplomatic architecture, describes it as a modern-day fortress. "Encircled by blast walls and cut off from the rest of Baghdad, it stands out like the crusader castles that once dotted the landscape of the Middle East."[13]

The presence of contractors presented a major headache for military commanders, who were wary of hired guns moving around in "their" battlespace. The U.S. military likes to maintain a monopoly on lethal force wherever it operates, and the heavily armed contractor convoys were not under their direct control. Revisions to defense contracting

regulations were supposed to tighten oversight of the army of contractors to make sure they complied with both local and U.S. laws, including
the Military Extraterritorial Jurisdiction Act, or MEJA, which theoreti-
cally allowed for prosecution under local laws of private contractors
employed by the military in foreign countries. But they did not resolve
the question of who, ultimately, had legal jurisdiction and control over
contractors in Iraq.

I accompanied an Erinys team on a trip to Camp Taji, a sprawling U.S.
military installation north of Baghdad that had once been a base for a Republican Guard tank division. The U.S. government had invested a serious
amount of money in base infrastructure, and the day's mission was to pick
up a "client," an engineer working on a construction project at Taji, and
deliver him safely to the Green Zone. The trip to Taji from downtown
Baghdad should have been a half-hour trip, but driving on Iraqi roads was
a risky affair. Insurgents were designing increasingly lethal roadside bombs,
and the contractors were particularly worried about a new threat, the
"explosively formed projectile," or EFP.

Unlike typical roadside bombs, made of an artillery shell buried beneath a road or concealed in some trash, an EFP was what some militaries called an "off-route mine," because it was placed beside a road. An
EEP was fabricated out of metal pipe and packed with a high-explosive
charge; the business end was sealed with a concave plate, or liner. When
the charge went off, the force of the blast turned the liner into a slug of
molten metal that could slice through the door of an armored vehicle at
supersonic speed. The EFPs were often tripped by passive infrared sen-
sors. When the beam was broken, the bomb went off.

The trip to Taji took an anxious two hours because of an emergency
detour. "That road is incredibly dangerous—it's perfect for setting up
an ambush," said one of the Russians. "The Americans and the Iraqis
patrol Route Irish [the Baghdad Airport road] all the time, but on that
road, you hardly see any patrols. By the end of the day, you're totally
wound up."

Driving through downtown Baghdad was a nightmare for ordinary
Iraqis as well. Contractor SUV motorcades drove aggressively, turning on
sirens to force other drivers to the side of the road. Get too close, and you
might get a warning shot. But there was a reason for the "tactical driving": If you didn't keep moving, you became a target. So when one of the
armored SUVs in the Erinys convoy got stuck traversing a low concrete

barrier, the shooters jumped out of the trucks to form a hasty roadblock, their rifles at the ready. One of the bodyguards, a lanky Ukrainian, stepped out to halt oncoming traffic. At least 6 feet 5, wearing full body armor and wraparound shades, he didn't need to point his weapon. He stood with his left hand raised, and the Iraqi drivers quickly stopped.

Fortunately, an Iraqi National Guard patrol was nearby. They quickly blocked all the civilian traffic merging from an access road and pulled around their truck, attached a chain, and towed the SUV free. The team members exchanged parting handshakes, boarded their vehicles, and turned back down the access road. We had to make a U-turn and reverse course through central Baghdad. As we sped away, I looked at the faces of the drivers in the opposite lane, where traffic was now backed up all the way to the next intersection; it was easy to see why Iraqis resented the contractors.

The military didn't like the contractors, either, at least not the armed ones. Colonel Peter Mansoor, an Iraq veteran and a member of the Petraeus brain trust, explained the dilemma to me at Fort Leavenworth in the fall of 2006: Logistics contractors like KBR fit neatly in the military chain of command. But the security firms "could not be controlled. They work for whoever hires them, they work under different rules of engagement than the military, they don't always have the same communications capabilities. They don't always have robust access to quick reaction forces—reinforcements—if they get into trouble."

Part of the problem, military officers realized, was that bodyguards' primary mission was to protect diplomats, civilian reconstruction experts, and other VIPs. They could be very good at their jobs, but at the expense of the larger nation-building mission. "Their limited role to protect the client may conflict with the overall mission, which is counterinsurgency," Mansoor said. "And if they push traffic off the roads or if they shoot up a car that looks suspicious—whatever it may be, they may be operating within their contract—[it's] to the detriment of the mission, which is to bring the people over to your side. I would much rather see basically all armed entities in a counterinsurgency operation fall under a military chain of command."

Members of the uniformed military could be held accountable for their actions: They were subject to the Uniform Code of Military Justice. If they used excessive or indiscriminate force, killed or injured civilians in violation of the rules of engagement, or engaged in any other serious crime, they could be court-martialed. The U.S. military also had a system of condolence payments to compensate people for damage to property or accidental deaths and injuries caused during combat operations. If a contractor ran a car off the road, or shot an innocent person—deliberately, or by accident—Iraqis had no real legal recourse.

Who could hold contractors accountable for their actions? In late 2005, they were not subject to the Uniform Code of Military Justice. In theory they could be prosecuted under the MEJA, which gave the Department of Justice the power to prosecute crimes committed overseas by contractors accompanying U.S. forces. In practice, however, MEJA was a poor enforcement tool. Federal prosecutors were unlikely to commit resources to investigate contractor misconduct in a distant war zone, and the Department of Justice did not have offices in Iraq set up to investigate contractor misdeeds. MEJA at the time was applied in only a few, exceptionally rare cases, and never against private security contractors. And then there was Coalition Provisional Authority Order 17, the get-out-of-jail-free card for contractors. Two days before the dissolution of the Coalition Provisional Authority, Paul Bremer signed CPA Order 17, which gave contractors blanket exemption from Iraqi law. It was in effect a form of diplomatic immunity for the foreign hired guns who were working in Iraq.

The management of Erinys liked to stress accountability: to their contract, to coalition forces, and to their internal corporate codes of conduct. They even had a system set up for paying compensation to Iraqis when their contractors were at fault in traffic incidents. Andy Melville, the country manager for Erinys, told a PBS *Frontline* documentary crew, "We have a contract with the United States [Army] Corps of Engineers, which is through the American Department of Defense. Most of the contractual stipulations are based on Army regulations, and they actually quote Army regulations, and we have to follow our contract very, very closely."[14]

But in the end, accountability was a fiction. The ROC system was essentially self-policing. Contractors reported their movements and escalation-of-force incidents to the ROC, and incident reports relied in part on the honor system. No one was even sure how many private security operators were working on behalf of the U.S. government in Iraq.

To Iraqis, the contractors seemed entirely above the law. And one private security company seemed more above the law than others. It had emerged as the main provider of security for the U.S. diplomatic mission in Iraq. Blackwater was founded by Erik Prince, a former Navy SEAL and heir to a Michigan auto parts fortune (his father's company invented the lighted vanity mirror for car window visors, among other things). Blackwater began in 1997 as a rather modest business: manufacturing steel targets and teaching combat shooting in a remote corner of northeastern North Carolina. Turnover was unremarkable—until September 12, 2001. After the 9/11 attacks the phone started ringing off the hook. Prince and several of his top executives tapped a network of former SEALs and other special operations veterans to bid for government bodyguard contracts.

The company's first big security client was the CIA. The agency needed high-end guard details for its widening operations in Afghanistan. In *Licensed to Kill*, his inside account of the post-9/11 boom in Blackwater's business, Robert Young Pelton writes, "The Global Response Staff, the CIA's security division, was overstretched, and they needed protection for their newly established Kabul station. The CIA had hired corporations for collection and other covert needs before, but they had rarely contracted out their field officers' security to private industry."[15]

Enter Blackwater. The company provided men to start protecting the remote outposts on the Afghan frontier, where operatives were pursuing the remnants of the al-Qaeda network. Prince even went over personally to Afghanistan as a security contractor for a few weeks in spring 2002. That stint of working for the CIA "energized him," Pelton wrote. "He loved the intrigue and excitement so much that the thirty-something head of the Prince family empire decided he wanted to join the CIA's Special Activities Division and enter the world of covert operations as a paramilitary."[16]

Things didn't work out as Prince hoped, however. He failed to pass the polygraph examination, so he focused instead on growing his business. Blackwater morphed from a small-time security contractor to a major provider of security services to the U.S. government. In 2001, it had federal contracts worth $736,906; by 2006 that figure had grown to $593.6 million. Between 2001 and 2006 Blackwater won contracts for U.S. government business worth over $1.1 billion.[17]

Prince was notoriously press-shy, but in early 2005 I watched him deliver his company's sales pitch at a conference on special operations and low-intensity conflict in Washington. It was a unique insight into the scale of Blackwater's operations in Iraq. In addition to its security details on the ground, the company had its own private air fleet. It operated MD-500 "Little Bird" small reconnaissance helicopters, complete with helicopter door gunners armed with M249 light machine guns, to give air cover to motorcades on the ground. In Afghanistan the company provided contract airlift for the U.S. military with CASA 212s, twin-engine turboprops that could take off and land from remote airstrips. They ferried essential personnel and equipment around the country, a mission similar to the one undertaken by Air America, the CIA front company, in Vietnam. At Blackwater's giant training facility in Moyock, North Carolina, they were burning through around a million rounds a month.

"Why private military firms?" Prince said. "Why do we exist? There have been a lot of defense contractors for a long time making gear. But not as much doing the kind of services that we provide."

Prince was advancing an argument that was commonly made by military contractors. The private sector had accompanied the military since the founding of the republic, from the camp sutlers who sold provisions at Valley Forge to European military professionals such as the Marquis de Lafayette, Friedrich Wilhelm von Steuben, and Tadeusz Kosciuszko, who were hired to help train and organize the Continental Army. But contractors were not just in the business of logistics support and equipment maintenance, Prince argued: He pointed to the American Volunteer Group, better known as the Flying Tigers, a wing of the Chinese nationalist air force that fought the Japanese prior to the entry of the United States into World War II. The Flying Tigers were technically employees of the Central Aircraft Manufacturing Company, an American company that was an antecedent of sorts of modern private military contractors. (After Pearl Harbor the group was disbanded and was succeeded by a regular military outfit.) Companies like KBR had capitalized on a push to outsource "nonmilitary" tasks such as laundry, logistics, and recreational facilities to private firms in the 1990s. Prince was making a more ambitious argument, that private companies like Blackwater could perform many of the core functions of the military, and they could do it more cheaply. He described one of the early assignments the company received, to provide security at a remote U.S. base in southwest Asia. A Blackwater team of 25 men replaced 166 active-duty soldiers: a 28-strong rifle platoon plus 138 other troops to provide headquarters, logistics support, and other administrative functions. "Everyone carries guns, just like Jeremiah rebuilding the temple in Israel—with a sword in one hand and a trowel in the other," Prince said. "They are the guys that keep the generators, water, food, communications, air conditioning, you name it. They run a whole base: 25 guys instead of 166. You can imagine the logistics, the simplicity of doing that."

It was about more than running bases on the cheap. Prince said that the private sector could take on many of the essential tasks of nation building and stability operations. The military, he suggested, could outsource things like traffic control, presence patrols, and convoys to a private army. "There's consternation in the DoD about increasing the permanent size of the Army; they wanted to add thirty thousand people—they talked about it costing anywhere from $3.6 billion to $4 billion to do that. By my math, that comes down to about $135,000 a soldier. And our ability to raise a contractor brigade, using vetted, trained and equipped, reliable third-country national soldiers led by one of our type guys, a nine-to-one ratio. We can do it, certainly cheaper."

It was a hardcore, free-market argument. Prince sounded like a disciple of Milton Friedman making an argument for private armies—something quite different than the limited defensive role of private security contractors. He cued up a slide showing an S-type Mercedes and a Trabant, the East German car that sounded as though it was powered by a lawnmower engine.

> Central planning, [a] noncompetitive, socialist market provided [a Trabant], versus the Mercedes, which is what a competitive, innovative, risk-rewarding culture built. And . . . you know, same culture, same language, same background. Different command structure. I don't believe the people we have in a private military firm are better—in fact, they are the same people that are on active duty. It's just a different set of bureaucracy, or lack of, that we deal with.

Prince did acknowledge one of the main arguments made against armed contractors: that they operated without any oversight or any jurisdiction. "As of 31 December [2004] that ended," he said. "The president signed a law, the Military Extraterritorial Jurisdiction Act, which previously applied to anyone on a defense contract, now it's any U.S. dollars that fund a contract overseas, that contractor can be brought to justice by the U.S. Justice Department."

In theory Prince was right. In the fiscal year 2005 Department of Defense Authorization Act, Congress amended MEJA to extend its jurisdictional coverage. The revisions tightened a loophole to extend jurisdiction to all contractors, not just those employed directly by the U.S. Defense Department. The legislation that created MEJA acknowledged that there had been a longstanding "jurisdictional gap" that had allowed crimes by battlefield contractors to go unpunished.

But there was still the problem of enforcement. The language of the report that accompanied the original bill when it was passed in 2000 was prescient:

> Often, the only remedy available to the United States Government with respect to military dependents and civilian employees and contractors who commit crimes in foreign countries is to limit their use of facilities on the installation where they live, or bar their entry onto the installation altogether, which often causes them to return to the United States. In any event, however, the fact that the person who committed the act may return to the United States does not give rise to any jurisdiction in the United States to try the crime he or she committed abroad.[18]

That is what happened when a Blackwater contractor shot and killed the local bodyguard of Vice President Adel Abdul Mahdi in Baghdad's Green Zone on Christmas Eve, 2006. The contractor, later identified in the press as Andrew Moonen, was off duty and had been drinking heavily when he wandered near the Iraqi prime minister's compound, got into an altercation with the bodyguard, and shot him three times.[19] The contractor fled the scene and was later apprehended by the International Zone police, who determined that he was too drunk for questioning. The following day, Blackwater fired him for cause—possession of a firearm while intoxicated—and on December 26, they whisked him out of the country on a flight to Jordan. The contractor then returned to the United States, a free man.

Stunningly, the State Department was informed of the incident and of Blackwater's arrangements to spirit Moonen out of the country. According to a Diplomatic Security incident report, the contractor was returned to the United States "under the authority of a DOS [Department of State] Regional Security Officer." In internal correspondence that followed, embassy officials discussed ways to paper over the incident. In an e-mail the day after the incident, the chargé d'affaires (the acting ambassador) urged the regional security officer to follow up and make sure the company did "all possible to assure that a sizeable compensation is forthcoming." A prompt apology and compensation, the chargé d'affaires reasoned, would be the "best way" to ensure that the Iraqis did not take measures to sanction Blackwater or bar them from operating in Iraq. He proposed a payment of $250,000, then $100,000. This prompted a diplomatic security officer to complain that such "crazy sums" would tempt Iraqis "to try to get killed so as to set up their families financially." The State Department and Blackwater agreed on a payment of $15,000 to the slain bodyguard's family. Summarizing the concerns of the Diplomatic Security Service, an official wrote: "This was an unfortunate event but we feel that it doesn't reflect on the overall Blackwater performance. They do an exceptional job under very challenging circumstances. We would like to help them resolve this so we can continue with our protective mission."[20]

In other words, the State Department's Regional Security Office in Baghdad was so preoccupied with protecting diplomats that it was willing to let Moonen walk free. Blackwater was performing its narrow mission magnificently, shielding U.S. diplomats from harm. Company officials often pointed out with pride that no diplomat in their care had ever been killed. But the risk-averse (and counterproductive for nation building) mentality of the diplomatic security apparatus had reached a logical extreme in Iraq. The incident was hushed up, although a slightly inaccurate report did air on the Al-Arabiya satellite television network identifying the murderer as a U.S. soldier. Blackwater continued operating in Iraq. That sent a message to Iraqis that one of our diplomats is worth a hundred of you.

In September 2007, a Blackwater security detail operating under the call sign Raven 23 responded to a call for backup from a second diplomatic security motorcade that was evacuating diplomats from a meeting in a compound in the Red Zone after a car bomb had gone off nearby. A first motorcade was already under way. Raven 23 was dispatched to Nisour Square, an area not far from the International Zone, to block traffic for the second motorcade. Seconds after Raven 23 entered the traffic circle, shooting started. Members of the team said they believed they were under attack by insurgents. They unleashed a hail of gunfire on civilian cars stopped outside the roundabout; at least thirty-four unarmed Iraqi civilians were killed or injured.

Before the Nisour Square incident, Blackwater had been a minor public-relations headache for the U.S. government. The company was already a favorite target of the antiwar left. It was secretive and militaristic and it cultivated a distinctly menacing corporate brand. As a former SEAL who sported a flag pin and severe military haircut, Erik Prince was a made-to-order caricature of the right-wing war profiteer. The scion of a Michigan Republican dynasty that bankrolled conservative causes, he had been a White House intern but found the administration of George H. W. Bush insufficiently conservative. The appearance of Blackwater operatives on the streets of New Orleans in the aftermath of Hurricane Katrina bolstered the company's sinister aura; to critics, Blackwater looked like a sort of Praetorian Guard for the Bush administration.

Nisour Square marked a turning point for private security companies in Iraq. For years, rage had been growing in Iraq over the foreign private security firms who operated with impunity on Iraqi roads. Iraqi politicians were quick to seize on public anger, and Prime Minister Nouri al-Maliki vowed to find the company responsible for the murder and put it out of work. The Iraqi government eventually revoked Blackwater's operating license and negotiated an end to the arrangement that had given contractors immunity from prosecution. The U.S. government began a belated push for better oversight of hired guns in Iraq.

In September 2007 Secretary of State Condoleezza Rice ordered a high-level security panel to review the practice of using private guards for diplomatic security in Iraq. The panel, led by Ambassador Patrick Kennedy, found serious failings. Contractors employed by the State Department did not properly coordinate their movements with the military, the embassy's Regional Security Office was not adequately sharing information with the military commanders, and few contractors had sufficient knowledge of Arabic. But "in-sourcing," giving the job of protecting diplomats back to the Bureau of Diplomatic Security, was not an option. The State Department did not have enough special diplomatic security agents to handle the job of running protective details in Iraq. It didn't even have enough people to exercise proper oversight of the hired guns. Likewise, the military did not have the manpower to spare to provide security escorts for diplomats. The panel also acknowledged there was no real framework for legal oversight and concluded that it was "unaware of any basis for holding non–Department of Defense contractors accountable under U.S. law," despite MEJA being on the books.[21]

The panel recommended a series of administrative remedies such as better communication and coordination, more diplomatic security personnel, clarification of legal jurisdiction. But those solutions did nothing to address the risk-averse culture of the State Department. The practice of diplomatic security was, at its core, antithetical to the nation-building mission, which required civilians to take risks and work outside the walls of the embassy. Even in relatively secure areas, the Baghdad-based Regional Security Office imposed strict limitations on where diplomatic officers could travel and what kinds of vehicles and convoys they could travel in, meaning that it was often difficult to get out to the field and do meaningful work. A Foreign Service officer who worked in two provinces in Iraqi Kurdistan as a provincial action officer explained the dilemma: "The embassy Regional Security Office imposed strict country-wide standards, but I was the only one doing those two provinces in econ [economics] and political . . . You are spending enormous amounts of energy on your [transportation], which is subtracting enormous amounts from your budget and your time."

The military took risks to accomplish its missions. The State Department, by contrast, responded to the Nisour Square incident with a lockdown, barring diplomats from travelling in Iraq by land, a move that brought into question the whole purpose of having a diplomatic mission there in the first place.[22] And the State Department's practice of relying on contractors to provide protective service did not change. Guards from Blackwater (later rebranded as the more innocuous-sounding Xe Services) continued to protect U.S. diplomatic convoys in Iraq, even though the company's license to operate there had been revoked. The State Department decided it would not renew Xe's Iraq contract, but the company's aviation wing continued to provide air cover for U.S. diplo-matic convoys well into the fall of 2009, two years after the Iraqi govern-ment had said Blackwater had to go.[23] Apparently, the State Department could not get by without them.*

---

*On December 31, 2009, in Washington, D.C., U.S. District Court Judge Ricardo Ur-bina dismissed charges against four former Blackwater guards over the Nisour Square shootings. The judge cited repeated missteps by prosecutors, who built their case around sworn statements given by the guards, who were promised immunity from prosecution after the shootings.[24] The same month, Xe (the renamed Blackwater) settled a civil case brought by the families of the victims, reportedly paying $100,000 for each of the Iraqis killed by its contractors.[25]

CHAPTER 10

Peace Corps on Steroids

The rust-flecked Toyota Land Cruiser skidded to an abrupt halt, and half a dozen armed men spilled out of the truck bed. The soldiers, wearing a motley assortment of khaki and forest-green camouflage, fanned out in the dirt, Kalashnikovs at the ready. A small group of boys who had been rolling old bicycle tires around the mud-walled courtyard stopped to watch the soldiers as they inched forward in the dirt, ready to return fire.

Captain Lassine Keita, a reed-thin officer in pressed desert fatigues, urged the soldiers on, and his men leapfrogged toward the ambush point to launch their counterattack. Then Keita, his spectacles pushed back on his forehead like a professor, stepped forward and waved his arms to stop the drill. The troopers clambered back in the pickup and prepared to make another circuit around the yard.

Keita was commander of the 512th Compagnie d'Infanterie Motori-sée, a Malian infantry unit that in 2007 was patrolling the country's Fifth Military Region, a vast territory that stretched across the northern deserts of Mali, reaching all the way to the borders of Algeria and Mauritania. The 512th was stationed at what some would consider the end of the world. Their training base was in Timbuktu, the fabled trading center at the very southern edge of the Sahara. At the intersection of ancient caravan routes, Timbuktu was once a center of Islamic scholarship, and over the centuries its leading families had preserved the city's priceless manuscripts in private libraries. Now it was an exotic tourist destination. Though the city had fallen on hard times, the phantasmagoric mud mosques and street markets still attracted adventurous, well-heeled travelers. It even hosted two world music festivals, Sahara Nights and the Festival in the Desert.

This part of Mali did not have a peaceful history. In the early twentieth century, it was a center of resistance against French colonial rule. In the early 1990s, portions of northern Mali and neighboring Niger were rocked by uprisings of the Touareg, nomadic Berbers who traditionally inhabited the Sahara and the Sahel. A "flame of peace" monument on the outskirts of Timbuktu marked the end of the most recent large-scale rebellion, in 1995, and the rusting barrels of weapons that were symbolically burned to mark the end of the conflict were embedded in the concrete. Fighting occasionally flared up. Just a few weeks earlier, government forces in northern Mali had engaged in a few gunfights with Touareg rebels led by Ibrahim Ag Bahanga, who had led two previous revolts against the government in the capital city of Bamako.

The training overseen by Keita reflected a newer threat faced by Mali's army. The expanses of the Sahara had become a staging ground for Islamic extremists because they could move easily between the porous, badly policed borders intersecting West Africa and North Africa. Four or five pickup trucks might rendezvous in a remote wadi, spend a week training with rifles or explosives, then disappear across the horizon. Extremist groups were also tied to narcotics and weapons trafficking rings, which often relied on old caravan routes that stretched across Libya, Chad, Mauritania, Mali, and Niger. Occasionally the militants were bold enough to confront local militaries. A year earlier, members of one faction of the Salafist Group for Preaching and Combat, a militant group known as GPSC (for Groupe Salafiste pour la Prédication et le Combat), attacked a Mauritanian military outpost near the border with Mali. The Mauritanians responded with force, chasing the insurgents across the border into Mali.

Keita's drill, called a "reaction to contact," was supposed to train the lightly armed Malian soldiers to respond to an ambush if they encountered insurgents on a long-range desert patrol. For Keita and his trainees, this was no run-of-the-mill training day. At the edge of the dusty parade ground, a few foreign visitors stood out, broad-shouldered men in digital-pattern Army combat uniforms. Their uniforms were "sterile"—they bore no name tapes or rank insignia, just U.S. ARMY on the left over the chest pocket and American flag patches on the right shoulder. All of the men wore wraparound shades. This was a training team from First Battalion, Third Special Forces Group—Green Berets—out of Fort Bragg, North Carolina, assigned to Special Operations Command Europe. The U.S. government was providing the trainers, the fuel for the trucks, and the extra ammunition for marksmanship practice.

Since 2003, the U.S. military had been quietly increasing its military-to-military ties with Mali. As part of the assistance, around two or three times a year a Special Forces team would deploy to this outpost near Timbuktu for three or six weeks of intensive instruction with the Malian military. The training began under the rubric of the Pan-Sahel Initiative, a post-9/11 border security and counterterrorism program started in 2003 by the State Department. The aims of the Pan-Sahel Initiative were straightforward: African soldiers would get schooling from some of the best infantry instructors in the world, and the Green Berets would get the opportunity to familiarize themselves with the cultures, terrain, and languages of four West African countries—Mali, Chad, Niger, and Mauritania. In 2005, the Pan-Sahel Initiative was renamed the Trans-Sahara Counter-Terrorism Partnership, or TSCTP, and now had a much more ambitious scope. With a budget of around $100 million per year, TSCTP would offer military aid to Nigeria and Senegal and also encourage the countries in the region to expand their security ties with Algeria, Morocco, and Tunisia.

The idea of the project was to make the region inhospitable to groups such as the GPSC, which formally aligned itself with al-Qaeda in 2006 and renamed itself Al Qaeda in the Land of the Islamic Maghreb, or AQIM.[1] This local insurgency fighting the Algerian government had become a regional franchise of a global terror organization, and the U.S. assistance to West Africa was supposed to help keep the region from becoming a base for extremists.

This Special Forces training mission coincided with a larger, three-week military exercise, called Flintlock 2007. Flintlock, held that year in Bamako, was a "command post exercise." It was built around a fictional (but quite plausible) scenario, the simultaneous staging of several cross-border incursions by a terror group, along with coordinated terror attacks in several cities. The goal of the exercise was to encourage representatives of regional militaries to share information with each other as the crisis unfolded. Military representatives from Burkina Faso, Chad, Mali, Mauritania, Morocco, Niger, Nigeria, Senegal, and Tunisia would all take part (Libya was invited, but declined to participate).

For African militaries, this kind of desktop exercise could have tangible professional benefits. It gave them a chance to work inside a modern, computerized command post. More important, participants from different countries could exchange cell-phone numbers with their counterparts. The next time there was a regional crisis or a violent border incident, a military officer or a border patrolman might be able to call his opposite number to coordinate a response. That kind of collaboration could have application for peacekeeping, disaster relief, and other kinds of emergencies.

Flintlock 2007 and the training exercise in Timbuktu were also part of a deepening U.S. military interest in the region. Part of the idea was to counter cross-border problems: terrorism, human trafficking, narcotics smuggling. But it was also what U.S. government officials liked to call "capacity building," helping vulnerable, impoverished governments in Africa build competent militaries and capable government institutions. That was a more sweeping state-building project, in which the U.S. military was taking the lead.

Colonel Mark Rosengard, a gruff Green Beret officer with a flat Boston accent, a thick black mustache, and a hockey player's build, was one of the officers observing from the sidelines in Timbuktu. As we watched the Malian troopers go through their paces on the training ground, he told me that the drill was a first step toward building a professional military for Mali. The country needed armed forces and border guards that were equipped to train and work in this austere, forbidding place, and capable of distinguishing between legitimate cross-border trade and more nefarious activity. "The important elements of security in this part of the world are pretty simple," he said. "[The Special Forces team] are here to help them establish procedure, how to shoot, move, and communicate more effectively."

Rosengard had long experience in the Balkans and Afghanistan, and he was observing this training mission as a representative of U.S. Special Operations Command Europe. The training in Timbuktu was in many respects a classic Special Forces "foreign internal defense" mission, an assignment known as Joint Combined Exchange Training, or JCET. Green Berets routinely performed these JCET missions around the globe.

But the mission to Timbuktu was taking place as the U.S. military was preparing to activate a brand-new military command for Africa, U.S. Africa Command, or AFRICOM. The new headquarters was slated to reach "initial operating capability" the following month, October 2007. This rollout was a sort of beta version of the organization, based out of U.S. European Command in Stuttgart. The command became a fully activated unitary command one year later, on October 1, 2008.

In some respects AFRICOM represented a simple streamlining and reorganization of U.S. military activity in Africa. Before AFRICOM, three different commands divided responsibility for watching Africa. U.S. European Command oversaw most of sub-Saharan Africa; it tended to view Africa as an extension of former European colonial territories. U.S. Central Command, focused primarily on the Middle East, was responsible for the countries bordering on the Red Sea. The island of Madagascar was under U.S. Pacific Command, a seeming afterthought. The creation of the new command signaled a major foreign policy shift. Instead of dealing with Africa through dozens of embassies, the U.S. government could approach the continent through a powerful, unified military command. The reasoning was the main problems in Africa were transnational. Migration, resource wars, ethnic conflict, HIV/AIDS—all cut across borders, and AFRICOM would offer a more coherent approach to dealing with them than the embassies could. That mission required a new kind of organization. Unlike a traditional military command, AFRICOM focused heavily on humanitarian and development issues. Its staff would include a large contingent of civilians, and one of the top officials, the deputy to the commander for civil-military affairs, would be a senior Foreign Service officer. After the failures of nation building in Iraq and Afghanistan, AFRICOM offered a clean slate, a hybrid civil-military organization optimized to respond to crises in the region before they required full-blown military intervention. Africa was the new laboratory for "getting it right."

AFRICOM's planners in the Pentagon envisioned its main goal as "preventive" security: Instead of stationing U.S. troops on the continent, the United States through AFRICOM would boost the ability of local governments to police their own borders, participate in peacekeeping operations, and, when necessary, organize the response to the next Somalia or Rwanda. It would also mean a new infusion of U.S. dollars on the continent, where the U.S. Agency for International Development had once been the primary vehicle for development assistance to Africa. Now, the new command would help direct millions more in "security assistance" funds to African governments, as well as oversee development projects. U.S. aid to the continent would take on a much more military flavor.

The training exercise in Mali was just one modest example. The U.S. teams were able to make the training in Timbuktu much more "event-intensive" by supplying ammunition for live-fire exercises and providing extra fuel for the trucks. The course of instruction was very basic: The Malian soldiers received classroom instruction on land navigation and the laws of armed conflict, practiced rifle marksmanship and communication, and took part in field exercises. But this modest investment could make a major difference for cash-strapped African militaries.

Still, the Malian military had a long way to go before they became self-sufficient. The U.S. trainers concluded the morning's exercise with a weapons inspection. While the Malian soldiers stood in formation, the Green Berets inspected their rifles, an assortment of corroded-looking SKS rifles and AK-47s. Across the courtyard, in a bare classroom, a medic gave a lecture on battlefield first aid. The Malians had no overhead projector or practice tools for the students. And it seemed difficult to maintain an atmosphere of military discipline as barefoot children wandered around the training grounds. While his colleagues examined the weapons, racking back the slides to inspect the breeches, the Green Beret team leader offhandedly muttered a joke: "They're probably surprised to see a truck with fuel."

The U.S. military had been an intermittent presence in Africa, but U.S. involvement in Africa ramped up dramatically after September 11, 2001. In late 2002, U.S. Marines established a task force at Camp Lemonier, a former French army outpost in Djibouti. The Djibouti task force, called Combined Joint Task Force–Horn of Africa, occupied a critical piece of geography near the Gulf of Aden and the Red Sea, along transit routes that might be used by al-Qaeda as they fled Central Asia or the Middle East. The task force was also heavily involved in Civil Affairs missions and military-to-military training, overseeing medical and veterinary clinics, digging wells, and providing security training for countries in the region. Still, momentum for this new Africa command did not really build within the Pentagon until after the invasion and occupation of Iraq. The experiences in Iraq and Afghanistan pushed military planners to embrace the tools of nation building and development, and laid bare the lack of civilian capability for repairing failed states. Like Iraq, Africa presented problems that defied simple military solutions, and the continent seemed to cry out for the "whole of government" treatment promoted by the counterinsurgents.

The idea of dividing up the globe into unified U.S. military commands dated back to the immediate postwar era, when the U.S. military began to confront its wartime ally, the Soviet Union. The original "Outline Command Plan" of 1946 established seven unified commands (Far East Command, Pacific Command, Alaskan Command, Northeast Command, Atlantic Fleet, Caribbean Command, and European Command). That scheme overlooked Africa entirely. It was not until 1952 that part of Africa was assigned to a unified geographic command, when European Command assumed responsibility for contingencies in France's *départments* in Algeria, along with the French colonies of Morocco, Tunisia, and Libya.[2]

That did not mean that the United States had no military involvement on the continent. During the Suez Crisis in 1956, a Marine battalion evacuated U.S. nationals from Alexandria, Egypt; in 1964, Belgian paratroopers parachuted out of U.S. transport planes during a hostage crisis in Stanleyville, Congo; and in 1986, President Ronald Reagan sent U.S. warships to confront Libya. U.S. involvement during the Cold War was not limited to brief military interventions: As part of its proxy war with the Soviet Union the United States provided long-term support to anti-Communist guerrillas such as Angola's UNITA, and for several decades the Army maintained a large listening post at Kagnew Station, near Asmara, Ethiopia (now part of Eritrea).

In the 1990s, U.S. military involvement in Africa saw a steady uptick. In response to widespread disorder in Zaïre in 1991, U.S. aircraft transported Belgian troops and equipment to Kinshasa; in 1992, U.S. forces evacuated Americans from Sierra Leone after the government was overthrown; U.S. aircraft evacuated noncombatants and diplomats during the 1994 Rwanda genocide. More emergency airlifts followed during crises in Liberia (1996), Congo and Gabon (1997), and Sierra Leone (1997 and 2000).[3] The proliferation of cheap small arms—particularly the ubiquitous AK-47 assault rifle, a rugged, simple weapon that any stoned teenager could operate—made local conflicts much more lethal, and the United Nations was often power-less to stop the violence. Peacekeeping missions such as the 25,000-strong UN force in the Democratic Republic of Congo or the African Union mis-sion in Somalia were often short of resources and had limited mandates. Terrorism was also a rising threat. A U.S. joint task force deployed to Kenya and Tanzania following the al-Qaeda–orchestrated bombings of U.S. embassies in 1998. The biggest involvement was in Somalia, where President George H. W. Bush first deployed armed forces in response to a humanitarian crisis in 1992. After the 1993 "Black Hawk down" debacle, in which nineteen U.S. servicemen were killed in a firefight in Mogadishu, President Bill Clinton ordered the U.S. task force home, but American forces returned briefly to Somalia again in March 1995 to assist in the withdrawal of UN forces. In the 1990s U.S. armed forces deployed to the continent at least eighteen times.[4]

The idea for a unified command for Africa gained momentum during the latter half of the 1990s, as the U.S. military witnessed a cascading series of crises in Africa. Civil wars in Liberia, Somalia, Sudan, Rwanda, and the Democratic Republic of the Congo cost millions of lives, and displaced millions more. The Rwanda genocide had forced something of a rethink in international relations theory, spurring arguments in favor of military intervention to halt mass atrocities. Military involvement in Africa could potentially be benign. A relatively small early intervention could stop a local conflict from turning into a mass outbreak of violence. Scott Feil, a retired Army officer, argued in a 1998 study that a five thousand–strong task force from a modern, Western military would have been enough to stop the killing in Rwanda.[5] Better yet, a longer-term presence in conflict-prone regions, coupled with swifter, more empow-ered international peacekeeping missions could keep such violence from starting in the first place.

In early 2001, Commander Richard Catoire, a naval aviator, wrote an article for *Parameters*, the journal of the Army War College, reflecting the Pentagon's new thinking on Africa:

> Because of the increased US engagement in sub-Saharan Africa, and because the current regional unified commands are princi-pally focused elsewhere, the time has come to rethink the Unified Command Plan as it regards Africa. The current plan cannot ef-fectively protect America's security interests on that continent. It

is unlikely to realize the articulated policy objectives of the United States in the region, and it should be revised to better secure those objectives.[6]

Catoire's article included a map of a proposed new command that would monitor all of the continent except five north African countries, which would remain under U.S. European Command. As Catoire outlined it, the United States would be stepping in to fill the shoes of France, which had provided much of the security assistance and training on the continent, especially to francophone countries, of which Mali was one. The piece also took note of new factors, particularly the rising dependence of the United States on African oil exports:

> The region has tremendous mineral wealth, huge hydro-electrical power reserves, and significant underdeveloped ocean resources. The better part of the world's diamonds, gold, and chromium are produced in countries at the southern end of the continent. Some 20 percent of America's oil now is imported from Africa. Copper, bauxite, phosphate, uranium, tin, iron ore, cobalt, and titanium are also mined in significant quantities. The waters off both coasts of the continent support huge fisheries. The continent's potential as a market and as a source of important commodities is great.[7]

In mid-2006, John Hillen, assistant secretary of state for political military affairs, was invited to working group meetings on AFRICOM at the Pentagon. From his post in the State Department, Hillen saw the push for AFRICOM as a reform initiative similar to the new Army and the Marine Corps counterinsurgency manual, an opportunity to bridge the "pol-mil divide" by forcing the military and civilian bureaucracies to work more closely together to integrate their efforts. "I always saw AFRICOM as a new kind of command, an interagency command that would be a better vehicle for delivering programs to Africa that were bent on nonkinetic goals than EUCOM had been," he said. "So to me it was very pragmatic. And I got Condi [Secretary of State Condoleezza Rice] on board; she said, 'Great, we'll play.'"

Hillen found an ally in the assistant secretary of state for African affairs, Jendayi Frazer, who was a strong supporter of the concept. Frazer had even included the idea of an Africa Command in Governor George

W. Bush's debate points during the 2000 election campaign. But Hillen and Frazer ran into resistance from the rank-and-file within the State Department's Bureau of African Affairs, where the new initiative was seen as another bureaucratic "land grab" by the Defense Department.

It was a legitimate concern. At the end of the day, AFRICOM was a powerful, well-resourced combatant command, and it exerted a serious gravitational pull. U.S. diplomats in the Middle East had long been aware that the military head of U.S. Central Command eclipsed them in power and resources. The new AFRICOM commander would have the same kind of resources at his or her disposal. Mindful of the power of the combatant commanders, planners rebalanced the design of AFRICOM by giving the State Department a seat at the table. The commander was assigned two deputies, one for military operations and one for political and economic affairs. The political and economic affairs slot would be taken by a career diplomat.

On February 6, 2007, President Bush made public his decision to create a new unified command for Africa, and directed the secretary of defense to have AFRICOM up and running by the end of fiscal year 2008. Bush cast the rationale for the new command in "soft power" terms, presenting it as a vehicle for humanitarian assistance and cooperation with African states. "This new command will strengthen our security cooperation with Africa and create new opportunities to bolster the capabilities of our partners in Africa," he said. "Africa Command will enhance our efforts to bring peace and security to the people of Africa and promote our common goals of development, health, education, democracy, and economic growth."[8]

Bush also promised to consult with African leaders on how the command should be structured. Over the next several months, military and diplomatic officials fanned out across the continent to sell the concept to African leaders. Despite efforts to sell AFRICOM as a primarily humanitarian and development-focused organization, African governments and their citizens were extremely wary of the Pentagon's intentions. To some, AFRICOM looked like a poorly disguised neocolonial scheme, and African governments were reluctant to host a large U.S. military headquarters.* In the late spring of 2007, U.S. officials, including representatives of

---

* A notable exception was Liberia. President Ellen Johnson Sirleaf offered to host AFRICOM headquarters, but as of fall 2010 the command was still based in Stuttgart.

the State Department and the military, paid visits to Ethiopia, Ghana, Kenya, Nigeria, Senegal, and South Africa to pitch the AFRICOM concept. Another delegation toured Africa that summer, but the diplomatic outreach did little to assuage concerns.

U.S. planners seemed to have willfully ignored the continent's history. "It was a complete and total disaster," Frazer later told me. The briefers kept changing the briefing slides on each stop of the tour, making it clear to African leaders that U.S. government agencies still had not reached internal agreement as to what, exactly, the mission of AFRICOM was, and how it was going to be organized. "The [lead briefer] was changing slides as he went along—as if the leaders don't talk to each other."

Part of the problem, Frazer said, was that the military was trying to design a command on Africa based on lessons from Iraq and Afghanistan. "If you don't know the African environment, you're prepared to impose any old structure on it, thinking, this'll work," Frazer said. "From my point of view, this sexy new design was Peace Corps on steroids. And we didn't need Peace Corps on steroids, what we needed was professional military doing the professional military engagement we had had, but more of it. Not something new and sexy and different. Give us something Africans already know."

The military tried to reach out to another key constituency, the foreign aid community. In May 2007, Rear Admiral Robert Moeller, director of the AFRICOM transition team, attended USAID's Advisory Committee on Voluntary Foreign Aid; he was there to present the concept to nongovernmental organizations and humanitarian relief groups. Principal Deputy Under Secretary of Defense for Policy Ryan Henry, who also attended the meeting, tried to reassure members of the USAID committee that AFRICOM would not be a typical military command, noting that it would draw as much as one quarter of its staff from civilian agencies of the U.S. government. Henry and Moeller also floated the idea of a "distributed" AFRICOM headquarters. Instead of a single AFRICOM headquarters on the continent, the new command would have several smaller regional hubs.

Lawmakers were skeptical. In an August 2007 hearing of the Senate Foreign Relations Committee, Senator Dick Lugar (R) of Indiana worried that the creation of AFRICOM would place a "disproportionately military emphasis" on Africa. AFRICOM also sent mixed messages about U.S. aims. In theory, U.S. military assistance to foreign nations was supposed to help reinforce principles such as civilian control of the military, but when men and women in uniform were the ones delivering humanitarian assistance and overseeing development projects, it sent a signal that the U.S. military, not its civilian agencies, called the shots in U.S. foreign policy. In fact, one southern African officer complained to *Jane's Defence Weekly*, the professional military journal, "We are told to leave our military legacies behind us to become true democracies, yet the world's biggest democracy is able to come into our sovereign territory with all of its military might; it is hypocritical and dangerous and not at all in Africa's best interests."[9]

In September 2007, South African officials announced they would not host AFRICOM; the Southern African Development Community, an organization representing fifteen southern African nations, also made it clear that they did not want a permanent U.S. command headquarters on their territories.[10] In fact, U.S.-led discussions about possible basing arrangements spurred speculation that the United States might have plans to overthrow unfriendly regimes or initiate regime change in dictatorships such as Zimbabwe.[11] From a public-relations standpoint, the rollout of the new command was botched. Despite efforts to reach out to the humanitarian aid and development community with reassurances that AFRICOM would focus on "nonkinetic" missions such as disaster relief, humanitarian aid, or professionalizing African armed forces, suspicions lingered that a more interventionist military agenda was at work. It didn't help that briefing papers circulated by the Defense Department said the command would "conduct limited operations" such as counterterrorism missions when necessary.

Many observers wondered whether the real reason U.S. policymakers had cooked up AFRICOM was to serve as a counterweight to China, which had been quietly but steadily increasing its presence on the continent through ambitious state-backed development assistance and investment schemes. China's expansion in Africa was remarkable. The Chinese invested in major infrastructure projects, building roads, bridges, and power plants in return for oil, mining, and other natural-resource concessions. Its activity in Africa was free of the poisonous legacy of colonialism that still lingered in relations between African states and former European colonizers. But human rights were not high on China's list, and Beijing was also willing to turn a blind eye to authoritarian regimes in Sudan, Zimbabwe, and other countries.

Marine Corps General James Jones helped pioneer the AFRICOM

concept while he was a four-star combatant commander of U.S. European Command. Shortly after retiring, Jones gave a speech in Washington in which he outlined some of the thinking behind the new dual-mission command:

> There are competitors out there . . . that are out-cycling us at a fairly rapid rate because they can make their decisions on a far more rapid basis [than we can]. One example of that . . . is the influence of China in Africa, which is very, very impressive from a standpoint of a sovereign nation able to take decisions quite rapidly . . . the process they go through is probably a lot shorter than ours. But if you're a unified commander and you're trying to render assistance somewhere or start a program . . . just about anywhere in my neck of the woods the past four years, it's a very frustrating and time-consuming proposition to get anything done, and to get anything done quickly.

Jones suggested that the new civil-military command of AFRICOM could help streamline the cumbersome processes of U.S. government, which he said have a "paralyzing effect" on foreign policy. "As we get more competitors on the playing field that out there—and believe me, they are out there as the world changes—we have to look at our systems, we have to look at our laws, our policies, our manipulations, the inner workings of the interagency to try to free up the giant that is the United States, that too often is captured, is restricted from moving in ways that this giant could."

To reach Timbuktu in October 2007, I hitched a ride from Bamako with representatives of U.S. Special Operations Command Europe. Our plane was a CASA 212, a boxy, utilitarian twin turboprop that was ideally suited for operating from primitive airstrips. The plane would take us from the lush, green plains of the Niger River valley to the thick brush and scrub of the southern edge of the Sahara.

The aircraft's tail number, I noticed, ended in BW—it was a Blackwater plane, part of the fleet of the company's Presidential Aviation airline. Blackwater provided contract aviation services to U.S. Special Operations Command, offering everything from airlift services in Africa to parachute training in the United States. The creation of AFRICOM and the military's new focus on nation building in Africa was sure to create another lucrative market for defense contractors who were looking for new business opportunities beyond Iraq and Afghanistan.

AFRICOM's unique structure and its emphasis on peacekeeping, development, and stability operations created demand for everything from logistics support and security to training and intelligence. John Wrenn, Blackwater's director of Global Stability Initiative and Corporate Communications, told me shortly before the full activation of AFRICOM in October 2008 that his company saw tremendous opportunities for a "strong partnership" between the new command and the private sector. Companies like Blackwater could provide everything from running medical clinics to overseeing civil engineering projects, military and law-enforcement training, and rule-of-law education. AFRICOM, said Wrenn, was "a lean organization, with a smaller command structure [than other military commands] to oversee the large area of operations. Since AFRICOM is a smaller organization, it will require a strong partnership with the private sector to effectively and efficiently direct and oversee U.S. engagement programs in Africa."

Erik Prince, Blackwater's founder, even envisioned a more ambitious new role on the continent for the private sector: as peacekeepers. Speaking in February 2005 in Washington, he floated the idea of Blackwater as peacekeepers-for-hire to replace U.N. blue helmets in Africa:

> One of the areas we see ourselves covering up more is contract peacekeeping in areas where the UN is, or where there's a lot of instability, sending a big, large-footprint conventional force is politically unpalatable. It's expensive, diplomatically difficult as well. We can put together a multinational professional force, supply it, manage it, lead it, put it under UN or NATO or U.S. control, however best we can, we can help stabilize a situation. I encourage people to go see . . . *Hotel Rwanda* . . . It's a great story—it's a sad story, it's pathetic. The UN let many people get slaughtered in a country the size of Vermont over a four-month period. Mostly by machetes. And it wouldn't have taken more than a couple hundred guys to stop it.

In the unfolding crisis in Darfur, Prince suggested that Blackwater operatives could provide an armed "quick reaction force," or QRF, to protect nongovernmental organizations, aid groups, and refugees from Sudan's feared *janjaweed* militia. If there was an atrocity in progress and the *janjaweed* needed to be stopped, Blackwater could move in and stop them. It was a cheaper proposition than funding UN peacekeepers. "I just challenge you: Are you getting your money's worth [from traditional UN peacekeeping]?" Prince said. "I think you can get a lot more done with a lot less."

In fact, Blackwater executives presented a plan for private-sector peacekeeping to the State and Defense departments and the National Security Council. The scheme, named the African Union Support program, was to create a ring of "persistent surveillance" around the camps for displaced Darfurians, using armed local or "third-country national" contractors and to provide Western supervisors and private logistics support. It was a swaggering, muscled-up vision of humanitarian aid— relief work as delivered by Arnold Schwarzenegger. Chris Taylor, the vice president of business development at Blackwater, presented the plan and spoke in broad terms about the proposal in industry forums. In an after-dinner speech at the 2006 annual meeting of the International Peace Operations Association, the main U.S. trade association for private security firms, Taylor argued for a private military role in humanitarian intervention. Once again Rwanda was the poster child: "Would the eight hundred thousand people killed in the Rwanda genocide have cared if their rescuers were from the private sector?" he said. But when Cofer Black, vice chairman of Blackwater, in 2006 raised the subject at an international military conference in Amman, Jordan, it created a wave of negative publicity. "We're low-cost and fast," Black was quoted as saying. "Who's going to let us play on their team?" The concept seemed to cross the line into creating a mercenary army with an overt combat role.[12]

Blackwater's swaggering talk of humanitarian soldiers-for-hire showed a remarkable lack of insight into Africa's recent history. In the 1960s and 1970s, white mercenaries such as "Mad" Mike Hoare and "Colonel" Bob Denard played a notorious role in postcolonial intrigues and coups. The market for armed force in Africa got another boost in the 1990s, when a controversial South African firm with the Bond-villain name of Executive Outcomes operated a private army for hire. It trained and later fought on behalf of the Angolan government against UNITA rebels and also helped rescue the government of Sierra Leone from a nihilistic militia known as the Revolutionary United Front. Executive Outcomes garnered some praise for its professionalism from Erik Prince, who noted admiringly that Executive Outcomes "had a good track record the first time they went into Sierra Leone." The company drew key personnel from veterans of apartheid era military and police units of South Africa and South-West Africa and the predominately Angolan 32 Battalion of the South African Army. Antimercenary legislation passed by the South African government in 1999 called the Regulation of Foreign Military Assistance Act effectively drove the company out of business.

Quasi-mercenary schemes forwarded by Blackwater's management may have seemed far-fetched, but U.S. private security firms in fact already had a significant foothold in Africa, largely through the African Contingency Operations Training and Assistance (ACOTA) program, a State Department–funded effort to help cash-strapped African militaries build militaries capable of contributing to UN peacekeeping missions. ACOTA was part of a larger U.S. program called the Global Peace Operations Initiative, which had a goal of training seventy-five thousand new peacekeepers worldwide by the end of 2010, a force to be drawn largely from the developing world. The bulk of this work was outsourced to the private sector. As the Government Accountability Office reported in June 2008, contractors provided the "majority" of ACOTA training in Africa. From the program's inception in 2004 to mid-2008, State Department–funded ACOTA contractors trained thousands of African peacekeepers, at a cost of around $98 million.[13] Northrop Grumman Information Technology designed training materials and conducted computer-simulated peacekeeping exercises for participating countries; DynCorp raised security forces; MPRI operated simulation centers. Once again, a core function of the government, training foreign militaries, was being outsourced to the private sector. This sent an ambiguous message to the recipients of aid about American motives and priorities.

Contractors also provided logistics support to the U.S. government in Africa through a State Department contract vehicle called AFRICAP (Africa Peacekeeping Program). Much like the Defense Department's LOGCAP (Logistics Civil Augmentation Program), which provided base operation and logistics support to military units in the Middle East and Central Asia, AFRICAP was a quick, relatively low-profile way to support military intervention in Africa. For example, in the summer of 2003, during a small-scale U.S. intervention in Liberia to protect the U.S. embassy in Monrovia, contractors provided support on the ground while a U.S. amphibious task force sailed from the East Coast to West Africa.

In a November 2003 after-dinner speech to the International Peace Operations Association, Theresa Whalen, deputy assistant secretary of defense for African affairs, told an audience of private security contractors that employing contractors in African contingencies "means that the U.S. can be supportive in trying to ameliorate regional crises without necessarily having to put U.S. troops on the ground, which is often times a very difficult political decision." Whalen said that in Liberia, contractors had helped speed up the U.S. response:

> If you look at the time between when the decision was made and when things got started on the ground in country, it was pretty darn short, a matter of weeks actually. And if you look at the time between when the Africans made the decision that they were going to send forces to Liberia at the end of July and then look at when we were actually getting the Africans on the ground, which was about the middle, or early August, again, very short. And in comparison if you look at the UN current deployment schedule, which is weeks behind, we were actually lightning fast. So there is a big advantage in being able to put the contractors on the ground and get things going fast.[14]

DynCorp and Pacific Architects and Engineers (a construction firm that was acquired by Lockheed Martin in 2006 and renamed PAE Government Services) won the original AFRICAP contract in 2003. In early 2008 the State Department announced it would tender the contract again, which would be worth approximately one billion dollars over five years. The contract was divided among four firms: PAE Government Services, AECOM, DynCorp, and Protection Strategies Incorporated.[15] But the U.S. government's dependence on private contractors in Africa once again raised serious questions about oversight. Contractors seemed to be performing many essential U.S. government tasks in Africa: training and advising foreign militaries, providing military mentors, and demobilizing former combatants. In some cases, they even performed oversight of other contractors. In fact, the State Department's ACOTA office was mostly staffed by contractors. According to the Government Accountability Office, the ACOTA staff comprised nine contractor employees and one federal employee. The GAO also raised serious questions about whether contractors were meeting targets for training peacekeepers, whether the State Department was properly able to assess the quality and effectiveness of the training, and whether trainees in U.S.-funded programs were being adequately screened for human rights abuses.[16]

Once again, responsibility for doing the government's job had been outsourced. Private profit, not smart foreign policy, seemed to be the guiding principle. And that did little to diminish suspicions in Africa as to American intentions.

About a week after the exercise in Timbuktu, a Malian army unit became pinned down in a protracted engagement with Touareg rebels led by Ibrahim Ag Bahanga. As fighting raged near the northern border post of Tinzaouatene, on the border with Algeria, the Malian government put in an emergency request to the U.S. military to resupply its troops with food rations. The U.S. government agreed, and dispatched a C-130 cargo plane that happened to be in Mali for an airborne exercise associated with Flintlock. It was a fairly straightforward task: The Malians supplied the rations, and the U.S Air Force provided the cargo pallets and the parachutes. During the second of two air-drop missions, the aircraft came under fire; the aircraft returned safely but was struck by rifle rounds, an unhappy reminder that nonlethal military assistance under the rubric of "building partnership capacity" came with some risks.

The rationale for U.S. support of the Malian military was counterterrorism: The mission was supposed to make Mali less vulnerable to transnational terrorist groups. It was not supposed to encourage the government in Bamako to resolve internal conflicts by force. In many respects the fighting in northern Mali was a domestic dispute between the Touareg minority and Mali's Bambara-speaking majority. The U.S. military had become, briefly, directly involved in a low-level civil war.

Adama Sacko, a former deputy in Mali's legislature, told me the clashes in northern Mali were a domestic problem, not a terrorist threat. "The problem in the north is very simple," he said. "It's a problem of poverty and development; it's not a problem of terrorism." Yet the Malian government seemed eager to cast its opponents as "terrorists" or extremists" in order to secure more U.S. support.

At the conclusion of the Flintlock exercise, I attended a press conference in Bamako hosted by the U.S. embassy and the Malian ministry of defense. It seemed a typically dull, stodgy event, as the U.S. ambassador, Terrence McCulley, issued a few platitudes about Mali's hospitality and the importance of partnership between nations. Then Mamadou Clazie Cissouma, the Malian minister of defense, veered a bit off-script. After thanking the participants in the Flintlock exercise, he launched into an angry denunciation of the "armed bandits" who had attacked military convoys and sown mines in the north. The politically correct facade of the Flintlock exercise had slipped.

Although U.S. officials were careful to emphasize the "preventative" and "nonkinetic" nature of AFRICOM, it did open the door to more direct military involvement. General William Ward, previously the deputy head of U.S. European Command, was AFRICOM's first four-star commander. Ward had served as a brigade commander during the Somalia intervention and had made clear his views about the military's role in Africa: It was to be driven by a sort of enlightened armed humanitarianism. In a 2007 article written for *Joint Forces Quarterly*, Ward described the searing experience of peacekeeping in the Horn of Africa: "Seeing the victims of the famine gave me stark reminders of why we were deployed there: to provide security to allow the international relief efforts to happen."[17]

The efforts to stabilize Somalia had ended in failure. In his article Ward suggested that in the future, the U.S. military would "have to be prepared to intervene early, with clear goals, authorities, and responsibilities understood by the parties to the conflict and among the international and interagency partners involved."[18] The conviction that the judicious application of military science and a willingness to intervene could somehow inoculate Africa from full-blown conflict seemed to be AFRICOM's guiding belief. This powerful new command could deliver aid to the continent in a way that no civilian relief agency could. It could draw upon the extraordinary logistics capabilities of the U.S. military to fly troops to a crisis in a hurry; it had a planning staff that could draw up sophisticated plans in an emergency; and it would have a sophisticated intelligence apparatus to anticipate conflict before it broke out. This vision of "smart power also pointed the way to future U.S. military intervention on the continent.

In May 2008, a few months before the full activation of AFRICOM, the Army hosted a war game at Carlisle Barracks, Pennsylvania, called Unified Quest 2008. There were around two hundred players: active-duty and retired military officers, Coast Guard personnel, NATO representatives, and a smattering of diplomats, intelligence officials, and other civilians. Unified Quest is an annual event whose purpose is to test the U.S. government's response to potential crises in the not-so-distant future. The focus of the 2008 game was conflict prevention. Participants tested scenarios that policymakers could face in an era of "persistent conflict" arising from the combined forces of globalization, competition for energy resources, population growth, and failing states.

Two of the scenarios took place in Africa. In one, Army Colonel Mark Forman played the role of the AFRICOM commander, responding to a hypothetical crisis in Nigeria sometime between 2013 and 2015. The Nigerian government is near collapse, and various factions are competing for power. In this scenario, AFRICOM operates as an "economy of force" headquarters; it has limited manpower and is only a small presence of the continent.

The second scenario was supposed to test how a fully configured AFRICOM could respond to a crisis in the Horn of Africa. James Embrey, a retired army colonel with the Army's Peacekeeping and Stability Operations Institute, played the head of a multinational task force that deploys to Somalia in 2025 to prop up an embattled government and fight off insurgents. The scenario was premised on the assumption that AFRICOM would command the full range of diplomatic, military, and conflict prevention tools by that time. "The supposition that we are making here is that the whole-of-government interagency planning and framework has been cured, there have been the proper structures built in terms of a special coordinator for reconstruction and stability," Embry explained. "And . . . the requisite civilian expertise in terms of Civilian Response Corps—additional subject matter experts that are almost like an interagency reserve force—have come online."

Embrey was describing the military's vision of the future: The U.S. government will have created a functioning civilian nation-building reserve on standby. The State Department has a deployable reserve, the military is skilled at reconstruction and stability operations, and hybrid "civil-military" commands such as AFRICOM are capable of coordinating the whole effort. Despite the lip service being paid to the "interagency" and "civil-military integration," it is clear that in this vision, the military is in charge. Brigadier General Barbara Fast, deputy director and chief of staff for the Army Capabilities Integration Center and deputy chief of staff for Army Training and Doctrine Command, told reporters quite explicitly that the Army wanted to communicate to civilian government agencies and foreign militaries to make the kind of investments and capabilities they will need in the future. "This is really a self-examination for us as an Army, and it's an introspective look that we hope to be able to offer the insights beyond the Army, both within the department and in the international arena writ large," she said.

Unified Quest was a forum for evangelizing another principle: humanitarian intervention. One prominent player in Unified Quest 2008 was Sarah Sewall, the Harvard professor and human rights advocate who had been instrumental in shaping the military's emerging counterinsurgency doctrine. A few months after Unified Quest 2008, the Carr Center for Human Rights Policy at the Kennedy School of Government unveiled a new initiative led by Sewall: the Mass Atrocity Response Operations, or MARO, Project. Cosponsored by the Army's Peacekeeping and Stability Operations Institute, the MARO Project was supposed to be a step-by-step guide for a military response to genocide or mass killings. According to Chris Taylor, a former private security executive who helped Sewall craft the document, it was written specifically as a blueprint for action for combatant commands such as AFRICOM to use the military as a "genocide prevention tool."

The MARO Project was inspired by "responsibility to protect," an emerging school of thought in international relations that calls for intervention by external actors if a state is unwilling, or unable, to stop genocide or mass killings. The guide even featured a hypothetical scenario on the African continent in Country X, a landlocked state in sub-Saharan Africa. Country X resembled Rwanda before the genocide. It was run by one ethnic group, Clan A, which was distributing weapons and broad-casting propaganda for a campaign of ethnic cleansing against another group, Clan B. The international community has limited time to act—weeks, perhaps days—before the mass killings begin. The MARO Project guide is supposed to spell out the options for intervening to halt the atrocities. Using this tool, the command could weigh the implications of sending in a rapid intervention force, understand the main operational tasks, and identify the desired end-state.

More important, the guide encourages civilian government agencies as well as allied nations to reorganize and become more closely involved in planning for such contingencies. The scenarios crafted by the MARO Project are hypothetical, but it is easy enough to spot real-world applications, especially after the creation of AFRICOM. In January 2009, the U.S. military became directly involved in planning and helping pay for a military offensive against the Lord's Resistance Army, a notorious rebel group in Uganda. It looked like a textbook case of "responsibility to protect": The LRA's messianic leader, Joseph Kony, was under indictment by the International Criminal Court for crimes against humanity; his cult-like army employed child soldiers and used rape as a weapon of war; and the LRA's reign of terror extended beyond Uganda's borders: north to Sudan, and east to the Democratic Republic of Congo and the Central African Republic.

Much as in Mali, the United States had quietly been providing counterterrorism training to Ugandan troops. In addition, as the *New York Times* later revealed, a team of seventeen advisers and analysts from AFRICOM worked closely with Ugandan officers to plan the offensive. They also provided intelligence, satellite phones, and $1 million in fuel. Despite the U.S. assistance, the operation was botched: Ugandan troops failed to block off the LRA's escape routes, and as the rebel fighters scattered, they embarked on a killing spree in nearby villages. An estimated nine hundred civilians were killed in a wave of massacres and reprisals.[19] The quiet, behind-the-scenes intervention in Uganda was a failure.

What was missing from the planning, and the scenarios, was some notion of balance between military and humanitarian capacity. U.S. foreign policy in Africa was quietly being militarized, but there was no parallel effort to beef up traditional aid and development efforts. There seemed to be no discussion within higher-echelon policy circles of trade, direct investment, or encouraging stronger bilateral ties within Africa. The new Africa command created its own internal logic. When the continent was viewed through the lens of preventive security, security became the sole goal.

CHAPTER 11

Windshield Ethnographers

On December 6, 2008, Lieutenant Colonel Pete Pierce was having a rough day. He had a meeting scheduled at noon with Hassan Shama, the chairman of the Sadr City District Advisory Council, but when Shama showed up at noon at the Iraqi Army checkpoint outside Forward Operating Base War Eagle, a U.S. outpost at an old police training center on the east side of the Tigris River, the soldiers would not let him to pass. Now Shama was angry: He had been waiting in his car for two hours.

Pierce marched into the office where Andre, one of his interpreters, was sprucing up a black vinyl couch with eau de cologne. "He's been delayed at the checkpoint," Pierce said, exasperated. "We had to call him and kiss his ass. He was stuck in traffic from ten o'clock to noon, and I promised to buy him lunch."

It was time for Plan B. Pierce would have to send someone out to the checkpoint to escort Shama on base—and order some kebabs. Fetching Shama fell to Abu Bassam, Pierce's Iraqi-American cultural advisor. "You go out to the checkpoint at two o'clock in your full battle rattle," he told Abu Bassam. "I'll get Sergeant Knox to go out with you to the checkpoint."

In civilian life, Pierce was a senior deputy district attorney in Orange County, California; in uniform, he maintained a weary, seen-it-all-before demeanor. In Baghdad, he led Human Terrain Team IZ3, a ten-person team attached to the Third Brigade Combat Team, Fourth Infantry Division. Pierce and his team were supposed to help the brigade manage its nonlethal operations. They provided cultural advice to the commander; helped the brigade's embedded Provincial Reconstruction Team, or e-PRT, allocate reconstruction funds; and identified key local leaders with whom the brigade commander, Colonel John Hort, could meet. It was all part of the Army's belated push for greater cultural awareness, an effort that had received official endorsement with the adoption of the Army-Marine Corps counterinsurgency manual in late 2006. Team IZ3 had recently organized five *iftar* dinners, meals to break the Ramadan fast, with tribal and religious sheikhs, local government officials and security forces, and members of the district advisory councils. It had also organized today's meeting with Shama.

The district advisory councils, referred to by the Americans as DACs, were local government bodies set up by the coalition following the invasion of Iraq in 2003. They had no lawmaking power or budget authority; their brief was to provide a form of local representative government. Neighborhood advisory councils, or NACs, selected representatives for the district-level council, and the DACs sent representatives to the Baghdad City Advisory Council. The DACs and the NACs also gave the U.S. presence a form of legitimacy, and provided a valuable interface between the U.S. military and local communities.

As its deputy chairman, Shama was a key player on the Sadr City DAC. Despite military commanders' wariness of Shama—Hort, the brigade commander, described him as initially "very anti-coalition"—Pierce and his teammates had persuaded the Army to work with him. Now things were a bit more cordial, although Shama still had a lot of complaints, particularly about the way the U.S. military was spending aid money inside Sadr City, part of the brigade's area of operations.

Sadr City was one of the most volatile places in Iraq. The densely populated Baghdad district had long been a stronghold for Shia militants, and a dangerous place for U.S. forces. Earlier in that spring of 2008, intense fighting had flared up around Sadr City after the Iraqi government launched an offensive in the southern city of Basra. Elements of Moqtada al-Sadr's Jaish al-Mahdi militia, designated "special groups" by the U.S. military, responded by using Sadr City as a launching pad for rocket attacks on the Green Zone. U.S. and Iraqi forces then launched a push into Sadr City, braving minefields and fighting street by street to retake the southern quadrant of the low-rise slum. U.S. forces then built a concrete wall along Al Quds Street that was supposed to push insurgent rocket teams beyond the reach of the Green Zone. North of the wall, tag teams of drones and attack helicopters loitered overhead, waiting to spot insurgent rocket and mortar teams. After two months of intense street fighting, the Iraqi government and the Jaish al-Mahdi concluded a truce, and Iraqi troops were able to take up positions inside the rest of Sadr City.

A few months after the ceasefire, a fragile sort of normalcy had returned to the area, and the U.S. military had begun aiming a firehose of development funds at the southern quadrant of Sadr City. In the eleven months since the arrival of the Third Brigade Combat Team, Fourth Infantry Division, in Baghdad in early 2008, the unit had spent around $72 million on public works projects in and around Sadr City. It hired local contractors to pick up trash, clear backed-up sewer lines, and repair downed power lines. On patrols, infantry officers were given "walking-around money." They were authorized to hand out $2,500 microgrants to jump-start local businesses that had lost inventory during the fighting. Seventy-two million was an astonishing amount of development money to focus on one section of one neighborhood. The United States had spent roughly the same amount on aid to all of Botswana in one year, 2008.

But the "save Sadr City fund" did not end the violence. In June 2008, a bomb was planted outside Shama's office. A group of Americans was meeting with Shama when the bomb detonated. Shama was wounded in the leg; the Americans, who were standing closer to the bomb, unwittingly shielded him from the blast. Four Americans were killed, along with six Iraqis and an Italian interpreter of Iraqi descent.[1] Two of the slain Americans were soldiers: Major Dwayne Kelley, a New Jersey state trooper and Army reservist, and Chief Warrant Officer Robert Hammett. Two were civilians: Steven Farley, a State Department contractor from Oklahoma and a member of the e-PRT, and Nicole Suveges, a member of Human Terrain Team IZ3.

When Suveges deployed to Iraq, in April 2008, Team IZ3 was part of an ambitious new experiment by the U.S. military to embed social scientists with combat brigades in Iraq and Afghanistan. Suveges was nearing completion of a Ph.D. in political science at Johns Hopkins University (her dissertation was titled "Markets and Mullahs: Global Networks,

Transnational Ideas and the Deep Play of Political Culture"), and she had worked in Iraq for two years, first as a polling expert and then as an advisor to Multi-National Corps Iraq. According to her colleagues, Suveges had been eager to join a Human Terrain Team; these teams were seen at the time as the cutting edge of counterinsurgency warfare and as the possible salvation of the U.S. military in Iraq.

But by December 2008, the military's program of embedding social scientists was in turmoil. Pierce had seen one member of his team killed, and he was in no mood to take any unnecessary risks. That day's meeting was no exception. When Shama finally reached the meeting two hours later, escorted through the checkpoint by Abu Bassam, the discussion quickly turned to the main item of business, the generators the brigade was installing to bring power to the southern neighborhoods of Sadr City. A major with the brigade's civil-military operations center was planning a trip to show members of the DAC where they were installed, and another IZ3 team member, Ben Rabitor, a young, slightly built social scientist, was enthusiastic about a chance to go out with the military team.

"I'd like to go on this mission!" he piped up.

"We'll see," Pierce replied drily. "I know you're anxious to get out beyond the wire, Ben, but"—Pierce paused for effect—"I guarantee by the end of your tour, you will never want to go out beyond the wire, okay? You will be all out-wired out!"

Ali Ghatteh, a deputy to Shama, had been listening in through an interpreter. He turned to Rabitor. "If you going to go out, grow out your beard and we are going to put you in a *dishdasha*," he said, referring to the traditional robe worn by men in Iraq. "And I can show you—I'll keep you safe in my area."

Rabitor sat up enthusiastically. It sounded like exactly the kind of thing a civilian anthropologist attached to the Army should be doing: blending in with the local community to help oversee a development project that might, if all went to plan, help restore stability to the area. "I'll be like *Iraqeen!*" he said.

Pierce, with the tone of a worried father, turned to Rabitor. "All right, Ben, you ain't doing anything like that while I'm here," he said.

The military that routed the Taliban in 2001 and decapitated the regime of Saddam Hussein in 2003 was a technologically superior force. It possessed overwhelming firepower, precision weaponry, and a global communications network. But this twenty-first-century force had blundered into Iraq and Afghanistan with only minimal understanding of the local cultural landscape. By the fall of 2006, with the adoption of the Army–Marine Corps counterinsurgency manual, the U.S. military was in theory taking the first steps toward reemphasizing the importance of cultural knowledge. In practice, these new nation builders were still struggling to understand the cultures they were dealing with in the Middle East and Central Asia. In a keynote address at the 2006 counterinsurgency conference in Washington, Eric Edelman, under secretary of defense for policy and a former ambassador, pointed to an essential new tool the U.S. government needed to deploy if it was to prevail in Iraq and Afghanistan, as well as in future conflicts: anthropology.

"In order to succeed in COIN [counterinsurgency] and stability operations, we must understand the cultures with which we are operating," he said.

> This is actually much more difficult than it sounds. Truly understanding another culture requires more than speaking a language or knowing certain social customs so that we do not offend our hosts. Certainly those things are important. But to truly have an impact, and to do more good than harm, we must understand the social power structures that informally govern societies as well as the internal motivations of the enemy and the people. In short, we need to develop an anthropological approach to understanding our enemies.

In Edelman's telling, ethnographic knowledge was in essence an intelligence tool, although perhaps not of the traditional sort. "Our intelligence processes and education and training systems must adapt to the need to obtain, analyze, and disseminate cultural knowledge," he said. "And by dissemination, I mean to everyone who needs it. It does no good for the military or anyone else to collect information if they do not share it with their interagency, coalition, private, and non-governmental partners."

When the can-do culture of the military applied itself to a technical problem, it could produce impressive technical results, particularly when it came to focusing the resources of the massive Pentagon procurement machine. The most dramatic example after September 11, 2001, was the creation of the Joint IED Defeat Organization, or JIEDDO, an organization within the Pentagon dedicated to countering the lethal roadside bomb threat in Iraq and Afghanistan.

At first, JIEDDO sank a large portion of its funds into technology, paying for myriad technical fixes to protect troops from IEDs. But despite the investment in defensive measures, the number of overall attacks continued to rise. JIEDDO began to shift its focus to stopping insurgent bomb-making cells, small, decentralized, secretive groups of part-time fighters who blended effortlessly into the local population. It was an approach that fused police work with anthropology: understanding the social context in which bomb makers operated, mapping out how they were organized, and learning how they interacted with the local population.

JIEDDO's new approach was presaged by a 2005 article in *Military Review*, the official journal of the Army's Combined Arms Center at Fort Leavenworth, written by Montgomery McFate, a policy fellow at the Office of Naval Research in Arlington, Virginia. In "Iraq: The Social Context of IEDs," McFate outlined ways that ethnographic knowledge could be applied to combating the problem of roadside bombs. "Because the insurgency is connected to the Sunni tribal system, certain sheiks probably know exactly where these explosives are stored," she wrote. "The sheiks are vulnerable in two ways: through their love of honor and through their love of money. Although they cannot be pressured to divulge the whereabouts of explosives through appeals to honor, because they see us as infidel adversaries, they are vulnerable to financial rewards. In Iraq, there is an old saying that you cannot buy a tribe, but you can certainly hire one."[2]

McFate suggested that the military units turn Iraq's traditional tribal patronage system to their advantage, bribing sheiks to buy their temporary loyalty and assistance: "In so doing, they [coalition forces] should be careful not to offer money as a 'reward' for divulging the whereabouts of explosives, but as a show of goodwill to the sheik, combined with a humble request for assistance."[3]

This idea of using social science to further military aims was intriguing, but cultural expertise could not simply be procured the same way the Army might buy a new radio or the Air Force might upgrade the camera on a spyplane. The government would need to enlist anthropologists and social scientists with serious professional expertise for this kind of effort.

In 2006, the Foreign Military Studies Office at Fort Leavenworth, Kansas, part of U.S. Training and Doctrine Command, launched a pilot program called the Human Terrain System, or HTS. The program grew directly out of the Pentagon's effort to counter roadside bombs. In December 2005, Army Colonel Steve Fondacaro, who headed JIEDDO, received a laptop loaded with ethnographic data and social network diagrams. The laptop was designed, in part by McFate, to help military commanders better understand local cultures they encountered in Iraq. Fondacaro concluded that the computer alone was useless. "I threw that shit out of there," he later told a *Wired* reporter, Noah Shachtman. "The last thing these guys needed was another gizmo . . . They needed a person, someone with knowledge of the society. An angel on their shoulder."[4]

The brigade commanders needed social scientists to provide advice, not a library loaded with ethnographic data. McFate helped come up with a revised plan for providing useful insights.[5] The idea was to set up five-person Human Terrain Teams, or HTTs, that would be embedded within the headquarters of brigades or regiments deployed to Iraq or Afghanistan. The civilian social scientists on the HTTs would provide cultural analysis for the commander. Able to link back to a "reachback center" at Fort Leavenworth, Kansas, for customized social science research, they would build a repository of local knowledge—customs and traditions, social network diagrams, economic data—as a lasting resource for commanders. Building up a database was a particularly important point. When a brigade rotated out of theater and a new unit arrived, the outgoing unit took a mountain of information with it, scribbled in notebooks, folded up on wall charts, and stored on memory sticks. A Human Terrain Team devoted to one area would provide "institutional memory," sparing military units the painful process of relearning everything from scratch.

Five teams were scheduled to deploy from Fort Leavenworth to Afghanistan and Iraq in the fall of 2006, as a "proof of concept." If all went as planned, HTTs would eventually be assigned to each deployed brigade or regimental combat team. McFate, then on staff at the Institute for Defense Analyses, was appointed as the senior social scientist for the program. She would be responsible for making the public case for this new, anthropological approach to winning the war at the September 2006 counterinsurgency conference in Washington.

It was a striking debut. Among the panelists in military dress uniform and Brooks Brothers suits, McFate stood out with her severe pixie hair-cut and stylish attire. Her professional biography described her as a "native of Marin County, California, where she grew up on a WWII naval ammunition barge that had been converted into a houseboat." It made an interesting contrast to the other panelists, whose biographies listed the usual bureaucratic highlights: service on bipartisan commissions, memberships with the Council on Foreign Relations, operational deployments, arms-control negotiations. She looked every inch the grown-up Goth punk, and her presentation and her style were meant to provoke. The U.S. military, she told attendees, had a "staggering lack of knowledge" about other countries and other societies, and in Iraq, the military's ignorance of local customs, traditions, and power relationships had been near-catastrophic. The national security establishment, too, needed the potent tools of social science that could help it understand its adversaries.

In "Anthropology and Counterinsurgency: The Strange Story of their Curious Relationship," published in *Military Review* in 2005, McFate argued that the military's lack of cultural mastery was a strategic weakness:

> Once called the "handmaiden of colonialism," anthropology has had a long, fruitful relationship with various elements of national power, which ended suddenly following the Vietnam War . . . The curious and conspicuous lack of anthropology in the national-security arena since the Vietnam War has had grave consequences for countering the insurgency in Iraq, particularly because political policy and military operations based on partial and incomplete cultural knowledge are often worse than none at all.[6]

To save the enterprise in Iraq from failure, McFate was arguing, the military needed to forge a new alliance with anthropology.

The rich history of anthropology as an instrument of national power can be traced back to the era of "high colonialism," when ethnographers, archaeologists, and cartographers traversed the globe to catalogue imperial possessions. As McFate noted, ethnography evolved as a practical tool for understanding and administering "native" societies during the heyday of imperialism:

> As early as 1908, anthropologists began training administrators of the Sudanese civil service. This relationship was quickly institutionalized: in 1921, the International Institute of African Languages and Cultures was established with financing from various colonial governments, and Lord Lugard, the former governor of Nigeria, became head of its executive council. The organization's mission was based on Bronislaw Malinowski's article, "Practical Anthropology," which argued that anthropological knowledge should be applied to solve the problems faced by colonial administrators, including those posed by "savage law, economics, customs, and institutions."[7]

But collaboration between anthropology and the state had a mixed record. In World War I social science research was used as a cover for espionage. In perhaps the most famous example, the Office of Naval Intelligence recruited Sylvanus Morley, a scholar of Mayan archaeology, to survey two thousand miles of remote Central American coastline in search of German submarine bases. Morley also produced almost a thousand pages of intelligence reporting and helped recruit several other archaeologists for clandestine missions.[8] The practice of spies using social science research as a cover was condemned by the prominent anthropologist Franz Boas, who saw it as a serious breach of professional ethics. In a letter published in the *Nation* in December 1919, Boas wrote, "A person . . . who uses science as a cover for political spying, who demeans himself to pose before a foreign government as an investigator and asks for assistance in his alleged researches in order to carry on, under this cloak, his political machinations, prostitutes science in an unpardonable way and forfeits the right to be classed as a scientist."[9]

According to David Price, a historian of anthropology and a critic of the Human Terrain System, the Boas affair "marked the beginning of American anthropology's public debates about the propriety of mixing anthropology with military and intelligence operations."[10] During World War II, however, many of those professional concerns were set aside as anthropologists joined in the war effort. Boas's most famous student, Margaret Mead, contributed to the National Research Council's

Committee on Food Habits, where she applied anthropological methods to food distribution and preparation in war-torn countries. She also published *And Keep Your Powder Dry: An Anthropologist Looks at America*, a patriotic volume on the American national character.[11] Mead's husband, the anthropologist Gregory Bateson, served with distinction in the Office of Strategic Services, the precursor to the CIA.[12]

In the one and a half decades after World War II, the military and academia once again became estranged. In December 1964, however, the Special Operations Research Office, a federally funded research institute at American University in Washington, wrote to scholars with an interest in social science research on conflict in the developing world to announce Project Camelot: "Project Camelot is a study whose objective is to determine the feasibility of developing a general social systems model which would make it possible to predict and influence politically significant aspects of social change in the developing nations of the world." The main objective of Project Camelot was to find ways to measure a country's vulnerability to "internal war," and come up with ways to counteract it.[13]

In the national-security jargon of the time, "internal war" was shorthand for Soviet-backed wars of national liberation fought in postcolonial societies. But the authors of a briefing paper prepared by the Army, which was providing the funds for Project Camelot research, put the objective in broader terms of nation building:

> The problem of insurgency is an integral part of the larger problem of the emergence of developing countries and their transition toward modernization . . . The indicated approach is to try to obviate the need for insurgency through programs for political, economic, social, and psychological development. Military support of such programs can be a significant factor in the nation-building process.[14]

Carefully applied U.S. assistance—sometimes economic, sometimes military—could influence the outcome in weak or endangered states, and prevent them from falling into the Soviet sphere. For this enterprise to succeed, however, the U.S. government needed to better understand the current cultural context of insurgency. The first Project Camelot field research was to be conducted in Latin America, but the main focus was

Vietnam, where the United States was becoming ever more deeply involved. Seymour Deitchman worked on Project Camelot as special assistant for counterinsurgency programs under Harold Brown, the director of Defense Research and Engineering. Project Camelot had originated in Brown's office. It duplicated some efforts being undertaken by the military services and the Advanced Research Projects Agency, the science arm of the Pentagon that was created after the Soviets launched Sputnik. Deitchman explained the rationale of Project Camelot in his memoir of the program, *The Best-Laid Schemes: A Tale of Social Research and Bureaucracy*:

> Historically, western nations in colonial times had a lode of data deriving from and relevant for the master-slave relationship between governors and governed. Such data were often not germane, and the learning problem was much more severe, in the more egalitarian relationship we had undertaken with the Vietnamese. We had insufficient knowledge to do the job as well as we wanted to, and while this may be typical of the international efforts of all nations, growing awareness led to a strong feeling at the highest levels of American government that we would have to do better.[15]

That sentiment—not *whether* the job should be done, but *how* to do it better—could easily describe the policymaking elite's discussions about Iraq forty years later. In essence, the Army wanted a new Project Camelot, but planners and policymakers conveniently overlooked the program's abject failure. When the left-wing press in Chile got wind of Project Camelot in mid-1965, lurid stories began to appear about U.S. "interventionism" and "espionage" under the guise of social-science research. To make matters worse, Project Camelot was seen as encroachment by the military on diplomatic turf: The State Department saw foreign policy and social science research as its domain, but the Pentagon was getting all the money.

A furor in Washington ensued after a front-page story by Walter Pincus of the *Washington Star* on July 27, 1965, "Army-State Department Feud Over Social Science Research in Chile," in which Pincus broke the news of the growing feud between the State Department and the Pentagon over the research the Army was conducting in Chile under the auspices of

Project Camelot. Pincus's reporting probably drew on a deliberate leak from Foggy Bottom (Deitchman noted that Pincus's story was based on a classified State Department cable). The controversy had as much to do with bureaucratic turf battle as it did with conspiracy theories: Project Camelot's Chilean study had been started without the knowledge of the U.S. ambassador in Santiago, who called for cancellation of the program. Press coverage was key to bringing Project Camelot to an untimely end, Deitchman noted:

> It brought the Camelot fiasco to the public's attention and stimulated the interest of members of Congress in DOD social research. It fed, if it did not trigger, the bureaucratic conflict between the State and Defense Departments. When all was over it could claim much of the credit for having brought the DOD's supposed misbehavior to public account.[16]

In many ways Project Camelot foreshadowed the controversy that followed the Human Terrain System from its inception. Like Project Camelot, the Human Terrain System arose from the intense frustration of military officials and policymakers with their inability to defeat relatively primitive insurgents. The United States was deeply engaged in giving aid to Iraq and Afghanistan, but it understood little about local antagonisms and local cultures in these and other countries. Washington policymakers rarely understood those dynamics, and any of the knowledge acquired during a twelve- or fifteen-month Army rotation (or in the case of a diplomat, a one-year tour) often had to be relearned when a new unit or a bureaucratic replacement arrived.

The Human Terrain System took things a step further than Project Camelot by embedding social scientists within military units. When the program became public, it almost immediately sparked controversy. Part of the problem was McFate's persona as an intellectual bomb thrower. As McFate saw it, anthropology had beaten a retreat to the Ivory Tower, where anthropologists' professional embrace of postmodernist theory led the discipline to continue a long slide toward irrelevance. In the 1960s and 1970s, she wrote, the anthropological community "refused to 'collaborate' with the powerful, instead vying to represent the interests of indigenous peoples engaged in neocolonial struggles ... Armed with critical hermeneutics, frequently backed up by self-reflexive neo-Marxism, anthropology began a brutal process of self-flagellation, to a degree almost unimaginable to anyone outside the discipline."[17]

In a 2006 *New Yorker* profile, McFate explained her collaboration with the military with a well-rehearsed line: "I'm engaged in a massive act of rebellion against my hippie parents."[18] But it was in equal part a rebellion against her profession.

In its search for qualified social scientists, the Army reverted to a familiar pattern: It outsourced. Army Training and Doctrine Command at Fort Monroe, Virginia, awarded a contract to BAE Systems, a major defense contractor, to run the Human Terrain System. Formed from the merger of British Aerospace and Marconi Electronic Systems, BAE Systems was a manufacturer of armored vehicles, naval guns, missile launchers, and artillery systems; it was a "systems integrator" for installing military electronics and communications gear. The company had no problem finding engineering talent, but it was perhaps not the ideal choice for luring qualified anthropologists from academia. Rather than reach out at academic conferences, it posted ads on military- and intelligence-oriented job boards and Monster.com. Of the first thirty-five social scientists who deployed to Iraq and Afghanistan, only about half had Ph.D.s. Of those, only seven were anthropologists.[19] Once again, finding manpower was the critical challenge in the nation-building enterprise.

The military's culture of secrecy clashed with the more free-spirited world of academia. Human Terrain research was supposed to draw from "open source" rather than classified information, but the teams worked inside military headquarters, a sensitive environment filled with classified maps, monitors, and equipment. The job required, at a minimum, a "secret" clearance; candidates would preferably obtain a "top secret" clearance. Background checks for a top-secret clearance are intrusive; they also require "cleared" individuals to sign what are, in effect, nondisclosure agreements. That kind of restriction could be a potential problem for an academic who was interested in writing and publishing freely. And it could also be an obstacle for social science researchers who traveled widely and had a great range of foreign contacts.

Such was the case with Zenia Helbig, a graduate student at the University of Virginia who joined the Human Terrain program in 2006.

Helbig was in many ways an ideal hire. She was a student of religious violence in the Muslim world, particularly in Shia communities, and her research had taken her twice to Iran, where she had briefly met Mahmoud Ahmadinejad, then the mayor of Tehran. Despite her travel to an "Axis of Evil" state, Helbig managed to receive an interim clearance. But she was suspended from the program after cracking a joke over a beer in a base parking lot during an exercise at Fort Hood, Texas ("Okay, if we invade Iran, that's where I draw the line, hop the border and switch sides," she recalls saying). Stripped of her clearance, Helbig became unable to work in any national security-related program.[20]

The Human Terrain System offered extremely lucrative pay packages, particularly for academics. The typical base salary for a Human Terrain Team member was around $115,000; when combined with hardship pay and other incentives for serving in a war zone, the take-home pay for a team member could climb as high as $300,000.[21] But the Army still had trouble recruiting. Part of the issue was professional resistance. In 2007, a group of anthropologists organized an ad hoc group called the Network of Concerned Anthropologists. They lobbied their colleagues to sign a pledge of nonparticipation in counterinsurgency programs. The pledge stated:

> U.S. military and intelligence agencies and military contractors have identified "cultural knowledge," "ethnographic intelligence," and "human terrain mapping" as essential to US-led military intervention in Iraq and other parts of the Middle East . . . Such work breaches relations of openness and trust with the people anthropologists work with around the world and, directly or indirectly, enables the occupation of one country by another. In addition, much of this work is covert. Anthropological support for such an enterprise is at odds with the humane ideals of our discipline as well as professional standards.[22]

The Network of Concerned Anthropologists' pledge was premised in large part on opposition to the war in Iraq. But the American Anthropology Association, the main professional body for anthropologists, raised broader ethical concerns. In October 2007, the "triple A" issued a statement condemning the program, saying that the Human Terrain System violated the ethical directive that anthropologists first "do no harm" to the individuals they study. "As members of HTS teams, anthropologists provide information and counsel to U.S. military field commanders," the statement read. "This poses a risk that information provided by HTS anthropologists could be used to make decisions about identifying and selecting specific populations as targets of U.S. military operations either in the short or long term."

Proponents of the Human Terrain System argued that the data they collected in the field was appropriately firewalled, and that it could not be tapped by military units for purposes of targeting. McFate stated in a 2008 interview:

> The S-2 [the military intelligence staff] can't come to the Human Terrain Team and say: "I need to find out x about this person." They literally can't do that. We don't want, as a program, the Human Terrain Teams, doing anything that's involved in lethal targeting. That's not their job . . . The military does not need our help to do that. They're the best in the world doing that. We're trying to be a resource for who their friends are.[23]

Then there was the nettlesome question of consent. Human Terrain Teams traveled in the field with heavily armed military units. When a researcher—in uniform, perhaps armed, and probably accompanied by a rifle platoon—stopped to interview an Afghan villager, it might seem more than just a little coercive. How much useful ethnographic or cultural information could be extracted under such conditions? Would villagers simply tell researchers what they wanted to hear? How, in the long term, did researchers expect to build rapport with ordinary people when they were swaddled in body armor, and carrying weapons? Social scientists training at Fort Leavenworth even learned the practice of "windshield ethnology"—observing groups from inside a vehicle.[24] But that sounded absurd. How much could you understand of a local community while gazing through the bulletproof windshield of an up-armored Humvee?

Despite these flaws, the program still seemed quite attractive to the military. Colonel Martin Schweitzer, commander of the Fourth Brigade, Eighty-second Airborne Division, told David Rohde of the *New York Times* that his unit had reduced their dependence on lethal operations by 60 percent since the Human Terrain Team was attached to his unit.

"We're looking at this from a human perspective, from a social scientist's perspective," he said. "We're not focused on the enemy. We're focused on bringing governance down to the people."[25]

Schweitzer's statistics were questionable: When David Price, a member of the Network of Concerned Anthropologists, filed a Freedom of Information Act request to look at the report supporting that claim, he received correspondence that merely restated the 60 percent figure, without an actual report to back up the statistic.[26] Still, it was a compelling idea. A little respect, compassion, and cultural sensitivity might save human lives. Instead of conducting an aggressive house-to-house search for bomb-making materials, a Human Terrain Team might be sent to coax information from a local community by offering to dig a well, resolve a tribal dispute, or redress some other local grievance. In parallel, the social scientists could teach soldiers to avoid cultural blunders that might injure local pride and motivate someone to shelter an insurgent, stash weapons, or attack coalition forces. Of course, it would be hard to measure progress. The effectiveness would be measured in roadside bombs that didn't go off. The concerned anthropologists might have worried about the purity of their profession, but the Human Terrain System, at least, seemed to offer a practical way of reducing harm to civilians.

That interest in the application of social science to resolving conflict seems to be what motivated Michael Bhatia, a scholar assigned to Human Terrain Team AF1 in Khowst Province, southeastern Afghanistan. A magna cum laude graduate of Brown University and a Marshall Scholar at St. Antony's College, Oxford, Bhatia joined the program in 2007 after working for several years as a researcher on Afghanistan. His doctoral dissertation, "The Mujahideen: A Study of Combatant Motives in Afghanistan, 1978–2005," was based on hundreds of interviews he conducted with current and former combatants throughout Afghanistan, as well as archival and media research. He had also worked as a UN observer in East Timor and an election monitor in Kosovo. Described by his thesis advisor at Brown as "an idealist and a realist," Bhatia went into the program with eyes open. "I am already preparing for both the real and ethical minefields," he wrote in an e-mail to friends shortly before deploying to Afghanistan.[27]

In early May 2008, Bhatia was riding in a convoy through a remote sector of Khowst Province, not far from the Pakistan border. That area had been the scene of a long-standing tribal feud, and Bhatia hoped that he could help initiate tribal negotiations that might spark reconciliation. The meeting would never take place. A roadside bomb struck the convoy's lead vehicle, and Bhatia was killed instantly. With Bhatia's death, the Human Terrain System lost the poster child for the program, an idealistic, articulate young researcher with serious experience in Afghanistan and a genuine interest in making military operations less lethal. It was the first of a series of deadly disasters for the program.

The main problem for Human Terrain Team IZ3, in Iraq, was electricity, not tribal politics. When major combat ended in Iraq in 2003, the U.S. military quickly discovered that one of the top complaints of the local population was power outages. During the summer months, when temperatures reached sweltering highs and the demand for cooling strained the electricity grid, neighborhoods received only two or three hours of power a day from municipal power. Things were a bit better in the winter, but residents still got power only about eight hours a day on the city grid. Power shortfalls exacerbated an already volatile situation in the capital. Power relations were constantly shifting. The government of Prime Minister Nouri al-Maliki had managed to broker a ceasefire with the Jaish al-Mahdi, but Sunni Arab leaders worried that the Shia-dominated coalition had long-term designs to exclude them from power.

The U.S.-led coalition was in the middle, and it was focused on trying to find the right people to work with at the local level. It had thrown money at these problems before, often with little result. But Colonel Hort, the commander of the Third Brigade Combat Team, Fourth Infantry Division, had made restoring essential services one of the priorities in the brigade's area of responsibility.

In the past, U.S. commanders used their emergency funds to put power generators on the ground in residential neighborhoods of Baghdad. It was a well-intentioned gesture, but those generators were only a short-term fix. They didn't come with maintenance, the government of Iraq and the local municipalities didn't provide fuel, and no one was charged with maintaining them over the longer term. Many generators were supplied with enough fuel for one month; once that was gone, the generators simply were left to rust away.

For Hort's power generation scheme to succeed in Sadr City, the brigade would have to do much more than install new generators or provide fuel. They would have to encourage the District Advisory Councils to exercise oversight, work with the central government to provide subsidized fuel, and make sure that the local community was invested in the upkeep. "With local power, it's about buy-in with the local government; it's about the Ministry of Oil agreeing to the fuel costs; it's about the neighborhood agreeing to take care of it," Hort said. "So it's a co-op. It's not just a generator that's being bought by U.S. taxpayers' money. It takes more time. You know, I can buy a generator probably tomorrow and put it on the ground—it'll last maybe two months, at that. Co-ops take about two to three months to really get moving. Where you get everybody's signature, everybody agrees to it, and that's the cultural thing you described. Everything's slower here, nothing is"—he snapped his fingers—"overnight."

That was where Human Terrain Team IZ3 came into the picture. They were supposed to identify the local leaders who could help make this arrangement work. It would require a laborious series of "meeting engagements" between the brigade's officers and local leaders such as the chairmen and deputy chairs of DACs, government officials, and tribal leaders. But it was more complicated than just identifying local counterparts. It also meant negotiating a byzantine system of local government that was a legacy of the administrative system created by Saddam Hussein.

For example, the government of Baghdad still essentially replicated the preinvasion Ba'ath regime model, in which the provincial council ran Baghdad via the Ba'ath Party. In 2008, the budget for the province still rested with the provincial council. The DAC, the democratically elected district council, had no budget, and no direct control over the *baladiya*, the public-works department for a particular area. The *baladiya*'s managers reported through the *amanat*—the municipal government—to the provincial council; they did not report directly to the DAC.

Another complicating factor was the remnants of Iraq's command economy. Like basic foodstuffs, generator fuel was subsidized by the state, and rations were issued by Iraq's Ministry of Oil, but much of the fuel ended up being sold on the street. The generators donated by the brigade were supposed to receive a certain amount of subsidized fuel, but there was little incentive to keep a neighborhood generator running when the operator could turn around and resell the subsidized fuel on the open market for a much higher price. This was a striking irony of U.S. involvement in Iraq: In order to keep the country from sliding into chaos, it had to prop up elements of Saddam Hussein's dysfunctional command economy and administrative structure.

To complicate matters further, the clock was ticking. Under a security framework that was negotiated between the United States and Iraq in late 2008, U.S. troops were to begin a gradual withdrawal from Iraq's cities by mid-2009. Within six months, the U.S. military would be moving to the periphery, and local communities would have to rely more and more on the provincial government and the national government and less and less on assistance from the United States. The costly U.S. investments in projects such as micro-power generation would be squandered if there was no Iraqi plan to sustain them. Things were moving swiftly, and the U.S. military needed to show progress.

Over the summer, Hort's Third Brigade had paid for nine new neighborhood generators for that part of Sadr City. So the news that Hassan Shama, now Sadr City DAC chairman, brought Pierce and his Human Terrain IZ3 team was not good: "We had a promise to deliver some generators, you may have delivered those generators and you may have left them, but I'm not aware of it—the council's not aware of it," Shama said.

Ali Ghatte, who headed the DAC's electricity committee and had accompanied Shama to the meeting, had counted only five generators. Another twist: they had no registration documents. In Iraq, a generator, like an automobile, came with registration papers. Without the papers, the DAC couldn't get subsidized fuel from the Ministry of Oil. Shama, a beefy, forty-something man in jeans and green and yellow polo shirt with closely cropped mustache and goatee, explained this complicated situation to Pierce and Ted Andrews, the Foreign Service officer who headed the e-PRT.

As the Americans listened through the interpreters, Shama shifted restlessly in his seat, and steadily began to raise his voice.

"Let me say this," Pierce said, trying to convey a sense of urgency. "Maybe we don't look like we are concerned. We're concerned with what you just told us, believe me."

Andrews, rising above the crosstalk, added, "We will have the Army confirm with you . . . and if there is some big mistake, we have a gentleman from the press here who can write all this down!"

Switching to English, Shama said, "I'm sorry, mister, this is the problem." Leaning energetically forward on his elbows, he resumed in Arabic. "This is how this thing's supposed to be done," he said. "If you have a quantity of generators, you should go to me and say you have those nine or ten generators. You tell us where the areas are that are most in need for them. Even if the Army is trying to put those generators up, they know who's the [council] member for the section they are working in. They should have grabbed him and told him [Ali Ghatte]. The Army may have placed the generator there, but nobody's aware of it. And nobody's watching the generators. So someone may have just come and taken it."

That worried Pierce. He called down to the brigade staff to sort out whether or not the generators had in fact been delivered or if they had in fact disappeared. A major from the brigade staff arrived shortly thereafter, looking confused.

"Let me do this as a district attorney here," Pierce told the major. "Here is the deal that we have discovered. First of all, Ali Ghatte is concerned about the actual location—and, frankly, security of the microgenerators. He's concerned, because we've given him in Arabic their location, and he says some of those are not in those *mahallas* [blocks] . . . Frankly, we're concerned that some of them have been taken. So that's a very significant issue."

Solving that first issue was fairly straightforward. The major would arrange to pick up Ghatte and Shama in an armored vehicle and show them where all the generators were. The second point, getting subsidized fuel, was a bit more complicated. They needed to get registration paperwork from Doctor Moayad Hamed, a Baghdad doctor who had built a lucrative postwar business as a contractor to the U.S. military. Doctor Moayad had won the contract to oversee the repair of Route Irish, the crucial Baghdad airport road. He had contracts for trash pickup, for street repair, even for painting bright murals to spruce up the concrete barriers that surrounded many residential neighborhoods. He had the contract for generators as well. The problem was, he was not turning over the paperwork.

Pierce said, "Ali Ghatte told us that he tried to talk to Doctor Moayad, and that for some reason Doctor Moayad is extremely reluctant to turn over the registration paperwork. Is that right?"

"That's true, we contacted them more than one time," Ghatte said.

Pierce, to the major, said sotto voce, "What I'm afraid is that he is turning around and using this registration paperwork to secure fuel and then selling it on the black market."

"Sure," the major whispered. "I'm tracking that."

Pierce then cleared his throat. "I do have a couple questions for the group. Will copies of the registrations suffice to get the fuel flowing?"

Shama and Ghatte agreed that, yes, a copy of the paperwork would suffice. After two hours of debate, a temporary solution had been reached—or so it seemed. Later that month, the generators still were not operating.

A few weeks after my visit with Human Terrain Team IZ3, I embedded with an Army infantry company at Joint Security Station Comanche, a small outpost manned by an Army infantry company inside Sadr City proper. First Sergeant Ethan Mizell, the company's senior NCO, told me the generators inside their patrol zone had been installed in August; the Iraqi government provided some test fuel, around a thousand liters. That supply ran out in less than three weeks, although the company donated some extra fuel to get people through the Eid festival after Ramadan. "They ran out of fuel in twenty days," Mizell said. "I gave it to them for the rest of the month because it was their holiday." After that, there was no more money from the Army to keep topping up the generator supply.

Captain Andrew Slack, the company commander, told me the Commander's Emergency Response Program funds had dried up on October 1, at the beginning of the new fiscal year. The Iraqis would be on their own. "You can sort of play Sim City: Come in and build some roads, repair buildings, spruce up a park or a school," he said. "That can be nice visually, but because we weren't so hooked up with the local leadership, we weren't as effective as we could have been."

In many respects Pete Pierce was the ideal person to lead Human Terrain IZ3. As a district attorney he was steeped in the intricacies of municipal politics; he also understood the organized crime–style networks underpinning the insurgency in Sadr City. But that was by accident, not by design. Pierce was recruited to run IZ3 because of his background in Military Intelligence and Civil Affairs; he was recruited by another reserve officer who was in his Civil Affairs unit, who had done a tour in Iraq with one of the senior managers of the Human Terrain System program. He was not a Middle East expert, and both he and the social scientists on

Human Terrain Team IZ3 relied heavily on Arabic interpreters to do their jobs.

For cultural insights, Pierce depended on his senior cultural adviser, Abu Bassam. An Iraqi Christian and Baghdad native, Abu Bassam had emigrated to the United States three decades ago and had returned to Iraq to work as an interpreter for U.S. military commanders. (Abu Bassam, or "father of Bassam" was the nickname he used when dealing with Iraqis.) A compactly built man with a neatly trimmed mustache, Abu Bassam had a gentle, low-key demeanor. Back in the United States, he was a retired engineer. Here, he was the key interpreter of the local scene, and a powerful broker between cultures.

"I am very much a fair broker to both sides," he told me while we waited for the meeting with Hassan Shama. "I don't want anybody to lose. A lot of money was wasted [on reconstruction projects] and we all know that."

The collaboration with Shama was a case in point. "Everyone hated him, the commander, the Americans," Abu Bassam said. "I convinced everyone we should work with him."

Abu Bassam may have emigrated to the States decades ago, but that didn't mean he had shed all of his Iraqi habits of thought. He had a low opinion of the Shia population of Sadr City. "The Shia mentality is different," he told me. "They are ghetto. They can sleep with their cousins, screw donkeys. I don't want to put them down—some of them are doctors, engineers, teachers. Now the Shia took over the government—what do they know how to do? Nothing. Administratively, they have nothing, no experience in governing."

During the years he had spent working for the U.S. military in Iraq, Abu Bassam had noticed a subtle shift under way. The U.S. military was getting smarter. "There was an attitude: Don't fight them with bullets. We need to be not more offensive, not more defensive. We need to listen." If the Human Terrain System had been in place in 2003, he concluded, "this all would have been different. We [the United States] don't know how to spend on projects. We need to run the military more as a business. The military never follows through on anything—so much money wasted, gone into bank accounts in Syria and Lebanon. We give a project a million dollars, and half a million dollars goes to militias."

This was the problem with spending money to pacify Iraq: The whole approach of paying large segments of the Iraqi population not to fight was extraordinarily susceptible to waste, fraud, and abuse. In Anbar Province and elsewhere, in a program called "Sons of Iraq," the U.S. military bank-rolled tribal militias to stop fighting American forces and keep order in their neighborhoods. Many of the "Sons" were former insurgents. Even-tually, the Iraqi government was supposed to absorb some of the "Sons" into regular security forces. In Baghdad, the U.S. government sponsored a host of make-work schemes and public works projects designed to keep fighting-age males on the U.S. payroll—and out of criminal gangs or in-surgent groups.

Fraud and waste were not limited to the military. USAID also lost track of millions of dollars. Take the Community Stabilization Program, a massive program started in May 2006 by USAID to complement coun-terinsurgency efforts in selected Iraqi cities. In a March 2008 audit, the agency's inspector general concluded that the program was extremely vulnerable to fraud. The report cited a letter from a USAID representa-tive on a Provincial Reconstruction Team in Baghdad that indicated that "millions of dollars" from trash pickup campaigns were being redirected to insurgents, as well as to corrupt community leaders. This source reck-oned that as much as half of the cash directed to cleanup campaigns in one area had been siphoned off by insurgents or corrupt officials. "If the source's estimates are correct—that 40 to 50 percent of payments for such projects were used for improper pay-offs—USAID may have al-ready been defrauded of $6.7 to $8.4 million, with another $3.4 to $4.3 million at risk absent any corrective action," the inspector general concluded—and this was in just one neighborhood of Baghdad, where $16.7 million in Community Stabilization Program funds had been disbursed.[28]

That was where the Human Terrain System entered the picture. It was not, as its academic critics liked to hint, a devilishly complex scheme to target Iraqis and Afghans for assassination, a sort of latter-day Phoenix Program, nor was it a version of COINTELPRO, the FBI's discredited domestic surveillance program that targeted antiwar groups and civil rights activists in the 1960s. Human Terrain IZ3's mission was an out-growth of the military's employment of cash as a weapon. The military needed better intelligence about how to spend the motherlode of recon-struction funds it was overseeing as part of the nation-building effort, and the Human Terrain System was tasked with obtaining it.

Human Terrain was, in short, an intelligence program. Not intelligence in the traditional sense, perhaps; instead, information with a practical military application. "Intelligence" was a taboo word for the Human Terrain System, and senior officials, like McFate, insisted that the teams were walled off from military intelligence. Yet the word cropped up in the field.

In a discussion with members of Human Terrain Team IZ3 around a picnic table at Forward Operating Base War Eagle, Pete Pierce, IZ3's leader, described the Human Terrain Team as having a clear role in collecting intelligence for the brigade's Civil Affairs operations.

"Well, we work with them on a constant basis," Pierce said. "So you could almost argue that we are"—Pierce paused, thinking—"the intelligence arm of Civil Affairs and the e-PRT, because they are the ones who control the budget. They are the ones who have the program to do reconstruction."

Robert Kerr, one of the social scientists on Pierce's team, swiftly moved to correct his boss. "The *information* arm," he clarified.

But in that conversation, Pierce repeatedly used the word "intelligence" to describe the kind of work they did. Asked what kinds of product they provided the commander after a key meeting with a local leader, he said, "We provide him with an intelligence . . ." He paused to clarify his language. "With an EXSUM, a summary of the meeting." In describing what kind of support he received from the "Reachback Center" analysts at Fort Leavenworth, he said, "If we go to these meetings and there's something we don't understand, about a tribe or about the political leadership or about the formation of the government of Iraq, then we request, you know, a report, a summary, or an intel product—I shouldn't say intel product—*information* product—from the Reachback Center."

So all the talk of the Human Terrain System being simple "open source" research was a polite fiction. The members of a Human Terrain Team worked for a military commander, they were located within a brigade headquarters, and information they shared, even if in the most general way, could help the commander sort out who was and was not the enemy. Lieutenant Colonel Gian Gentile, who commanded an armored reconnaissance squadron in Baghdad in 2006 and who described himself as "greatly in favor" of the program, pointed out that Human Terrain analysis would on some level allow commanders to understand who the enemy was in the area his unit operated in. "Don't fool yourself," he wrote Marcus Griffin, a Human Terrain Team member working in Iraq. "These Human Terrain Teams whether they want to acknowledge it or not, in a generalized and subtle way, do at some point contribute to the collective knowledge of a commander which allows him to target and kill the enemy in the Civil War in Iraq . . . So stop sugarcoating what these teams do and end up being a part of; to deny this fact is to deny a reality of the wars in Iraq and Afghanistan."[29]

Nicole Suveges, who was killed in the Sadr City advisory council bombing, would not be the last Human Terrain Team casualty. On November 4, 2008, two Human Terrain Team members, Don Ayala and Paula Loyd, were on a foot patrol in the village of Chehel Gazi, Afghanistan. Loyd, a social scientist, approached Abdul Salam, a local man carrying a fuel jug, and struck up a conversation about the price of gasoline. Without warning, the man doused Loyd in a flammable liquid and set her on fire. Soldiers rolled Loyd in a ditch to put out the flames; Abdul Salam was captured and restrained in plastic flexcuffs. When Ayala learned about the extent of Loyd's injuries, he walked over to the Afghan man, still bound at the wrists, and executed him with a pistol shot to the head.

Loyd died of her injuries after two agonizing months in an Army hospital.[30] Ayala pled guilty to the revenge killing; a U.S. District Court judge sentenced him to five years probation and a $12,500 fine.[31] The incident further tarnished the reputation of the program. In February 2009, morale further plummeted after the program's managers suddenly announced a major change. Team members would have to convert from well-compensated contractor status to a less well compensated government employee status, or they would have to resign. The move was supposed to be in response to the agreement struck between the Iraqi and U.S. governments to lift legal immunity for contractors, but it did not sit well with team members. Around one third of the program's deployed workforce quit.

That same spring, Major Ben Connable, a Marine Corps officer, authored a devastating critique of the Human Terrain System in *Military Review*, the same publication that had introduced the concept to a military audience two and a half years earlier. As a foreign area officer, or FAO, Connable understood the military's need to learn about foreign cultures. FAOs were supposed to be the military's resident experts on local cultures; they had language training and advanced degrees in area studies or international relations. But the Human Terrain approach of hiring civilian social scientists on contract had been a disaster, he contended. In the article, "All Our Eggs in a Broken Basket: How the Human Terrain System Is Undermining Sustainable Military Cultural Competence," he argued that the military needed to develop its own culturally literate officers in-house. That would further a commonsense aim of remedying the military's devastating lack of cultural knowledge without all the blowback from recruiting anthropologists and other social scientists. Connable asked:

> Why is it necessary to create a separate program, costing (at a minimum) tens of millions of dollars, to assign these personnel to the very staffs at which they were trained to serve? What do the Human Terrain Team FAO and CA [Civil Affairs] officers bring to the table that organic FAO and CA officers do not? If HTS can find these qualified officers, why can't the U.S. military services?[32]

But boosting the military's cultural I.Q. would have been too logical, and by now the Human Terrain System had taken on a life of its own in the Pentagon bureaucracy. U.S. Africa Command had quietly begun recruiting to staff a new "sociocultural cell" that would be attached to the new regional military headquarters. A "research and risk management firm" called Archimedes Global, Inc., was selected to recruit contractor teams. As the military ramped up its involvement in Afghanistan, the Army quietly moved to expand the program. In June 2009, a $40 million expansion of the program appeared in a story posted by the Thirty-fourth Infantry Division at its Web site—buried in a photo caption.[33]

Despite setbacks and failures, and the general inability to find the right people for the job, the U.S. military's embrace of social science showed no sign of diminishing. The approach was seen as the key to fighting a smarter war. But the Human Terrain System ignored a larger problem. The U.S. military was fighting an away game, operating in cultures it didn't understand, in places undergoing violent social change. They were the outsiders. All the anthropological expertise in the world couldn't fix that.

CHAPTER 12

Obama's War

On July 15, 2009, Admiral Mike Mullen, the chairman of the Joint Chiefs of Staff, boarded a Chinook helicopter bound for Pushghar, a village in Afghanistan's remote Panjshir Valley. Mullen was in Afghanistan as part of a morale-boosting United Service Organizations tour of U.S. bases in the Middle East and Central Asia. Accompanied by Don Shula, an NFL Hall of Famer, and other celebrities, Mullen and his entourage visited Kirkuk, Iraq; Bagram, Afghanistan; and the USS *Ronald Reagan*, deployed in the Persian Gulf. His detour to the Panjshir, however, was not for a meet-and-greet with the troops. The admiral was on a different mission: He was on his way to attend a ribbon-cutting at a girls' school.

The Panjshir girls' school had been opened by Greg Mortenson, author of the bestseller *Three Cups of Tea* and founder of the nonprofit Central Asia Institute, which promoted girls' education in rural Pakistan and Afghanistan. Members of the Panjshir Provincial Reconstruction Team, which was funding a dozen education projects throughout the province, also attended the opening ceremony.[1] The admiral had brought the *New York Times* columnist and globalization theorist Thomas Friedman along for the ride.[2] A visit by the top uniformed officer in the U.S. military to this rural schoolhouse would show how fully the U.S. military had embraced the concept of armed humanitarianism.

The morning of the ceremony, I hitched a ride to the Panjshir with an

Army security detail that was providing backup for Mullen's visit. The Panjshir Valley was considered "permissive," meaning the risk of attack was low. The high-walled valley had been a famous redoubt against both the Soviets and the Taliban, and the tough, warlike Panjshiris took pride in protecting their guests. Nevertheless, the Army dispatched a small security force to the Panjshir to provide backup security for Mullen's visit. The security force, led by Staff Sergeant Gabriel Castillo, would be the "quick reaction force" on hand in case anything went wrong.

The security force rolled out from Bagram Air Base in a convoy of Mine Resistant Ambush Protected (MRAP) vehicles, the behemoth, blast-proof trucks the military had procured in massive numbers to shield troops from roadside bombs.* Castillo, a muscular close-protection specialist from El Paso, Texas, gave the security team a short predeparture briefing. At the time, all roads to the Panjshir were considered "green" (relatively safe) but the soldiers were to be on the lookout for possible attackers, particularly when crossing through Kapisa Province, between Bagram and the gateway to the Panjshir. In late May, a Humvee carrying members of the Panjshir Provincial Reconstruction Team had been hit by a suicide car bomber while passing through Kapisa. Four members of the team were killed. It was a reminder that although the mission in the Panjshir Valley was primarily humanitarian, there were still serious risks.

The supersized armored trucks may have been well suited for Iraq's extensive highway network, but they definitely were not designed with Afghanistan's primitive roads in mind. The two-lane highway through the Panjshir was reasonably well paved, but the convoy also had to navigate village streets that were at some points barely wider than the trucks themselves. As the convoy weaved along narrow switchback roads, the MRAP driver leaned on the horn, scattering the occasional flock of fat-tailed sheep or gaggle of children playing in the road. A miscalculation

---

* MRAP procurement began in earnest in November 2006, more than three years after the invasion of Iraq. With some prodding from Secretary of Defense Robert Gates, buying the vehicles soon became the Pentagon's top spending priority. By mid-2009, the military had taken delivery of more than 16,000 of the million-dollar-plus vehicles, and the military had ordered a more nimble, offroad version for Afghanistan service, called the MRAP-All Terrain Vehicle. Though smaller, the M-ATV was still a beast, weighing in at twelve tons.

on one of the turns, and the trucks could easily tumble to the bottom of a ravine.

After passing through the main gateway to the valley, the crews removed the barrels of their heavy .50-caliber machine guns. More than anything it was a gesture of trust. Traveling guns-up in the Panjshir would definitely have sent the wrong signal. Nonetheless, the Army lieutenant who was hitching a ride with the team in the back of one of the MRAPs wasn't particularly happy. "I don't like that," he said. "I just came from Kapisa."

After a bumpy hour-and-a-half ride, the crew reached their destination. They parked in the motor pool of Forward Operating Base Lion, the small base for the Panjshir PRT, and waited. FOB Lion looked quite different from most military outposts I had seen in Iraq or Afghanistan. It was not surrounded by intimidating concrete walls or a perimeter of sand-filled HESCO barricades but was quite open and accessible, with just a simple gate and some concertina wire across the entrance. Pickup trucks, not massive armored vehicles, were parked in the motor pool. It was intriguing to see a U.S. base in Afghanistan that didn't look like Fortress America.

The convoy had arrived early; I wandered around the small camp and talked with some of the team members. Matthew Burns, a U.S. Army Corps of Engineers representative on the PRT, had come to the valley after stints working in Jalalabad and Kabul. When he first heard about how the PRT operated—driving around in pickups, not living behind walls, he was skeptical, to say the least. "When I first heard about it, no HESCOS, soft-skin vehicles, I didn't want anything to do with it," he said.

This was a very different sort of approach to the heavily armed nation building I had seen in Iraq. After years of watching the U.S. military armoring up to do a humanitarian mission, the Panjshir PRT seemed to offer a tantalizing glimpse of a different way of doing business. For nation builders used to living behind blast walls and commuting to their jobs in the Red Zone, that took some getting used to. Burns was honest about the adjustment. "My boss used to call me phobic," he said. "It took me a while to get used to it."

Burns soon found that working in the relatively peaceful Panjshir allowed for more hands-on development work. Instead of being holed up inside a camp and venturing out once or twice a week under heavy security to visit construction sites or oversee projects, members of the PRT here could get out in the valley every day. Burns and his teammates could visit a project site—a school being refurbished, a clinic under construction—as many as three times a week. For someone who was a general contractor by trade and who liked to see results, it was satisfying to watch progress every day. "It's phenomenal," he said with evident satisfaction. "We've done eighty site visits in three months. Sometimes we'll have a dozen in a day."

In Kabul, by contrast, Burns considered himself lucky if he got out once a week. There he had to travel "up-armored," with three body-guards accompanying his team. In the Panjshir, things were much closer to traditional development work. Team members could venture out in trucks or even, in some of the more remote districts, on horseback. A Corps of Engineers manager had his kayak sent over so he could paddle the Panjshir River. Aside from the rifles and the uniforms, the Pro-vincial Reconstruction Team looked like a civilian-run development scheme.

In 2009 about $40 million in projects were under way in the Panjshir Valley, and about another $20 million worth were in the pipeline. The main projects were schools and health clinics; the team was also bringing electricity to the valley with micro hydro power. Renewable energy was a big theme: They installed solar panels on all major project buildings, es-pecially the clinics. PRT members also gave practical advice and hands-on instruction while the projects were under way. Afghan bricklayers and carpenters still used rocks suspended from strings to make sure their structures were built to a true vertical. The engineers taught them to use more modern tools. "It's a golden opportunity to train these guys on ce-ment work and brickwork," Burns said.

Panjshir seemed to offer a glimpse of what the rest of Afghanistan could look like: a peaceful, relatively stable province that was a magnet for reconstruction and development work. Returning from his visit to the Panjshir, Friedman gushed about his heartstring-tugging visit to Morten-son's school, writing in a *New York Times* op-ed on July 18, 2009:

> I must say, after witnessing the delight in the faces of those little Afghan girls crowded three to a desk waiting to learn, I found it very hard to write, "Let's just get out of here." Indeed, Mortenson's efforts remind us what the essence of the "war on terrorism" is

about. It's about the war of ideas within Islam—a war between religious zealots who glorify martyrdom and want to keep Islam untouched by modernity and isolated from other faiths, with its women disempowered, and those who want to embrace modernity, open Islam to new ideas and empower Muslim women as much as men.

But Panjshir was the exception in Afghanistan, not the rule. The isolated valley was populated almost exclusively by ethnic Tajiks and thus was ethnically quite homogeneous—and it was home to many of the powerful military commanders and intelligence officials who had dominated Afghanistan's security ministries. Panjshiris were not a population at risk from Islamic extremism; their young men were not being recruited as suicide bombers. But seeing the schoolgirls of Pushghar, with their expectant smiles, it was tempting to view the massive U.S. military involvement here as a progressive enterprise, a mission to rescue the daughters of Afghanistan, save "Muslim progressives" from extremists, and project Western hopes and expectations on the country. It was an image that could be used to justify an American generation's worth of blood and treasure.

As the security team stood by, I spotted three helicopters soaring high, heading northeast through the valley. It was Mullen's Chinook, escorted by two Black Hawks. For a moment I contemplated the cost of ferrying the admiral to see Mortenson's school: fueling, flying, and maintaining three helicopters in a combat zone; sending a couple of squads of highly trained soldiers in million-dollar-trucks to the Panjshir. It seemed an awfully expensive way to lift a country out of poverty.

On December 1, 2009, President Barack Obama announced his decision to escalate the war in Afghanistan by sending an additional thirty thousand troops, which would bring the total U.S. force there to just under one hundred thousand by mid-2010. "Our troop commitment in Afghanistan cannot be open-ended," he said, "because the nation that I am most interested in building is our own." The following day, Secretary of Defense Robert Gates made the same point, telling the Senate Armed Services Committee, "This approach is not open-ended nation building." But while the administration excised the phrase "nation building" from the talking points, that was precisely what the involvement in Afghanistan had become. Whether it was soldiers teaching better planting techniques to Afghan farmers, diplomats and aid consultants advising local leaders, or Provincial Reconstruction Teams building roads, digging wells, and repairing schools, Afghanistan had become a major nation-building effort. Moreover, the exit strategy—building capable Afghan security institutions and transferring responsibility to them—was, by definition, a state-building project.

The escalation of the Afghanistan war underscored the continuity between the foreign policies of Obama and his predecessor, George W. Bush. By the end of Bush's term, his gamble of doubling down by sending more troops to Iraq had delivered some results. Violence in Iraq had dropped precipitously from previous levels, and the United States and Iraq negotiated a new security pact at the end of 2008 that called for the departure of U.S. troops by 2011. The surge validated the counterinsurgents theory: The U.S. military could prevail in this kind of conflict, if given the right tools. But it was an oversimplified take on events. The steep drop in violence was due to several factors, including the troop increase, a rift between al-Qaeda and Sunni tribes, and a ceasefire by Moqtada al-Sadr's Jaish al-Mahdi militia. Segregation and ethnic cleansing also played a major role: The process had somewhat played itself out, and so the triggers of violence had been eliminated.* By late 2008, the sectarian lines between neighborhoods had hardened, and Baghdad was a divided city. Millions of Iraqis remained outside the country, waiting out the conflict as refugees. The country continued to suffer from major political violence, and 2009 closed with a string of deadly suicide bomb attacks.

The Iraq surge had a curious knock-on effect. Despite the failure to turn Iraq into an oasis of stability and democracy in the Middle East, it gave the military and foreign policy establishment confidence that the United States could succeed at nation building, and transform a society.

In Beltway foreign-policy circles, attention quickly shifted away from Iraq to another unresolved crisis: Afghanistan and its increasingly chaotic

---

* A *New England Journal of Medicine* study published in mid-2009 concluded that murder after abduction was the leading cause of civilian deaths in Iraq between 2003 and 2008. Of the nearly twenty thousand murder victims accounted for in the study, nearly one third showed signs of torture.[3]

neighbor, Pakistan. After several years of being considered a "forgotten war," Afghanistan commanded the attention of the new administration. Within weeks of taking office Obama pledged to launch a top-to-bottom review of strategy in the region. The Taliban was resurgent, threatening the central government in Afghanistan, and by the end of Bush's term the United States had quietly stepped up a secret war in Pakistan, using armed Predator drones to strike the bases of Islamic militants who operated in Pakistan's remote tribal territories. In addition, in late 2009 the U.S. government promised a massive aid package of $7.5 billion to Pakistan over the following five years. The money was slated for high-visibility infrastructure projects, health and education projects, and building Pakistani government institutions.

The continuity between the Bush and Obama administrations was shaped in part by the consensus the nation builders had helped forge within the policymaking establishment. Just a few days before Obama's inauguration, Secretary of State Condoleezza Rice, Secretary of Defense Robert Gates, and USAID Administrator Henrietta Fore signed off on the U. S. government's new Interagency Counterinsurgency Guide, the handbook for policymakers that is supposed to reassert the primacy of "soft power." It was the culmination of two years of effort by the counterinsurgency guru David Kilcullen and his allies, and was a major victory for the nation builders. Getting two cabinet secretaries and an agency head to sign off on it was a tacit admission of failure by the Bush administration— that it had wasted years in Iraq and Afghanistan.

After the Republican defeat in November 2008, Kilcullen had toyed with the idea of getting Rice to hold off on signing the document. With her permission he had talked with the Obama transition team after the election victory, advising them on counterinsurgency issues. But he decided it was a good thing to push for high-level signatures before the close of the Bush era. An economic crisis was looming, and the new administration might not focus on the project.

The signing of this new document was significant for a number of reasons. First, the guide was signed at the highest level, lending weight to a document that was supposed to distill the principles of counterinsurgency doctrine and the lessons from Iraq and Afghanistan. Second, the guide was completed in time for the new administration, which was larded with true believers in nation building. Michele Flournoy, a former Clinton official whom the administration selected as the Pentagon's new policy chief, was a powerful advocate of the concept of global counterinsurgency. In early 2007, she had cofounded the Center for a New American Security, or CNAS, a think tank that attracted some of the most prominent counterinsurgency theorists and practitioners, including the former armor officer John Nagl; the former Marine Corps infantry officer Nathaniel Fick; Tom Ricks, the author of *Fiasco*, the influential critique of the U.S. military's performance in Iraq; and the counterinsurgency blogger Andrew Exum.*

CNAS was part of a new establishment in Washington that rallied to the new counterinsurgency consensus. But the most important factor for securing a seamless transition was Obama's decision to keep Gates on as his secretary of defense. Gates had been called in to salvage the situation in Iraq, and in the process he became a forceful advocate for mastering the tasks of what he called "nation-building under fire."[4]

During his tenure, Gates sent a message to the Pentagon's procurement bureaucracy and to the defense industry that nation building would not be going out of fashion anytime soon. Despite nearly a decade at war, the military services had continued to push for new equipment designed for war against sophisticated, high-tech adversaries, as if they harbored a deep inner wish for a great-power war or a revived Soviet Union, not the relatively low-tech, manpower-intensive business of rebuilding failed states.

Gates's message was delivered to the civilian bureaucracy as well. In February 2009, the new administration kicked off a sixty-day policy review of Afghanistan and Pakistan strategy. Possible options included sending tens of thousands of more troops to Afghanistan and delivering billions more in aid to Pakistan. This approach would require another "whole-of-government" effort. Addressing soldiers at Fort Drum, New York, Admiral Mike Mullen, the chairman of the Joint Chiefs of Staff, said it was time for a "commensurate surge" of diplomats and civilian experts to reinforce the military campaign to stabilize Afghanistan. The civilians were supposed to fill posts on Provincial Reconstruction Teams and new district-level advisory teams. The strategy was formally known as the "civilian uplift," as the word "surge" was too closely associated with

---

* Kilcullen also landed briefly at CNAS: He worked on his book *The Accidental Guerrilla: Fighting Small Wars in the Midst of a Big One* at CNAS in 2008 before moving on to a private consulting firm.[5]

Iraq; it was supposed to double the number of U.S. government civilians deployed to Afghanistan to around nine hundred.[6] For the nation builders, the arrival of the Obama administration offered another chance to "get it right." The experiment in Iraq was drawing to a close, with all U.S. forces scheduled to withdraw by the end of 2011, but Afghanistan was seen as the new laboratory for applying all the lessons learned in Mesopotamia and refined in Washington.

In the spring of 2009, General David McKiernan, the top U.S. general in Afghanistan, was unceremoniously relieved of his command. General Stanley McChrystal, an ascetic Special Forces officer, was announced as his replacement. McKiernan was generally viewed as a competent commander, but the consensus among the counterinsurgency cognoscenti was that he was not sufficiently innovative. Washington needed someone who was more schooled in the principles of armed social work. Equally important, the Obama administration wanted to put its imprimatur on the Afghanistan campaign. In late February the president signed off on an initial troop increase. An additional seventeen thousand U.S. troops started heading to Afghanistan, and within a few months, the figure rose to around twenty-one thousand.

The administration now viewed Afghanistan and Pakistan as a single problem (now referred to with the annoying policy wonk shorthand, "Af-Pak"). The main sources of Taliban financing and recruitment were in Pakistan; al-Qaeda's top leadership, including Osama bin Laden and Ayman al Zawahiri, were believed to have found refuge inside Pakistan's Federally Administered Tribal Areas; and a homegrown Taliban movement was gaining momentum inside Pakistan itself. Conventional wisdom now held that fixing Afghanistan would require a parallel effort in Pakistan. For fiscal year 2009, the administration put in an emergency spending request for a $2.4 billion assistance package for Pakistan, a bigger chunk of change than either Iraq or Afghanistan received in the same budget supplemental. That amount included four hundred million dollars to build Pakistani counterinsurgency forces and nearly a billion ($921 million) to pay for diplomatic security upgrades in Afghanistan and Pakistan, including a new fortified embassy in Pakistan. The president appointed Richard Holbrooke as his special representative for Afghanistan and Pakistan.

In June 2009, the Center for a New American Security, the new Washington think tank that had ties to the Obama administration's national

security team, published a report on Afghanistan policy titled "Triage."
It argued for a further increase in troops and a civilian surge to seize the
initiative from the Taliban. The report—written by David Killcullen;
Ahmed Humayun, a CNAS researcher; and Andrew Exum, the smart,
plugged-in former Army captain who founded the influential counterinsurgency blog Abu Muqawama—caught the eye of General Stanley
McChrystal, who had been tapped one month earlier as the top U.S.
commander in Afghanistan. When McChrystal decided to launch a
sweeping, top-down review of Afghanistan strategy, he invited Exum,
who served in Afghanistan in 2002 as an Army Ranger, to join his assessment team. McChrystal invited other Beltway policy wonks to Afghanistan to take part in a sixty-day review of strategy and operations,
including Fred Kagan of the neoconservative American Enterprise Institute; two top members of the centrist foreign policy establishment,
Anthony Cordesman of the Center for Strategic and International Studies
(a former national security assistant to Republican Senator John McCain
on the Senate Armed Services Committee), and Stephen Biddle of the
Council on Foreign Relations (Biddle had served on Petraeus's Iraq Joint
Strategic Assessment Team).[7] Sarah Chayes, a National Public Radio correspondent and Peace Corps veteran turned Kandahar-based humanitarian, also worked as a "special advisor" to McChrystal.

The strategy review was a deft public relations move. After returning
from their Pentagon-organized visit to Afghanistan, members of the strategic assessment group served as an advance guard for McChrystal's upcoming request for a significant increase in troops and a commitment of
more resources. The think-tankers were banging the drum for reinforcements even before McChrystal's assessment was made public in late September by means of a leak to Bob Woodward of the *Washington Post*.
Cordesman, in an op-ed in the *Washington Post* on August 31, wrote, "Almost every expert on the scene has talked about figures equivalent to three
to eight more brigade combat teams—with nominal manning levels that
could range from 2,300 to 5,000 personnel each."[8] Winning the hearts and
minds of Washington's foreign policy elite seemed as much the goal as re-
vamping the strategy on the ground.

In Washington, it looked as though a dream team was being assembled
to revamp Afghanistan strategy, and most of the foreign policy establishment rallied around a consensus: The Afghanistan mission had suffered

from strategic neglect; more resources were needed; and it needed a bigger push for "governance," wonk-speak for more civilian advisors. McChrystal's review showed that a new nation-building orthodoxy had taken hold in Washington. Afghanistan, in the view of the new administration, was the "good war," a mission that had been neglected by the Bush administration in its rush to launch a preemptive war in Iraq. Afghanistan was primarily a nation-building mission now, not the punitive expedition launched against al-Qaeda in 2001. Building a functioning state in Afghanistan was the goal.

Shortly after assuming command, McChrystal issued a tactical directive, a sort of mission statement that would guide operations on the ground. In its sanitized form—made available for public release with sensitive military information redacted—it echoed all the main themes of the nation-building mission. It emphasized the importance of cultural sensitivity and mastering the human terrain:

> Our strategic goal is to defeat the insurgency threatening the stability of Afghanistan. Like any insurgency, there is a struggle for the support and will of the population. Gaining and maintaining that support must be our overriding operational imperative—and the ultimate objective of every action we take.
>
> We must fight the insurgents, and will use the tools at our disposal to both defeat the enemy and protect our forces. But we will not win based on the number of Taliban we kill, but instead on our ability to separate insurgents from the center of gravity—the people. That means we must respect and protect the population from coercion and violence—and operate in a manner which will win their support.

Most important, McChrystal imposed serious restrictions on the use of force. He curtailed the use of artillery and close air support (CAS), military tools that had the most potential to kill innocent civilians: "Commanders must weigh the gain of using CAS against the cost of civilian casualties, which in the long run make mission success more difficult and turn the Afghan people against us."

McChrystal also made clear that U.S. and coalition forces would not conduct searches in Afghan homes unaccompanied by Afghan national security forces; they would not fire on mosques or religious sites; and they would respect the unique cultural sensitivities concerning Afghan women. A few weeks after issuing this initial guidance, McChrystal and his advisors took things even further, introducing guidelines that would discourage "tactical driving"—aggressive, "guns-up" convoys—by coalition security forces, especially in Kabul. McChrystal distributed additional counterinsurgency guidance that would govern day-to-day interactions with Afghans. As he traveled around the field, McChrystal also tried to set a different tone: He was almost never seen wearing a helmet or body armor. It telegraphed an image of trust to Afghans, and sent the U.S. military a message as well. They would have to adopt a less aggressive posture. More than eight years after arriving in Afghanistan, it seemed that the United States was finally starting to get a grip on the situation.

By mid-2009, the U.S. presence in Afghanistan had taken on a new kind of permanence, and Bagram Air Base, the logistics hub for the war effort, had been transformed in the process. When I first visited the airfield in the spring of 2002, Bagram was a temporary outpost for a temporary mission, a primitive tent city on the edge of a minefield. By 2009, the main road through the center of camp, once a rutted dirt track, had been paved over with smooth asphalt. Renamed Disney Drive, after the Army specialist killed in early 2002 while clearing scrap metal from the aircraft hangar, the street had strict speed limits, and pedestrians on the sidewalk were required to wear reflective safety belts after dark.

Bagram, now known by the acronym BAF (the military referred to the base as Bagram Airfield), had infrastructure. It also had rules. "Seatbelts are mandatory for all vehicle occupants," flashed an electronic sign parked across from the main dining facility. The sign also offered other safety tips: "Use of headphones while walking or running on BAF is prohibited"; "Smoke detectors save lives—be sure to check yours."

Living standards had improved dramatically since the United States first occupied Bagram. Soldiers no longer lined up for trays of powdered eggs and creamed chipped beef; the troops could eat three meals a day in a gleaming, all-you-can-eat dining facility, courtesy of the Army logistics contractor KBR.* For variety, they could also visit a Burger King, a Pizza Hut, or a Popeye's chicken franchise. In their spare time they could sip shakes and smoothies from Orange Julius or linger over a latté from Green Beans Coffee. For a touch of the exotic, they could visit a row of souvenir shops and carpet vendors run by the Army & Air Force Exchange Service. Bagram even featured a day spa run by a Korean company where efficient Kyrgyz women worked as hairdressers, manicurists, and masseuses. Signs inside the massage booths warned sternly against attempting any sexual contact. A piece of strip-mall America had been transplanted to the Shomali Plain.

BAF was the nerve center of the new U.S. mission in Afghanistan. By midsummer of 2009, the population of Bagram Air Base hovered at around twenty thousand troops and contractors, and the base that had been on the frontlines between the Taliban and the Northern Alliance was now the main logistics and support hub for a fresh influx of U.S. troops into Afghanistan.

The rural communities around Bagram had been a focal point of the U.S. government's first hesitant steps toward nation-building since 2002, when Civil Affairs teams and USAID launched their quick-impact projects on the Shomali Plain. The region had been on the receiving end of U.S. largesse for nearly eight years, and it had come a long way. The highway from Kabul to Bagram, once a narrow, cratered road, was now a busy thoroughfare lined with shops and filling stations. New electrical transmission lines ran parallel to the road, and construction seemed everywhere in evidence, with rebar springing up from the unfinished second floors of new concrete buildings.

Bagram was what front-line soldiers referred to disparagingly as "FOB-istan," the comfortable rear-echelon life of the forward operating base, and the culture of petty rules that came with it. It was a "hat and salute"

---

* By the summer of 2009, fewer of the red lanyards worn by KBR workers were seen. That July, the Army awarded two giant task orders to the service firms Fluor and Dyn-Corp to build and run bases in Afghanistan. The work was divided along geographic lines: Fluor got the northern part of Afghanistan, and DynCorp, the southern half. All told the work was worth a potential $15 billion over five years, depending on how many troops would eventually be sent to Afghanistan. The new task orders reflected the Army's shift away from the controversial Logistics Civil Augmentation Program III contract, which had given KBR a lock on base operations in Iraq and Afghanistan and had helped give battlefield contracting a bad name.

zone, meaning troops had to comply with strict uniform standards and salute their superiors, just as they would when garrisoned at home. And the "safety culture" was smothering. In addition to posted speed limits and constant reminders about the dangers of negligent weapons discharges, residents of Bagram could be reprimanded for the pettiest of infractions, such as jogging with sunglasses on or wearing sleeveless shirts in the dining facility. Even the short-order cooks making omelets at breakfast labored in front of a sign: NO EGGS OVER LIGHT. For final official touch, a laminated copy of the memorandum from a food safety officer was taped to the sneeze guard.

The safety culture of Bagram had a curious side effect: It made the world "outside the wire," beyond the floodlit confines of the base, seem all the more dangerous and forbidding. Bagram could look like a warped military version of a United Colors of Benetton ad, with cafeteria workers from Bangladesh and the Philippines, construction managers from Bosnia, helicopter pilots from Poland, masseuses and manicurists from Kyrgyzstan. But for most people based on Bagram, interactions with Afghans were rare. The Afghans were there, but they were almost invisible, working as manual laborers on construction gangs, set apart by the red "escort required" badges, and watched over by escorts or armed guards. They looked like prison road crews. Of course, there was "Afghan music night," featuring a traditional musician, Bismullah Jan. This was perhaps the closest some on BAF would come to an encounter with Afghan culture.

Despite the progress, the U.S. military still seemed to be struggling to win friends and build goodwill, even in this relatively secure, prosperous part of Afghanistan. When the world outside the base was seen as the Red Zone, it was not surprising that relations with the local community would often be fraught with tension. In late July 2005, a demonstration outside Bagram turned into a riot after six villagers were detained by U.S. forces during operations in surrounding Parwan Province (the arrested men were reportedly in possession of a rocket-propelled grenade, a rocket launcher, a Kalashnikov assault rifle, and a selection of bomb-making materials). First, local residents threw stones at a passing U.S. convoy; then, as the SUVs sped into the base, the crowd rushed a checkpoint gate guarded by Afghan troops, who reportedly dispersed protesters with sticks and shots fired in the air.[9] The trust built with the communities around Bagram was fragile. The base housed a major detention facility, and in early 2005, revelations surfaced about prisoner abuse there, including the deaths of two detainees.[10] The goodwill earned by digging wells and building schools could be easily undermined.

More troublesome were the occasional rocket and mortar attacks on the base. Insurgents were still infiltrating villages in the area. Some of them were thought to be aligned with Hizb-e-Islami Gulbuddin, the militant party of the mujahideen commander Gulbuddin Hekmatyar, a recipient of U.S. weapons and funding during the Soviet-Afghan war. Occasionally, the insurgents managed to fire off a 107mm rocket or a mortar in the direction of the base. Usually the rockets were propped up on rocks or rails in the surrounding hills and set off by timer, and they often fell short of their target. But the attacks were still an annoyance, and once in a while the insurgents did hit the mark. In July 2009 a rocket attack claimed the lives of two soldiers.

In the summer of 2009, the job of policing the villages in the surrounding area fell to Task Force Gladius, manned by soldiers from the Army's Eighty-second Airborne Division Special Troops Battalion. The task force took a very practical approach to securing the region: They promised jobs and reconstruction dollars in return for information and intelligence in the local communities. This "Bagram outreach program" was a classic example of the quasi-development mission the Army had taken on in Afghanistan. The village of Qaleh Dewana, an ethnic Pashtun settlement not far from Bagram, was one of the places where insurgents could find safe haven and also stash rockets or bomb-making materials. On a late July morning, I tagged along with Captain Derek Henson, the commander of Headquarters Company, on a KLE ("key leader engagement"), a meeting with village elders in Qaleh Dewana. The village had been overlooked in the past by coalition patrols, and military intelligence wanted Henson to "target" the village: By building some rapport in Qaleh Dewana, the theory went, the military would make locals more willing to feed intel tips to the coalition.* "Usually if we give them a little help, they're more willing to help," Henson said. "In this village, the issue is that they don't have a lot of work; they have to go to Pakistan for work, and we are concerned that people may be infiltrating back to the village with them, or may be recruited while in Pakistan."

---

*An unfortunate use of the word "target." In military-speak, "targeting" can mean building relationships ("targeting a local leader" means arranging a meeting) or taking lethal action.

The convoy rolled out, once again in heavy Mine-Resistant Ambush Protected vehicles. The Pentagon had spent billions on the hulking trucks, which were purpose-built to protect troops from roadside bombs. Built with higher suspensions and v-shaped hulls that would direct blast away from the passengers, the MRAP saved lives, but they were massive, intimidating vehicles. As the giant trucks trundled through the narrow alleys of the mud-walled village, the troopers in my vehicle opened hatches in the top and scanned the crowd, rifles at the ready. They were being pursued by a small mob of dust-caked Afghan boys, curious to catch a glimpse of the soldiers riding around in the high-tech trucks. The hydraulic doors of the trucks noisily opened like a mechanical drawbridge, and the troopers dismounted. Swathed in body armor, wearing wraparound shades, they looked almost like visitors from another planet.

Accompanied by his interpreter, a thin, unhappy-looking Afghan nicknamed Arnold, the company commander and his security team trudged off to the house of Sayed Mohammad, the village elder. At the house they sent an older man to look for Sayed Mohammad; for security reasons, the troopers could not give notice of their visit. The elder arrived a few minutes later, accompanied by Commander Bashir, a former *mujahid* who lived in the village. Henson had mastered the Afghan custom of inquiring after the health of his host; now, after exchanging a few pleasantries and sipping some tea, the men got down to business. Bashir, the former commander, did most of the talking. He was not happy with the assistance the coalition had offered his village so far. "Our people need jobs," he said. "And you're supposed to help everyone. You guys help the Dari [ethnic Tajik] people working inside the base. But you don't help the Pashtun people."

The biggest complaint seemed to be the way the military was doling out its aid money. "All the dollars are going to Kandahar, that's why I'm angry," he said, referring to the money and military resources the United States had poured on the restless southern province. "If we grew opium you would help us!"

"Stop complaining," Henson replied through his interpreter. "And let me help you."

Henson explained that he could help some of the men in the village get coveted red badges to work as day laborers on the base, but he added that he could not guarantee any jobs. "I can't hire them, and I can't make anyone hire them," he said. "I'll do my best to assist . . . You know there are hundreds of villages around here and we'll try to assist everyone as best we can."

Bashir was not satisfied. He ostentatiously waved a slip of paper that was scrawled with the phone number of a Lieutenant Delage, from the French army. "The French gave me a number but they never pick up the phone," he complained.

Henson responded by giving them his local cell phone number. "Give 'em your number too, Arnold."

Arnold—a young man from the Bagram area—did not look very pleased with that command. At one point during the conversation, Bashir pointed directly at Arnold and whispered something in Sayed Moham-mad's ear. Arnold turned to me and said, with a pleading look, "They know me, all of them. This is the problem."

It was frustrating to watch the exchange. Half of the dialogue was lost in translation, and Arnold was more than a bit preoccupied by the fact that he had been identified as working for the Americans. It could poten-tially put him or his family in danger. In any case, building local relation-ships was a Sisyphean task. In another six or eight months, a new unit would rotate in, and another young officer would replace Henson. He would have to introduce himself to Sayed Mohammad and Commander Bashir, and they might have the same conversation. The approach of Task Force Gladius was in line with counterinsurgency theory, to a point. They rolled in occasionally to a village, handed out some humanitarian aid, made some contacts. But they did not establish any lasting presence in these villages. At night, insurgents would be free to return to Qaleh Dewana.

Things were not rosy in Charikar, Parwan's provincial capital, either. On another morning, I went along with a Police Mentoring Team on a visit to the Afghan National Police Headquarters, where the team was help-ing supervise the creation of an emergency-response center being set up in advance of the presidential elections. On the way into town, the con-voy of MRAPs was pelted with stones. Charikar, a market town, was a stronghold of Abdul Bashir Salangi, a Northern Alliance warlord who had fought the Taliban, and was a nominally friendly city, so it was sur-prising to get such a hostile reception. Major Steve Olson, the head of the team, mentioned the stone-throwing incident over tea and cookies with the deputy police chief of the province, General Faqir Ahmad: "Sir, I wanted to ask you. This morning, as we were coming into the city, people were throwing some rocks at us. Are people upset at us?"

The problem wasn't with the Police Mentoring Team, the general explained, it was with a company of Army Military Police who also patrolled the area. On a Thursday night, they had intruded on a wedding celebration in the village of Qalanderkhel, outraging the locals. And the day before, the MPs had nearly caused a riot in Charikar. During a visit to the city to do an assessment of polling sites for the upcoming election, the MPs had attempted to detain a young woman, a Canadian of Afghan descent who was visiting the town. She had been spotted taping the convoy with a video camera, something considered a fair pretext for detention by coalition forces. When the MPs tried to put her in their vehicle, however, hundreds of locals quickly gathered, incensed that an Afghan woman was being manhandled by foreign soldiers.

"She may have filmed them by mistake," Ahmad conceded. "But they got her hand and tried to put her in an MRAP. It has a bad effect . . . These people are pissed off right now."

Plucking an Afghan woman from the street, justified or not, was a major affront, and the MPs had completely misread the situation. They were accompanied by a contingent of Afghan National Police, who had tried to persuade them to deal with the problem in a more subtle way, but they had insisted on questioning the woman on the street, while the crowd grew angrier. It was precisely the kind of situation that General McChrystal's new tactical directive was designed to help the coalition avoid.

The major promised to look into the situation. But the police chief was still simmering about the incident. He laid the blame on one of the MPs—he didn't know his name, but said he recognized him by his jug ears. "He looks like this," the translator said, putting his fingers behind his ears to make them stick out. "I don't know his name, but it's MPs, and it's Eighty-second," the general said. "We can make sure. If she's a Talib, we'll arrest her, and turn her over. That was the whole issue there. Six hundred people got together yesterday when it happened. That is the only team that bothers these people."

And there was another final insult. The MPs had run across an Afghan man wearing Army-issue pants. Troops were concerned about insurgents disguising themselves as coalition soldiers, but this young man was innocently wearing a pair of surplus trousers. The MPs stopped the young man in the street and stripped him of his pants, a grave insult in this conservative community.

"You can kill an Afghan, but you cannot take his pants off," the police commander said. "In front of the community, it's a bad idea."

"I'll speak with my higher headquarters," the major replied.

The police chief clucked his tongue. "Everywhere they go they create problems," he said. "Every time he sends one Ranger [truck] with ANP [Afghan National Police], they know that they have ANP and they can arrest anyone who is a problem. They are making this Parwan situation bad."

An influx of new troops and a focus on social work were consistent with counterinsurgency theory, which called for a bigger presence in Afghanistan's towns and villages. But in practice, that meant more convoys on the road, more potential for escalationof-force incidents, and more chances for miscommunication. The counterinsurgency strategy also called for a massive investment in Afghan infrastructure: roads, dams, and power generation projects. But development, like security, did not instantly translate to success.

After the year he spent spreading the gospel of counterinsurgency during the Iraq surge, the Australian counterinsurgency specialist David Kilcullen shifted his attention to Afghanistan. While leading the effort to write the counterinsurgency handbook for civilian policymakers, he traveled to Afghanistan, where he spent extensive time in the field with Provincial Reconstruction Teams and coalition and Afghan units. In a post on the Small Wars Journal Web site in April 2008, he introduced his recent work in Afghanistan with an almost lyrical passage in which he reminisced about his early days teaching infantry tactics to British platoon commanders on the plains of rural England and south Wales. Noting that the old Roman mile-castles and military roads could still be seen on the modern landscape, he wrote: "Like the Romans, counterinsurgents through history have engaged in road-building as a tool for projecting military force, extending governance and the rule of law, enhancing political communication and bringing economic development, health and education to the population . . . But the political impact of road-building is even more striking than its tactical effect."[11]

It was a simple, attractive argument: Roads equaled economic development and central control. They connected isolated rural populations to the central government, and provided a means for the counterinsurgency force to cause the ink-blot of security to spread. Kilcullen was particularly effusive about what he saw in Afghanistan's Kunar Province. While acknowledging that road construction could have "negative security and political effects, especially when executed unthinkingly or in an un-coordinated fashion," he called what he saw in Kunar "a coordinated civil-military activity based on a political strategy of separating the insurgent from the people and connecting the people to the government. In short, this is a political maneuver with the road as a means to a political end."[12]

By 2009, road projects had become the single biggest investment by coalition forces in Afghanistan. Major General Jeffrey Schloesser, the commander of the Combined Joint Task Force 101, told reporters in a June 2009 briefing that his forces had committed around $300 million of the total pool of $485 million in the Commander's Emergency Response Program funds to laying asphalt. "Roads still remain our biggest investment, just like last year," he said. "They have a huge impact, as you know. They connect communities . . . to themselves, so they can have an economy. They connect the village to the government. And they help to increase the access to the larger cities and towns in Afghanistan."

All told, Schloesser said, the task force had undertaken three hundred road projects and had paved or planned to pave two thousand kilometers of road. One of the more ambitious road projects begun in the summer of 2009 was the Parwan-to-Bamyan road, a major project for the north of Afghanistan that would link the isolated highland province of Bamyan with the rest of Afghanistan, and help create an alternative northern transportation route for the country. It was of strategic importance as well. The main highway linking Afghanistan to the southern ports of Pakistan passed through the vulnerable Khyber Pass, and supply convoys passing through Pakistan had come under increased attack by militants.

Bamyan Province was home to the Hazaras, Afghanistan's most oppressed and downtrodden minority group, most of them Shia Muslims. Subjugated by the country's Pashtun rulers and relegated to manual labor, they often worked as housemaids or night watchmen in Kabul. In their home province, they scratched out a living from subsistence farming.

During their rule, the Taliban visited terrible violence on the Hazaras, in some cases systematically singling out Hazara men and boys for execution. The province was also the scene of the Taliban's most dramatic act of vandalism: the destruction of the giant Buddha statues in Bamyan Valley in 2001. Things had improved little since the fall of the Taliban. The province rarely seemed to command the attention of the central government, and in terms of development, Bamyan remained pretty much off the grid.

A new highway, it was thought, would not only connect the impoverished dwellers of Bamyan to markets but also, more important, bring them closer to the capital. The journey to Parwan Province, just north of Kabul, usually took twelve or fourteen hours by car; when the new highway was finished, travel time would be reduced to two or three hours. It was a major undertaking that would turn the dingy market town of Charikar into a central hub for travel, and create a bypass around the Salang Tunnel, the main north–south link in Afghanistan.

Responsibility for managing the road projects in Bamyan fell to the Bamyan Provincial Reconstruction Team, a 150-strong contingent of the New Zealand military based at a former Soviet airstrip just outside the town of Bamyan. The Bamyan PRT was generally seen as one of the more successful civil-military teams. New Zealand's soldiers had plenty of experience on peacekeeping operations; Kiwis had been deployed on peacekeeping operations and U.N. missions in around a dozen countries, including East Timor, the Solomon Islands, and Kosovo. They had a reputation for a low-key approach that was less aggressive than the Americans'. Equally important, the province's political leader, Habiba Surabi—Afghanistan's first female governor—was a strong proponent of development work. Around 125 different projects were under way in the province, with a total value of around forty million dollars. Some projects were modest in scale, such as flood protection walls, footbridges, school repairs, and wells. The largest share of funding came from the U.S. military, which was helping fund the more ambitious projects like the Parwan-to-Bamyan road.

Like the Panjshir, Bamyan was relatively peaceful and stable, but in the weeks before I arrived, the province had seen what Group Captain Greg Elliot, the Bamyan PRT commander, called an "uptick in kinetic activity": some roadside bombs, a recent firefight at a police outpost. The Bamyan PRT had five liaison teams stationed at remote outposts, and a security patrol in the northeast region had recently been caught in a so-phisticated ambush. Before I arrived at Kiwi Base, the team had been on lockdown for several days before over a security alert. According to one civilian on the team, everyone was "keyed up" because of the upcoming presidential elections and concerns that the Taliban were looking for a target in the north to demonstrate that they could strike anywhere.

Most of the recent violence had been confined to the northeast of Bamyan, near the border with Baghlan Province, where the Bamyan PRT was finishing a district roadbuilding project to the town of Madar. A ribbon-cutting ceremony was being planned to celebrate the completion of the road, as well as to inaugurate the western portion of the Parwan-to-Bamyan road. It would be an important photo opportunity for the coalition. To reach the far northeast corner of the province required a day-long journey. Helicopters were in short supply, and it took a bone-jarring eight-hour drive to reach the Bamyan PRT's remote patrol base.

I hitched a ride with two of the team's engineers, New Zealand army Captain Paul Mead, a combat engineer, and Mike Doherty of the U.S. Army Corps of Engineers. They did not have their own vehicles, so they rode along with a security patrol that was heading to the northeastern patrol base. On the way, they were planning to stop and visit some other projects. It was the best chance for them to measure the progress of the construction work the coalition was funding in the province.

The engineers' first stop was at a district government center where laborers were spreading asphalt coating on the roof. Mead and Doherty clambered up a rickety ladder to inspect their work. Doherty praised the contractor, but pointed out a number of improvements that needed to be made at the work site: Clean up those wood shavings; don't leave planks with nails sticking up; make sure that the ladder is fixed.

After their walk-through, the engineers spotted some workers getting ready to mix some concrete in a wheelbarrow, a cost-cutting measure that would save diesel used to run their mixer. Doherty politely scolded the contractor. "You shouldn't mix it in a wheelbarrow. The contract doesn't allow hand-mixed concrete."

As the convoy wound farther north, the engineers stopped at more work sites, including a basic health clinic in the village of Ghandak, where they sat down to talk about building a flood wall with Nematul-lah, the clinic director, and the head of the local *shura*, or council. It was a further occasion for diplomacy. Mead began his meeting with a short, well-rehearsed speech: "The New Zealand PRT is committed to helping the people of Ghandak, and it's important that we have the full participation of the *shura* and the community in this project."

Mead asked about the concertina wire they put around the clinic's wall: Had it made the community feel safer?

"The wires on the wall are very good," Nematullah said. "During the middle of the night the patients feel safer. And the walls stop the dogs."

"This is good to hear," Mead said. "The next thing that our friends from Afghan Bamaco are going to do is put up a flood protection wall for the clinic." He introduced a local contractor, who ceremoniously unrolled a sheaf of blueprints.

Village leaders were less than enthusiastic about that plan. "If you put the wall there, there'll be arguments with the farmers," said Mohammad Daoud, the village elder. "We want a flood protection wall along the riverbank."

The design of flood protection walls was a serious issue. In another village, Der Sheng, the two engineers inspected another flood wall that had caused a small disaster. The Der Sheng flood wall—perhaps built by an earlier rotation of the PRT, perhaps by a nongovernmental organization, no one was quite sure—had channeled the water into a "pinch point" that sent water hurtling down the valley at high velocity. It churned up the foundation of the flood wall and scoured out the floor of the channel, dragging along rock, soil, and boulders that covered up arable land further down the valley. People could go hungry because of good intentions.

Doherty, a Corps of Engineers flood-protection expert, spoke up: "This is what we want to do with the wall. Make sure that it's wide enough to accommodate the river. If the channel is too narrow, the velocity of the water will increase."

The interpreter struggled with the technical explanation, and the Afghans were still unconvinced. "I appreciate your concern that you have," said Mead. "However, in my experience—and Mike is an expert in America in flood protection—we believe it's not best if the flood wall is by the river. I ask that you trust the PRT engineers and the design that we've come up with."

The extended discussion was part of the frustrating but very necessary process of winning local commitment to the project; it required patience from the engineers, who had seen the results of poorly conceived or badly executed aid work. After debating for an hour and a half,

Daoud relented. "We believe you and trust in your experience," he said, shaking the hands of the engineers. "But the people are not happy with this."

Doherty and Mead seemed to care deeply about their job, and they had to work hard to convince the security teams, usually composed of younger, ready-for-action infantrymen, that these protracted negotiations were the primary mission. On a visit to a district subgovernor's office under construction in the provincial center of Sayghan, Doherty had to argue with the patrol commander, who wanted him to hurry up and wrap up a meeting with a local building contractor.

One of the soldiers called over the radio, "The boss wants to know when we're done. We've got other patrols to do."

Mike snapped back, "Tell him I haven't been here for a month. This trip is for me."

"But we've got patrols to do."

"I know, but if he's got a problem, we can talk it through later."

For the engineers, it was a constant battle: Trying to win the trust of Afghans, and trying to persuade the other soldiers that this was a mission that deserved their time. They also had to remind the security teams about winning hearts and minds. Despite the generally lower level of violence here, the security teams often drove at high speeds through villages or refused to take off their intimidating wraparound shades when interacting with ordinary Afghans.

During their long-range patrol in the northeast, the engineers overnighted at a small patrol base shared with a contingent of U.S. Military Police from Fort Hood, Texas. The MPs were there to train the local contingent of Afghan National Police. When not on a training mission, they played Ping-Pong or worked out in a weight room. At night they watched DVDs on a projector. There were few other distractions. This small base had no Internet or morale phones for calls home, so the troopers devised other entertainment. One diversion was the "man-jammy challenge": When someone lost at Ping-Pong with a score of zero, they had to run around the perimeter of the small camp in a *shalwar kameez*, the long tunic and baggy pants worn by Afghan men. The soldiers claimed their adopted camp dogs were trained to attack anyone in man-jammies, which would double the entertainment value. It didn't quite work that way in practice. When a soldier who lost at Ping-Pong emerged from behind the HESCO barrier in his *shalwar kameez*, the dog lunged after him, then stopped to sniff his hand and lick it. "She recognized him," said one MP with disappointment. Despite the NATO command's pronouncements, cultural sensitivity was not their strong suit.

That night, as we set out our cots under the stars at the remote patrol base, a weary Doherty finally unburdened himself. He was frustrated not by the interminable negotiations with the Afghans, but by his work with the military. Even though this was primarily a reconstruction mission, he worried that testosterone-filled infantrymen were not suited for the job. "The Kiwis are supposed to be the low-key ones!" he said, shaking his head. "And they are so coarse and heavy-handed. Their language is so crude. Even if Afghans don't understand English, they can tell. The muscles and the tattoos, the wraparound shades, the body language. They have this contempt for the locals."

It wasn't just the New Zealanders who had that attitude, Doherty said. "Remember the movie *The Beast*?" he asked, referring to a Hollywood film about a Soviet tank crew in Afghanistan. "I watched that at the base in Qalat. And you know the opening scene, where the helicopters come in and destroy the village? The U.S. soldiers all cheered. And the Afghan staff watched."

We discussed the day's patrol. While driving back to base, the soldiers sped through the village nearest to the patrol base, kicking up an enormous cloud of dust. I saw more than a few sidelong glances at the convoy. "It's so inconsiderate," Doherty said. "And one inconsiderate gesture can erase all the months of good work."

Doherty's biggest concern, though, was the road to Madar, where the ribbon-cutting ceremony was to take place in two days. Local contractors had bulldozed over part of the local bazaar and paved over some of the fields without compensating anyone. The road looked great on paper. It was a deliverable result, and would be a public relations boost for the coalition, but the local residents were still simmering. Worse still, the local government had no budget or equipment to maintain and repair the roads. Unless they received continued subsidy, the roads would quickly fall into disrepair. "You have colonels in Bagram making decisions about the inches of asphalt, and they have no clue," Doherty said with a sigh.

Two days later, top officers were helicoptered in from Bagram for the road-opening ceremony, which also marked the launch of the western portion of the Parwan-to-Bamyan road. The event was presided over by Habiba Surabi, the governor of Bamyan Province. Surabi appeared at the ribbon-cutting with Colonel Scott Spellmon, the commander of Task Force Warrior, and Group Captain Elliot, the PRT commander, who was photographed at the ribbon cutting wearing a traditional lambskin cap and a woolen cloak.

It was a marvelous photo opportunity, but the goodwill did not last. A few days after the ceremony, Abdullah Abdullah, an Afghan presidential candidate, paid a visit to the province for a campaign event. When Surabi's car arrived at the checkpoint outside the event, her guards emerged from the vehicle, only to have the U.S. MPs draw their weapons on them. Surabi was infuriated; I later learned that she called all government officials in Kabul demanding that the Americans leave Bamyan. Colonel Spellmon, the commander of Task Force Warrior, flew up to Bamyan to smooth things over, but also warned the locals that if the Americans left, they would take all their money with them.

The school visit in the Panjshir was not a mere photo opportunity intended to win over the Beltway elites with images of progress; the valley was not a Potemkin village. The Bagram outreach was a genuine effort to win friends and influence people in the communities around a vital base. Road projects were some measure of progress, even if they weren't sustainable. But to replicate this success throughout Afghanistan would require a generation-long military commitment and a generation-long investment by the U.S. taxpayer. It would require a military and diplomatic apparatus that was completely reorganized around a new mission of building the rudiments of a functioning Afghan state. It would be armed development work on a massive scale, involving combat troops, military advisors, cultural and development experts, and local administrators, in a reprise of the "successful" Iraq strategy. It meant more troops would live out among the population, away from the fortified sanctuary of the forward operating base, and commanders would turn on a stream of development money through the Commander's Emergency Response Program. And this time, civilian agencies would have to chip in on a much larger scale and step up to the task of administering a state down to the district level. Could this be done? Or was the ribbon-cutting scene in the Panjshir girls' school just a symbol of an elusive dream?

Since 2001, Congress has appropriated more than $50 billion for humanitarian and reconstruction aid to Afghanistan, yet all the money spent in Afghanistan has not guaranteed success. Violence was on the rise in the summer of 2009; August 2009 was the deadliest month on record for U.S. troops, but by June 2010 the security situation had deteriorated further. In fact, the infusion of aid was to some extent enabling the corruption that was undermining support for the Afghan government. It was fairly common knowledge that the increase in aid had created more opportunities for kickbacks and bribery. For example, the owner of an Afghan logistics firm casually disclosed to me in 2008 that he was spending $5,000 to pay off militia commanders every time he sent a fuel convoy to Kandahar. But the U.S. government was slow to act. In September 2009, prompted in part by an investigation in the online newspaper *GlobalPost*, USAID launched a belated investigation into allegations that money for highway and bridge projects was ending up in the hands of Taliban commanders, who extracted protection money from roadbuilders.[13] But increased oversight could never be enough, given the sheer volume of dollars arriving in Afghanistan. Even Secretary of Defense Robert Gates acknowledged this reality in a press conference with President Hamid Karzai, saying: "I do have concerns that with the billions and billions of dollars coming into Afghanistan from the international community, that that assistance itself has become one of those sources of corruption."

In a damning report published in March 2008, Matt Waldman, a policy and advocacy advisor with Oxfam, a British charity, reckoned that international assistance accounted for 90 percent of public expenditures in Afghanistan. Yet the Afghan government didn't know how one third of all aid to the country, around $5 billion, had been allocated since 2001. What's more, much of the aid being pledged to Afghanistan was being repatriated in the form of aid contractor salaries and corporate overhead costs. The cost of a single expatriate consultant working for one of the myriad private consulting companies was between $250,000 and $500,000 per year, and Waldman estimated that 40 percent of aid went back to donor countries in one form or another.[14] The U.S. military was spending close to a hundred million dollars a day in Afghanistan, yet the average volume of aid spent by all donors since 2001 was just seven million dollars a day.[15]

The reconstruction business in Afghanistan has opened extraordinary opportunities for international consulting firms and well-connected Afghan contractors. According to Waldman, companies have enjoyed profit margins of 20 percent and sometimes take home as much as 50 percent of the contract amount. The reconstruction projects run out of Bagram were just one glimpse of the marvelous opportunities for greed that the Afghanistan surge has created.

The reconstruction racket seems to be enriching a small and select group of well-connected Afghan officials, many of whom are former warlords. General Baba Jan, the Northern Alliance commander who once escorted reporters to the frontlines of the fighting at Bagram, has been said to enjoy a postwar retirement as a Bagram contractor.[16] Coalition officers told me that the governor of one province was suspected of skimming reconstruction funds. Other officials have been implicated in bulldozing the houses of refugees in Kabul's Sherpur district to make way for the expensive new homes of government ministers and former warlords.[17] Seen through the eyes of ordinary people, nation-building in Afghanistan seemed to benefit everyone—foreign aid workers, well-connected local officials, Afghan construction firms—except them.

Afghanistan offered a new laboratory for a "whole-of-government" approach to nation building, but it seemed doubtful that the civilian bureaucracy could rise to that challenge. The Civilian Response Corps, created in response to the nation-building fiascos in both Iraq and Afghanistan, was still in its infancy, and the military ended up shouldering the burden once again in Afghanistan. As 2009 drew to a close, the administration had still fallen short of its target to have nearly a thousand government experts in Afghanistan by year's end to support Obama's civilian "surge." By October 2009, only 575 civilians were in Afghanistan, and most of these were still in Kabul and rarely left their secure compounds.[18]

Foreign Policy Out of Balance

Over the past decade, the United States has become more deeply involved in nation building than at any point since the Marshall Plan. Iraq was the turning point. Confronted with the failures of the Coalition Provisional Authority and the early occupation, the military rediscovered the principles of population-centric counterinsurgency, an approach that translated in practice to armed social work. But the military establishment overcompensated. As the Pentagon took on a greater share of diplomatic and development work, foreign policy became dangerously out of balance.

This approach had its successes. This notion of a better war probably saved the United States from outright defeat, and helped contain Iraq's sectarian violence. But the dominant reading of the Iraq surge—that we somehow managed to "get it right" by applying enough resources and ingenuity to the problem—not only overlooks the larger question of whether we should have intervened in the first place, but also raises the question of whether we could be successful in the long term. This relentless focus on fixing two failed states also meant we were less prepared to handle another foreign policy crisis elsewhere on the globe: an outbreak of war on the Korean peninsula, a nuclear confrontation between India and Pakistan, a localized conflict in Central Asia that threatens to become a regional conflagration.

That was the fatal flaw in the whole enterprise. The nation-building missions in Iraq and Afghanistan were too big to fail. Both involvements became so large and so costly that they edged out all other priorities in national security. The cost of keeping a large troop contingent in Afghanistan was the perfect case in point: The mountainous, landlocked country is at the end of a long and difficult supply route. It has no ports, abysmal infrastructure, and difficult neighbors. Factoring in the astronomical cost of transporting fuel, it currently costs around a million dollars a year to keep a single U.S. soldier stationed there.[1] And that number doesn't include the intangibles: U.S. officials expend countless hours negotiating complex overflight and supply deals with countries in the region to keep the hellishly complex supply lines open, sometimes cutting deals with very unsavory regimes. Yet they have to persist, because U.S. lives are at stake and because the commitment is so enormous.

This approach shares another flaw with many other imperial adventures: a sort of hubris, a belief we can remake the world in our image. This was the operating assumption behind "shock and awe," the idea that regime change in Baghdad or Kabul would automatically create functioning democracies friendly to U.S. interests and inhospitable to global terrorists. Nation building is based on a similarly utopian idea: that development work and poverty alleviation in combination with military action can get at the underlying causes of political violence.

The nation builders were some of the best and the brightest: smart, soul-searching people who sought answers to why the United States was failing so miserably to secure the peace in Afghanistan and Iraq. The Obama administration was packed with true believers in this cause. The Center for a New American Security, the think tank that emerged as a feeder for the new administration's national security team, was the intellectual home to a military reform movement that fully embraced the idea of using military force not just to defeat armies but also to transform societies.

That belief in the power of nation building ignores many of the broader lessons of the postcolonial era. Advocates of counterinsurgency point to many historical precedents for military success: the British campaigns in Kenya or in Malaya; the French victory over the Algerian National Liberation Front in the Battle of Algiers; the U.S. involvement in Vietnam in the early 1970s. But they often overlook the end result, the withdrawal of foreign forces and the establishment of independent states. And proponents of this idea often skirt around what should be the fundamental question: *when* to intervene, not *how* to intervene. If the United States props up a government that is illegitimate, kleptocratic or unwilling to reform, then no amount of U.S. blood or treasure can save the situation.

After nine years of war in Afghanistan, the United States is only belatedly coming to this realization. In July 2010, after replacing General Stanley McChrystal as the top U.S. commander in Afghanistan, General David Petraeus issued new guidance to his troops that underscored how much of a problem corruption had become in Afghanistan. "Money is ammunition; don't put it in the wrong hands," the guidance states. "Pay close attention to the impact of your spending and understand who benefits from it. And remember, you are who you fund. How you spend is often more important than how much you spend."[2] Coming from the man who was an enthusiastic early convert to using cash as a weapon in Iraq, it was a remarkable admission that U.S. military assistance can, inadvertently, help fund an insurgency.

The manpower-intensive approach of the nation builders also shows how throwing more resources at the problem can undermine our long-term goals. The successful campaign to unseat the Taliban in 2001 was led by a relatively small force of Special Operations troops and CIA operatives whose low-key operating style and almost invisible presence ensured there would be little friction with ordinary Afghans. But even before the Obama administration announced a surge of forces to Afghanistan in late 2009, the mission there had quietly and steadily expanded. When the military establishes an airfield, it requires a "force protection" element to protect it and contractors to sustain it. That in turn requires a larger logistics tail to support all those boots on the ground. As the base grows, it requires more convoys to keep the place supplied. Dangerous supply lines must be avoided, which means more aircraft are needed to ferry people and equipment around. Before you know it, you are expanding the airfield. The military has a marvelous phrase used to describe this phenomenon: the "self-licking ice cream cone," something that exists to serve itself.

The greater the military presence, the more potential for deadly encounters between the military and the population they are supposed to protect. Today, the presence of U.S. military convoys on the roads is a constant source of tension in Afghanistan. Even Kabul, once a hospitable base for the NATO-led International Security Assistance Force, has seen a backlash against foreign troops. A deadly July 2010 traffic incident involving State Department contractors led to violent street protests not far from the U.S. embassy in Kabul; every accidental shooting at a checkpoint or misdirected air strike further inflames the population and gives insurgents more fodder for propaganda. Supersizing our commitment only serves to undermine the mission in the long run.

And there's the question about whether we really even understand the long-term mission. A rich literature exists about the European colonial experience, but Americans seem to lack the same gift for self-scrutiny. In his 1936 autobiographical short story, "Shooting an Elephant," George Orwell described his moment of awakening when he was serving as an imperial policeman in Burma. Standing in front of the elephant, rifle in hand, he realized the hollowness and futility of the European presence and of his role as an enforcer of colonial law. The colonial policeman seems to be the lead actor in the scene, but it's all charade, an illusion of mastery and control. Larger local forces are at work.

Compared with the characters of Orwell's Burmese days, we make pretty poor imperialists. As a nation, we're relatively incurious about other cultures, terrible at acquiring foreign languages, and generally focused on our own shrill domestic politics. That's not necessarily a bad thing, but it leaves us poorly equipped for this kind of work.

Not for lack of trying. The embrace of cultural knowledge, the investment in development projects, and the experiments in fusing civilian and military functions were all worthwhile experiments. But at their core, they were a way to attack a single problem: the twenty-first-century insurgent armed with the improvised explosive device. To begin tackling that threat, the military needed to understand the communities the insurgents operated in, win friends among the local population, and make sure that development funds were spent wisely. Insurgent violence, however, is a symptom of underlying political conflict. All too often, we ignored the politics driving the insurgencies.

In Iraq, we unseated a regime that had favored the Sunni Arab minority. By upending the established political order, we helped kick off a latent sectarian conflict. In Afghanistan, the Kabul government's conflict with the largely Pashtun Taliban drew us into a regional power struggle.

Rather than aiming for a realistic end-state, our ambitions of creating functioning democracies and refashioning tribal societies meant we doubled down in both Iraq and Afghanistan. And the more resources the U.S. government threw at the client state (or to use today's euphemism, a "host nation"), the more it created the potential for waste and the growth of kleptocracy. It created a corrosive aid dependency that in the long run can undermine the legitimacy of the government the United States was trying to prop up.

Afghanistan is the textbook example of a country that has become a charity case. For fiscal year 2010, Congress appropriated $6.6 billion for the Afghan Security Forces Fund—money to train, equip, and sustain the operations of the Afghan National Army, the Afghan National Police and other security agencies. Afghanistan's total annual budget revenue, according to the *CIA World Factbook*, is $890 million. Not surprisingly, Afghan President Hamid Karzai admitted in December 2009 that Afghanistan did not expect to be able to sustain its own security forces for another fifteen to twenty years. Not being able to sustain its own forces means the Afghan government may in a few short years be faced with a large pool of unemployed men with guns. And all the money we pour into training and advising those men could have unintended—and possibly quite violent—consequences.

Despite those flaws, the armed humanitarians were motivated by a desire to do the right thing. Rebuilding Iraq, for instance, was better than invading and walking away. But while acknowledging the flaws, it's absolutely essential that we do not discard lessons acquired at such extraordinary cost in blood and treasure. We need to be able to do these kinds of things but do them intelligently, and well. And in the coming years, we may also have to do them on a much more modest scale. Scaling back may actually improve outcomes.

In July 1972, Colonel Edward Chamberlain, the senior advisor for the Forty-fourth Special Tactical Zone, Military Assistance Command-Vietnam, wrote a confidential debriefing report. The conventional U.S. involvement in South Vietnam was winding down, and U.S. combat troops were being withdrawn. Chamberlain sketched out some of the main lessons he had drawn from the advisory mission. His advice was prescient:

In any future involvements, we must never allow ourselves to become so emotionally involved that we lose our freedom of action. In short, we must be able to quickly extricate ourselves the minute it becomes apparent that the government we are assisting either cannot or will not institute the reforms or actions we deem essential to success. This is of course a political decision but the Army has an important role to play by insuring that we do not oversubscribe ourselves by requesting too much manpower or material for our client . . . This is the hardest thing of all to practice, because caught up in the enthusiasm and challenges posed by such a conflict, most Army officers at every level are going to be aggressive and determined to succeed regardless of cost. Therefore, any officer or commander who advocates less than an all-out effort is quickly going to be in trouble with his peers, his bosses, and his subordinates, unless we make it perfectly clear from the outset that involvement is limited and will stay limited regardless of success or failure. Easy to say, virtually impossible to practice. Yet somehow we must. There will be another Vietnam whether we like it or not, and the factors which insured our involvement here, even though currently disputed, will arise again and continue to arise so long as we are a global power.

Less is more in nation building, Chamberlain is saying. Involvements must be limited, because the more resources you throw at the problem, the less likely the nation you are assisting will ever be self-sufficient. If a government relies completely on outside assistance, it will be incapable of defending itself when the United States eventually turns off the money taps.

In the future, modest commitments may be the only available course of action. Diminishing budgets, rising deficits, and economic pressure may force a much-needed correction, and compel policymakers to try to do more with less resources. There will be new Afghanistans, and new Iraqs. But committing fifty billion dollars and one hundred thousand troops to rebuilding another country seems unthinkable. In Haiti, after the earthquake in January 2010, the U.S. military staged a rapid and astonishing drawdown, avoiding the temptations of "mission creep." At the beginning of February 2010, around twenty thousand U.S. troops were on the ground or in the waters just off Haiti. By June 1, 2010, that presence had been reduced to a liaison office of about eight uniformed personnel. That was an example of getting it right. The U.S. military was the only organization that was equipped to respond to a disaster of that scale. But it didn't end up owning the problem. Rebuilding Haiti would be a task for the international community, aid agencies, the private sector, and Haitians themselves.

That less-is-more approach is key to restoring balance within the military. Critics of the "cult of counterinsurgency" have pointed out that a focus on nation building neglects the basics of defense, by creating a military primarily trained and equipped to staff occupations, not fight and win wars. The United States needs a Navy that maintains a global presence to protect trade, commerce, and shipping; an Air Force that protects U.S. airspace and can project power anywhere in the world; an Army and Marine Corps that can win decisively on land; and real alliances—not "coalitions of the billing"—to join the United States in future contingencies. One can look to the Israeli experience in Lebanon in its 2006 war against Hezbollah for a lesson in the dangers of neglecting conventional military might. After years of constabulary duty in the West Bank and Gaza, the Israeli military's conventional warfighting skills were rusty, and Israeli military planners were not prepared for high-intensity conflict against an adversary armed with some of the latest anti-armor weapons.

Even as counterinsurgency came into fashion, some generals were beginning to fret about the military's readiness for high-end warfare. In January 2007, General William Wallace, head of Army Training and Doctrine Command, aired concerns about the Army's readiness for high-end warfare, suggesting that some combat skills may have atrophied because of the overemphasis on counterinsurgency. As an example, Wallace noted that a significant number of captains in an advanced armor course—10 to 15 percent—had never fired a tank gun. "It's not a huge number," he said, "but it's enough to cause us to think about whether there are some things institutionally we ought to do to maintain a hedge against the potential for high-intensity, combined-arms operations."

A renewed focus on conventional military power does not, however, mean discarding the costly lessons of Iraq and Afghanistan. Whatever strategic threats the United States might face in the future, the military will still be involved in internal wars, humanitarian crises, and stability operations. Training and equipping for those missions will continue to be an important task for the military, but it must not be the primary goal.

Building effective states can take decades, and requires a class of people who are committed to it. It's not a task that can be accomplished primarily by the military. But as experience in Iraq and Afghanistan showed, civilian agencies simply lack the personnel—and the expeditionary capability—to handle nation building in the world's most violent neighborhoods.

This is more than an issue of manpower and money. Again, it's a question of balance. The military has been asked to do double duty as armed humanitarians. We need to begin a national conversation about returning this mission to its rightful place within the civilian agencies of government. If this is going to be a long-term mission for the U.S. government, it needs to be on an affordable scale, because the American public has limited patience for supporting expensive military operations involving the deployment of tens or hundreds of thousands of troops.

But we are still a long way from developing a real cadre of people who can handle this job. With the Marshall Plan, the State Department had the lead, but the contemporary U.S. diplomatic corps lacks the manpower—and the organizational culture—for this new era of armed development work. If we hope to succeed at this mission, the government needs to have real nation builders on call with real-world skills, not an army of contractors. And Congress needs to fund them.

In practice, that means fully funding a civilian nation-building reserve, not just creating a standby group of federal bureaucrats who provide the civilian window-dressing for military operations. It would give Americans outside of government the chance to volunteer for humanitarian relief missions or stability operations not as contractors, but as temporary government hires, available on short notice to go overseas. At the end of his term, George W. Bush requested $248.6 million to begin funding a reserve (i.e., non-government civilian) component of the Civilian Response Corps for fiscal year 2009, but that request was not funded by Congress. And that was tragically shortsighted: While that amount is significant, it is only a fraction of what the U.S. taxpayer spends each year on contractors to support nation-building missions. It would cost less than buying a pair of F-35 Joint Strike Fighters.

During the 2008 election, in fact, the Obama-Biden campaign expanded upon Bush's concept of a civilian nation-building reserve, calling for the creation of a twenty-five-thousand-strong Civilian Assistance Corps, something described in a campaign fact sheet as a "corps of civilian volunteers with special skill sets (doctors, lawyers, engineers, city planners, agriculture specialists, police, etc.) . . . organized to provide each federal agency with a pool of volunteer experts willing to deploy in times of need at home and abroad." The document suggests how deeply the ideas of nation building had taken hold in Washington, but it also showed how efforts to create a proper civilian nation-building force have fallen short in practice. Within the State Department's Office of the Coordinator for Reconstruction and Stabilization (S/CRS), efforts to stand up the Civilian Response Corps with an active, standby and reserve component have moved ahead only haltingly. Two years after Bush called for the creation of a civilian reserve in early 2007, the active (i.e., full-time) component of the corps had only ten full-time employees. As of mid-2009, some money was supposed to be available to begin hiring the first of around 250 federal employees who would help staff the active component of the Civilian Response Corps more fully, and the Foreign Service Institute was preparing a four-week-long training curriculum for standby (federal reserve) members of the CRC. Funding for the real civilian reserve pool—which would draw on social workers, police officers, lawyers, doctors and engineers—had not materialized.

Not surprisingly, institutional resistance to the nation-building mission is strong. Within some segments of the Foreign Service, hope persisted that the business of nation building and the unending cycle of war-zone assignment would go away once Bush left office. They viewed the war in Iraq as a one-time foreign policy adventure, an experiment that would not be repeated. The Iraq mission had required the State Department to staff the most massive embassy in the world and establish outposts throughout Iraq's provinces. Leaving Iraq might obviate the need for a permanent cadre of professional nation builders. After all, Barack Obama, the victor in the 2008 election, campaigned on a promise to end the war there.

At Secretary of State Hillary Clinton's first "town hall" meeting with State Department employees on February 4, 2009, Steve Kashkett, who represented the American Foreign Service Association, the Foreign

Service's union, asked if diplomats could expect a return to the status quo ante. "As you know, over the past six years, thousands of our colleagues have volunteered to serve in the two war zones of Iraq and Afghanistan—Iraq in particular, where we've created the largest U.S. diplomatic mission in history," he said. "But the cost of doing this has been to take people away from all of our other diplomatic missions around the world, which have been left understaffed and with staffing gaps."

Kashkett then asked, "Have you had any discussions yet about reducing the size of our diplomatic mission in Iraq down to that of a normal diplomatic mission?" Clinton evaded giving a direct answer. But the diplomats who hoped for a drawdown should have given the Obama campaign platform a closer read. The new Democratic administration embraced the nation-building mission as well, and there would be no return to "normal" diplomatic affairs. This mission is not going away for the foreseeable future.

For the United States to succeed at this, however, we need more than just manpower. We need a different mindset. For starters, we need a serious rethink of diplomatic security, which has been the Achilles' heel of the nation-building mission. The world can be a dangerous place, and U.S. embassies and diplomatic installations are a terrorist target. But the relentless focus on protecting U.S. diplomats and officials had created a situation that seemed to make diplomacy and development work impossible. Restoring some balance to the mission means there must be some acceptance of risk.

Contracted security has been a disaster both in terms of oversight and effectiveness. In February 2009, in a belated attempt at reform, the State Department began a recruiting drive to find people to supervise their protective details in Iraq, Afghanistan, and other dangerous places. The idea was to boost oversight of its contracted guard force, whose deployment had proven a public-relations disaster for the U.S. government and angered so many Iraqis and Afghans. As part of the plan, the department created a new position, Security Protective Specialists, or SPSs, who would serve on renewable one-year contracts with the Department's Bureau of Diplomatic Security. This crop of new hires would augment its fifteen-hundred-strong force of Diplomatic Security agents, who had been stretched thin by the requirements for post-9/11 security and the push for more muddy-boots diplomacy. The SPSs were supposed to provide an important new layer of accountability. Security Protective Specialists would essentially work as shift supervisors for contract security guards. The new position was deliberately designed to lure private security contractors away from firms like DynCorp, Blackwater, and Triple Canopy.

So how many stepped forward for the job? According to government auditors, exactly four. Diplomatic Security officials reported having difficulty filling the positions because they compete with private security contractors for new hires and, at the end of September 2009, only ten positions had been filled. The proposed base pay for a Security Protective Specialist was $52,221 per year. Even when factoring in overseas allowances and danger pay, that salary would be a pittance compared to the six-figure pay a U.S. operator for a private firm would expect to earn working on contract for the State Department. Outsourcing had once again confounded oversight.

But rather than focusing on improved oversight of its contracted guard force, the U.S. government needs to part with the Fortress America mindset. The United States does require a cadre of dedicated nation builders who are prepared to work in dangerous and difficult places, and they need the training and the mind-set to be responsible for their own security. The military has taken hesitant first steps toward shedding the "force protection" mind-set that once kept troops sequestered inside large forward-operating bases, commuting to the war. The State Department needs to shift its focus from staffing giant fortified compounds in conflict zones. Paying lip service to being "population centric" is no substitute for living outside the wire, sharing the same risks and standards of living as the populations we are supposed to defend. When diplomatic personnel are sequestered inside costly fortresses, they can't succeed at the tasks of traditional diplomacy or conflict prevention. They need to be trained, and prepared, to work in dangerous places without the military or an army of hired guns.

We are still a long way from getting the scale and the balance right in nation building. The rise of the armed humanitarians was in part a rebellion by rank-and-file members of the government and the military who felt the institutions they belonged to were ill equipped for the missions in Iraq and Afghanistan. The failures of postwar planning spurred a grassroots movement to reform the military and the national security establishment from within, a phenomenon enabled by the tools of social networking and online communication. Crucially, this movement had the backing of senior leaders such as Secretary of Defense Robert Gates, who believed that the Defense Department needed to shift in a "different strategic direction," toward fighting and winning irregular war. His decision to stay on in the Obama administration helped ensure that those concepts would take root within the national-security establishment.

Iraq and Afghanistan offered the United States a laboratory for something new and remarkable: a sort of enlightened militarism. But although the U.S. military has in some respects begun to master "soft power," this approach is still the wrong instrument for nation building. Development and diplomatic agencies are the proper tools for nation building, but so long as agencies like USAID and the Foreign Service lack the personnel or the in-house expertise to run ambitious development programs, and the ability to work independently in conflict zones, much of the actual work will be outsourced to the Beltway bandits, private-sector and not-for-profit aid contractors. In the end, diplomacy and development is supposed to be a job for public servants, not for the private sector, much as national defense is the job of the uniformed military, not contractors.

When nation building becomes an attractive line of business for contractors, it's more likely to become a permanent feature of foreign policy, thanks to the revolving door between government service and private-sector contracting. Companies like Northrop Grumman and Lockheed Martin, which made their names building ships and fighter aircraft, opened business lines dedicated to supporting "soft power" missions around the globe, such as training foreign security forces and logistics and technical support. Thomas Barnett, the Pentagon theorist who was one of the earliest people to recognize this shift, capitalized on the move himself: He left government and joined a corporate and government consulting firm called Enterra Solutions, which offered "strategic advisory services" like "nation-state building" and "development-in-a-box."

One tempting solution seems to be "insourcing"—taking jobs that have been contracted out to the private sector and returning them to their "rightful place" in the federal bureaucracy. After a two-decade experiment in outsourcing, a reassertion of essential government functions would resolve some problems of accountability. But the idea that we will become more effective nation builders by creating more jobs within dysfunctional, risk-averse bureaucracies is magical thinking, and the idea that the complex problems of Afghanistan can be solved by applying a bureaucratic fix—"harmonizing the interagency," "breaking down stovepipes," "bridging the civil-military divide," and so on—is an illusion. And it ignores the fact that nation-building missions such as those in Iraq and Afghanistan have become so large, and so unwieldy, that they begin to undermine our intentions.

As of this writing, several initiatives are under way to better reorganize and realign the agencies of defense, diplomacy, and development for the tasks of nation building. In November 2009, Stuart Bowen, the U.S. special inspector general for Iraq reconstruction, floated a detailed proposal for a "U.S. Office for Contingency Operations" that would be charged with leading the federal government's armed nation-building efforts. The concept would be to create a hybrid civil-military organization within the federal government that reports to both the State Department and the Pentagon. Bowen likened it to a sort of "international FEMA" that would create a "permanent, fully accountable, empowered interagency management office" with "full responsibility for managing the relief and reconstruction component" of future military contingencies.[3] Such proposals, while well-intentioned, are merely bureaucratic fine-tuning. They ignore the real cost and consequences of these kinds of interventions.

The new doctrine of armed humanitarianism, and the reorganization of government around the tasks of nation building, creates more, not less, temptation to intervene in failed states. If we take at face value the assertion by Defense Secretary Gates—that the best approach is the "indirect" one of building the institutions of partner governments and their security forces—the question becomes this: How do we avoid costly, ultimately self-defeating commitments?

Over the past decade, and with little fanfare, we have managed do this kind of mission without a massive U.S. military presence. In the Philippines, for example, U.S. Special Operations forces have been running a low-key advisory mission since 2002. Joint Special Operations Task Force-Philippines has only around six hundred personnel, and they are limited to training missions and Civil Affairs projects. It's the traditional foreign internal defense approach: The military of the Philippines has to take the initiative, with behind-the-scenes support from U.S. advisors. It demonstrates that there are ways to conduct a counterinsurgency campaign without a large foreign force and in a way that is mindful of nationalist sensitivities. In Pakistan, we are waging a covert war using drones and a handful of advisors to take on al-Qaeda and its allies. The heavy presence of foreign troops and advisors might only destabilize the situation, which is something to be avoided in a country armed with nuclear weapons.

In El Salvador, veterans of the Vietnam conflict made a similarly wise effort to avoid a massive U.S. presence that would ultimately have undermined the self-reliance of the local government. The same has been true for Georgia, which has also been an important recipient of U.S. military assistance and training since 2002. U.S. military assistance to Georgia had its downside: It gave Georgia's government overconfidence about its military capabilities, its ability to take back the secessionist territories of Abkhazia and South Ossetia by force, and the U.S. willingness to intervene on its behalf during its brief, ruinous war with Russia in 2008. But U.S. assistance also helped build functioning security institutions, reinforced the rule of law, and helped move Georgia out from the bottom of the transparency index. While Georgia suffered a serious defeat in 2008, it has better prospects in the longer term for becoming a functioning market economy and democracy than many of its neighbors.

Reorganizing government around the ambitious goals of "global counterinsurgency" or "stability operations" currently demands a massive, quasi-colonial bureaucracy, a large constabulary army, and long-term occupation of failed states. As President Obama weighed a troop increase in Afghanistan, an anonymous Pentagon official complained to *Slate*: "Counterinsurgency has become synonymous with nation building . . . We have to change that."[4] How, exactly, can that be achieved? It would be ludicrous to believe that the United States can simply step away, avoid nation building altogether, and somehow free ourselves from foreign entanglements. The U.S. military maintains a global force that protects global shipping lanes, guards strategic airspace, and enables free trade. And in limited instances, it can provide that crucial margin of security that allows aid and development to flourish.

But the real mission of living and working with populations that are vulnerable to extremists requires a degree of cultural sophistication that we are not even close to attaining. After the Soviets launched Sputnik, the United States began a crash effort to fund engineering and science. If the main existential threat to the United States does come from militant extremism in places like Afghanistan, Iraq, or Somalia, then we need a decades-long investment in real social science research, language studies, and higher education, not cheap solutions delivered by contractors. Long term, continuing the kinds of nation-building projects we are involved in today without contractors would require a massive realignment of our foreign policy objectives, or a reinstatement of the draft.

The real locus of U.S. ingenuity is in places like Silicon Valley and New York, not Washington. Mobilizing capital to invest in developing countries is far superior to exporting aid workers with guns. Some of the most innovative thinkers in aid and development are now broadly skeptical of the ability of state institutions and multilateral organizations to foster effective development. As Ashraf Ghani, the former finance minister of Afghanistan, put it: "A dollar in private investment is equal to twenty dollars of aid."[5] Rebuilding broken states is not purely a task for the military or for government consultants.

The American public has, in the end, been divorced from the reality of nation building. While boots were on the ground in places like Iraq and Afghanistan, Americans were at the mall. When a small fraction of the population was engaged in the bloody business of repairing war-torn, failed states, the class of nation builders had become estranged from the American people, widening the divide between civilian and military. We have failed to have a national conversation about the real cost of this commitment, the limits of what nation building can and cannot achieve, and what place nation building plays within the larger national interest.

Acknowledgments

Anton Mueller, my editor at Bloomsbury, helped shape this book from its inception. I am immensely grateful for his enthusiasm, his guiding vision, and his belief in the importance of this subject. I am also indebted to Michelle Tessler, a wonderful literary agent and incisive reader.

This book grew out of a decade spent covering U.S. military operations around the globe. As I followed the U.S. involvement in Afghanistan, and then in Iraq, I saw the military taking on more and more nonmilitary tasks: building roads, digging wells, and repairing schools. Over time, it became clear that these were not unusual cases. Armed development work was the new norm, and I wanted to tell this story from the point of view of the practitioners: the people putting themselves in harm's way as part of this ambitious experiment.

It would have been impossible to tell this story without the active assistance of many men and women in uniform, as well as civilian employees of the military. The relationship between reporters and the Pentagon's public-affairs apparatus can sometimes be adversarial, but units in the field often showed extraordinary willingness to open up to me. This speaks to their democratic values and respect for an independent press.

At Fort Riley, Kansas, Army Sergeant First Class Ken McCooey helped arrange my stay at FOB Army Strong, and Army Lieutenant Colonel Eric Borgeson and the members of Team Mohican were kind enough to let me follow them through part of their training. At Fort Leavenworth, Kansas, Stephen Nolan and Army Colonel Steve Boylan lined up a series of valuable interviews.

In 2002, Army Major Bryan Hilferty set an excellent precedent, encouraging an open-door policy for military reporters at Bagram Airfield, Afghanistan. Army Lieutenant Lory Stevens and Captain Scot Keith helped organize several Afghanistan embeds in the summer of 2009, and understood the focus of my reporting. Air Force Major David Faggard opened many doors as well. In 2004, Army Captain Jacob Larkowich and Lieutenant Steve McKeon of Alpha Company, 1–4 Infantry, part of the first U.S. contingent under the NATO International Security Assistance Force in Afghanistan, brought me along on a security mission outside of Kabul. And in 2008, Lieutenant Colonel Tony Henderson, commander of First Battalion, Sixth Marines, and Captain Charles O'Neill, commander of Bravo Company, First Battalion, Sixth Marine Regiment, hosted me in Helmand Province. Thanks are also due to Major Kelly Frushour, public affairs chief for the Twenty-fourth Marine Expeditionary Unit, and Colonel Peter Petronzio, commander of the Twenty-fourth Marine Expeditionary Unit.

In Washington, Navy Lieutenant Jennifer Cragg of the Pentagon's new media directorate played a key role in helping ensure that online reporters had fair access to important news stories. Jaime Wood and Army Lieutenant Colonel Holly Silkman showed great patience and persistence in helping arrange my visit to Timbuktu. Tom Cooney and Todd Calongne of the State Department organized several key interviews.

In Baghdad, Army Lieutenant Colonel Craig Simonsgaard and the members of his transition team brought me along on their missions in Sadr City. Major Michael Humphreys and Scott Flenner of the Army's Third Brigade Combat Team, Fourth Infantry Division, helped facilitate my stay at FOB War Eagle. Air Force Major Jason "Fitz" Kirkpatrick and Tarah Hollingsworth organized a unique 2007 visit to Iraq. Steve Bird helped arrange a 2005 visit to Baghdad. In Kabul, I enjoyed the support of Gillian Sandford, Wali Azizi, Wahidullah Amani, and many other friends at the Institute for War and Peace Reporting. David Trilling, Sanjar Qiam, Saira Shah, and Hugo MacPherson were great companions in 2004.

During my research, I also relied on Michael Bear Kleinman, Nancy Lindborg, and Roman Ponos for insights into the world of aid and development. I'm also indebted to Lynda Granfield, Dan Green, and Ramon Negron, who helped explain the mission of the Provincial Reconstruction Teams, and the German Marshall Fund of the United States, which helped support one of my trips to Afghanistan.

Many friends provided valuable comments and criticism on various chapters and drafts. Thanks go to Noah Shachtman, my friend and co-writer at Danger Room, *Wired*'s national security blog: an immensely talented writer who helped refine an early version of the manuscript. Kris Alexander, Sally Cooper, Steven Lee Myers, Jonathan Hayes, Kathryn Schulz, and Askold Krushelnycky all provided me with key feedback. Tara McKelvey, Robert Wall, Richard Whittle, Greg Renoff, and Kathleen Kuehnast offered encouragement and advice during the writing process. Sean Allen and Nikolai Firtich were patient friends. Thanks also to the staff at the library of the Massachusetts Institute of Technology, where I conducted some of the background research.

My gratitude as well to Evan Hansen of *Wired*; Peter Felstead and Nick Brown of *Jane's Defence Weekly* and *International Defence Review*; Pavel Bykov of *Expert*; Llewellyn King of King Publishing; John Robinson of *Defense Daily*; June Thomas of *Slate*; and Chuck Holmes of Cox News.

My father, Brien Hodge, served in Vietnam as an Army advisor in the Mekong Delta region from September 1967 to September 1968. His experiences during his tour helped inform my reading of history. My mother, Marjorie Hodge, and my sisters, Miriam and Naomi, gave tremendous encouragement during my travels.

Finally, I am forever grateful to my wife, Sharon, whose support has been beyond measure. She has been a sounding board for every story idea, a capable editor of every draft, my closest friend and collaborator. Without her, I would not have had the courage to start. This book is dedicated to her.

Notes

Prologue

1 John Kruzel, "Colonel Describes Orderly Traffic at Haiti Airport," American Forces Press Service, January 17, 2010.

2 Kelly Webster, "Lessons from a Military Humanitarian in Port-au-Prince, Haiti," Small Wars Journal, March 28, 2010, http://smallwarsjournal.com/blog/journal/docs-temp/401-webster.pdf.

3 Yochi Dreazen, "Military Finds an Unlikely Advisor in School-Building Humanitarian," Wall Street Journal, December 26, 2008.

4 Lin Wells, "Tides Week One Summary by Lin Wells," Star-Tides blog, http://star-tides.blogspot.com/2007/10/below-is-summary-of-first-week-of-tides.html.

5 Donna Miles, "Obama Cites Responsibility to 'Get It Right' in Iraq, Afghanistan," American Forces Press Service, February 28, 2009.

6 Robert Gates, National Defense University (Washington, D.C.), Speech, September 29, 2008, www.defense.gov/speeches/speech.aspx?speechid=1279.

7 John Hillen, "Superpowers Don't Do Windows," Orbis, Spring 1997, http://www.fpri.org/americavulnerable/03.SuperpowersDontDoWindows.Hillen.pdf.

8 Special Inspector General for Iraq Reconstruction, "Hard Lessons: The Iraq Reconstruction Experience," report, February 2, 2009, www.sigir.mil/files/HardLessons/Hard_Lessons-Report.pdf.

9 Special Inspector General for Afghanistan Reconstruction, "Quarterly Report to the United States Congress," April 30, 2010, www.sigar.mil/pdf/quarterlyreports/Apr2010/SIGARapril_Lores.pdf.

10 Robert Gates, "Eisenhower Library (Defense Spending)," speech, May 8, 2010, www.defense.gov/speeches.aspx?speechID=1467.

11 Ken Dilanian, "Clinton: U.S. Will Try to Repair Broken Aid," *USA Today*, April 1, 2009.

12 USAID, "Budget Justification FY 2001," www.usaid.gov/pubs/bj2001.

13 Max Boot, "The Case for American Empire: The Most Realistic Response to Terrorism Is for America to Embrace Its Imperial Role," *Weekly Standard*, October 12, 2001.

14 American Foreign Service Association, "AFSANET: Telling Our Story: October 17, 2007," factsheet, www.afsa.org/101707presupdate.cfm.

15 See Organisation for Economic Co-operation and Development, "The United States: Development Assistance Committee Peer Review," 2006, www.oecd.org/dataoecd/61/57/37885999.pdf.

16 Corine Hegland, "Pentagon, State Struggle to Define Nation-Building Roles," *National Journal*, April 30, 2007.

17 An updated version of this document, dated September 16, 2009, is available at www.dtic.mil/whs/directives/corres/pdf/300005p.pdf.

18 August Cole, "Defense Firms Look to Fill Gaps as U.S. Policy Shifts," *Wall Street Journal*, March 2, 2009.

19 Nina Serafino, "Peacekeeping and Related Stability Operations: Issues of U.S. Military Involvement," Congressional Research Service report, July 13, 2006, www.history.navy.mil/library/online/peacekeep_stab%20ops.htm#evolution.

20 Michael Siegl, "Clarity and Culture in Stability Operations." *Military Review* 87, no. 6, November–December 2007.

Part I: Winning the War, Losing the Peace

1. Absolute Beginners

1 Patrick Cockburn, "Cluster Bombs over Charicar," *The Independent*, October 5, 2001.

2 For photos of the Salang Pass, see the Web site for former students and teachers of the American International School of Kabul, www.aisk.org/aisk/return2kabul200501.php.

3 Linette Albert, "Afghanistan: A Perspective," in Louis Dupree and Linette Albert, eds., *Afghanistan in the 1970s* (New York: Praeger, 1974), p. 254.

4 Ibid.

5 U.S. Government Accounting Office, "Contingency Operations: Army Should Do More to Control Contract Cost in the Balkans," report to the U.S. Senate, September 2000.

6 U.S. Army Corps of Engineers, factsheet on LOGCAP I, "Transatlantic Program Center's Involvement in the First Contract Awarded for the Logistics Civil Augmentation Program (1991–1997)," www.tac.usace.army.mil/Organization/lcap.html.

7 Dana Priest, *The Mission: Waging War and Keeping Peace with America's Military* (New York: Norton, 2003), p. 387.

8 James Dao, "G.I.'s Fight Afghan Devastation with Plaster and Nails," *New York Times*, June 24, 2002.

9 Sandra Erwin, "Civil Affairs," *National Defense*, May 2005.

10 Sean Naylor, "Demand Skyrocketing for Active-Duty Civil Affairs Brigade," *Defense News*, October 5, 2001.

11 Chemonics, "Helping Rebuild Lives in Afghanistan," press release, www.chemonics.com/projects/default.asp?content_id={17C6D697-B36B-4B95-8A3F-424816235E18}.

12 Ken Dilanian, "Short-Staffed USAID Tries to Keep Pace," *USA Today*, February 1, 2009.

13 Ruben Berrios, *Contracting for Development: The Role of For-Profit Development Contractors in U.S. Foreign Development Assistance* (Westport, Conn.: Praeger, 2000), pp. 1–2.

14 Matt Steinglass, "The Pitfalls of Pacification," GlobalPost.com, March 27, 2009, www.globalpost.com/dispatch/vietnam/090327/the-pitfalls-pacification?page=0,2.

15 Berrios, *Contracting for Development*, pp. 7–8.

16 For a list of USAID implementation partners in Ukraine, see http://ukraine.usaid.gov/link.shtml.

17 Matt Bivens, "Aboard the Gravy Train: In Kazakhstan, the Farce That Is U.S. Foreign Aid," *Harper's*, August 1997.

18 Ibid.

19 Janine Wedel, "The Harvard Boys Do Russia," *The Nation*, June 1, 1998.

20 Zachary Seward, "Harvard to Pay $26.5 Million in HIID Settlement," *Harvard Crimson*, July 29, 2005.

21 Joel Hafvenstein, *Opium Season: A Year on the Afghan Frontier* (Guilford, Conn.: Lyons Press, 2007), p. 61.

22 Gary Berntsen and Ralph Pezzullo, *Jawbreaker: The Attack on Bin Laden and Al-Qaeda: A Personal Account by the CIA's Field Commander* (New York: Crown, 2005), pp. 194–95.

23 Luke Harding and Matthew Engel, "U.S. Bomb Blunder Kills 30 at Afghan Wedding," *Guardian*, July 2, 2002.

24 Philip Smucker, "Liabilities of Using Afghan Informants," *Christian Science Monitor*, December 21, 2001.

25 "Deputy Secretary Wolfowitz Town Hall Meeting at Bagram Air Base," July 15, 2002, Department of Defense news transcript.

2. The PowerPoint Warrior

1 Donald Rumsfeld, "DOD Acquisition and Logistics Excellence Week Kickoff—Bureaucracy to Battlefield," remarks delivered at the Pentagon, September 10, 2001, www.defense.gov/speeches/speech.aspx?speechid=430.

2 Arthur Cebrowski and John Garstka, "Network-Centric Warfare: Its Origin and Future," *Proceedings*, January 1998.

3 Thomas Barnett, "The Seven Deadly Sins of Network-Centric Warfare," *Proceedings*, January 1999.

4 Charles Krulak, "The Strategic Corporal: Leadership in the Three Block War," *Marines Magazine*, January 1999.

5 Thomas Barnett, *The Pentagon's New Map: War and Peace in the Twenty-first Century* (New York: Berkley, 2005), p. 180.

6 Ibid., p. 181.

7 George Gedda, "Bush Administration Speeds Up Help to Colombian Military," Associated Press, February 22, 2002.

8 Paul Quinn-Judge, "Inside al-Qaeda's Georgia Refuge," *Time*, October 19, 2002.

9 Thomas P. M. Barnett, "The Pentagon's New Map: It Explains Why We're Going to War, and Why We'll Keep Going to War," *Esquire*, March 2003.

3. "Beat 'em Up and Go Home"

1 Office of the Under Secretary of Defense for Acquisition, Technology, and Logistics, "Report of the Defense Science Board Task Force on Patriot System Performance," January 2005, www.acq.osd.mil/dsb/reports/ADA435837.pdf.

2 "Deputy Secretary Wolfowitz Interview with Sam Tannenhaus [*sic*], *Vanity Fair*," May 9, 2003, Department of Defense news transcript.

3 Ryan Chilcote, "Commander Shows Restraint, Prevents Unnecessary Violence," CNN.com, http://edition.cnn.com/SPECIALS/2003/iraq/heroes/chrishughes.html.

4 Christopher Hughes, *War on Two Fronts: An Infantry Commander's War in Iraq and the Pentagon* (Drexel Hill, Pa.: Casemate, 2007), pp. 106–11.

5 Jim Garamone, "U.S. Army Trains Free Iraqi Forces in Hungary," American Forces Press Service, February 23, 2003, www.defenselink.mil/news/newsarticle.aspx?id=29394.

6 Linda Robinson and Kevin Whitelaw, "Deploying the 'Free Iraqi Forces': What Role for the Arriving Anti-Saddam Iraqi Fighters?" *U.S. News & World Report*, April 7, 2003.

7 Christopher Griffin, "Revenge of the Staff Weenie: Mining the Military Bureaucracy for Nuggets of Humor," *Armed Forces Journal*, October 2006, www.armedforcesjournal.com/2006/10/2098845.

8 Jim Dwyer, "American Soldiers, at the Behest of an Iraqi Officer, Topple a Hussein Statue," *New York Times*, April 4, 2003.

9 Nathaniel Fick, *One Bullet Away: The Making of a Marine Officer* (New York: Mariner Books, 2006), pp. 237–39.

10 Ibid.

11 Fick, *One Bullet Away*, pp. 303–4.

12 U.S. Department of Defense, "Pre-war Planning for Post-war Iraq," at Department of Defense Air University Web site, "Lessons Learned," www.au.af.mil/au/awc/awcgate/dod/postwar_iraq.htm.

13 "CONPLAN AURORA (releasable) 06-260," CENTCOM Information Portal, Case H06-260, http://www2.centcom.mil/sites/foia/rr/default.aspx.

14 Kurt Schork, "Mission-Minded Dallas Man Confronts Disasters Hurting Third World's Poor," *Dallas Morning News*, July 1991.

15 Donald Wright and Colonel Timothy Reese with the Contemporary Operations Study Team, *On Point II: Transition to the New Campaign—The United States Army in Operation Iraqi Freedom, May 2003—January 2005* (Fort Leavenworth, Kans.: Combat Studies Institute Press, U.S. Army Combined Arms Center, 2008), p. 150.

16 John Guardiano, "'Bush Good, Saddam Bad!': A Marine Reports from Iraq, Where Things Are Far Better Than the Media Let On," *Wall Street Journal*, August 19, 2003.

17 Peter Ford and Seth Stern, "Humanitarian Aid to Iraq Proves One of War's Biggest Obstacles," *Christian Science Monitor*, March 28, 2003.

18 Nick Cater, "Oxfam to Refuse Government Iraq Aid," *Guardian*, March 4, 2003.

19 Jack Epstein, "Charities at Odds with Pentagon," *San Francisco Chronicle*, June 14, 2003.

20 See "USAID Press Releases," April 2 and April 11, 2003, www.usaid.gov/press/releases/2003.

21 Andrew Natsios, "Agency Takes Right Approach," *USA Today*, March 31, 2003.

22 Peter Mansoor, *Baghdad at Sunrise: A Brigade Commander's War in Iraq* (New Haven: Yale University Press, 2008), pp. 53–54.

23 Ibid., p. 27.

24 Jim Krane, "GOP Operatives Lead at Iraq Press Office," Associated Press, April 4, 2004.

25 Ariana Eunjung Cha, "In Iraq, the Job Opportunity of a Lifetime," *Washington Post*, May 23, 2004.

26 Ray LeMoine and Jeff Neumann with Donovan Webster, *Babylon by Bus* (New York: Penguin, 2006), p. 44.

27 Ibid., p. 76.

28 Colonel Lloyd Sammons, interview by Larry Plotkin, of the United States Institute of Peace Association for Diplomatic Studies and Training Iraq Experience Project, October 1, 2004, transcript at www.usip.org/files/file/resources/collections/histories/iraq/sammons.pdf.

4. The Other War

1 Carlotta Gall, "The Reach of War: U.S. Woman and Girl, 12, Die in Attack by Afghan Bomber," *New York Times*, October 24, 2004.

2 Borhan Younus, "The Death of a Little Street-Seller," Pajhwok Afghan News, November 27, 2004.

3 Safia Milad, "Kabul Suicide Bomber Revealed," Pajhwok Afghan News, November 8, 2004.

4 Casey Vinall, "Joe Collins: Career Officer, Deputy Assistant Defense Secretary," American Forces Press Service, June 23, 2003, www.defenselink.mil/news/newsarticle.aspx?id=28841.

5 "Deputy Assistant Secretary Collins Media Roundtable on Afghanistan," December 19, 2002, U.S. Department of Defense, news transcript, www.defenselink.mil/transcripts/transcript.aspx?transcriptid=2942.

6 "Britain's Armed Forces: Losing Their Way?" *Economist*, January 29, 2009.

7 Carlotta Gall, "Serbs on Edge After Rally by Albanians in a Kosovo City," *New York Times*, February 23, 2000.

8 J. Alexander Thier, "Afghanistan," in William Durch, ed., *Twenty-First-Century Peace Operations* (Washington, D.C.: U.S. Institute of Peace Press, 2006), p. 495.

9 Barbara Stapleton, "The Provincial Reconstruction Team Plan in Afghanistan: A New Direction?," paper presented at the symposium State Reconstruction and International Engagement in Afghanistan, Center for Development Research (ZEF), Bonn, May 30–June 1, 2003, www.ag-afghanistan.de/arg/arp/stapleton.pdf.

10 "Deputy Assistant Secretary of Defense Joseph Collins Media Roundtable on Afghanistan," December 19, 2002, Department of Defense transcript, http://www.defense.gov/transcripts/transcript.aspx?transcriptid=2942.

11 "Deputy Assistant Secretary of Defense Joseph Collins Media Roundtable on Afghanistan."

12 Nicolaus Mills, *Winning the Peace: The Marshall Plan and America's Coming of Age as a Superpower* (New York: John Wiley, 2008), p. 184.

13 Ibid., p. xi.

14 Marc Kaufman, "Afghanistan Still Groping for Order," *Washington Post*, April 15, 2003.

15 "Deputy Assistant Secretary of Defense Joseph Collins Media Roundtable on Afghanistan."

16 Jane Barry with Anna Jefferys, "A Bridge Too Far: Aid Agencies and the Military in Humanitarian Response," Humanitarian Practice Network paper, January 2002, http://reliefweb.int/rw/lib.nsf/db900sid/LGEL-5FKHH5/$file/odi-bridge-jan02.pdf?openelement.

17 Carlotta Gall, "A Nation at War: Aid Workers; In Afghanistan, Helping Can Be Deadly," *New York Times*, April 5, 2003.

18 Agency Coordinating Body for Afghan Relief, "NGOs Alarmed by Lack of Media Coverage Following Execution of ICRC Staff Member," press release, March 31, 2003, www.reliefweb.int/rw/rwb.nsf/db900sid/ACOS-64D2SU?OpenDocument.

19 Sarah Chayes, *The Punishment of Virtue: Inside Afghanistan After the Taliban* (New York: Penguin Press, 2006), p. 236.

20 Ibid., pp. 237–38.

21 Noor Khan, "Helicopter Crashes in Southern Afghanistan After Coming Under Fire," Associated Press, February 22, 2004.

5. Cash as a Weapon

1 "Secretary, Rumsfeld Town Hall Meeting in Kuwait," December 8, 2004, Department of Defense transcript, www.defense.gov/transcripts/transcript.aspx?transcriptid=1980.

2 Lieutenant Colonel Mark Martins, "The Commander's Emergency Response Program," *Joint Forces Quarterly*, no. 37 (Second Quarter, 2005): 47.

3 Special Inspector General for Iraq Reconstruction, "Hard Lessons: The Iraq Reconstruction Experience," report, February 2009, www.sigir.mil/files/HardLessons/Hard_Lessons-Report.pdf, p. 79.

4 Martins, "Commander's Emergency Response Program," p. 48.

5 Special Inspector General for Iraq Reconstruction, "Hard Lessons," p. 87.

6 Ibid., p. vii.

7 "101st Airborne Division Commander Live Briefing from Iraq," May 13, 2003, Department of Defense news briefing, www.defenselink.mil/tran scripts/transcript.aspx?transcriptid=2601.

8 Colonel Lloyd Sammons, interview by Larry Plotkin, see chapter 3, note 28.

9 Michael Knights, "Lessons from Mosul," *PolicyWatch*, no. 950 (Washington, D.C.: Washington Institute for Near East Policy), January 27, 2005.

10 Sergeant First Class Doug Sample, "Task Force Commander Says Insurgents 'Desperate, Isolated,'" American Forces Press Service, March 9, 2004.

11 Daniel Gonzales, John Hollywood, et al., *Networked Forces in Stability Operations: 101st Airborne Division, 3/2 and 1/25 Stryker Brigades in Northern Iraq* (Santa Monica, Calif.: RAND Corporation, 2007).

12 Colonel Lloyd Sammons, interview by Plotkin.

13 Gonzales, Hollywood, et al., *Networked Forces in Stability Operations*.

14 U.S. General Accounting Office, "Defense Transformation: Army's Evaluation of Stryker and M113A3 Infantry Carrier Vehicles Provided Sufficient Data for Statutorily Mandated Comparison," publication GAO-03-671, May 2003, www.gao.gov/new.items/d03671.pdf.

15 "Coalition Provisional Authority Order Number 45: Non-Governmental Organizations."

16 Integrated Regional Information Network, Iraq: "NGO registration causes controversy," January 13, 2004, www.irinnews.org/Report.aspx?Re portID=23334.

17 Ray LeMoine and Jeff Neumann, *Babylon by Bus* (New York: Penguin Press, 2006), p. 85.

18 Juliana Gittler, "14th Cavalry delivers backpacks to kids at remote Iraqi school," *Stars & Stripes*, European edition, November 8, 2004.

Part II: History Lessons

6. The Phoenix Rises

1 William Arkin, "The Pentagon Unleashes a Holy Warrior," *Los Angeles Times*, October 16, 2003.

2 U.S. Department of Defense, Office of the Inspector General, "Alleged Improprieties Related to Public Speaking: Lieutenant General William G. Boykin, U.S. Army, Deputy Under Secretary of Defense for Intelligence," report prepared by the Directorate for Investigations of Senior Officials, August 5, 2004, www.dodig.mil/fo/Foia/ERR/ho/3189967206.pdf.

3 William Colby with James McCargar, *Lost Victory* (Chicago: Contemporary Books, 1989), pp. 330–33.

4 Ibid., p. 16.

5 John Nagl, *Learning to Eat Soup with a Knife: Counterinsurgency Lessons from Malaya and Vietnam* (Chicago: University of Chicago Press, 2005), p. ix.

6 Ibid.

7 Ibid., p. xiii.

8 David Petraeus, "The American Military and the Lessons of Vietnam: A Study of Military Influence and the Use of Force in the Post-Vietnam Era," Ph.D. diss., Princeton University, 1987.

9 See Robert Komer, *The Malayan Emergency in Retrospect: Organization of a Successful Counterinsurgency Effort* (Santa Monica, Calif.: RAND Corporation, 1972).

10 Sylvia Ellis, *Britain, America and the Vietnam War* (Westport, Conn.: Praeger, 2004), p. 2.

11 Sir Robert Thompson, "Squaring the Error," *Foreign Policy*, April 1968.

12 Robert Thompson, *Peace Is Not at Hand* (New York: David McKay, 1974), p. 71.

13 Colby and McCargar, *Lost Victory*, p. 263.

14 Robert Komer, *Bureaucracy Does Its Thing: Institutional Constraints on U.S-GVN Performance in Vietnam* (Santa Monica, Calif.: RAND Corporation, 1972), pp. v–ix.

15 Thompson, *Peace Is Not at Hand*, p. 59.

16 Ibid., p. 35.

17 Colby and McCargar, *Lost Victory*, p. 91.

18 Komer, *Bureaucracy Does Its Thing*, p. 113.

19 Ibid., p. 115.

20 Ibid., p. xi.

21 Nguyen Van Thieu, letter to President Richard Nixon, March 20, 1973, The American Presidency Project, www.presidency.ucsb.edu/ws/index.php? pid=3790.

22 Lewis Sorley, *Vietnam Chronicles: The Abrams Tapes, 1968–1972* (Lubbock, Texas: Texas Tech University Press, 2004), p. 354.

23 Ibid.

24 Marc Leepson, "The Heart and Mind of USAID's Vietnam Mission," *Foreign Service Journal*, April 2000.

25 Eliot Cohen, *Citizens and Soldiers: The Dilemmas of Military Service* (Ithaca, N.Y.: Cornell University Press, 1985), p. 107.

7. The Accidental Counterinsurgents

1 David Galula, *Counterinsurgency Warfare: Theory and Practice* (Westport, Conn.: Praeger Security International, 2006), p. 62.

2 Elaine Grossman, "To Understand Insurgency in Iraq: Read Something Old, Something New," *Inside the Pentagon*, December 2, 2004.

3 Kris Hundley, "Strategic Control, by the Book," *St. Petersburg Times*, October 4, 2005.

4 "More Than 80 Dead in Apparent Reprisals," CNN.com, March 14, 2006, www.cnn.com/2006/WORLD/meast/03/14/iraq.main/index.html.

5 Dan Baum, "Battle Lessons: What the Generals Don't Know," *New Yorker*, January 17, 2005.

6 Brigadier Nigel Aylwin-Foster, "Changing the Army for Counterinsurgency Operations," *Military Review*, November–December 2005.

7 David Kilcullen, "Twenty-Eight Articles: Fundamentals of Company-Level Counterinsurgency," March 2006, http://usacac.army.mil/cac2/coin/repository/28_Articles_of_COIN-Kilcullen%28Mar06%29.pdf.

8 Vince Crawley, "The Battle of 73 Easting," *Stars & Stripes*, June 7, 2003 (Desert Storm commemorative edition), www.stripes.com/news/from-the-s-s-archives-the-battle-of-the-73-easting-1.6319.

9 "Secretary of Defense Robert Gates Testimony Before the House Armed Services Committee, April 15, 2008," http://armedservices.house.gov/pdfs/FC041508/GatesTestimony041508.pdf.

Part III: Theory into Practice

8. Wingtips on the Ground

1 "DoD News Briefing—Secretary Rumsfeld and Gen. Myers," June 30, 2003, Department of Defense transcript, www.defense.gov/transcripts/transcript .aspx?transcriptid=2767.

2 House Committee on Armed Services, Subcommittee on Oversight and Investigation, *Agency Stovepipes vs. Strategic Agility: Lessons We Need to Learn from Provincial Reconstruction Teams in Iraq and Afghanistan*, report, April 2008, www.armedservices.house.gov/Reports/PRT_Report.pdf.

3 Karen DeYoung, "Envoys Resist Forced Iraq Duty," *Washington Post*, November 1, 2007.

4 See Noah Shachtman, "Diplos Cry in Their Milk over Iraq Assignments," November 1, 2007, www.wired.com/dangerroom/2007/11/diplos-cry-in-t.

5 John Matel, "A Letter from Iraq to My Overwrought Colleagues," Dipnote (the official blog of the State Department), November 7, 2007, http://blogs .state.gov/index.php/entries/iraq_colleagues.

6 David Kilcullen, *The Accidental Guerrilla: Fighting Small Wars in the Midst of a Big One* (New York: Oxford University Press, 2009), p. 119.

7 Kilcullen, "Twenty-eight Articles: Fundamentals of Company-Level Counterinsurgency."

8 Joanna Jolly, "Army's Hand Seen in East Timor Border Ambush," *Guardian*, October 11, 1999.

9 Tom Morton, "Perils of Peacekeeping," ABC Radio National broadcast, October 29, 2006, transcript at www.abc.net.au/rn/backgroundbriefing/sto ries/2006/1772988.htm.

10 Combat camera footage, archived at www.youtube.com/watch?v=5jLEAJ mAwjE.

11 Kilcullen, *Accidental Guerrilla*, pp. 120–22.

12 Eythan Sontag and Keith Mines, "First Response: Transformational Diplomacy in Darfur," *State Magazine*, June 2007.

9. Kalashnikovs for Hire

1 Congressional Budget Office, "Contractors' Support of U.S. Operations in Iraq," August 2008.

2 Justin Elliott, "How Many Private Contractors Are There in Afghanistan? Military Gives Us a Number," *TPM Muckraker*, December 2, 2009, http://

tpmmuckraker.talkingpointsmemo.com/2009/12/so_how_many_private_contractors_are_there_in_afgha.php.

3 T. Christian Miller, "Iraq Convoy Got Go-Ahead Despite Threat," *Los Angeles Times*, September 3, 2007.

4 Jane Loeffler, *The Architecture of Diplomacy: Building America's Embassies* (New York: Princeton Architectural Press, 1998), p. 4.

5 Ibid., p. 8.

6 The Inman Report. The report is available at the Federation of American Scientists Web site: www.fas.org/irp/threat/inman/index.html.

7 "Statement of Ambassador Richard Griffin, Assistant Secretary of State, Bureau of Diplomatic Security, Department of State, before the House Committee on Oversight and Government Reform, October 2, 2007," www.reform.democrats.house.gov/documents/20071002145249.pdf.

8 U.S. Government Accountability Office, "Rebuilding Iraq: Actions Needed to Improve Use of Private Security Providers," report no. GAO-05-737, July 2005, www.gao.gov/new.items/d05737.pdf.

9 Neil King, Jr., and Yochi Dreazen, "Amid Chaos in Iraq, Tiny Security Firm Found Opportunity," *Wall Street Journal*, August 13, 2004.

10 "Statement of Ambassador Richard Griffin," p. 3.

11 United States Department of State and Broadcasting Board of Governors Office of Inspector General, Middle East Regional Office, "Performance Audit of the Triple Canopy Contract for Personal Protective Services in Iraq," report no. MERO-A-09-08, August 2009, http://oig.state.gov/documents/organization/135559.pdf.

12 Elizabeth Williamson, "How Much Embassy Is Too Much?" *Washington Post*, March 2, 2007.

13 Jane Loeffler, "Fortress America," *Foreign Policy*, September–October 2007.

14 Andy Melville, interviewed by Martin Smith for "Private Warriors," *Frontline*, PBS, broadcast June 23, 2005, interview transcript, www.pbs.org/wgbh/pages/frontline/shows/warriors/interviews/melville.html.

15 Robert Young Pelton, *Licensed to Kill: Hired Guns in the War on Terror* (New York: Crown, 2006), p. 37

16 Ibid., p. 40.

17 "Memorandum, October 1, 2007, to the Members of the House Committee on Oversight and Government Reform, re: Additional Information about Blackwater USA," staff memorandum, http://graphics8.nytimes.com/packages/pdf/national/20071001121609.pdf. The memorandum, compiled by the committee's Democratic staff, was based largely on internal Blackwater e-mail messages and State Department documents.

18 Report from the House Committee on the Judiciary accompanying H.R. 3380, amending title 18, United States Code, www.justice.gov/criminal/hrsp/docs/07-20-2000-meja-act.pdf.

19 John Broder, "Ex-Paratrooper Is Suspect in Blackwater Killing," *New York Times*, October 4, 2007.

20 "Memorandum, October 1, 2007," p. 11.

21 Patrick Kennedy, "Report of the Secretary of State's Panel on Personal Protective Services in Iraq," October 2007.

22 Ned Parker, "U.S. Limits Diplomats' Travel in Iraq," *Los Angeles Times*, September 19, 2007.

23 Matthew Lee, "Blackwater Security Contractors Still in Iraq," Associated Press, April 20, 2009.

24 Charlie Savage, "Judge Drops Charges from Blackwater Deaths in Iraq," *New York Times*, December 31, 2009.

25 Mike Baker, "Blackwater Settles Series of Civil Lawsuits," Associated Press, January 7, 2010.

10. Peace Corps on Steroids

1 See, for example, Andrew Hansen and Lauren Vriens, "Al-Qaeda in the Islamic Maghreb (AQIM) or L'Organisation Al-Qaïda au Maghreb Islamique (Formerly Salafist Group for Preaching and Combat or Groupe Salafiste pour la Prédication et le Combat)," Backgrounder, Council on Foreign Relations, July 21, 2009, www.cfr.org/publication/12717.

2 Richard Catoire, "A CINC for Sub-Saharan Africa? Rethinking the Unified Command Plan," *Parameters*, Winter 2000–2001, pp. 102–17.

3 Lauren Ploch, "Africa Command: U.S. Strategic Interests and the Role of the U.S. Military in Africa," Congressional Research Service Report for Congress, April 3, 2010, www.fas.org/sgp/crs/natsec/RL34003.pdf, pp. 35–39.

4 Ibid.

5 Scott Feil, "Preventing Genocide: How the Early Use of Force Might Have Succeeded in Rwanda," report to the Carnegie Commission on Preventing Deadly Conflict, April 1998.

6 Catoire, "CINC for Sub-Saharan Africa."

7 Ibid.

8 "President Bush Creates a Department of Defense Unified Combatant Command for Africa," February 6, 2007, White House press release.

9 Lauren Gelfand, "Air of Unease Remains as U.S. Africa Command Becomes Fully Operational," *Jane's Defence Weekly*, September 29, 2008.

10 Shaun Benton, "US to Shed Light on AFRICOM," SouthAfrica.info, September 21, 2007, www.safrica.info/africa/africom-210907.htm.

11 Kitsepile Nyathi, "Plans to Base U.S. Africa Command in Botswana Causes Tension," *Nation* (Kenya), September 13, 2007.

12 Bill Sizemore, "Private Army Is Ready for Hire, Company Says," *Virginian-Pilot*, March 31, 2006.

13 U.S. Government Accountability Office, "Peacekeeping: Thousands Trained but United States Is Unlikely to Complete All Activities by 2010 and Some Improvements Are Needed," Report to Congressional Committees, report no. GAO-08-754, June 26, 2008, www.gao.gov/new.items/d08754.pdf.

14 "Theresa Whelan, Deputy Assistant Secretary of Defense for African Affairs, Remarks to IPOA [International Peace Operations Association] dinner, November 19, 2003, Washington, D.C.," http://policy.defense.gov/sections/policy_offices/isa/africa/IPOA.htm.

15 "AFRICAP Recompete," awards notice posted on FedBizOpps.gov (Federal Business Opportunities), www.fbo.gov/index?tab=core&s=opportunity&mode=form&id=8c9852ce91f1fe6c3e79273f0b04e500&tabmode=list.

16 U.S. Government Accountability Office, "Peacekeeping."

17 William Ward, "Toward a Horizon of Hope: Considerations for Long-Term Stability in Postconflict Situations," *Joint Force Quarterly*, no. 45 (Second Quarter 2007).

18 Ibid.

19 Jeffrey Gettleman and Eric Schmitt, "U.S. Aided a Failed Plan to Rout Ugandan Rebels," *New York Times*, February 6, 2009.

11. Windshield Ethnographers

1 Alissa Rubin and Mudhafer al-Husaini, "Baghdad Blast Kills Four Americans," *New York Times*, June 25, 2008.

2 Montgomery McFate, "Iraq: The Social Context of IEDs," *Military Review*, May–June 2005.

3 Ibid.

4 Noah Shachtman, "Army Anthropologist's Controversial Culture Clash," *Wired*, October 2008.

5 Jacob Kipp, Lester Grau, Karl Prinslow, and Captain Dan Smith, "The

Human Terrain System: A CORDS for the 21st Century," *Military Review*, September–October 2006.

6 Montgomery McFate, "Anthropology and Counterinsurgency: The Strange Story of Their Curious Relationship," *Military Review*, March–April 2005.

7 Ibid.

8 David Price, *Anthropological Intelligence: The Deployment and Neglect of American Anthropology in the Second World War* (Durham, N.C.: Duke University Press, 2008), pp. 9–10.

9 Ibid., pp. 11–13.

10 Ibid., p. 14.

11 See "National Character," a subsection of "Margaret Mead: Human Nature and the Power of Culture," Library of Congress exhibition, www.loc.gov/exhibits/mead/oneworld-char.html.

12 Price, *Anthropological Intelligence*, p. 239.

13 Irving Louis Horowitz, ed., *The Rise and Fall of Project Camelot: Studies in the Relationship between Social Science and Practical Politics* (Cambridge, Mass.: MIT Press, 1967), p. 47.

14 Ibid., p. 51.

15 Seymour Deitchman, *The Best-Laid Schemes: A Tale of Social Research and Bureaucracy* (Cambridge, Mass.: MIT Press, 1976), p. 16.

16 Ibid., pp. 169–70.

17 McFate, "Anthropology and Counterinsurgency."

18 George Packer, "Knowing the Enemy: Can Social Scientists Redefine the 'War on Terror'?" *New Yorker*, December 18, 2006.

19 Sharon Weinberger, "The Pentagon's Culture Wars," *Nature*, October 2, 2008.

20 Zenia Helbig, "Memorandum: Human Terrain System Program; U.S. Army Training and Doctrine Command," letter to Representative Ike Skelton, chairman of the House Armed Services Committee, and Representative Henry Waxman, chairman of the House Committee on Oversight and Government Reform, September 13, 2007, www.brama.com/news/press/2007/12/070913HelbigCongressMemo.pdf.

21 David Glenn, "Former Human Terrain System Participant Describes Program in Disarray," *Chronicle of Higher Education*, December 5, 2007.

22 "Pledge of Non-participation in Counter-insurgency," http://sites.google.com/site/concernedanthropologists.

23 Montgomery McFate, quoted in Weinberger, "The Pentagon's Culture Wars."

24 Lee Hill Kavanaugh, "Army Takes Human Terrain to Heart," *Kansas City Star*, October 14, 2008.

25 David Rohde, "Army Enlists Anthropology in War Zones," *New York Times*, October 5, 2007.

26 Weinberger, "The Pentagon's Culture Wars," pp. 583–85.

27 Adam Geller, "One Man's Odyssey from Campus to Combat," *Army Times*, March 16, 2009.

28 USAID, Office of Inspector General, "Audit of USAID/Iraq's Community Stabilization Program," audit report number E-267-08-001-P, March 18, 2008, www.usaid.gov/oig/public/fy08rpts/e-267-08-001-p.pdf.

29 Roberto Gonzalez, *American Counterinsurgency: Human Science and the Human Terrain* (Chicago: Prickly Paradigm Press, 2009), p. 68.

30 Noah Shachtman, "Third 'Human Terrain' Researcher Dead," Wired.com, Danger Room, January 8, 2009, www.wired.com/dangerroom/2009/01/third-human-ter.

31 Noah Shachtman, "No Jail Time for Army Contractor in Revenge Killing," Wired.com, Danger Room, May 8, 2009, www.wired.com/dangerroom/2009/05/no-jail-time-in-human-terrain-slaying.

32 Major Ben Connable, "All Our Eggs in a Broken Basket: How the Human Terrain System is Undermining Sustainable Military Cultural Competence," *Military Review*, March–April 2009.

33 Private First Class J. P. Lawrence, "Army Deploys Social Scientists to Study Iraqi Culture," 34th Infantry Division news article, June 4, 2009, www.theredbulls.org/article116.

12. Obama's War

1 Captain Stacie Shafran, "Girls' School Opens in Panjshir," American Forces Press Service, July 21, 2009.

2 Thomas Friedman, "Teacher, Can We Leave Now? No," *New York Times*, July 17, 2009.

3 Madelyn Hsiao-Rei Hicks, Hamit Dardagan, et al., "The Weapons That Kill Civilians—Deaths of Children and Noncombatants in Iraq, 2003–2008," *New England Journal of Medicine*, April 16, 2009.

4 Secretary of Defense Robert M. Gates, "National Defense University (Washington, D.C.)," speech, September 29, 2008, www.defense.gov/speeches/speech.aspx?speechid=1279.

5 "David Kilcullen Joins CNAS as a Senior Fellow," CNAS press release, November 19, 2008.

6 Kenneth Katzman, "Afghanistan: Politics, Government Formation and Performance," Congressional Research Service Report for Congress, June 26, 2009, http://fpc.state.gov/documents/organization/127030.pdf.

7 Laura Rozen, "Winning Hearts and Minds: All of McChrystal's Advisors," Foreignpolicy.com, July 31, 2009.

8 Anthony Cordesman, "How to Lose in Afghanistan," *Washington Post*, August 31, 2009.

9 "U.S. Military Moves to Defuse Tension after Afghan Riot," Associated Press, July 27, 2005.

10 Tim Golden, "In U.S. Report, Brutal Details of 2 Afghan Inmates' Deaths," *New York Times*, May 20, 2005.

11 David Kilcullen, "Political Maneuver in Counterinsurgency: Roadbuilding in Afghanistan," Small Wars Journal, April 24, 2008, http://smallwars journal.com/blog/2008/04/political-maneuver-in-counteri.

12 Ibid.

13 Jean MacKenzie, "Are U.S Taxpayers Funding the Taliban?" *GlobalPost*, September 2, 2009, www.globalpost.com/dispatch/afghanistan/090902/usaid-taliban-funding.

14 Matt Waldman, "Aid Effectiveness in Afghanistan," paper, ACBAR (Agency Coordinating Body for Afghan Relief), Advocacy Series, March 2008, www.acbar.org/ACBAR%20Publications/ACBAR%20Aid%20Effective ness%20%2825%20Mar%2008%29.pdf.

15 Anthony Cordesman, "The New Metrics of Afghanistan: The Data Needed to Support, Shape, Clear, Hold, and Build," Center for Strategic and International Studies commentary, August 10, 2009, www.opera tionspaix.net/IMG/pdf/CSIS-New-Metrics-Afghanistan_2009-08-07_.pdf.

16 Patrick Cockburn, "A Land Darkened by the Shadow of the Taliban," *Independent*, May 3, 2009.

17 Revolutionary Association of Afghan Women, "Crime and Barbarism in Shirpur by Afghan Ministers and High Authorities," report, www.rawa.org/land2.htm.

18 Elizabeth Bumiller and Mark Landler, "Civilian Goals Largely Unmet in Afghanistan," *New York Times*, October 11, 2009.

Conclusion

1 Christopher Drew, "High Costs Weigh on Troop Debate for Afghanistan War," *New York Times*, November 14, 2009.

2 "New COMISAF/ USFOR-A Commander Issues Counterinsurgency Guidance," July 27, 2010, http://www.defpro.com/daily/details/625/.

3 Spencer Ackerman, "Proposal Circulates on New Civilian-Military Agency," *Washington Independent*, November 3, 2009, http://washingtonindependent.com/66183/proposal-circulates-on-new-civilian-military-agency.

4 John Dickerson, "Defining Afghanistan Down: The President's New Strategy Will Include a New View of What's Possible," *Slate*, October 28, 2009, www.slate.com/id/2233835.

5 Ashraf Ghani, "Ashraf Ghani on Rebuilding Broken States," July 2005, TED video, www.ted.com/talks/ashraf_ghani_on_rebuilding_broken_states.html.

Select Bibliography

Books

Alderson, Andrew. *Bankrolling Basra: The Incredible Story of a Part-Time Soldier, $1 Billion and the Collapse of Iraq.* London: Constable & Robinson, 2007.

Barnett, Thomas. *The Pentagon's New Map: War and Peace in the Twenty-first Century.* New York: Berkley Books, 2005.

Berntsen, Gary, and Ralph Pezzullo. *Jawbreaker: The Attack on Bin Laden and Al-Qaeda: A Personal Account by the CIA's Field Commander.* New York: Crown, 2005.

Berrios, Ruben. *Contracting for Development: The Role of For-Profit Development Contractors in U.S. Foreign Development Assistance.* Westport, Conn.: Praeger, 2000.

Bowden, Mark. *Black Hawk Down: A Story of Modern War.* New York: Atlantic Monthly Press, 1999.

Burgess, Anthony. *The Long Day Wanes: A Malayan Trilogy.* New York: W. W. Norton, 1992.

Chandrasekaran, Rajiv. *Imperial Life in the Emerald City: Inside Iraq's Green Zone.* New York: Alfred A. Knopf, 2006.

Chatterjee, Pratap. *Halliburton's Army: How a Well-Connected Texas Oil Company Revolutionized the Way America Makes War.* New York: Nation Books, 2009.

Chayes, Sarah. *The Punishment of Virtue: Inside Afghanistan after the Taliban.* New York: Penguin Press, 2006.

Cohen, Eliot. *Citizens and Soldiers: The Dilemmas of Military Service.* Ithaca, N.Y.: Cornell University Press, 1985.

Colby, William, with James McCargar. *Lost Victory.* Chicago: Contemporary Books, 1989.

Cooper, Sally. *A Burqa and a Hard Place: Three Years in the New Afghanistan.* Sydney: Pan Macmillan Australia, 2008.

Deitchman, Seymour. *The Best-Laid Schemes: A Tale of Social Research and Bureaucracy.* Cambridge, Mass.: MIT Press, 1976.

DiPrizio, Robert. *Armed Humanitarians: U.S. Interventions from Northern Iraq to Kosovo.* Baltimore: Johns Hopkins University Press, 2002.

Dockery, Martin. *Lost in Translation: Vietnam: a Combat Advisor's Story.* New York: Presidio Press, 2003.

Dupree, Louis, and Linette Albert, eds. *Afghanistan in the 1970s.* New York: Praeger, 1974.

Durch, William, ed. *Twenty-First Century Peace Operations.* Washington, D.C.: U.S. Institute of Peace Press, 2006.

Easterly, William. *The White Man's Burden: Why the West's Efforts to Aid the Rest Have Done So Much Ill and So Little Good.* New York: Penguin, 2006.

Ellis, Sylvia. *Britain, America and the Vietnam War.* Westport, Conn.: Praeger, 2004.

Evans, Gareth. *The Responsibility to Protect: Ending Mass Atrocity Crimes Once and for All.* Washington, D.C.: Brookings Institution Press, 2008.

Exum, Andrew. *This Man's Army: A Soldier's Story from the Front Lines of the War on Terrorism.* New York: Gotham Books, 2004.

Ferguson, Niall. *Empire: The Rise and Demise of the British World Order and the Lessons for Global Power.* New York: Basic Books, 2003.

Fick, Nathaniel. *One Bullet Away: The Making of a Marine Officer.* New York: Mariner Books, 2006.

Galula, David, *Counterinsurgency Warfare: Theory and Practice.* Westport, Conn.: Praeger Security International, 2006.

Ghani, Ashraf, and Clare Lockhart. *Fixing Failed States: A Framework for Rebuilding a Fractured World.* New York: Oxford University Press, 2008.

Gonzalez, Roberto. *American Counterinsurgency: Human Science and the Human Terrain.* Chicago: Prickly Paradigm Press, 2009.

Hafvenstein, Joel. *Opium Season: A Year on the Afghan Frontier.* Guilford, Conn.: Lyons Press, 2007.

Horne, Alistair. *A Savage War of Peace: Algeria, 1954–1962.* New York: New York Review of Books, 2006.

Horowitz, Irving Louis, ed. *The Rise and Fall of Project Camelot: Studies in the Relationship between Social Science and Practical Politics.* Cambridge, Mass.: MIT Press, 1967.

Hughes, Christopher. *War on Two Fronts: An Infantry Commander's War in Iraq and the Pentagon.* Drexel Hill, Pa.: Casemate, 2007.

Kaplan, Robert. *Hog Pilots, Blue Water Grunts: The American Military in the Air, at Sea, and on the Ground.* New York: Vintage Departures, 2008.

Karnow, Stanley. *Vietnam: A History.* Revised and updated. New York: Penguin Books, 1997.

Kilcullen, David. *The Accidental Guerrilla: Fighting Small Wars in the Midst of a Big One.* New York: Oxford University Press, 2009.

Komer, Robert. *Bureaucracy Does Its Thing: Institutional Constraints on U.S-GVN Performance in Vietnam.* Santa Monica, Calif.: RAND Corporation, 1972.

Komer, Robert. *The Malayan Emergency in Retrospect: Organization of a Successful Counterinsurgency Effort.* Santa Monica, Calif.: RAND Corporation, 1972.

Krepinevich, Andrew. *The Army and Vietnam.* Baltimore: Johns Hopkins University Press, 1986.

LeMoine, Ray, and Jeff Neumann, with Donovan Webster. *Babylon by Bus.* New York: Penguin Press, 2006.

Loeffler, Jane. *The Architecture of Diplomacy: Building America's Embassies.* New York: Princeton Architectural Press, 1998.

Mansoor, Peter. *Baghdad at Sunrise: A Brigade Commander's War in Iraq.* New Haven: Yale University Press, 2008.

Marston, Daniel, and Carter Malkasian, eds. *Counterinsurgency in Modern Warfare.* Oxford and New York: Osprey, 2008.

Mills, Nicolaus. *Winning the Peace: The Marshall Plan and America's Coming of Age as a Superpower.* New York: John Wiley, 2008.

Mortenson, Greg, and David Oliver Relin. *The Three Cups of Tea: One Man's Mission to Promote Peace . . . One School at a Time.* New York: Viking, 2006.

Murphy, Cullen. *Are We Rome? The Fall of an Empire and the Fate of America.* New York: Houghton Mifflin, 2007.

Nagl, John. *Learning to Eat Soup with a Knife: Counterinsurgency Lessons from Malaya and Vietnam.* Westport, Conn.: Praeger, 2005.

Neumann, Ronald. *The Other War: Winning and Losing in Afghanistan.* Washington, D.C.: Potomac Books, 2009.

Odom, William. *On Internal War: American and Soviet Approaches to Third World Clients and Insurgents.* Durham, N.C.: Duke University Press, 1992.

Pelton, Robert Young. *Licensed to Kill: Hired Guns in the War on Terror.* New York: Crown, 2006.

Peters, Gretchen. *Seeds of Terror: How Heroin Is Bankrolling the Taliban and al Qaeda*. New York: Thomas Dunne Books, 2009.

Power, Samantha. *"A Problem from Hell": America and the Age of Genocide*. New York: Basic Books, 2002.

Price, David. *Anthropological Intelligence: The Deployment and Neglect of American Anthropology in the Second World War*. Durham, N.C.: Duke University Press, 2008.

Priest, Dana. *The Mission: Waging War and Keeping Peace with America's Military*. New York: W. W. Norton, 2003.

Ricks, Thomas. *Fiasco: The American Military Adventure in Iraq*. New York: Penguin Press, 2006.

Rieff, David. *A Bed for the Night: Humanitarianism in Crisis*. New York: Simon & Schuster, 2002.

Rosen, Nir. *In the Belly of the Green Bird: The Triumph of the Martyrs in Iraq*. New York: Free Press, 2006.

Scahill, Jeremy. *Blackwater: The Rise of the World's Most Powerful Mercenary Army*. New York: Nation Books, 2007.

Sheehan, Neil. *A Bright Shining Lie: John Paul Vann and America in Vietnam*. New York: Vintage Books, 1988.

Singer, P. W. *Corporate Warriors: Rise of the Privatized Military Industry*. Ithaca, N.Y.: Cornell University Press, 2003.

Sorley, Lewis. *Vietnam Chronicles: The Abrams Tapes, 1968–1972*. Lubbock, Texas: Texas Tech University Press, 2004.

Stewart, Rory. *The Prince of the Marshes—And Other Occupational Hazards of a Year in Iraq*. New York: Harvest, 2007.

Thompson, Sir Robert. *Peace Is Not at Hand*. New York: David McKay, 1974.

Wedel, Janine. *Collision and Collusion: The Strange Case of Western Aid to Eastern Europe 1989–1998*. New York: St. Martin's Press, 1998.

Wright, Donald, and Timothy Reese, with the Contemporary Operations Study Team. *On Point II: Transition to the New Campaign—The United States Army in Operation Iraqi Freedom, May 2003–January 2005*. Fort Leavenworth, Kans.: Combat Studies Institute Press, U.S. Army Combined Arms Center, 2008.

Wrong, Michela. *"I Didn't Do It for You": How the World Betrayed a Small African Nation*. New York: HarperCollins, 2005.

Oral Histories

U.S. Institute of Peace, Association for Diplomatic Studies and Training Iraq Experience Project, www.usip.org/resources/oral-histories-iraq-experience-project.

Manuals and Handbooks

Field Manual 3–24, Counterinsurgency
Field Manual 3–07, Stability Operations
Field Manual 3–0, Operations
U.S. Army Escalation of Force Handbook, Center for Army Lessons Learned Publication 07–21, July 2007.
U.S. Government Counterinsurgency Guide, January 2009.

Index

Note on the Author

Nathan Hodge is a Washington, D.C.-based writer who specializes in defense and national security. He has reported from Iran, Iraq, Afghanistan, Russia, and a number of other countries in the Middle East and former Soviet Union. He is the author, with Sharon Weinberger, of *A Nuclear Family Vacation*, and his work has appeared in *Slate*, the *Financial Times*, *Foreign Policy*, and many other newspapers and magazines.